15.99

Case Studies in Contemporary Criticism

KT-426-565

Heart of Darkness

Case Studies in Contemporary Criticism

SERIES EDITOR: Ross C Murfin

Case Studies in Contemporary Criticism

SERIES EDITOR: Ross C Murfin, *Southern Methodist University*

JOSEPH CONRAD
Heart of Darkness

Complete, Authoritative Text with
Biographical, Historical, and Cultural Contexts,
Critical History, and Essays from
Contemporary Critical Perspectives

THIRD EDITION

EDITED BY
Ross C Murfin
Southern Methodist University

Bedford/St. Martin's
BOSTON ♦ NEW YORK

For Bedford/St. Martin's

Senior Executive Editor: Stephen A. Scipione
Editorial Associate: Kate Mayhew
Production Associate: Samuel Jones
Senior Marketing Manager: Adrienne Petsick
Project Management: DeMasi Design and Publishing Services
Cover Design: Donna Lee Dennison
Cover Art: Sunrise over Zaire Rainforest © Karl Ammann/CORBIS
Composition: Jeff Miller Book Design
Printing and Binding: Haddon Craftsmen, Inc., an RR Donnelley & Sons
 Company

President: Joan E. Feinberg
Editorial Director: Denise B. Wydra
Editor in Chief: Karen S. Henry
Director of Marketing: Karen R. Soeltz
Director of Production: Susan W. Brown
Associate Director, Editorial Production: Elise S. Kaiser
Manager, Publishing Services: Andrea Cava

Library of Congress Control Number: 2010932771

Manufactured in the United States of America.

5 4 3 2 1 0
f e d c b a

For information, write: Bedford/St. Martin's, 75 Arlington Street, Boston, MA
02116   (617-399-4000)

ISBN-13: 978-0-312-45753-2

Acknowledgments

Published and distributed outside North America by
PALGRAVE MACMILLAN
Houndmills, Basingstoke, Hampshire RG21 6XS
Companies and representatives throughout the world.
ISBN-13: 978-0-230-33345-1
ISBN-10: 0-230-33345-1
A catalogue record for this book is available from the British Library.

About the Series

Volumes in the Case Studies in Contemporary Criticism series introduce college students to critical and theoretical trends in literary studies. Each volume reprints the complete text of a significant literary work, together with critical essays that approach the work from different theoretical perspectives and editorial matter that introduces both the literary work and the critics' theoretical perspectives.

The volume editor of each Case Study selects and prepares an authoritative text of a classic work, writes introductions (sometimes supplemented by cultural documents) that place the work in biographical and historical context, and surveys the critical responses to the work since its original publication. Thus situated biographically, historically, and critically, the work is subsequently examined in several critical essays that have been written or chosen with students in mind. The essays show theory in practice; whether written by established scholars or exceptional young critics, they demonstrate how theoretical approaches can generate compelling readings of great literature.

As series editor, I have prepared introductions to the critical essays and to the theoretical approaches they entail. The introductions, accompanied by bibliographies, explain and historicize the principal concepts, major figures, and key works of particular theoretical approaches as a prelude to discussing how they pertain to the critical essays that follow. It is my hope that the introductions will reveal to students that effective criticism — including their own — is informed by a set of coherent assumptions that can be not only articulated but also modified and extended through comparison of different theoretical approaches. Finally, I have included a glossary of key terms that recur in these volumes and in the discourse of contemporary theory and criticism.

I would like to thank Supryia M. Ray, with whom I wrote *The Bedford Glossary of Critical and Literary Terms*, for her invaluable help in revising introductions to the critical approaches represented in this volume.

Ross C Murfin
Southern Methodist University
Series Editor

About This Volume

Part One of this volume reprints the text of *Heart of Darkness* from the 1921 Heinemann edition of Conrad's *Collected Works* — the last version of the text that Conrad approved.

Part Two includes documents and illustrations providing cultural contexts for *Heart of Darkness*. Part Three features a critical history of the novella, plus six contemporary critical essays representing deconstruction; feminist, gender, and queer theory; and new historicist, postcolonial, and psychoanalytic approaches to Conrad's most famous tale.

New to This Edition

I undertook a third edition to make this Case Study of *Heart of Darkness* a more useful and current resource for introducing students to the latest trends in contemporary criticism. Two new essays combine perspectives presented earlier in the volume. The Cultural Documents and Illustrations section is entirely new to this edition, as is the introduction to postcolonial criticism. All of the introductions and bibliographies to the critical approaches have been significantly revised. A new, coauthored critical history now extends into the twenty-first century.

Acknowledgments

I am indebted to those whose comments have improved the introductions to the critical approaches: Shari Benstock, Patrick Brantlinger,

Janice Carlisle, Steven Mailloux, J. Hillis Miller, Margot Norris, John Paul Riquelme, and Brook Thomas. I am deeply grateful to the authors of the critical essays, especially Gabrielle McIntire, who combines post-colonial, feminist, and gender criticism with queer theory; Tony C. Brown, who merges historicist and postcolonial perspectives with that of psychoanalytic criticism; and Kayla Walker Edin, who prepared and wrote the Cultural Documents and Illustrations section and coauthored with me the new and updated critical history. Walker Edin and I both gratefully acknowledge the work of a former undergraduate student at Southern Methodist University, Katie Lanning, who as part of a senior project did the initial work of researching and assembling cultural and critical documents, several of which are featured in this volume. For her help in updating the bibliographies that follow my introductions to the various critical approaches, I would like to thank Supryia M. Ray, whose work was supported by the E. A. Lilly Distinguished Professorship in English at Southern Methodist University.

I continue to appreciate the exemplary help of people at Bedford/ St. Martin's, especially Joan Feinberg, Steve Scipione, Kate Mayhew, Emily Berleth, and Linda DeMasi of DeMasi Design and Publishing.

This book is dedicated to two miracles that have recently changed my life unexpectedly and dramatically: my wife Heather Lynn Flabiano and my daughter Makenna Ross Murfin.

Contents

PART THREE

Heart of Darkness:
A Case Study in Contemporary Criticism

PART ONE

Heart of Darkness:
The Complete Text

Introduction: Biographical and Historical Contexts

Polish, not English, was the language Joseph Conrad grew up speaking. English wasn't even his second language: French was. The fact that Conrad achieved fame in his third language is testimony to his genius — genius that could be contained neither by linguistic barriers nor by national boundaries. Early political persecution and exile failed to stifle it; even the loss of family and deep personal unhappiness could only restrain it temporarily.

Conrad was christened Josef Konrad Nalecz Korzeniowski. Both his mother, Ewa, and his father, Apollo, were descended from wealthy Polish families. Born in 1857 — "in the 85th year of Muscovite Oppression," as his father put it — Josef found himself, from childhood on, a person without a country. In 1772 Poland had been divided up among Russia, Prussia, and Austria, only to be redivided in 1793 and 1795.

Thus, although Conrad was born into the landed gentry of Polish culture (in what had become a western Russian province), his childhood years were full of uncertainty. His headstrong, talented father, a poet and translator of French and English literature, was dedicated to the cause of Polish independence from Russia. Just before a Polish uprising was quelled in 1863, Apollo was arrested and exiled to the village of Vologda, hundreds of miles north of Moscow.

The trip to Vologda nearly killed young Josef, and the brutal winters there hastened the demise of both his parents. Ewa died of tuberculosis in 1865, her despairing husband shortly thereafter, in 1869. Josef, who was but twelve years old, was adopted by his mother's uncle, an at once firm but indulgent gentleman named Tadeusz Bobrowski.

Uncle Tadeusz cared well for his orphaned nephew, sending him first to school in Krakow, later to Geneva with a tutor. But the young Conrad could adjust neither to the rigors of school life nor to the personal attentions of his private teacher, who continually tried to reform his pupil's romantic views on life and the world. Finally, the exasperated Josef persuaded his Uncle Tadeusz to let him join the French merchant navy.

The four years following were more adventure-filled, but apparently no more satisfying, than the earlier, teenage years. Conrad sailed to the West Indies and Venezuela, squandered a small fortune, lost in love, got involved in a gun-running venture for the Carlists (who were seeking to seize the throne of Spain for Carlos de Bourbon), and attempted suicide in 1878. That same year, French immigration authorities prevented him from continuing as a sailor on merchant marine vessels.

This last turn of events seems in the long run to have been a fortunate one, since Conrad was to sail for the next sixteen years on British ships and to become a British subject in 1887. Conrad's metamorphosis from a French sailor to an English one caused him to master the language in which he would ultimately choose to write his novels. The greatest of these — including *Heart of Darkness*, *Lord Jim*, *Nostromo*, *The Secret Agent*, and *Victory* — have been, almost since their publication, ranked with the most powerful and poetic novels ever written in English.

Like other geniuses, Conrad had a way of turning disadvantage into advantage. He made unconventional, poetic use of a language he was forced to master by circumstance. A lesser talent would have been blunted by twenty trying years of life on deck; Conrad transformed his experiences into art.

From his years in the East and West Indies, he gained the atmosphere as well as the insights into human nature that he was to draw upon while writing works from *Almayer's Folly* (published in 1895, when Conrad was in his thirties) to *The Rescue* (published in 1920, four years before Conrad's death).

But it was not only in the East and West Indies that Conrad came by the store of experiences that were later to be metamorphosed into art. Indeed, the voyage that seems to have had the greatest impact on Conrad's life and art was not by sea at all — or at least the most memorable part of the trip was not. That was the expedition that saw Conrad far up the Congo River on a rusty steamboat with a shrill whistle.

Conrad had begun writing *Almayer's Folly*, his first novel, in 1889, just before commencing the trip up to Stanley (now Boyoma) Falls in 1890. In spite of the near-torturous nature of the journey, he managed to make continual progress on the book while en route. The trip from Boma to Stanley Falls and back was one of the last Conrad ever made as a sailor. It marked, in a sense, the beginning of a brief but crucial period of his life, a period that came to an end in 1894, the year his beloved Uncle Tadeusz died. For it was then that Conrad decided to devote himself to writing full time. Shortly after making that decision, he was to marry Jessie George. The troubled Pole without a clear-cut family, nationality, language, love, or even calling in life was now Joseph Conrad, a British subject, husband, and writer.

The present-day Democratic Republic of the Congo, one of the largest nations in Africa, was known as the Belgian Congo from 1908 until 1960, when it gained its independence. The Congo visited by Conrad and by the narrator of *Heart of Darkness* was officially called "L'État Indépendent du Congo" (customarily if roughly translated into English as "the Congo Free State"). But Belgian the Congo was, from 1885 on, thanks to a conference called in Berlin in 1884 by Otto von Bismarck, first chancellor of the newly formed German Empire.

Not that Belgium had opened up the Congo to European exploration, exploitation, and development. The celebrated Scot Dr. David Livingstone had gone there in 1856, to be "found" by the Americanized Welshman Henry Morton Stanley in 1871. Livingstone and Stanley, moreover, had been preceded by Portuguese, Dutch, and French pioneers. In fact, until 1876, King Léopold II of Belgium had merely sat back and watched with interest. In that year, though, this ambitious and notoriously immoral monarch of a nation less than fifty years old made his first move. He organized a meeting in Brussels to discuss a plan "to open to civilization the only part of our globe where Christianity has not yet penetrated and to pierce the darkness which envelops the entire population" (Hennessy 13).

Bismarck, who had gradually come to realize that no nation would win anything if all were drawn into a territorial, theological, or trade war, eventually called his own conference in Berlin. To the surprise of astute political forecasters throughout the Western world, Bismarck's 1884 convention resulted in a decision to make the Congo the personal property of Léopold II. All the king had to do was guarantee that all nations would be permitted to trade freely there, that taxes and tariffs would not be collected, and that nations would not be granted monopolies on particular items of trade. Léopold, who ended up shirking most of his commitments, staunchly defended his actions in the Congo even in the face of mounting international outcry and crippling debt as his financial backers pulled their support. In a will written in 1889, he bequeathed the territory to Belgium in exchange for a government loan of 150 million francs. As it turned out, in light of the turn of events and the shift in public opinion, Belgium annexed the Congo in 1908, a year before Léopold died.

While the Congo Free State became the Belgian Congo, immediate change occurred in name only. After all, the Congo had been all but Belgian since long before 1908. And it had been ruled by a tyrant whose promise to bring civilization to Africa had turned out to be little more than a cruel joke. Léopold had divided the country into sixteen districts, each governed by a commissioner who rendered the local chiefs impotent. Some of these officials went on to build personal fortunes by collecting taxes from the natives, and since few of the natives had anything to give but their labor, the commissioners were, in effect, slaveholders, and the Congolese were slaves in all but name. Léopold, in turn, received a portion of all profits made by his administrators, so it was in his interest to make sure that when Africans rebelled against the sentries who guarded them while they worked out their taxes, they be taught a swift and brutal lesson.

Reports of atrocities were drifting back to Europe within a few years after Léopold had been granted proprietorship. Baptist missionaries duped by the king's stated goal of Christianizing the Congo were among the first to cry foul. But the Congo was far from Europe, and the damning reports from scattered missionaries were relatively few and far between. And anyway, people wondered in Europe, wasn't it inevitable that the lives of some Africans would be lost? When natives rebelled, weren't the sentries merely protecting themselves, or at worst doing their duty? King Léopold assured his people that their "agents" were "profoundly reluctant to use force." However, he explained, unfortunate incidents were bound to happen, since many of the sentries were "wretched negroes" with "sanguinary habits" recruited from the local population, natives who were, in other words, prone to turn viciously on their own people (Burrows 286).

Many of the station managers and traders that Léopold refers to as his agents were drawn from the ranks of the Belgian army, and by 1890 they had, with Léopold's blessing, given the lie to their king's promise that the Congo would be a free-trade territory. Ivory, the most valuable commodity, had become a Belgian monopoly; non-Belgian traders caught carrying it could be summarily shot, either by Léopold's army-trained representatives or by their sentries. Among these sentries were natives "freed" from their black slaveowners and offered "protection" by the white invaders. They had to work seven years for their new master, wherever he chose to send them, for whatever wages he sought to bestow, and in whatever conditions he saw fit to provide.

Why did Conrad go to such a place? Since the mid-1870s, he had been sailing the high seas, mainly on English ships. Why would he want to ride a leaky Belgian steamboat upriver into the troubled heart of Africa when the open seas led to a whole world of places whose names surely conjured up more images of romance and adventure?

Part of the answer can perhaps be found in Conrad's late essay "Geography and Some Explorers," in which he recalls that, as an adolescent, he had been particularly fascinated by stories of polar explorers. Of Leopold McClintock's book *The Voyage of the "Fox" in the Arctic Seas* (1859), Conrad writes: "There could hardly have been imagined a better book for letting in the breath of the stern romance of polar exploration. . . . The great spirit of the realities of the story sent me off on the romantic explorations of my inner self" ("Geography" 16–17).

Another, complementary explanation of why Conrad wanted to visit King Léopold's troubled Congo may lie in the same essay, in the paragraphs that tell of a lifelong fascination with maps. By age thirteen, he recalls, he was "addicted" to "map-gazing," much as other people become hooked on stargazing. "And it was Africa," Conrad writes, "the Continent out of which the Romans used to say some new thing was always coming," that seemed particularly fascinating. So much of that continent was unknown and unexplored that maps of whole regions of it would be covered by "exciting spaces of white paper." Thus, owing to its "regions unknown," the "heart of Africa" as represented by maps was "white and big" ("Geography" 19–20).

At about the age of sixteen, Conrad made a public commitment to travel someday to unknown Africa. "One day," he recalls, "putting my finger on a spot in the very middle of the then white heart of Africa, I declared that some day I would go there" ("Geography" 24). Long before he was sixteen and even before he read *The Voyage of the "Fox" in the Arctic Seas*, though, Conrad had expressed his intention to do what he finally did in 1890 on the steamer *Roi des Belges*. In his late, autobiographical retrospective entitled *Some Reminiscences*, Conrad claims that the decision was made during childhood:

It was in 1868, when I was nine years old or thereabouts, that while looking at a map of Africa of the time and putting my finger on the blank space then representing the unsolved mystery of the continent, I said to myself with absolute assurance and an amazing audacity which are no longer in my character now:

"When I grow up I shall go there." (41)

Conrad then says that he gave that proclamation no further thought until, more than twenty years later, the opportunity to travel up the Congo River to Stanley Falls actually presented itself. For Stanley Falls was the very spot on the map he had pointed at in 1868: "the blankest of blank spaces on the earth's figured surface" (*Reminiscences* 41).

These various personal records suggest that Conrad decided to go to the Congo for several closely related reasons. In part because the interior of Africa had been represented by cartographers as a mysterious white blankness, and in part because tales of polar exploration had equated white blankness with the unknown and explorers of the white wilderness with true heroism, Conrad associated the Congo with the unknown and equated a voyage there with the most important, heroic kind of voyage. Tales of seamen wandering the South Pacific were tales of the "acquisitive spirit," of those urged on by "the desire of trade . . . or loot," whereas the "aims" of the polar explorers were "as pure as the air of those high latitudes" ("Geography" 14). If mere stories of such men sent Conrad "off on . . . explorations of [his] inner self," how much more he was likely to learn about his own nature and human nature in general by traveling into the great expanse of white that lay beyond the colored, mapped areas of Africa.

There is an obvious irony in Conrad's implicit association of the unknown Congo, hot and humid home of a dark race, with whiteness and the arctic. Another irony emerges as we read Conrad's novel set in the Congo: the aims of several white "explorers" portrayed in it were morally black as pitch — not at all like the "pure" aims of arctic wayfarers in search of the Northwest Passage. So obvious are these ironies that they were, obviously, intended.

Still, we must remember that the Conrad who wrote not *Heart of Whiteness* but, rather, *Heart of Darkness* — the Conrad who still later penned *Some Reminiscences* and the essay on maps and explorers — was an older and wiser Conrad than the young man who set sail from France on the sixth of May, 1890, for the Congolese coast. Conrad could not have known until he actually experienced the Congo just how much its "explorers" were prompted by the desire for "loot." The Congo was supposed to be a relatively free, peaceable state, open to all traders and therefore free not only of the murderous violence but also of the slavery found in so many other areas of the world.

Conrad had to discover, personally, just how false that supposition was. In seeing how easily Europeans who set forth in ships to enlighten and civilize can corrupt and destroy, Conrad came to a profound realization about human nature: whiteness and light may turn out to be blackness and darkness, and blackness and darkness may be relatively pure. In learning that hard lesson, Conrad also discovered something profound about himself: that it was as a writer, not as a merchant sailor, that he wanted to explore the world — especially the inner world of "civilized" humanity.[1] Thus, even though Conrad could not have been prepared to find what he found in the Congo by white spaces on a map, tales of polar exploration, or accounts of the Congo Free State that amounted to a king's whitewash, he did, in a sense, find in the Congo exactly what, as a schoolboy, he had somehow sensed he would find: the mysterious unknown, self-knowledge, and even, it seems fair to say, his destiny.

There were, of course, practical reasons why Conrad decided to go to the Congo. Fated though it seems he was by the promise he had made in childhood to go there, drawn as he was to the idea of discovering something about himself while voyaging into uncharted territory, Conrad was also attracted to the Congo because it promised a much-needed source of financial support (Conrad had used up his inheritance by the age of twenty-one) and because there, it seemed, he would be not just a sailor but a captain. He had briefly served as master of an Australian vessel, but it was not until 1886 that he had passed the examination qualifying him for a commission certified by the British Board of Trade.

In 1889 Conrad approached Albert Thys, managing director of the Société Anonyme Belge pour le Commerce du Haut-Congo, in the hope that Thys could procure him a position commanding a steamer plying the Congo River. But Conrad also looked into other positions that, had they materialized, would have sent him back to the West Indies as a captain. Neither destination beckoned immediately; Thys had nothing to offer, perhaps because Conrad wanted a long-term commitment. "A short visit would not be worth the trouble and expense of leaving

---

[1]Frederick Karl develops this idea in *Joseph Conrad: The Three Lives* (New York: Farrar, 1979). I am indebted to Karl not only for this idea but also for bringing together illuminating excerpts from Conrad's letters and diary, some of which are quoted below.

[Europe] for," he remarked to Thys in a letter dated December 27, 1889 (Karl 276).

With no immediate prospects, Conrad decided to visit Uncle Tadeusz in the Ukraine, then to return to England by way of Brussels, where he hoped not only to reassert his interest in a Congo command but also to visit with his "Aunt" Marguerite and "Uncle" Aleksander Poradowska. (Uncle Aleksander was actually Conrad's cousin; Aunt Marguerite, a writer of novels and short stories, was related to Conrad only by marriage.) Hearing that Aleksander was ill and failing fast, Conrad changed his plans and went to Brussels first. He arrived on February 5, 1890; two days later his cousin died. Although Conrad was soon to enter a close relationship and correspondence with Marguerite, he left her before her husband was buried, traveling to Warsaw, then to Lublin, and finally to Kazimierowka, where he stayed with Uncle Tadeusz for two months.

In spite of Tadeusz's attempt to discourage him from his interest in a Congo command, Conrad returned to Brussels on April 26, 1890. There he learned that a steamer captain named Freiesleben had died in the Congo and that a command was available. Actually, Conrad's turn in luck was due to far more than the death of the ship's captain; Aunt Marguerite had, with Conrad's permission, used her considerable influence on several important men involved in the colonization effort, including Thys. After signing with Thys, Conrad headed for a French port, from which he shipped for Boma, the main port of entry to the Congo.

Conrad wrote letters back to Marguerite Poradowska, so we have a fair idea of what his journey to the heart of the "Haut-Congo" was like — or at least the first, easiest part of his journey. He was working on *Almayer's Folly* and thinking constantly of his "aunt," who seems to have been not only a mother figure but also a woman whose image raised romantic possibilities in his mind. ("You have endowed my life with new interest, new affection," he tells her in a letter mailed from Libreville [Karl 285].) Conrad arrived at his destination on June 12, after an interminable-seeming sea voyage down the African coast. The trip, from Bordeaux to Boma on the *Ville de Maceio*, had taken more than a month.

Forty miles from Boma, in Matadi, Conrad met Roger Casement, who had come to the Congo Free State thinking that he would abolish the slave trade carried on by Arabs in the area and establish a railway that would link the coastal region with Stanley (now Malebo) Pool, where the Congo River becomes navigable and stays navigable all the way inland to Stanley (Boyoma) Falls. When he met Conrad in the spring of 1890, Casement was beginning the railway project, as yet unaware (like Conrad) that many of King Léopold's men were using the natives as slave labor. Conrad shared a room with Casement for almost a month, at the end of which he began the overland journey made arduous by the lack of a railway and fresh water, and by the presence of what turned out to be three virtual plagues: heat, mosquitoes, and one of Léopold's agents, Prosper Harou.

The trip to Stanley Pool had to be made by foot: "Not an ass here," Conrad joked in a letter to Marguerite, "except your very humble servant" (Karl 289). But there were other things to see along the way, not beasts of burden but evidence that men and women were being treated worse than animals. Conrad kept a diary in which he recorded these sights and sounds: "Saw at a camp place the dead body of a Backongo. Shot? Horrid smell" [July 3]. "Saw another dead body lying by the path in an attitude of meditative repose. . . . At night when the moon rose heard shouts and drumming in distant villages. Passed a bad night" [July 4].

Agent Harou, apparently, passed a worse one: "H. lame and not in very good form," Conrad wrote in his diary on July 25. "Passed a skeleton tied up to a post," Conrad was to write some days later; "put [Harou] in hammock" (Karl 290–92).

Harou's crippling lameness made the trip more difficult for everyone, but it was far from the most disappointing development to try Conrad's spirits during the thirty-six-day trip that ended on August 2. On July 29, Conrad met a man named Louette who was transporting another sick agent back in the direction of Boma. From Louette Conrad learned that the steamer he had been hired to command now lay sunk on the bottom of the river. Having come all the way from Belgium to captain *The Florida*, Conrad suddenly learned that he would be shipping upriver not as a captain but as a sailor on the *Roi des Belges*.

Rather miraculously, Conrad had continually been writing *Almayer's Folly* while making the torturous overland trek. Although work had proceeded fitfully, something definite had been accomplished. The loss of a command was a serious blow to Conrad and may have made him prefer the slow progress of writing to the unpredictable vagaries besetting a would-be captain. Certainly, the period commencing just before Conrad's arrival at Kinshasa marked the beginning of a period of disillusionment — with Africa, with life on deck, with colonial trade, and with white European agents running trading stations throughout the Congo. Conrad seems to have particularly disliked Camille Delcommune, the manager of the station at Kinshasa, whom he later called "a common ivory dealer with base instincts" (Karl 294). To Conrad's dismay, Delcommune decided to make the trip on the *Roi des Belges* all the way to the Inner Station at Stanley Falls, where an agent named Klein lay desperately ill. That four-week trip and the return downriver to Kinshasa with the corpse of Klein seem not only to have cured Conrad's weakness for life aboard ship but also to have very nearly robbed him of all taste for life in general. "Everything here is repellent to me," he wrote to Marguerite once the round trip had been completed. "Men and things, but above all men" (Karl 294).

Conrad, who wished to leave Africa as quickly as possible, got out of his contract with the Société Anonyme Belge pour le Commerce du Haut-Congo. A terrible case of dysentery that he had picked up on his journey turned out to be an adequate excuse. Perhaps fearing that it wouldn't be adequate, Conrad had written Brussels to ask Marguerite to inform Albert Thys that the Société had failed to live up to its terms: a command had been promised, whereas in fact Conrad had served only as mate, except for a brief period during the return trip, when Captain L. R. Koch was even sicker than Conrad was.

What Conrad couldn't wriggle out of was his Congo experience; it seems to permeate *Heart of Darkness*, even though the novel wasn't begun for almost a decade following its author's departure from Africa. Some of the parallels between *Heart of Darkness* and Conrad's Congo adventure are so obvious that it may be tempting to think of the novel as a thinly veiled autobiography.

It may be tempting, but it may also be treacherous, for reasons that have perhaps been best articulated by formalist critics. A work of art, formalists would argue, is not undigested experience; rather, it is characterized by *form*. That characteristic form is to be discovered by finding the patterns and relationships that exist within the work itself, not the connections that may seem to exist between the work and its author's life story.

Still, even formalists would not have us be unaware of those connections. For one thing, we have to know that connections exist before we can affirm or deny their ultimate significance. For another, knowing the biographical background of a text helps us to better appreciate the text's *difference*; that is, the shape it has been given by the artist's imagination. And there is still another reason to become aware of the parallels between Conrad's Congo experience and Marlow's. With such an awareness comes the possibility of deciding that the formalist view is too narrow, too limiting.

To summarize the parallels briefly: Marlow, the novel's protagonist and narrator, tells his listeners about his childhood passion for maps and about his declared intention to go, someday, to the blank heart of Africa. He describes how, years later, he signed up for a Congo command in the office of a "great man" — "pale plumpness in a frock-coat" — after receiving some behind-the-scenes help from "an aunt, a dear enthusiastic soul." Whereas Conrad got his command due to the death of a captain named Freiesleben, Marlow is signed on shortly after the demise of the unlucky Captain Fresleven.

Marlow's description of his sea voyage down the African coast ("Every day looked the same") reads like Conrad's diary, and his description of an overland journey from a company station not far from the African coast to the "Central Station" repeats many of Conrad's experiences in traveling from Matadi to Kinshasa, by Stanley Pool. Heat and mosquitoes and the lack of water are mentioned, as is "a white companion" who becomes so sick with fever that he has to be "carried in a hammock slung under a pole." A corpse like the one Conrad was shocked to see while on his overland trek turns up in *Heart of Darkness*: "Can't say I saw any road or any upkeep," Marlow recalls, "unless the body of a middle-aged negro, with a bullet hole in the forehead, upon which I absolutely stumbled . . . may be considered as a permanent improvement."

Marlow, like Conrad, learns that an accident has befallen the steamer that he was to have commanded; like Conrad he journeys upriver to retrieve a sick agent who dies on board shortly after being rescued. And Marlow is accompanied on his travels by a man who must have been modeled on Camille Delcommune, the station manager at Kinshasa whom Conrad referred to as "a common ivory dealer with base instincts." (Marlow calls the manager of the Central Station, who accompanies him upriver to the Inner Station, "a common trader" with "no learning and no intelligence.")

But the differences between Conrad's experiences and those of Charlie Marlow are as striking as the similarities. To begin with, there is the matter of Marlow himself, a thoroughly English Everyman — not a Polish intellectual who happens to be a sailor, too. Marlow is a recognizable kind of guy, one perfectly capable of joking that a corpse may be a road improvement, and one made more than a little uncomfortable by the efforts made in his behalf by his aunt: "Would you believe it?" he asks the other men listening to his story, "I, Charlie Marlow, set the women to work — to get a job."

Other differences abound. The "great man" who hires Marlow is not named Thys — in fact, no names are given for Marlow's aunt, the station manager modeled on Delcommune, or the "white companion" who becomes sick and has to be carried much as Prosper Harou became lame and unable to walk. The ship Marlow travels upriver on is left similarly unnamed, as is the "Company" that Conrad knew as the Société Anonyme Belge pour le Commerce du Haut-Congo. No character in the novel bears more than a passing resemblance to Roger Casement, whom Conrad stayed with in Matadi. Whereas Conrad didn't get to captain a ship, thanks to the damage done to his intended vessel, Marlow waits months for rivets and repairs that eventually allow him to command his steamboat. Marlow retrieves Kurtz only to have him die on his ship; Anton Klein was the name of the agent who died on Conrad's ship. But whereas all we know about Klein is that he had fallen ill near Stanley Falls, Kurtz is a marvelously mysterious imaginative creation, a kind of Everyman, like Marlow ("All Europe contributed to the making of Kurtz," Marlow says, when the matter of his lineage comes up), but a mythological demon figure as well. Critics have often compared him to Faust and to Satan.

Kurtz is, then, someone who exceeds the dimensions of anyone Conrad met in the Congo, just as the Africa in *Heart of Darkness* is far more than a continent — it has universal dimensions. There are minor characters, too, who testify to Conrad's ability not just to transcribe reality but to invent a world full of powerful significances. In the area that corresponds to the place where Conrad met Casement, Marlow meets a wonderfully sleazy accountant whom he describes as a "hairdresser's dummy." There is a station manager modeled after Delcommune, but his agent, characterized as a "papier-mâché Mephistopheles," seems to be pure invention. Even more fascinating is the Russian mindlessly loyal to the murderous Kurtz, a harlequin figure "covered with patches all over, with bright patches, blue, red, and yellow — patches on the back, patches on the front, patches on elbows, on knees; coloured binding round his jacket, scarlet edging at the bottom of his trousers." These characters are not part of any diary or historical record; rather, they are masterful touches in a great work of novelistic art.

Not all of the artfulness of *Heart of Darkness* is to be found in its characters. Part of the creative complexity of the work lies in the form Conrad's narrative takes; that is to say, in the way the story is told. After all, we are not told the tale of a trip to Africa by an omniscient, authorial narrator. Instead, we find ourselves reading a story within a story. We must learn about Kurtz and the harlequin, the hairdresser's dummy and the Eldorado Explorers, from a nameless, anonymous source, a man who repeats the tale he says Charlie Marlow told him and four other men one night sitting on a cruising yawl anchored in the River Thames.

Thus, part of the meaning of the story is the way we learn about "reality" through other people's accounts of it, many of which are, themselves, twice-told tales. Part of the meaning of the novel, too, is the possibly unreliable nature of our teachers; Marlow is the source of our story, but he is also a character within the story we read, and a flawed one at that. Marlow's macho comments about women and his insensitive reaction to the "middle-aged negro" with a "bullet-hole in the forehead" cause us to refocus our critical attention, to shift it from the story being retold to the storyteller whose supposedly autobiographical yarn is being repeated.

Because we occasionally judge Marlow negatively, we find ourselves having to take certain passages ironically, and the ironic distance that we experience between ourselves and our narrator is another important difference between a novel like *Heart of Darkness* and a diary or a history book. Irony, after all, makes possible a complex form of humor in which we find ourselves laughing at as well as with the chronicler. It is irony, too, that causes us to apprehend something profound about the human self: namely, its capacity to understand or "see through" others while remaining self-destructively ignorant about its own identity. We see what Marlow shows us, but we also see Marlow, and one of the things about him we can see is his blindness to his own nature.

Marlow interrupts the story he tells to the Lawyer, the Accountant, the Chief of Companies, and the person who retells his story to put it this way: "Of course in this you fellows see more than I could then. You see me, whom you know. . . ." What he fails to mention is that his listeners "see" different things, for the Marlow known to each of them is surely different from the one known to all the others. We, as readers, enjoy the same privilege — and suffer the same predicament — as Marlow's auditors. What we "see in" the story depends on the nature and extent of our knowledge. Knowledge of Conrad's life may lead us to "see" Marlow's story as Conrad's own. Further knowledge — of formalist theory, for instance — may cause us to decide that Marlow is, after all, an artificial construct: a narrator, and an unreliable one at that. But there is still more to know about Conrad and his times — for example, the kind of knowledge that psychoanalytic, feminist, and new historicist critics would bring to bear. And there is more, too, to see in literary art than formalist theorists have seen in it. Deconstructors, for instance, would make us aware not of the definite form of a text but, rather, of its surprisingly contradictory elements. Reader-response critics might argue that a work of art is what we make of it. Each of these ways of knowing (which are explored in Part Three of this edition) causes us to see more in Marlow's story than the Lawyer, the Accountant, or the Chief of Companies did—perhaps even more than Conrad did. But one thing is sure: each of these ways of knowing brings a different kind of light and color to *Heart of Darkness*.

WORKS CITED

Burrows, Guy. *The Land of the Pigmies*. London: Pearson, 1898. Print.

Conrad, Joseph. "Geography and Some Explorers." *Last Essays*. Ed. Richard Curle. London: Dent, 1926. Print.

———. *Some Reminiscences*. London: Eveleigh Nash, 1912. Print.

Hennessy, Maurice. *Congo: A Brief History and Appraisal*. New York: Praeger, 1961. Print.

Karl, Frederick. *Joseph Conrad: The Three Lives*. New York: Farrar, 1979. Print.

Heart of Darkness

I

The *Nellie*, a cruising yawl, swung to her anchor without a flutter of the sails, and was at rest. The flood had made, the wind was nearly calm, and being bound down the river, the only thing for it was to come to and wait for the turn of the tide.

The sea-reach of the Thames stretched before us like the beginning of an interminable waterway. In the offing the sea and the sky were welded together without a joint, and in the luminous space the tanned sails of the barges drifting up with the tide seemed to stand still in red clusters of canvas sharply peaked, with gleams of varnished sprits. A haze rested on the low shores that ran out to sea in vanishing flatness. The air was dark above Gravesend,° and farther back still seemed condensed into a mournful gloom, brooding motionless over the biggest, and the greatest, town on earth.

The Director of Companies was our captain and our host. We four affectionately watched his back as he stood in the bows looking to seaward. On the whole river there was nothing that looked half so nautical. He resembled a pilot, which to a seaman is trustworthiness personified. It was difficult to realise his work was not out there in the luminous estuary, but behind him, within the brooding gloom.

Gravesend: A town on the Thames estuary.

Between us there was, as I have already said somewhere, the bond of the sea. Besides holding our hearts together through long periods of separation, it had the effect of making us tolerant of each other's yarns — and even convictions. The Lawyer — the best of old fellows — had, because of his many years and many virtues, the only cushion on deck, and was lying on the only rug. The Accountant had brought out already a box of dominoes, and was toying architecturally with the bones. Marlow sat cross-legged right aft, leaning against the mizzenmast. He had sunken cheeks, a yellow complexion, a straight back, an ascetic aspect, and, with his arms dropped, the palms of hands outwards, resembled an idol. The Director, satisfied the anchor had good hold, made his way aft and sat down amongst us. We exchanged a few words lazily. Afterwards there was silence on board the yacht. For some reason or other we did not begin that game of dominoes. We felt meditative, and fit for nothing but placid staring. The day was ending in a serenity of still and exquisite brilliance. The water shone pacifically; the sky, without a speck, was a benign immensity of unstained light; the very mist on the Essex marshes was like a gauzy and radiant fabric, hung from the wooded rises inland, and draping the low shores in diaphanous folds. Only the gloom to the west, brooding over the upper reaches, became more sombre every minute, as if angered by the approach of the sun.

And at last, in its curved and imperceptible fall, the sun sank low, and from glowing white changed to a dull red without rays and without heat, as if about to go out suddenly, stricken to death by the touch of that gloom brooding over a crowd of men.

Forthwith a change came over the waters, and the serenity became less brilliant but more profound. The old river in its broad reach rested unruffled at the decline of day, after ages of good service done to the race that peopled its banks, spread out in the tranquil dignity of a waterway leading to the uttermost ends of the earth. We looked at the venerable stream not in the vivid flush of a short day that comes and departs for ever, but in the august light of abiding memories. And indeed nothing is easier for a man who has, as the phrase goes, "followed the sea" with reverence and affection, than to evoke the great spirit of the past upon the lower reaches of the Thames. The tidal current runs to and fro in its unceasing service, crowded with memories of men and ships it has borne to the rest of home or to the battles of the sea. It had known and served all the men of whom the nation is proud, from Sir Francis Drake to Sir John Franklin, knights all, titled and untitled — the great knights-errant of the sea. It had borne all the ships whose names are like jewels flashing in the night of time, from the *Golden Hind* returning with her round flanks full of treasure, to be visited by the Queen's Highness and thus pass out of the gigantic tale, to the *Erebus* and *Terror*, bound on other conquests — and that never returned. It had known the ships and the men. They had sailed from Deptford, from Greenwich, from Erith — the adventurers and the settlers; kings' ships and the ships of men on 'Change; captains, admirals, the dark "interlopers" of the Eastern trade, and the commissioned "generals" of East India fleets.° Hunters for gold or pursuers of fame, they all had gone out on that stream, bearing the sword, and often the torch, messengers of the might within the land, bearers of spark from the sacred fire. What greatness had not floated on the ebb of that river into the mystery of an unknown earth! . . . The dreams of men, the seed of commonwealths, the germs of empires.

The sun set; the dusk fell on the stream, and lights began to appear along the shore. The Chapman lighthouse, a three-legged thing erect on a mud-flat, shone strongly. Lights of ships moved in the fairway — a great stir of lights going up and going down. And farther west on the upper reaches the place of the monstrous town was still marked ominously on the sky, a brooding gloom in sunshine, a lurid glare under the stars.

"And this also," said Marlow suddenly, "has been one of the dark places of the earth."

He was the only man of us who still "followed the sea." The worst that could be said of him was that he did not represent his class. He was a seaman, but he was a wanderer too, while most seamen lead, if one may so express it, a sedentary life. Their minds are of the stay-at-home order, and their home is always with them — the ship; and so is their country — the sea. One ship is very much like another, and the sea is always the same. In the immutability of their surroundings the foreign shores, the foreign faces, the changing immensity of life, glide past, veiled not by a sense of mystery but by a slightly disdainful ignorance; for there is nothing mysterious to a seaman unless it be the sea itself, which is the mistress of his existence and as inscrutable as Destiny. For the rest, after his hours of work, a casual stroll or a casual spree on shore suffices to unfold for him the secret of a whole continent, and generally he finds the secret not worth knowing. The yarns of seamen have a

---

Sir Francis Drake . . . fleets: Drake (c. 1540–1596) commanded the *Golden Hind*, and Sir John Franklin (1786–1847) led the ships *Erebus* and *Terror* on an ill-fated expedition to find the Northwest Passage. Deptford, Greenwich, and Erith are ports between London and Gravesend.

direct simplicity, the whole meaning of which lies within the shell of a
cracked nut. But Marlow was not typical (if his propensity to spin yarns
be excepted), and to him the meaning of an episode was not inside like
a kernel but outside, enveloping the tale which brought it out only as a
glow brings out a haze, in the likeness of one of these misty halos that
sometimes are made visible by the spectral illumination of moonshine.

His remark did not seem at all surprising. It was just like Marlow. It
was accepted in silence. No one took the trouble to grunt even; and
presently he said, very slow:

"I was thinking of very old times, when the Romans first came here,
nineteen hundred years ago — the other day. . . . Light came out of this
river since — you say Knights? Yes; but it is like a running blaze on a
plain, like a flash of lightning in the clouds. We live in the flicker — may
it last as long as the old earth keeps rolling! But darkness was here yesterday. Imagine the feelings of a commander of fine — what d'ye call
'em? — trireme in the Mediterranean, ordered suddenly to the north;
run overland across the Gauls in a hurry; put in charge of one of these
craft the legionaries — a wonderful lot of handy men they must have
been too — used to build, apparently by the hundred, in a month or
two, if we may believe what we read. Imagine him here — the very end
of the world, a sea the colour of lead, a sky the colour of smoke, a kind
of ship about as rigid as a concertina — and going up this river with
stores, or orders, or what you like. Sandbanks, marshes, forests, savages — precious little to eat fit for a civilised man, nothing but Thames
water to drink. No Falernian wine° here, no going ashore. Here and
there a military camp lost in a wilderness, like a needle in a bundle of
hay — cold, fog, tempests, disease, exile, and death — death skulking
in the air, in the water, in the bush. They must have been dying like flies
here. Oh yes — he did it. Did it very well, too, no doubt, and without
thinking much about it either, except afterwards to brag of what he had
gone through in his time, perhaps. They were men enough to face the
darkness. And perhaps he was cheered by keeping his eye on a chance
of promotion to the fleet at Ravenna by and by, if he had good friends
in Rome and survived the awful climate. Or think of a decent young
citizen in a toga — perhaps too much dice, you know — coming out
here in the train of some prefect, or tax-gatherer, or trader, even, to
mend his fortunes. Land in a swamp, march through the woods, and in
some inland post feel the savagery. The utter savagery had closed round
him — all that mysterious life of the wilderness that stirs in the forest,

---

Falernian wine: Wine celebrated by the Latin poet Horace (65 B.C.E.–8 B.C.E.).

in the jungles, in the hearts of wild men. There's no initiation either into such mysteries. He has to live in the midst of the incomprehensible, which is also detestable. And it has a fascination, too, that goes to work upon him. The fascination of the abomination — you know. Imagine the growing regrets, the longing to escape, the powerless disgust, the surrender, the hate."

He paused.

"Mind," he began again, lifting one arm from the elbow, the palm of the hand outwards, so that, with his legs folded before him, he had the pose of a Buddha preaching in European clothes and without a lotus-flower — "Mind, none of us would feel exactly like this. What saves us is efficiency — the devotion to efficiency. But these chaps were not much account, really. They were no colonists; their administration was merely a squeeze, and nothing more, I suspect. They were conquerors, and for that you want only brute force — nothing to boast of, when you have it, since your strength is just an accident arising from the weakness of others. They grabbed what they could get for the sake of what was to be got. It was just robbery with violence, aggravated murder on a great scale, and men going at it blind — as is very proper for those who tackle a darkness. The conquest of the earth, which mostly means the taking it away from those who have a different complexion or slightly flatter noses than ourselves, is not a pretty thing when you look into it too much. What redeems it is the idea only. An idea at the back of it; not a sentimental pretence but an idea; and an unselfish belief in the idea — something you can set up, and bow down before, and offer a sacrifice to. . . ."

He broke off. Flames glided in the river, small green flames, red flames, white flames, pursuing, overtaking, joining, crossing each other — then separating slowly or hastily. The traffic of the great city went on in the deepening night upon the sleepless river. We looked on, waiting patiently — there was nothing else to do till the end of the flood; but it was only after a long silence, when he said, in a hesitating voice, "I suppose you fellows remember I did once turn fresh-water sailor for a bit," that we knew we were fated, before the ebb began to run, to hear about one of Marlow's inconclusive experiences.

"I don't want to bother you much with what happened to me personally," he began, showing in this remark the weakness of many tellers of tales who seem so often unaware of what their audience would best like to hear; "yet to understand the effect of it on me you ought to know how I got out there, what I saw, how I went up that river to the place where I first met the poor chap. It was the farthest point of navigation and the culminating point of my experience. It seemed somehow to throw a kind of light on everything about me — and into my thoughts. It was sombre enough too — and pitiful — not extraordinary in any way — not very clear either. No, not very clear. And yet it seemed to throw a kind of light.

"I had then, as you remember, just returned to London after a lot of Indian Ocean, Pacific, China Seas — a regular dose of the East — six years or so, and I was loafing about, hindering you fellows in your work and invading your homes, just as though I had got a heavenly mission to civilise you. It was very fine for a time, but after a bit I did get tired of resting. Then I began to look for a ship — I should think the hardest work on earth. But the ships wouldn't even look at me. And I got tired of that game too.

"Now when I was a little chap I had a passion for maps. I would look for hours at South America, or Africa, or Australia, and lose myself in all the glories of exploration. At that time there were many blank spaces on the earth, and when I saw one that looked particularly inviting on a map (but they all look that) I would put my finger on it and say, When I grow up I will go there. The North Pole was one of these places, I remember. Well, I haven't been there yet, and shall not try now. The glamour's off. Other places were scattered about the Equator, and in every sort of latitude all over the two hemispheres. I have been in some of them, and . . . well, we won't talk about that. But there was one yet — the biggest, the most blank, so to speak — that I had a hankering after.

"True, by this time it was not a blank space any more. It had got filled since my boyhood with rivers and lakes and names. It had ceased to be a blank space of delightful mystery — a white patch for a boy to dream gloriously over. It had become a place of darkness. But there was in it one river especially, a mighty big river, that you could see on the map, resembling an immense snake uncoiled, with its head in the sea, its body at rest curving afar over a vast country, and its tail lost in the depths of the land. And as I looked at the map of it in a shopwindow it fascinated me as a snake would a bird — a silly little bird. Then I remembered there was a big concern, a Company for trade on that river. Dash it all! I thought to myself, they can't trade without using some kind of craft on that lot of fresh water — steamboats! Why shouldn't I try to get charge of one? I went on along Fleet Street,° but could not shake off the idea. The snake had charmed me.

Fleet Street: A major street in London known for business and journalism.

"You understand it was a Continental concern, that Trading Society; but I have a lot of relations living on the Continent, because it's cheap and not so nasty as it looks, they say.

"I am sorry to own I began to worry them. This was already a fresh departure for me. I was not used to get things that way, you know. I always went my own road and on my own legs where I had a mind to go. I wouldn't have believed it of myself; but, then — you see — I felt somehow I must get there by hook or by crook. So I worried them. The men said, 'My dear fellow,' and did nothing. Then — would you believe it? — I tried the women. I, Charlie Marlow, set the women to work — to get a job. Heavens! Well, you see, the notion drove me. I had an aunt, a dear enthusiastic soul. She wrote: 'It will be delightful. I am ready to do anything, anything for you. It is a glorious idea. I know the wife of a very high personage in the Administration, and also a man who has lots of influence with,' etc. etc. She was determined to make no end of fuss to get me appointed skipper of a river steamboat, if such was my fancy.

"I got my appointment — of course; and I got it very quick. It appears the Company had received news that one of their captains had been killed in a scuffle with the natives. This was my chance, and it made me the more anxious to go. It was only months and months afterwards, when I made the attempt to recover what was left of the body, that I heard the original quarrel arose from a misunderstanding about some hens. Yes, two black hens. Fresleven — that was the fellow's name, a Dane — thought himself wronged somehow in the bargain, so he went ashore and started to hammer the chief of the village with a stick. Oh, it didn't surprise me in the least to hear this, and at the same time to be told that Fresleven was the gentlest, quietest creature that ever walked on two legs. No doubt he was; but he had been a couple of years already out there engaged in the noble cause, you know, and he probably felt the need at last of asserting his self-respect in some way. Therefore he whacked the old nigger mercilessly, while a big crowd of his people watched him, thunderstruck, till some man — I was told the chief's son — in desperation at hearing the old chap yell, made a tentative jab with a spear at the white man — and of course it went quite easy between the shoulder-blades. Then the whole population cleared into the forest, expecting all kinds of calamities to happen, while, on the other hand, the steamer Fresleven commanded left also in a bad panic, in charge of the engineer, I believe. Afterwards nobody seemed to trouble much about Fresleven's remains, till I got out and stepped into his shoes. I couldn't let it rest, though; but when an opportunity offered at last to meet my predecessor, the grass growing through his ribs was tall enough to hide his bones. They were all there. The supernatural being had not been touched after he fell. And the village was deserted, the huts gaped black, rotting, all askew within the fallen enclosures. A calamity had come to it, sure enough. The people had vanished. Mad terror had scattered them, men, women, and children, through the bush, and they had never returned. What became of the hens I don't know either. I should think the cause of progress got them, anyhow. However, through this glorious affair I got my appointment, before I had fairly begun to hope for it.

"I flew around like mad to get ready, and before forty-eight hours I was crossing the Channel to show myself to my employers, and sign the contract. In a very few hours I arrived in a city that always makes me think of a whited sepulchre. Prejudice no doubt. I had no difficulty in finding the Company's offices. It was the biggest thing in the town, and everybody I met was full of it. They were going to run an oversea empire, and make no end of coin by trade.

"A narrow and deserted street in deep shadow, high houses, innumerable windows with venetian blinds, a dead silence, grass sprouting between the stones, imposing carriage archways right and left, immense double doors standing ponderously ajar. I slipped through one of these cracks, went up a swept and ungarnished staircase, as arid as a desert, and opened the first door I came to. Two women, one fat and the other slim, sat on straw-bottomed chairs, knitting black wool. The slim one got up and walked straight at me — still knitting with downcast eyes — and only just as I began to think of getting out of her way, as you would for a somnambulist, stood still, and looked up. Her dress was as plain as an umbrella-cover, and she turned round without a word and preceded me into a waiting-room. I gave my name, and looked about. Deal table in the middle, plain chairs all round the walls, on one end a large shining map, marked with all the colours of a rainbow. There was a vast amount of red — good to see at any time, because one knows that some real work is done in there, a deuce of a lot of blue, a little green, smears of orange, and, on the East Coast, a purple patch, to show where the jolly pioneers of progress drink the jolly lager-beer. However, I wasn't going into any of these. I was going into the yellow. Dead in the centre. And the river was there — fascinating — deadly — like a snake. Ough! A door opened, a white-haired secretarial head, but wearing a compassionate expression, appeared, and a skinny forefinger beckoned me into the sanctuary. Its light was dim, and a heavy writing-desk squatted in the middle. From behind that structure came out an impression of pale plumpness in a frock-coat. The great man himself. He was five feet six, I should judge, and had his grip on the handle-end of ever so many millions. He shook hands, I fancy, murmured vaguely, was satisfied with my French. *Bon voyage.*

"In about forty-five seconds I found myself again in the waiting-room with the compassionate secretary, who, full of desolation and sympathy, made me sign some document. I believe I undertook amongst other things not to disclose any trade secrets. Well, I am not going to.

"I began to feel slightly uneasy. You know I am not used to such ceremonies, and there was something ominous in the atmosphere. It was just as though I had been let into some conspiracy — I don't know — something not quite right; and I was glad to get out. In the outer room the two women knitted black wool feverishly. People were arriving, and the younger one was walking back and forth introducing them. The old one sat on her chair. Her flat cloth slippers were propped up on a foot-warmer, and a cat reposed on her lap. She wore a starched white affair on her head, had a wart on one cheek, and silver-rimmed spectacles hung on the tip of her nose. She glanced at me above the glasses. The swift and indifferent placidity of that look troubled me. Two youths with foolish and cheery countenances were being piloted over, and she threw at them the same quick glance of unconcerned wisdom. She seemed to know all about them and about me too. An eerie feeling came over me. She seemed uncanny and fateful. Often far away there I thought of these two, guarding the door of Darkness, knitting black wool as for a warm pall, one introducing, introducing continuously to the unknown, the other scrutinising the cheery and foolish faces with unconcerned old eyes. *Ave!* Old knitter of black wool. *Morituri te salutant.*° Not many of those she looked at ever saw her again — not half, by a long way.

"There was yet a visit to the doctor. 'A simple formality,' assured me the secretary, with an air of taking an immense part in all my sorrows. Accordingly a young chap wearing his hat over the left eyebrow, some clerk I suppose — there must have been clerks in the business, though the house was as still as a house in a city of the dead — came from somewhere upstairs, and led me forth. He was shabby and careless, with ink-stains on the sleeves of his jacket, and his cravat was large and billowy, under a chin shaped like the toe of an old boot. It was a little too early for the doctor, so I proposed a drink, and thereupon he developed a vein of joviality. As we sat over our vermuths he glorified the

---

Ave! . . . Morituri te salutant: "Greetings! . . . We who are about to die salute you."

Company's business, and by and by I expressed casually my surprise at
him not going out there. He became very cool and collected all at once.
'I am not such a fool as I look, quoth Plato to his disciples,' he said
sententiously, emptied his glass with great resolution, and we rose.

"The old doctor felt my pulse, evidently thinking of something else
the while. 'Good, good for there,' he mumbled, and then with a certain
eagerness asked me whether I would let him measure my head. Rather
surprised, I said Yes, when he produced a thing like callipers and got the
dimensions back and front and every way, taking notes carefully. He
was an unshaven little man in a threadbare coat like a gaberdine, with
his feet in slippers, and I thought him a harmless fool. 'I always ask
leave, in the interests of science, to measure the crania of those going
out there,' he said. 'And when they come back too?' I asked. 'Oh, I
never see them,' he remarked; 'and, moreover, the changes take place
inside, you know.' He smiled, as if at some quiet joke. 'So you are going
out there. Famous. Interesting too.' He gave me a searching glance,
and made another note. 'Ever any madness in your family?' he asked, in
matter-of-fact tone. I felt very annoyed. 'Is that question in the interests of science too?' 'It would be,' he said, without taking notice of my
irritation, 'interesting for science to watch the mental changes of individuals, on the spot, but . . .' 'Are you an alienist?'° I interrupted. 'Every
doctor should be — a little,' answered that original imperturbably. 'I
have a little theory which you Messieurs who go out there must help
me to prove. This is my share in the advantages my country shall reap
from the possession of such a magnificent dependency. The mere wealth
I leave to others. Pardon my questions, but you are the first Englishman
coming under my observation . . .' I hastened to assure him I was not
in the least typical. 'If I were,' said I, 'I wouldn't be talking like this
with you.' 'What you say is rather profound, and probably erroneous,'
he said, with a laugh. 'Avoid irritation more than exposure to the sun.
Adieu. How do you English say, eh? Good-bye. Ah! Good-bye. Adieu.
In the tropics one must before everything keep calm.' . . . He lifted a
warning forefinger. . . . *Du calme, du calme. Adieu.*'

"One thing more remained to do — say goodbye to my excellent
aunt. I found her triumphant. I had a cup of tea — the last decent cup
of tea for many days — and in a room that most soothingly looked just
as you would expect a lady's drawing-room to look, we had a long quiet
chat by the fireside. In the course of these confidences it became quite
plain to me I had been represented to the wife of the high dignitary,

alienist: A doctor concerned with psychological disturbances.

and goodness knows to how many more people besides, as an exceptional and gifted creature — a piece of good fortune for the Company — a man you don't get hold of every day. Good Heavens! and I was going to take charge of a two-penny-halfpenny river-steamboat with a penny whistle attached! It appeared, however, I was also one of the Workers, with a capital — you know. Something like an emissary of light, something like a lower sort of apostle. There had been a lot of such rot let loose in print and talk just about that time, and the excellent woman, living right in the rush of all that humbug, got carried off her feet. She talked about 'weaning those ignorant millions from their horrid ways,' till, upon my word, she made me quite uncomfortable. I ventured to hint that the Company was run for profit.

" 'You forget, dear Charlie, that the labourer is worthy of his hire,' she said brightly. It's queer how out of touch with truth women are. They live in a world of their own, and there had never been anything like it, and never can be. It is too beautiful altogether, and if they were to set it up it would go to pieces before the first sunset. Some confounded fact we men have been living contentedly with ever since the day of creation would start up and knock the whole thing over.

"After this I got embraced, told to wear flannel, be sure to write often, and so on — and I left. In the street — I don't know why — a queer feeling came to me that I was an impostor. Odd thing that I, who used to clear out for any part of the world at twenty-four hours' notice, with less thought than most men give to the crossing of a street, had a moment — I won't say of hesitation, but of startled pause, before this commonplace affair. The best way I can explain it to you is by saying that, for a second or two, I felt as though, instead of going to the centre of a continent, I were about to set off for the centre of the earth.

"I left in a French steamer, and she called in every blamed port they have out there, for, as far as I could see, the sole purpose of landing soldiers and custom-house officers. I watched the coast. Watching a coast as it slips by the ship is like thinking about an enigma. There it is before you — smiling, frowning, inviting, grand, mean, insipid, or savage, and always mute with an air of whispering, Come and find out. This one was almost featureless, as if still in the making, with an aspect of monotonous grimness. The edge of a colossal jungle, so dark green as to be almost black, fringed with white surf, ran straight, like a ruled line, far, far away along a blue sea whose glitter was blurred by a creeping mist. The sun was fierce, the land seemed to glisten and drip with steam. Here and there greyish-whitish specks showed up clustered inside the white surf, with a flag flying above them perhaps — settlements some centuries old, and still no bigger than pin-heads on the untouched expanse of their background. We pounded along, stopped, landed soldiers; went on, landed custom-house clerks to levy toll in what looked like a God-forsaken wilderness, with a tin shed and a flagpole lost in it; landed more soldiers — to take care of the custom-house clerks presumably. Some, I heard, got drowned in the surf; but whether they did or not, nobody seemed particularly to care. They were just flung out there, and on we went. Every day the coast looked the same, as though we had not moved; but we passed various places — trading places — with names like Gran' Bassam, Little Popo; names that seemed to belong to some sordid farce acted in front of a sinister back-cloth. The idleness of a passenger, my isolation amongst all these men with whom I had no point of contact, the oily and languid sea, the uniform sombreness of the coast, seemed to keep me away from the truth of things, within the toil of a mournful and senseless delusion. The voice of the surf heard now and then was a positive pleasure, like the speech of a brother. It was something natural, that had its reason, that had a meaning. Now and then a boat from the shore gave one a momentary contact with reality. It was paddled by black fellows. You could see from afar the white of their eyeballs glistening. They shouted, sang; their bodies streamed with perspiration; they had faces like grotesque masks — these chaps; but they had bone, muscle, a wild vitality, an intense energy of movement, that was as natural and true as the surf along their coast. They wanted no excuse for being there. They were a great comfort to look at. For a time I would feel I belonged still to a world of straightforward facts; but the feeling would not last long. Something would turn up to scare it away. Once, I remember, we came upon a man-of-war anchored off the coast. There wasn't even a shed there, and she was shelling the bush. It appears the French had one of their wars going on thereabouts. Her ensign dropped limp like a rag; the muzzles of the long six-inch guns stuck out all over the low hull; the greasy, slimy swell swung her up lazily and let her down, swaying her thin masts. In the empty immensity of earth, sky, and water, there she was, incomprehensible, firing into a continent. Pop, would go one of the six-inch guns; a small flame would dart and vanish, a little white smoke would disappear, a tiny projectile would give a feeble screech — and nothing happened. Nothing could happen. There was a touch of insanity in the proceeding, a sense of lugubrious drollery in the sight; and it was not dissipated by somebody on board assuring me earnestly there was a camp of natives — he called them enemies! — hidden out of sight somewhere.

"We gave her her letters (I heard the men in that lonely ship were dying of fever at the rate of three a day) and went on. We called at some more places with farcical names, where the merry dance of death and trade goes on in a still and earthy atmosphere as of an overheated catacomb; all along the formless coast bordered by dangerous surf, as if Nature herself had tried to ward off intruders; in and out of rivers, streams of death in life, whose banks were rotting into mud, whose waters, thickened into slime, invaded the contorted mangroves, that seemed to writhe at us in the extremity of an impotent despair. Nowhere did we stop long enough to get a particularised impression, but the general sense of vague and oppressive wonder grew upon me. It was like a weary pilgrimage amongst hints for nightmares.

"It was upward of thirty days before I saw the mouth of the big river. We anchored off the seat of the government. But my work would not begin till some two hundred miles farther on. So as soon as I could I made a start for a place thirty miles higher up.

"I had my passage on a little sea-going steamer. Her captain was a Swede, and knowing me for a seaman, invited me on the bridge. He was a young man, lean, fair, and morose, with lanky hair and a shuffling gait. As we left the miserable little wharf, he tossed his head contemptuously at the shore. 'Been living there?' he asked. I said, 'Yes.' 'Fine lot these government chaps — are they not?' he went on, speaking English with great precision and considerable bitterness. 'It is funny what some people will do for a few francs a month. I wonder what becomes of that kind when it goes up country?' I said to him I expected to see that soon. 'So-o-o!' he exclaimed. He shuffled athwart, keeping one eye ahead vigilantly. 'Don't be too sure,' he continued. 'The other day I took up a man who hanged himself on the road. He was a Swede, too.' 'Hanged himself! Why, in God's name?' I cried. He kept on looking out watchfully. 'Who knows? The sun too much for him, or the country perhaps.'

"At last we opened a reach. A rocky cliff appeared, mounds of turned-up earth by the shore, houses on a hill, others with iron roofs, amongst a waste of excavations, or hanging to the declivity. A continuous noise of the rapids above hovered over this scene of inhabited devastation. A lot of people, mostly black and naked, moved about like ants. A jetty projected into the river. A blinding sunlight drowned all this at times in a sudden recrudescence of glare. 'There's your Company's station,' said the Swede, pointing to three wooden barrack-like structures on the rocky slope. 'I will send your things up. Four boxes did you say? So. Farewell.'

"I came upon a boiler wallowing in the grass, then found a path leading up the hill. It turned aside for the boulders, and also for an undersized railway truck lying there on its back with its wheels in the air. One was off. The thing looked as dead as the carcass of some animal. I came upon more pieces of decaying machinery, a stack of rusty rails. To the left a clump of trees made a shady spot, where dark things seemed to stir feebly. I blinked, the path was steep. A horn tooted to the right and I saw the black people run. A heavy and dull detonation shook the ground, a puff of smoke came out of the cliff, and that was all. No change appeared on the face of the rock. They were building a railway. The cliff was not in the way or anything; but this objectless blasting was all the work going on.

"A slight clinking behind me made me turn my head. Six black men advanced in a file, toiling up the path. They walked erect and slow, balancing small baskets full of earth on their heads, and the clink kept time with their footsteps. Black rags were wound round their loins, and the short ends behind waggled to and fro like tails. I could see every rib, the joints of their limbs were like knots in a rope; each had an iron collar on his neck, and all were connected together with a chain whose bights swung between them, rhythmically clinking. Another report from the cliff made me think suddenly of that ship of war I had seen firing into a continent. It was the same kind of ominous voice; but these men could by no stretch of imagination be called enemies. They were called criminals, and the outraged law, like the bursting shells, had come to them, an insoluble mystery from the sea. All their meagre breasts panted together, the violently dilated nostrils quivered, the eyes stared stonily uphill. They passed me within six inches, without a glance, with that complete, deathlike indifference of unhappy savages. Behind this raw matter one of the reclaimed, the product of the new forces at work, strolled despondently, carrying a rifle by its middle. He had a uniform jacket with one button off, and seeing a white man on the path, hoisted his weapon to his shoulder with alacrity. This was simple prudence, white men being so much alike at a distance that he could not tell who I might be. He was speedily reassured, and with a large, white, rascally grin, and a glance at his charge, seemed to take me into partnership in his exalted trust. After all, I also was a part of the great cause of these high and just proceedings.

"Instead of going up, I turned and descended to the left. My idea was to let that chain-gang get out of sight before I climbed the hill. You know I am not particularly tender; I've had to strike and to fend off. I've had to resist and to attack sometimes — that's only one way of resisting — without counting the exact cost, according to the demands of such sort of life as I had blundered into. I've seen the devil of violence, and the devil of greed, and the devil of hot desire; but, by all the stars! these were strong, lusty, red-eyed devils, that swayed and drove men — men, I tell you. But as I stood on this hillside, I foresaw that in the blinding sunshine of that land I would become acquainted with a flabby, pretending, weak-eyed devil of a rapacious and pitiless folly. How insidious he could be, too, I was only to find out several months later and a thousand miles farther. For a moment I stood appalled, as though by a warning. Finally I descended the hill, obliquely, towards the trees I had seen.

"I avoided a vast artificial hole somebody had been digging on the slope, the purpose of which I found it impossible to divine. It wasn't a quarry or a sandpit, anyhow. It was just a hole. It might have been connected with the philanthropic desire of giving the criminals something to do. I don't know. Then I nearly fell into a very narrow ravine almost no more than a scar in the hillside. I discovered that a lot of imported drainage-pipes for the settlement had been tumbled in there. There wasn't one that was not broken. It was a wanton smash-up. At last I got under the trees. My purpose was to stroll into the shade for a moment; but no sooner within than it seemed to me I had stepped into the gloomy circle of some Inferno. The rapids were near, and an uninterrupted, uniform, headlong, rushing noise filled the mournful stillness of the grove, where not a breath stirred, not a leaf moved, with a mysterious sound — as though the tearing pace of the launched earth had suddenly become audible.

"Black shapes crouched, lay, sat between the trees, leaning against the trunks, clinging to the earth, half coming out, half effaced within the dim light, in all the attitudes of pain, abandonment, and despair. Another mine on the cliff went off, followed by a slight shudder of the soil under my feet. The work was going on. The work! And this was the place where some of the helpers had withdrawn to die.

"They were dying slowly — it was very clear. They were not enemies, they were not criminals, they were nothing earthly now — nothing but black shadows of disease and starvation, lying confusedly in the greenish gloom. Brought from all the recesses of the coast in all the legality of time contracts, lost in uncongenial surroundings, fed on unfamiliar food, they sickened, became inefficient, and were then allowed to crawl away and rest. These moribund shapes were free as air — and nearly as thin. I began to distinguish the gleam of the eyes under the trees. Then, glancing down, I saw a face near my hand. The black bones reclined at full length with one shoulder against the tree, and slowly the eyelids rose and the sunken eyes looked up at me, enormous and vacant, a kind of blind, white flicker in the depths of the orbs, which died out slowly. The man seemed young — almost a boy — but you know with them it's hard to tell. I found nothing else to do but to offer him one of my good Swede's ship's biscuits I had in my pocket. The fingers closed slowly on it and held — there was no other movement and no other glance. He had tied a bit of white worsted round his neck — Why? Where did he get it? Was it a badge — an ornament — a charm — a propitiatory act? Was there any idea at all connected with it? It looked startling round his black neck, this bit of white thread from beyond the seas.

"Near the same tree two more bundles of acute angles sat with their legs drawn up. One, with his chin propped on his knees, stared at nothing, in an intolerable and appalling manner: his brother phantom rested its forehead, as if overcome with a great weariness; and all about others were scattered in every pose of contorted collapse, as in some picture of a massacre or a pestilence. While I stood horror-struck, one of these creatures rose to his hands and knees, and went off on all-fours towards the river to drink. He lapped out of his hand, then sat up in the sunlight, crossing his shins in front of him, and after a time let his woolly head fall on his breastbone.

"I didn't want any more loitering in the shade, and I made haste towards the station. When near the buildings I met a white man, in such an unexpected elegance of get-up that in the first moment I took him for a sort of vision. I saw a high starched collar, white cuffs, a light alpaca jacket, snowy trousers, a clean necktie, and varnished boots. No hat. Hair parted, brushed, oiled, under a green-lined parasol held in a big white hand. He was amazing, and had a pen-holder behind his ear.

"I shook hands with this miracle, and I learned he was the Company's chief accountant, and that all the book-keeping was done at this station. He had come out for a moment, he said, 'to get a breath of fresh air.' The expression sounded wonderfully odd, with its suggestion of sedentary desk-life. I wouldn't have mentioned the fellow to you at all, only it was from his lips that I first heard the name of the man who is so indissolubly connected with the memories of that time. Moreover, I respected the fellow. Yes; I respected his collars, his vast cuffs, his brushed hair. His appearance was certainly that of a hairdresser's dummy; but in the great demoralisation of the land he kept up his appearance. That's backbone. His starched collars and got-up shirt-fronts were achievements of character. He had been out nearly three years; and, later, I could not help asking him how he managed to sport such linen. He had just the faintest blush, and said modestly, 'I've been teaching one of the native women about the station. It was difficult. She had a distaste for the work.' Thus this man had verily accomplished something. And he was devoted to his books, which were in apple-pie order.

"Everything else in the station was in a muddle, — heads, things, buildings. Strings of dusty niggers with splay feet arrived and departed; a stream of manufactured goods, rubbishy cottons, beads, and brass-wire set into the depths of darkness, and in return came a precious trickle of ivory.

"I had to wait in the station for ten days — an eternity. I lived in a hut in the yard, but to be out of the chaos I would sometimes get into the accountant's office. It was built of horizontal planks, and so badly put together that, as he bent over his high desk, he was barred from neck to heels with narrow strips of sunlight. There was no need to open the big shutter to see. It was hot there too; big flies buzzed fiendishly and did not sting, but stabbed. I sat generally on the floor, while, of faultless appearance (and even slightly scented), perching on a high stool, he wrote, he wrote. Sometimes he stood up for exercise. When a truckle-bed with a sick man (some invalided agent from up-country) was put in there, he exhibited a gentle annoyance. 'The groans of this sick person,' he said, 'distract my attention. And without that it is extremely difficult to guard against clerical errors in this climate.'

"One day he remarked, without lifting his head, 'In the interior you will no doubt meet Mr. Kurtz.' On my asking who Mr. Kurtz was, he said he was a first-class agent; and seeing my disappointment at this information, he added slowly, laying down his pen, 'He is a very remark-able person.' Further questions elicited from him that Mr. Kurtz was at present in charge of a trading-post, a very important one, in the true ivory-country, at 'the very bottom of there. Sends in as much ivory as all the others put together . . .' He began to write again. The sick man was too ill to groan. The flies buzzed in a great peace.

"Suddenly there was a growing murmur of voices and a great tramp-ing of feet. A caravan had come in. A violent babble of uncouth sounds burst out on the other side of the planks. All the carriers were speak-ing together, and in the midst of the uproar the lamentable voice of the chief agent was heard 'giving it up' tearfully for the twentieth time that day. . . . He rose slowly. 'What a frightful row,' he said. He crossed the room gently to look at the sick man, and returning, said to me, 'He does not hear.' 'What! Dead?' I asked, startled. 'No, not yet,' he answered, with great composure. Then, alluding with a toss of the head to the tumult in the station-yard, 'When one has got to make correct entries, one comes to hate those savages — hate them to death.' He remained thoughtful for a moment. 'When you see Mr. Kurtz,' he went on, 'tell him for me that everything here' — he glanced at the desk — 'is very satisfactory. I don't like to write to him — with those messengers of ours you never know who may get hold of your letter — at that Central Station.' He stared at me for a moment with his mild, bulging eyes. 'Oh, he will go far, very far,' he began again. 'He will be a somebody in the Administration before long. They, above — the Council in Europe, you know — mean him to be.'

"He turned to his work. The noise outside had ceased, and presently in going out I stopped at the door. In the steady buzz of flies the homeward-bound agent was lying flushed and insensible; the other, bent over his books, was making correct entries of perfectly correct transactions; and fifty feet below the doorstep I could see the still tree-tops of the grove of death.

"Next day I left that station at last, with a caravan of sixty men, for a two-hundred-mile tramp.

"No use telling you much about that. Paths, paths, everywhere; a stamped-in network of paths spreading over the empty land, through long grass, through burnt grass, through thickets, down and up chilly ravines, up and down stony hills ablaze with heat; and a solitude, a solitude, nobody, not a hut. The population had cleared out a long time ago. Well, if a lot of mysterious niggers armed with all kinds of fearful weapons suddenly took to travelling on the road between Deal and Gravesend, catching the yokels right and left to carry heavy loads for them, I fancy every farm and cottage thereabouts would get empty very soon. Only here the dwellings were gone too. Still, I passed through several abandoned villages. There's something pathetically childish in the ruins of grass walls. Day after day, with the stamp and shuffle of sixty pair of bare feet behind me, each pair under a 60-lb. load. Camp, cook, sleep; strike camp, march. Now and then a carrier dead in harness, at rest in the long grass near the path, with an empty water-gourd and his long staff lying by his side. A great silence around and above. Perhaps on some quiet night the tremor of far-off drums, sinking, swelling, a tremor vast, faint; a sound weird, appealing, suggestive, and wild — and perhaps with as profound a meaning as the sound of bells in a Christian country. Once a white man in an unbuttoned uniform, camping on the path with an armed escort of lank Zanzibaris,° very hospitable and festive — not to say drunk. Was looking after the upkeep

---

Zanzibaris: Mercenaries from the African Zanzibar nation.

of the road, he declared. Can't say I saw any road or any upkeep, unless the body of a middle-aged negro, with a bullet-hole in the forehead, upon which I absolutely stumbled three miles farther on, may be considered a permanent improvement. I had a white companion too, not a bad chap, but rather too fleshy and with the exasperating habit of fainting on the hot hillsides, miles away from the least bit of shade and water. Annoying, you know, to hold your own coat like a parasol over a man's head while he is coming to. I couldn't help asking him once what he meant by coming there at all. 'To make money, of course. What do you think?' he said scornfully. Then he got fever, and had to be carried in a hammock slung under a pole. As he weighed sixteen stone° I had no end of rows with the carriers. They jibbed, ran away, sneaked off with their loads in the night — quite a mutiny. So, one evening, I made a speech in English with gestures, not one of which was lost to the sixty pairs of eyes before me, and the next morning I started the hammock off in front all right. An hour afterwards I came upon the whole concern wrecked in a bush — man, hammock, groans, blankets, horrors. The heavy pole had skinned his poor nose. He was very anxious for me to kill somebody, but there wasn't the shadow of a carrier near. I remembered the old doctor — 'It would be interesting for science to watch the mental changes to individuals, on the spot.' I felt I was becoming scientifically interesting. However, all that is to no purpose. On the fifteenth day I came in sight of the big river again, and hobbled into the Central Station. It was on a back water surrounded by scrub and forest, with a pretty border of smelly mud on one side, and on the three others enclosed by a crazy fence of rushes. A neglected gap was all the gate it had, and the first glance at the place was enough to let you see the flabby devil was running that show. White men with long staves in their hands appeared languidly from amongst the buildings, strolling up to take a look at me, and then retired out of sight somewhere. One of them, a stout, excitable chap with black moustaches, informed me with great volubility and many digressions, as soon as I told him who I was, that my steamer was at the bottom of the river. I was thunderstruck. What, how, why? Oh, it was 'all right.' The 'manager himself' was there. All quite correct. 'Everybody had behaved splendidly! splendidly!' — 'You must,' he said in agitation, 'go and see the general manager at once. He is waiting!'

"I did not see the real significance of that wreck at once. I fancy I see it now, but I am not sure — not at all. Certainly the affair was too

sixteen stone: 224 pounds.

stupid — when I think of it — to be altogether natural. Still . . . But at the moment it presented itself simply as a confounded nuisance. The steamer was sunk. They had started two days before in a sudden hurry up the river with the manager on board, in charge of some volunteer skipper, and before they had been out three hours they tore the bottom out of her on stones, and she sank near the south bank. I asked myself what I was to do there, now my boat was lost. As a matter of fact, I had plenty to do in fishing my command out of the river. I had to set about it the very next day. That, and the repairs when I brought the pieces to the station, took some months.

"My first interview with the manager was curious. He did not ask me to sit down after my twenty-mile walk that morning. He was commonplace in complexion, in feature, in manners, and in voice. He was of middle size and of ordinary build. His eyes, of the usual blue, were perhaps remarkably cold, and he certainly could make his glance fall on one as trenchant and heavy as an axe. But even at these times the rest of his person seemed to disclaim the intention. Otherwise there was only an indefinable, faint expression of his lips, something stealthy — a smile — not a smile — I remember it, but I can't explain. It was unconscious, this smile was, though just after he had said something it got intensified for an instant. It came at the end of his speeches like a seal applied to the words to make the meaning of the commonest phrase appear absolutely inscrutable. He was a common trader, from his youth up employed in these parts — nothing more. He was obeyed, yet he inspired neither love nor fear, nor even respect. He inspired uneasiness. That was it! Uneasiness. Not a definite mistrust — just uneasiness — nothing more. You have no idea how effective such a . . . a . . . faculty can be. He had no genius for organising, for initiative, or for order even. That was evident in such things as the deplorable state of the station. He had no learning, and no intelligence. His position had come to him — why? Perhaps because he was never ill . . . He had served three terms of three years out there . . . Because triumphant health in the general rout of constitutions is a kind of power in itself. When he went home on leave he rioted on a large scale — pompously. Jack ashore — with a difference — in externals only. This one could gather from his casual talk. He originated nothing, he could keep the routine going — that's all. But he was great. He was great by this little thing that it was impossible to tell what could control such a man. He never gave that secret away. Perhaps there was nothing within him. Such a suspicion made one pause — for out there there were no external checks. Once when various tropical diseases had laid low almost every 'agent' in the station, he was heard to say, 'Men who come out here should have no entrails.' He sealed the utterance with that smile of his, as though it had been a door opening into a darkness he had in his keeping. You fancied you had seen things — but the seal was on. When annoyed at meal-times by the constant quarrels of the white men about precedence, he ordered an immense round table to be made, for which a special house had to be built. This was the station's mess-room. Where he sat was the first place — the rest were nowhere. One felt this to be his unalterable conviction. He was neither civil nor uncivil. He was quiet. He allowed his 'boy' — an overfed young negro from the coast — to treat the white men, under his very eyes, with provoking insolence.

"He began to speak as soon as he saw me. I had been very long on the road. He could not wait. Had to start without me. The up-river stations had to be relieved. There had been so many delays already that he did not know who was dead and who was alive, and how they got on — and so on, and so on. He paid no attention to my explanations, and, playing with a stick of sealing-wax, repeated several times that the situation was 'very grave, very grave.' There were rumours that a very important station was in jeopardy, and its chief, Mr. Kurtz, was ill. Hoped it was not true. Mr. Kurtz was . . . I felt weary and irritable. Hang Kurtz, I thought. I interrupted him by saying I had heard of Mr. Kurtz on the coast. 'Ah! So they talk of him down there,' he murmured to himself. Then he began again, assuring me Mr. Kurtz was the best agent he had, an exceptional man, of the greatest importance to the Company; therefore I could understand his anxiety. He was, he said, 'very, very uneasy.' Certainly he fidgeted on his chair a good deal, exclaimed, 'Ah, Mr. Kurtz!' broke the stick of sealing-wax and seemed dumbfounded by the accident. Next thing he wanted to know 'how long it would take to' . . . I interrupted him again. Being hungry, you know, and kept on my feet too, I was getting savage. 'How can I tell?' I said. 'I haven't even seen the wreck yet — some months, no doubt.' All this talk seemed to me so futile. 'Some months,' he said. 'Well, let us say three months before we can make a start. Yes. That ought to do the affair.' I flung out of his hut (he lived all alone in a clay hut with a sort of verandah) muttering to myself my opinion of him. He was a chattering idiot. Afterwards I took it back when it was borne in upon me startlingly with what extreme nicety he had estimated the time requisite for the 'affair.'

"I went to work the next day, turning, so to speak, my back on that station. In that way only it seemed to me I could keep my hold on the redeeming facts of life. Still, one must look about sometimes; and then

I saw this station, these men strolling aimlessly about in the sunshine of the yard. I asked myself sometimes what it all meant. They wandered here and there with their absurd long staves in their hands, like a lot of faithless pilgrims bewitched inside a rotten fence. The word 'ivory' rang in the air, was whispered, was sighed. You would think they were pray-ing to it. A taint of imbecile rapacity blew through it all, like a whiff from some corpse. By Jove! I've never seen anything so unreal in my life. And outside, the silent wilderness surrounding this cleared speck on the earth struck me as something great and invincible, like evil or truth, waiting patiently for the passing away of this fantastic invasion.

"Oh, those months! Well, never mind. Various things happened. One evening a grass shed full of calico, cotton prints, beads, and I don't know what else, burst into a blaze so suddenly that you would have thought the earth had opened to let an avenging fire consume all that trash. I was smoking my pipe quietly by my dismantled steamer, and saw them all cutting capers in the light, with their arms lifted high, when the stout man with moustaches came tearing down to the river, a tin pail in his hand, assured me that everybody was 'behaving splen-didly, splendidly,' dipped about a quart of water and tore back again. I noticed there was a hole in the bottom of his pail.

"I strolled up. There was no hurry. You see the thing had gone off like a box of matches. It had been hopeless from the very first. The flame had leaped high, driven everybody back, lighted up everything — and collapsed. The shed was already a heap of embers glowing fiercely. A nigger was being beaten near by. They said he had caused the fire in some way; be that as it may, he was screeching most horribly. I saw him, later, for several days, sitting in a bit of shade looking very sick and trying to recover himself: afterwards he arose and went out — and the wilderness without a sound took him into its bosom again. As I approached the glow from the dark I found myself at the back of two men, talking. I heard the name of Kurtz pronounced, then the words 'take advantage of this unfortunate accident.' One of the men was the manager. I wished him a good evening. 'Did you ever see anything like it — eh? it is incredible,' he said, and walked off. The other man remained. He was a first-class agent, young, gentlemanly, a bit reserved, with a forked little beard and a hooked nose. He was stand-offish with the other agents, and they on their side said he was the manager's spy upon them. As to me, I had hardly ever spoken to him before. We got into talk, and by and by we strolled away from the hissing ruins. Then he asked me to his room, which was in the main building of the station. He struck a match, and I perceived that this young aristocrat had not only a silver-mounted dressing-case but also a whole candle all to himself. Just at that time the manager was the only man supposed to have any right to candles. Native mats covered the clay walls; a collection of spears, assegais,° shields, knives, was hung up in trophies. The business entrusted to this fellow was the making of bricks — so I had been informed; but there wasn't a fragment of a brick anywhere in the station, and he had been there more than a year — waiting. It seems he could not make bricks without something, I don't know what — straw maybe. Anyway, it could not be found there, and as it was not likely to be sent from Europe, it did not appear clear to me what he was waiting for. An act of special creation perhaps. However, they were all waiting — all the sixteen or twenty pilgrims of them — for something; and upon my word it did not seem an uncongenial occupation, from the way they took it, though the only thing that ever came to them was disease — as far as I could see. They beguiled the time by backbiting and intriguing against each other in a foolish kind of way. There was an air of plotting about that station, but nothing came of it, of course. It was as unreal as everything else — as the philanthropic pretence of the whole concern, as their talk, as their government, as their show of work. The only real feeling was a desire to get appointed to a trading-post where ivory was to be had, so that they could earn percentages. They intrigued and slandered and hated each other only on that account — but as to effectually lifting a little finger — oh no. By Heavens! there is something after all in the world allowing one man to steal a horse while another must not look at a halter. Steal a horse straight out. Very well. He has done it. Perhaps he can ride. But there is a way of looking at a halter that would provoke the most charitable of saints into a kick.

"I had no idea why he wanted to be sociable, but as we chatted in there it suddenly occurred to me the fellow was trying to get at something — in fact, pumping me. He alluded constantly to Europe, to the people I was supposed to know there — putting leading questions as to my acquaintances in the sepulchral city, and so on. His little eyes glittered like mica discs — with curiosity — though he tried to keep up a bit of superciliousness. At first I was astonished, but very soon I became awfully curious to see what he would find out from me. I couldn't possibly imagine what I had in me to make it worth his while. It was very pretty to see how he baffled himself, for in truth my body was full only of chills, and my head had nothing in it but that wretched steamboat business. It was evident he took me for a perfectly shameless prevaricator.

---

assegais: Thin spears designed to be thrown.

At last he got angry, and, to conceal a movement of furious annoyance, he yawned. I rose. Then I noticed a small sketch in oils, on a panel, representing a woman, draped and blindfolded, carrying a lighted torch. The background was sombre — almost black. The movement of the woman was stately, and the effect of the torchlight on the face was sinister.

"It arrested me, and he stood by civilly, holding an empty half-pint champagne bottle (medical comforts) with the candle stuck in it. To my question he said Mr. Kurtz had painted this — in this very station more than a year ago — while waiting for means to go to his trading-post. 'Tell me, pray,' said I, 'who is this Mr. Kurtz?'

" 'The chief of the Inner Station,' he answered in a short tone, looking away. 'Much obliged,' I said, laughing. 'And you are the brickmaker of the Central Station. Every one knows that.' He was silent for a while. 'He is a prodigy,' he said at last. 'He is an emissary of pity, and science, and progress, and devil knows what else. We want,' he began to declaim suddenly, 'for the guidance of the cause entrusted to us by Europe, so to speak, higher intelligence, wide sympathies, a singleness of purpose.' 'Who says that?' I asked. 'Lots of them,' he replied. 'Some even write that; and so *he* comes here, a special being, as you ought to know.' 'Why ought I to know?' I interrupted, really surprised. He paid no attention. 'Yes. To-day he is chief of the best station, next year he will be assistant-manager, two years more and . . . but I daresay you know what he will be in two years' time. You are of the new gang — the gang of virtue. The same people who sent him specially also recommended you. Oh, don't say no. I've my own eyes to trust.' Light dawned upon me. My dear aunt's influential acquaintances were producing an unexpected effect upon that young man. I nearly burst into a laugh. 'Do you read the Company's confidential correspondence?' I asked. He hadn't a word to say. It was great fun. 'When Mr. Kurtz,' I continued severely, 'is General Manager, you won't have the opportunity.'

"He blew the candle out suddenly, and we went outside. The moon had risen. Black figures strolled about listlessly, pouring water on the glow, whence proceeded a sound of hissing; steam ascended in the moonlight; the beaten nigger groaned somewhere. 'What a row the brute makes!' said the indefatigable man with the moustaches, appearing near us. 'Serve him right. Transgression — punishment — bang! Pitiless, pitiless. That's the only way. This will prevent all conflagrations for the future. I was just telling the manager . . .' He noticed my companion, and became crestfallen all at once. 'Not in bed yet,' he said, with a kind of servile heartiness; 'it's so natural. Ha! Danger — agitation.' He vanished. I went on to the river-side, and the other followed me. I heard a scathing murmur at my ear, 'Heaps of muffs — go to.' The pilgrims could be seen in knots gesticulating, discussing. Several had still their staves in their hands. I verily believe they took these sticks to bed with them. Beyond the fence the forest stood up spectrally in the moonlight, and through the dim stir, through the faint sounds of that lamentable courtyard, the silence of the land went home to one's very heart — its mystery, its greatness, the amazing reality of its concealed life. The hurt nigger moaned feebly somewhere near by, and then fetched a deep sigh that made me mend my pace away from there. I felt a hand introducing itself under my arm. 'My dear sir,' said the fellow, 'I don't want to be misunderstood, and especially by you, who will see Mr. Kurtz long before I can have that pleasure. I wouldn't like him to get a false idea of my disposition. . . .'

"I let him run on, this papier-mâché Mephistopheles, and it seemed to me that if I tried I could poke my forefinger through him, and would find nothing inside but a little loose dirt, maybe. He, don't you see, had been planning to be assistant-manager by and by under the present man, and I could see that the coming of that Kurtz had upset them both not a little. He talked precipitately, and I did not try to stop him. I had my shoulders against the wreck of my steamer, hauled up on the slope like a carcass of some big river animal. The smell of mud, of primeval mud, by Jove! was in my nostrils, the high stillness of primeval forest was before my eyes; there were shiny patches on the black creek. The moon had spread over everything a thin layer of silver — over the rank grass, over the mud, upon the wall of matted vegetation standing higher than the wall of a temple, over the great river I could see through a sombre gap glittering, glittering, as it flowed broadly by without a murmur. All this was great, expectant, mute, while the man jabbered about himself. I wondered whether the stillness on the face of the immensity looking at us two were meant as an appeal or as a menace. What were we who had strayed in here? Could we handle that dumb thing, or would it handle us? I felt how big, how confoundedly big, was that thing that couldn't talk and perhaps was deaf as well. What was in there? I could see a little ivory coming out from there, and I had heard Mr. Kurtz was in there. I had heard enough about it too — God knows! Yet somehow it didn't bring any image with it — no more than if I had been told an angel or a fiend was in there. I believed it in the same way one of you might believe there are inhabitants in the planet Mars. I knew once a Scotch sailmaker who was certain, dead sure, there were people in Mars. If you asked him for some idea how they looked and behaved, he would get shy and mutter something about 'walking on all-fours.' If you as much as smiled, he would — though a man of sixty — offer to fight you. I would not have gone so far as to fight for Kurtz, but I went for him near enough to a lie. You know I hate, detest, and can't bear a lie, not because I am straighter than the rest of us, but simply because it appals me. There is a taint of death, a flavour of mortality in lies — which is exactly what I hate and detest in the world — what I want to forget. It makes me miserable and sick, like biting something rotten would do. Temperament, I suppose. Well, I went near enough to it by letting the young fool there believe anything he liked to imagine as to my influence in Europe. I became in an instant as much of a pretence as the rest of the bewitched pilgrims. This simply because I had a notion it somehow would be of help to that Kurtz whom at the time I did not see — you understand. He was just a word for me. I did not see the man in the name any more than you do. Do you see him? Do you see the story? Do you see anything? It seems to me I am trying to tell you a dream — making a vain attempt, because no relation of a dream can convey the dream-sensation, that commingling of absurdity, surprise, and bewilderment in a tremor of struggling revolt, that notion of being captured by the incredible which is of the very essence of dreams. . . ."

He was silent for a while.

". . . No, it is impossible; it is impossible to convey the life-sensation of any given epoch of one's existence — that which makes its truth, its meaning — its subtle and penetrating essence. It is impossible. We live, as we dream — alone. . . ."

He paused again as if reflecting, then added:

"Of course in this you fellows see more than I could then. You see me, whom you know. . . ."

It had become so pitch dark that we listeners could hardly see one another. For a long time already he, sitting apart, had been no more to us than a voice. There was not a word from anybody. The others might have been asleep, but I was awake. I listened, I listened on the watch for the sentence, for the word, that would give me the clue to the faint uneasiness inspired by this narrative that seemed to shape itself without human lips in the heavy night-air of the river.

". . . Yes — I let him run on," Marlow began again, "and think what he pleased about the powers that were behind me. I did! And there was nothing behind me! There was nothing but that wretched, old, mangled steamboat I was leaning against, while he talked fluently about 'the necessity for every man to get on.' 'And when one comes

out here, you conceive, it is not to gaze at the moon.' Mr. Kurtz was a
'universal genius,' but even a genius would find it easier to work with
'adequate tools — intelligent men.' He did not make bricks — why,
there was a physical impossibility in the way — as I was well aware; and
if he did secretarial work for the manager, it was because 'no sensible
man rejects wantonly the confidence of his superiors.' Did I see it? I saw
it. What more did I want? What I really wanted was rivets, by Heaven!
Rivets. To get on with the work — to stop the hole. Rivets I wanted.
There were cases of them down at the coast — cases — piled up —
burst — split! You kicked a loose rivet at every second step in that station yard on the hillside. Rivets had rolled into the grove of death. You
could fill your pockets with rivets for the trouble of stooping down —
and there wasn't one rivet to be found where it was wanted. We had
plates that would do, but nothing to fasten them with. And every week
the messenger, a lone negro, letter-bag on shoulder and staff in hand,
left our station for the coast. And several times a week a coast caravan
came in with trade goods — ghastly glazed calico that made you shudder only to look at it, glass beads value about a penny a quart, confounded spotted cotton handkerchiefs. And no rivets. Three carriers
could have brought all that was wanted to set that steamboat afloat.

"He was becoming confidential now, but I fancy my unresponsive
attitude must have exasperated him at last, for he judged it necessary to
inform me he feared neither God nor devil, let alone any mere man.
I said I could see that very well, but what I wanted was a certain quantity of rivets — and rivets were what really Mr. Kurtz wanted, if he had
only known it. Now letters went to the coast every week. . . . 'My dear
sir,' he cried, 'I write from dictation.' I demanded rivets. There was a
way — for an intelligent man. He changed his manner; became very
cold, and suddenly began to talk about a hippopotamus; wondered
whether sleeping on board the steamer (I stuck to my salvage night and
day) I wasn't disturbed. There was an old hippo that had the bad habit
of getting out on the bank and roaming at night over the station
grounds. The pilgrims used to turn out in a body and empty every rifle
they could lay hands on at him. Some even had sat up o' nights for him.
All this energy was wasted, though. 'That animal has a charmed life,' he
said; 'but you can say this only of brutes in this country. No man — you
apprehend me? — no man here bears a charmed life.' He stood there
for a moment in the moonlight with his delicate hooked nose set a little
askew, and his mica eyes glittering without a wink, then, with a curt
Good-night, he strode off. I could see he was disturbed and considerably puzzled, which made me feel more hopeful than I had been for

days. It was a great comfort to turn from that chap to my influential
friend, the battered, twisted, ruined, tin-pot steamboat. I clambered on
board. She rang under my feet like an empty Huntley & Palmer biscuit-
tin kicked along a gutter; she was nothing so solid in make, and rather
less pretty in shape, but I had expended enough hard work on her to
make me love her. No influential friend would have served me better.
She had given me a chance to come out a bit — to find out what I could
do. No, I don't like work. I had rather laze about and think of all
the fine things that can be done. I don't like work — no man does —
but I like what is in the work — the chance to find yourself. Your own
reality — for yourself, not for others — what no other man can ever
know. They can only see the mere show, and never can tell what it really
means.

"I was not surprised to see somebody sitting aft, on the deck, with
his legs dangling over the mud. You see I rather chummed with the few
mechanics there were in that station, whom the other pilgrims naturally despised — on account of their imperfect manners, I suppose. This
was the foreman — a boiler-maker by trade — a good worker. He was
a lank, bony, yellow-faced man, with big intense eyes. His aspect was
worried, and his head was as bald as the palm of my hand; but his hair
in falling seemed to have stuck to his chin, and had prospered in the
new locality, for his beard hung down to his waist. He was a widower
with six young children (he had left them in [the] charge of a sister of
his to come out there), and the passion of his life was pigeon-flying. He
was an enthusiast and a connoisseur. He would rave about pigeons.
After work hours he used sometimes to come over from his hut for a
talk about his children and his pigeons; at work, when he had to crawl
in the mud under the bottom of the steamboat, he would tie up that
beard of his in a kind of white serviette° he brought for the purpose. It
had loops to go over his ears. In the evening he could be seen squatted
on the bank rinsing that wrapper in the creek with great care, then
spreading it solemnly on a bush to dry.

"I slapped him on the back and shouted 'We shall have rivets!' He
scrambled to his feet exclaiming 'No! Rivets!' as though he couldn't
believe his ears. Then in a low voice, 'You . . . eh?' I don't know why we
behaved like lunatics. I put my finger to the side of my nose and nodded mysteriously. 'Good for you!' he cried, snapped his fingers above
his head, lifting one foot. I tried a jig. We capered on the iron deck. A
frightful clatter came out of that hulk, and the virgin forest on the other

serviette: Napkin.

bank of the creek sent it back in a thundering roll upon the sleeping station. It must have made some of the pilgrims sit up in their hovels. A dark figure obscured the lighted doorway of the manager's hut, vanished, then, a second or so after, the doorway itself vanished too. We stopped, and the silence driven away by the stamping of our feet flowed back again from the recesses of the land. The great wall of vegetation, an exuberant and entangled mass of trunks, branches, leaves, boughs, festoons, motionless in the moonlight, was like a rioting invasion of soundless life, a rolling wave of plants, piled up, crested, ready to topple over the creek, to sweep every little man of us out of his little existence. And it moved not. A deadened burst of mighty splashes and snorts reached us from afar, as though an ichthyosaurus° had been taking a bath of glitter in the great river. 'After all,' said the boiler-maker in a reasonable tone, 'why shouldn't we get the rivets?' Why not, indeed! I did not know of any reason why we shouldn't. 'They'll come in three weeks,' I said confidently.

"But they didn't. Instead of rivets there came an invasion, an infliction, a visitation. It came in sections during the next three weeks, each section headed by a donkey carrying a white man in new clothes and tan shoes, bowing from that elevation right and left to the impressed pilgrims. A quarrelsome band of footsore sulky niggers trod on the heels of the donkey; a lot of tents, camp-stools, tin boxes, white cases, brown bales would be shot down in the courtyard, and the air of mystery would deepen a little over the muddle of the station. Five such instalments came, with their absurd air of disorderly flight with the loot of innumerable outfit shops and provision stores, that, one would think, they were lugging, after a raid, into the wilderness for equitable division. It was an inextricable mess of things decent in themselves but that human folly made look like the spoils of thieving.

"This devoted band called itself the Eldorado Exploring Expedition, and I believe they were sworn to secrecy. Their talk, however, was the talk of sordid buccaneers: it was reckless without hardihood, greedy without audacity, and cruel without courage; there was not an atom of foresight or of serious intention in the whole batch of them, and they did not seem aware these things are wanted for the work of the world. To tear treasure out of the bowels of the land was their desire, with no more moral purpose at the back of it than there is in burglars breaking into a safe. Who paid the expenses of the noble enterprise I don't know; but the uncle of our manager was leader of that lot.

ichthyosaurus: Giant prehistoric reptile.

"In exterior he resembled a butcher in a poor neighbourhood, and his eyes had a look of sleepy cunning. He carried his fat paunch with ostentation on his short legs, and during the time his gang infested the station spoke to no one but his nephew. You could see these two roaming about all day long with their heads close together in an everlasting confab.

"I had given up worrying myself about the rivets. One's capacity for that kind of folly is more limited than you would suppose. I said Hang! — and let things slide. I had plenty of time for meditation, and now and then I would give some thought to Kurtz. I wasn't very interested in him. No. Still, I was curious to see whether this man, who had come out equipped with moral ideas of some sort, would climb to the top after all, and how he would set about his work when there."

II

"One evening as I was lying flat on the deck of my steamboat, I heard voices approaching — and there were the nephew and the uncle strolling along the bank. I laid my head on my arm again, and had nearly lost myself in a doze, when somebody said in my ear, as it were: 'I am as harmless as a little child, but I don't like to be dictated to. Am I the manager — or am I not? I was ordered to send him there. It's incredible.' . . . I became aware that the two were standing on the shore alongside the forepart of the steamboat, just below my head. I did not move; it did not occur to me to move: I was sleepy. 'It *is* unpleasant,' grunted the uncle. 'He has asked the Administration to be sent there,' said the other, 'with the idea of showing what he could do; and I was instructed accordingly. Look at the influence that man must have. Is it not frightful?' They both agreed it was frightful, then made several bizarre remarks: 'Make rain and fine weather — one man — the Council — by the nose' — bits of absurd sentences that got the better of my drowsiness, so that I had pretty near the whole of my wits about me when the uncle said, 'The climate may do away with this difficulty for you. Is he alone there?' 'Yes,' answered the manager; 'he sent his assistant down the river with a note to me in these terms: "Clear this poor devil out of the country, and don't bother sending more of that sort. I had rather be alone than have the kind of men you can dispose of with me." It was more than a year ago. Can you imagine such impudence?' 'Anything since then?' asked the other hoarsely. 'Ivory,' jerked the nephew; 'lots of it — prime sort — lots — most annoying, from him.' 'And with that?' questioned the heavy rumble. 'Invoice,' was the reply fired out, so to speak. Then silence. They had been talking about Kurtz.

"I was broad awake by this time, but, lying perfectly at ease, remained still, having no inducement to change my position. 'How did that ivory come all this way?' growled the elder man, who seemed very vexed. The other explained that it had come with a fleet of canoes in charge of an English half-caste clerk Kurtz had with him; that Kurtz apparently intended to return himself; the station being by that time bare of goods and stores, but after coming three hundred miles, had suddenly decided to go back, which he started to do alone in a small dugout with four paddlers, leaving the half-caste to continue down the river with the ivory. The two fellows there seemed astounded at anybody attempting such a thing. They were at a loss for an adequate motive. As for me, I seemed to see Kurtz for the first time. It was a distinct glimpse: the dugout, four paddling savages, and the lone white man turning his back suddenly on the headquarters, on relief, on thoughts of home — perhaps; setting his face towards the depths of the wilderness, towards his empty and desolate station. I did not know the motive. Perhaps he was just simply a fine fellow who stuck to his work for its own sake. His name, you understand, had not been pronounced once. He was 'that man.' The half-caste, who, as far as I could see, had conducted a difficult trip with great prudence and pluck, was invariably alluded to as 'that scoundrel.' The 'scoundrel' had reported that the 'man' had been very ill — had recovered imperfectly. . . . The two below me moved away then a few paces, and strolled back and forth at some little distance. I heard: 'Military post — doctor — two hundred miles — quite alone now — unavoidable delays — nine months — no news — strange rumours.' They approached again, just as the manager was saying, 'No one, as far as I know, unless a species of wandering trader — a pestilential fellow, snapping ivory from the natives.' Who was it they were talking about now? I gathered in snatches that this was some man supposed to be in Kurtz's district, and of whom the manager did not approve. 'We will not be free from unfair competition till one of these fellows is hanged for an example,' he said. 'Certainly,' grunted the other; 'get him hanged! Why not? Anything — anything can be done in this country. That's what I say; nobody here, you understand, *here* can endanger your position. And why? You stand the climate — you outlast them all. The danger is in Europe; but there before I left I took care to ——' They moved off and whispered, then their voices rose again. 'The extraordinary series of delays is not my fault. I did my possible.' The fat man sighed, 'Very sad.' 'And the pestiferous absurdity of his talk,' continued the other; 'he bothered me enough when he was here. "Each station should be like a beacon on the road towards better things, a centre for trade of course, but also for humanising, improving, instructing." Conceive you — that ass! And he wants to be manager! No, it's ——' Here he got choked by excessive indignation, and I lifted my head the least bit. I was surprised to see how near they were — right under me. I could have spat upon their hats. They were looking on the ground, absorbed in thought. The manager was switching his leg with a slender twig: his sagacious relative lifted his head. 'You have been well since you came out this time?' he asked. The other gave a start. 'Who? I? Oh! Like a charm — like a charm. But the rest — oh, my goodness! All sick. They die so quick, too, that I haven't the time to send them out of the country — it's incredible.' 'H'm. Just so,' grunted the uncle. 'Ah! my boy, trust to this — I say, trust to this.' I saw him extend his short flipper of an arm for a gesture that took in the forest, the creek, the mud, the river — seemed to beckon with a dishonouring flourish before the sunlit face of the land a treacherous appeal to the lurking death, to the hidden evil, to the profound darkness of its heart. It was so startling that I leaped to my feet and looked back at the edge of the forest, as though I had expected an answer of some sort to that black display of confidence. You know the foolish notions that come to one sometimes. The high stillness confronted these two figures with its ominous patience, waiting for the passing away of a fantastic invasion.

"They swore aloud together — out of sheer fright, I believe — then, pretending not to know anything of my existence, turned back to the station. The sun was low; and leaning forward side by side, they seemed to be tugging painfully uphill their two ridiculous shadows of unequal length, that trailed behind them slowly over the tall grass without bending a single blade.

"In a few days the Eldorado Expedition went into the patient wilderness, that closed upon it as the sea closes over a diver. Long afterwards the news came that all the donkeys were dead. I know nothing as to the fate of the less valuable animals. They, no doubt, like the rest of us, found what they deserved. I did not inquire. I was then rather excited at the prospect of meeting Kurtz very soon. When I say very soon I mean it comparatively. It was just two months from the day we left the creek when we came to the bank below Kurtz's station.

"Going up that river was like travelling back to the earliest beginnings of the world, when vegetation rioted on the earth and the big trees were kings. An empty stream, a great silence, and impenetrable forest. The air was warm, thick, heavy, sluggish. There was no joy in the brilliance of sunshine. The long stretches of the waterway ran on, deserted, into the gloom of overshadowed distances. On silvery sand-banks hippos and alligators sunned themselves side by side. The broadening waters flowed through a mob of wooded islands; you lost your way on that river as you would in a desert, and butted all day long against shoals, trying to find the channel, till you thought yourself bewitched and cut off for ever from everything you had known once — somewhere — far away — in another existence perhaps. There were moments when one's past came back to one, as it will sometimes when you have not a moment to spare to yourself; but it came in the shape of an unrestful and noisy dream, remembered with wonder amongst the overwhelming realities of this strange world of plants, and water, and silence. And this stillness of life did not in the least resemble a peace. It was the stillness of an implacable force brooding over an inscrutable intention. It looked at you with a vengeful aspect. I got used to it afterwards; I did not see it any more; I had no time. I had to keep guessing at the channel; I had to discern, mostly by inspiration, the signs of hidden banks; I watched for sunken stones; I was learning to clap my teeth smartly before my heart flew out, when I shaved by a fluke some infernal sly old snag that would have ripped the life out of the tin-pot steamboat and drowned all the pilgrims; I had to keep a look-out for the signs of dead wood we could cut up in the night for the next day's steaming. When you have to attend to things of that sort, to the mere incidents of the surface, the reality — the reality, I tell you — fades. The inner truth is hidden — luckily, luckily. But I felt it all the same; I felt often its mysterious stillness watching me at my monkey tricks, just as it watches you fellows performing on your respective tight-ropes for — what is it? half a crown a tumble —— "

"Try to be civil, Marlow," growled a voice, and I knew there was at least one listener awake besides myself.

"I beg your pardon. I forgot the heartache which makes up the rest of the price. And indeed what does the price matter, if the trick be well done? You do your tricks very well. And I didn't do badly either, since I managed not to sink that steamboat on my first trip. It's a wonder to me yet. Imagine a blindfolded man set to drive a van over a bad road. I sweated and shivered over that business considerably, I can tell you. After all, for a seaman, to scrape the bottom of the thing that's supposed to float all the time under his care is the unpardonable sin. No one may know of it, but you never forget the thump — eh? A blow on the very heart. You remember it, you dream of it, you wake up at night

and think of it — years after — and go hot and cold all over. I don't
pretend to say that steamboat floated all the time. More than once
she had to wade for a bit, with twenty cannibals splashing around and
pushing. We had enlisted some of these chaps on the way for a crew.
Fine fellows — cannibals — in their place. They were men one could
work with, and I am grateful to them. And, after all, they did not eat
each other before my face: they had brought along a provision of hippo-
meat which went rotten, and made the mystery of the wilderness stink
in my nostrils. Phoo! I can sniff it now. I had the manager on board and
three or four pilgrims with their staves — all complete. Sometimes we
came upon a station close by the bank, clinging to the skirts of the
unknown, and the white men rushing out of a tumble-down hovel,
with great gestures of joy and surprise and welcome, seemed very
strange — had the appearance of being held there captive by a spell.
The word 'ivory' would ring in the air for a while — and on we went
again into the silence, along empty reaches, round the still bends,
between the high walls of our winding way, reverberating in hollow
claps the ponderous beat of the stern-wheel. Trees, trees, millions of
trees, massive, immense, running up high; and at their foot, hugging
the bank against the stream, crept the little begrimed steamboat, like a
sluggish beetle crawling on the floor of a lofty portico. It made you feel
very small, very lost, and yet it was not altogether depressing, that feeling. After all, if you were small, the grimy beetle crawled on — which
was just what you wanted it to do. Where the pilgrims imagined it
crawled to I don't know. To some place where they expected to get
something, I bet! For me it crawled towards Kurtz — exclusively; but
when the steam-pipes started leaking we crawled very slow. The reaches
opened before us and closed behind, as if the forest had stepped lei-
surely across the water to bar the way for our return. We penetrated
deeper and deeper into the heart of darkness. It was very quiet there. At
night sometimes the roll of drums behind the curtain of trees would
run up the river and remain sustained faintly, as if hovering in the air
high over our heads, till the first break of day. Whether it meant war,
peace, or prayer we could not tell. The dawns were heralded by the
descent of a chill stillness; the woodcutters slept, their fires burned low;
the snapping of a twig would make you start. We were wanderers on a
prehistoric earth, on an earth that wore the aspect of an unknown
planet. We could have fancied ourselves the first of men taking possession of an accursed inheritance, to be subdued at the cost of profound
anguish and of excessive toil. But suddenly, as we struggled round a
bend, there would be a glimpse of rush walls, of peaked grass-roofs, a

burst of yells, a whirl of black limbs, a mass of hands clapping, of feet
stamping, of bodies swaying, of eyes rolling, under the droop of heavy
and motionless foliage. The steamer toiled along slowly on the edge
of a black and incomprehensible frenzy. The prehistoric man was cursing us, praying to us, welcoming us — who could tell? We were cut off
from the comprehension of our surroundings; we glided past like phantoms, wondering and secretly appalled, as sane men would be before an
enthusiastic outbreak in a madhouse. We could not understand because
we were too far and could not remember, because we were travelling
in the night of first ages, of those ages that are gone, leaving hardly a
sign — and no memories.

"The earth seemed unearthly. We are accustomed to look upon the
shackled form of a conquered monster, but there — there you could
look at a thing monstrous and free. It was unearthly, and the men
were —— No, they were not inhuman. Well, you know, that was the
worst of it — this suspicion of their not being inhuman. It would come
slowly to one. They howled and leaped, and spun, and made horrid
faces; but what thrilled you was just the thought of their humanity —
like yours — the thought of your remote kinship with this wild and
passionate uproar. Ugly. Yes, it was ugly enough; but if you were man
enough you would admit to yourself that there was in you just the faintest trace of a response to the terrible frankness of that noise, a dim
suspicion of there being a meaning in it which you — you so remote
from the night of first ages — could comprehend. And why not? The
mind of man is capable of anything — because everything is in it, all the
past as well as all the future. What was there after all? Joy, fear, sorrow,
devotion, valour, rage — who can tell? — but truth — truth stripped of
its cloak of time. Let the fool gape and shudder — the man knows, and
can look on without a wink. But he must at least be as much of a man
as these on the shore. He must meet that truth with his own true
stuff — with his own inborn strength. Principles? Principles won't do.
Acquisitions, clothes, pretty rags — rags that would fly off at the first
good shake. No; you want a deliberate belief. An appeal to me in this
fiendish row — is there? Very well; I hear; I admit, but I have a voice
too, and for good or evil mine is the speech that cannot be silenced. Of
course, a fool, what with sheer fright and fine sentiments, is always safe.
Who's that grunting? You wonder I didn't go ashore for a howl and a
dance? Well, no — I didn't. Fine sentiments, you say? Fine sentiments
be hanged! I had no time. I had to mess about with white-lead and
strips of woollen blanket helping to put bandages on those leaky steam-
pipes — I tell you. I had to watch the steering, and circumvent those

snags, and get the tin-pot along by hook or by crook. There was surface-truth enough in these things to save a wiser man. And between whiles I had to look after the savage who was fireman. He was an improved specimen; he could fire up a vertical boiler. He was there below me, and, upon my word, to look at him was as edifying as seeing a dog in a parody of breeches and a feather hat, walking on his hind legs. A few months of training had done for that really fine chap. He squinted at the steam-gauge and at the water-gauge with an evident effort of intrepidity — and he had filed teeth too, the poor devil, and the wool of his pate shaved into queer patterns, and three ornamental scars on each of his cheeks. He ought to have been clapping his hands and stamping his feet on the bank, instead of which he was hard at work, a thrall to strange witchcraft, full of improving knowledge. He was useful because he had been instructed; and what he knew was this — that should the water in that transparent thing disappear, the evil spirit inside the boiler would get angry through the greatness of his thirst, and take a terrible vengeance. So he sweated and fired up and watched the glass fearfully (with an impromptu charm, made of rags, tied to his arm, and a piece of polished bone, as big as a watch, stuck flatways through his lower lip), while the wooded banks slipped past us slowly, the short noise was left behind, the interminable miles of silence — and we crept on, towards Kurtz. But the snags were thick, the water was treacherous and shallow, the boiler seemed indeed to have a sulky devil in it, and thus neither that fireman nor I had any time to peer into our creepy thoughts.

"Some fifty miles below the Inner Station we came upon a hut of reeds, an inclined and melancholy pole, with the unrecognisable tatters of what had been a flag of some sort flying from it, and a neatly stacked wood-pile. This was unexpected. We came to the bank, and on the stack of firewood found a flat piece of board with some faded pencil-writing on it. When deciphered it said: 'Wood for you. Hurry up. Approach cautiously.' There was a signature, but it was illegible — not Kurtz — a much longer word. Hurry up. Where? Up the river? 'Approach cautiously.' We had not done so. But the warning could not have been meant for the place where it could be only found after approach. Something was wrong above. But what — and how much? That was the question. We commented adversely upon the imbecility of that telegraphic style. The bush around said nothing, and would not let us look very far, either. A torn curtain of red twill hung in the doorway of the hut, and flapped sadly in our faces. The dwelling was dismantled; but we could see a white man had lived there not very long ago. There remained a rude table — a plank on two posts; a heap of rubbish reposed in a dark corner, and by the door I picked up a book. It had lost its covers, and the pages had been thumbed into a state of extremely dirty softness; but the back had been lovingly stitched afresh with white cotton thread, which looked clean yet. It was an extraordinary find. Its title was, *An Inquiry into some Points of Seamanship*, by a man Towser, Towson — some such name — Master in His Majesty's Navy. The matter looked dreary reading enough, with illustrative diagrams and repulsive tables of figures, and the copy was sixty years old. I handled this amazing antiquity with the greatest possible tenderness, lest it should dissolve in my hands. Within, Towson or Towser was inquiring earnestly into the breaking strain of ships' chains and tackle, and other such matters. Not a very enthralling book; but at the first glance you could see there a singleness of intention, an honest concern for the right way of going to work, which made these humble pages, thought out so many years ago, luminous with another than a professional light. The simple old sailor, with his talk of chains and purchases, made me forget the jungle and the pilgrims in a delicious sensation of having come upon something unmistakably real. Such a book being there was wonderful enough; but still more astounding were the notes pencilled in the margin, and plainly referring to the text. I couldn't believe my eyes! They were in cipher! Yes, it looked like cipher. Fancy a man lugging with him a book of that description into this nowhere and studying it — and making notes — in cipher at that! It was an extravagant mystery.

"I had been dimly aware for some time of a worrying noise, and when I lifted my eyes I saw the wood-pile was gone, and the manager, aided by all the pilgrims, was shouting at me from the river-side. I slipped the book into my pocket. I assure you to leave off reading was like tearing myself away from the shelter of an old and solid friendship.

"I started the lame engine ahead. 'It must be this miserable trader — this intruder,' exclaimed the manager, looking back malevolently at the place we had left. 'He must be English,' I said. 'It will not save him from getting into trouble if he is not careful,' muttered the manager darkly. I observed with assumed innocence that no man was safe from trouble in this world.

"The current was more rapid now, the steamer seemed at her last gasp, the stern-wheel flopped languidly, and I caught myself listening on the tiptoe for the next beat of the float, for in sober truth I expected the wretched thing to give up every moment. It was like watching the last flickers of a life. But still we crawled. Sometimes I would pick out a tree a little way ahead to measure our progress towards Kurtz by, but I lost it invariably before we got abreast. To keep the eyes so long on one thing was too much for human patience. The manager displayed a beautiful resignation. I fretted and fumed and took to arguing with myself whether or no I would talk openly with Kurtz; but before I could come to any conclusion it occurred to me that my speech or my silence, indeed any action of mine, would be a mere futility. What did it matter what anyone knew or ignored? What did it matter who was manager? One gets sometimes such a flash of insight. The essentials of this affair lay deep under the surface, beyond my reach, and beyond my power of meddling.

"Towards the evening of the second day we judged ourselves about eight miles from Kurtz's station. I wanted to push on; but the manager looked grave, and told me the navigation up there was so dangerous that it would be advisable, the sun being very low already, to wait where we were till next morning. Moreover, he pointed out that if the warning to approach cautiously were to be followed, we must approach in daylight — not at dusk, or in the dark. This was sensible enough. Eight miles meant nearly three hours' steaming for us, and I could also see suspicious ripples at the upper end of the reach. Nevertheless, I was annoyed beyond expression at the delay, and most unreasonably too, since one more night could not matter much after so many months. As we had plenty of wood, and caution was the word, I brought up in the middle of the stream. The reach was narrow, straight, with high sides like a railway cutting. The dusk came gliding into it long before the sun had set. The current ran smooth and swift, but a dumb immobility sat on the banks. The living trees, lashed together by the creepers and every living bush of the undergrowth, might have been changed into stone, even to the slenderest twig, to the lightest leaf. It was not sleep — it seemed unnatural, like a state of trance. Not the faintest sound of any kind could be heard. You looked on amazed, and began to suspect yourself of being deaf — then the night came suddenly, and struck you blind as well. About three in the morning some large fish leaped, and the loud splash made me jump as though a gun had been fired. When the sun rose there was a white fog, very warm and clammy, and more blinding than the night. It did not shift or drive; it was just there, standing all round you like something solid. At eight or nine, perhaps, it lifted as a shutter lifts. We had a glimpse of the towering multitude of trees, of the immense matted jungle, with the blazing little ball of the sun hanging over it — all perfectly still — and then the white shutter came down again, smoothly, as if sliding in greased grooves. I ordered the chain, which we had begun to heave in, to be paid out again. Before it stopped running with a muffled rattle, a cry, a very loud cry, as of infinite desolation, soared slowly in the opaque air. It ceased. A complaining clamour, modulated in savage discords, filled our ears. The sheer unexpectedness of it made my hair stir under my cap. I don't know how it struck the others: to me it seemed as though the mist itself had screamed, so suddenly, and apparently from all sides at once, did this tumultuous and mournful uproar arise. It culminated in a hurried outbreak of almost intolerably excessive shrieking, which stopped short, leaving us stiffened in a variety of silly attitudes, and obstinately listening to the nearly as appalling and excessive silence. 'Good God! What is the meaning ——?' stammered at my elbow one of the pilgrims — a little fat man, with sandy hair and red whiskers, who wore side-spring boots, and pink pyjamas tucked into his socks. Two others remained open-mouthed a whole minute, then dashed into the little cabin, to rush out incontinently and stand darting scared glances, with Winchesters at 'ready' in their hands. What we could see was just the steamer we were on, her outlines blurred as though she had been on the point of dissolving, and a misty strip of water, perhaps two feet broad, around her — and that was all. The rest of the world was nowhere, as far as our eyes and ears were concerned. Just nowhere. Gone, disappeared; swept off without leaving a whisper or a shadow behind.

"I went forward, and ordered the chain to be hauled in short, so as to be ready to trip the anchor and move the steamboat at once if necessary. 'Will they attack?' whispered an awed voice. 'We will all be butchered in this fog,' murmured another. The faces twitched with the strain, the hands trembled slightly, the eyes forgot to wink. It was very curious to see the contrast of expressions of the white men and of the black fellows of our crew, who were as much strangers to that part of the river as we, though their homes were only eight hundred miles away. The whites, of course greatly discomposed, had besides a curious look of being painfully shocked by such an outrageous row. The others had an alert, naturally interested expression; but their faces were essentially quiet, even those of the one or two who grinned as they hauled at the chain. Several exchanged short, grunting phrases, which seemed to settle the matter to their satisfaction. Their head-man, a young, broad-chested black, severely draped in dark-blue fringed cloths, with fierce nostrils and his hair all done up artfully in oily ringlets, stood near me. 'Aha!' I said, just for good fellowship's sake. 'Catch 'im,' he snapped, with a bloodshot widening of his eyes and a flash of sharp teeth — 'catch 'im. Give 'im to us.' 'To you, eh?' I asked; 'what would you do with them?' 'Eat 'im!' he said curtly, and, leaning his elbow on the rail,

looked out into the fog in a dignified and profoundly pensive attitude.
I would no doubt have been properly horrified, had it not occurred to
me that he and his chaps must be very hungry: that they must have
been growing increasingly hungry for at least this month past. They
had been engaged for six months (I don't think a single one of them
had any clear idea of time, as we at the end of countless ages have. They
still belonged to the beginnings of time — had no inherited experience
to teach them, as it were), and of course, as long as there was a piece of
paper written over in accordance with some farcical law or other made
down the river, it didn't enter anybody's head to trouble how they
would live. Certainly they had brought with them some rotten hippo-
meat, which couldn't have lasted very long, anyway, even if the pilgrims
hadn't, in the midst of a shocking hullabaloo, thrown a considerable
quantity of it overboard. It looked like a high-handed proceeding; but
it was really a case of legitimate self-defence. You can't breathe dead
hippo waking, sleeping, and eating, and at the same time keep your
precarious grip on existence. Besides that, they had given them every
week three pieces of brass wire, each about nine inches long; and the
theory was they were to buy their provisions with that currency in river-
side villages. You can see how *that* worked. There were either no villages, or the people were hostile, or the director, who like the rest of us
fed out of tins, with an occasional old he-goat thrown in, didn't want
to stop the steamer for some more or less recondite reason. So, unless
they swallowed the wire itself, or made loops of it to snare the fishes
with, I don't see what good their extravagant salary could be to them.
I must say it was paid with a regularity worthy of a large and honour-
able trading company. For the rest, the only thing to eat — though it
didn't look eatable in the least — I saw in their possession was a few
lumps of some stuff like half-cooked dough, of a dirty lavender colour,
they kept wrapped in leaves, and now and then swallowed a piece of,
but so small that it seemed done more for the look of the thing than for
any serious purpose of sustenance. Why in the name of all the gnaw-
ing devils of hunger they didn't go for us — they were thirty to five —
and have a good tuck-in for once, amazes me now when I think of it.
They were big powerful men, with not much capacity to weigh the
consequences, with courage, with strength, even yet, though their skins
were no longer glossy and their muscles no longer hard. And I saw that
something restraining, one of those human secrets that baffle probabil-
ity, had come into play there. I looked at them with a swift quickening
of interest — not because it occurred to me I might be eaten by them
before very long, though I own to you that just then I perceived —

in a new light, as it were — how unwholesome the pilgrims looked, and I hoped, yes, I positively hoped, that my aspect was not so — what shall I say? — so — unappetising: a touch of fantastic vanity which fitted well with the dream-sensation that pervaded all my days at that time. Perhaps I had a little fever too. One can't live with one's finger everlastingly on one's pulse. I had often 'a little fever,' or a little touch of other things — the playful paw-strokes of the wilderness, the preliminary trifling before the more serious onslaught which came in due course. Yes; I looked at them as you would on any human being, with a curiosity of their impulses, motives, capacities, weaknesses, when brought to the test of an inexorable physical necessity. Restraint! What possible restraint? Was it superstition, disgust, patience, fear — or some kind of primitive honour? No fear can stand up to hunger, no patience can wear it out, disgust simply does not exist where hunger is; and as to superstition, beliefs, and what you may call principles, they are less than chaff in a breeze. Don't you know the devilry of lingering starvation, its exasperating torment, its black thoughts, its sombre and brooding ferocity? Well, I do. It takes a man all his inborn strength to fight hunger properly. It's really easier to face bereavement, dishonour, and the perdition of one's soul — than this kind of prolonged hunger. Sad, but true. And these chaps too had no earthly reason for any kind of scruple. Restraint! I would just as soon have expected restraint from a hyena prowling amongst the corpses of a battlefield. But there was the fact facing me — the fact dazzling, to be seen, like the foam on the depths of the sea, like a ripple on an unfathomable enigma, a mystery greater — when I thought of it — than the curious, inexplicable note of desperate grief in this savage clamour that had swept by us on the river-bank, behind the blind whiteness of the fog.

"Two pilgrims were quarrelling in hurried whispers as to which bank. 'Left.' 'No, no; how can you? Right, right, of course.' 'It is very serious,' said the manager's voice behind me; 'I would be desolated if anything should happen to Mr. Kurtz before we came up.' I looked at him, and had not the slightest doubt he was sincere. He was just the kind of man who would wish to preserve appearances. That was his restraint. But when he muttered something about going on at once, I did not even take the trouble to answer him. I knew, and he knew, that it was impossible. Were we to let go our hold of the bottom, we would be absolutely in the air — in space. We wouldn't be able to tell where we were going to — whether up or down stream, or across — till we fetched against one bank or the other — and then we wouldn't know at first which it was. Of course I made no move. I had no mind for a smash-up. You couldn't imagine a more deadly place for a shipwreck. Whether drowned at once or not, we were sure to perish speedily in one way or another. 'I authorise you to take all the risks,' he said, after a short silence. 'I refuse to take any,' I said shortly; which was just the answer he expected, though its tone might have surprised him. 'Well, I must defer to your judgment. You are captain,' he said, with marked civility. I turned my shoulder to him in sign of my appreciation, and looked into the fog. How long would it last? It was the most hopeless look-out. The approach to this Kurtz grubbing for ivory in the wretched bush was beset by as many dangers as though he had been an enchanted princess sleeping in a fabulous castle. 'Will they attack, do you think?' asked the manager, in a confidential tone.

"I did not think they would attack, for several obvious reasons. The thick fog was one. If they left the bank in their canoes they would get lost in it, as we would be if we attempted to move. Still, I had also judged the jungle of both banks quite impenetrable — and yet eyes were in it, eyes that had seen us. The river-side bushes were certainly very thick; but the undergrowth behind was evidently penetrable. However, during the short lift I had seen no canoes anywhere in the reach — certainly not abreast of the steamer. But what made the idea of attack inconceivable to me was the nature of the noise — of the cries we had heard. They had not the fierce character boding of immediate hostile intention. Unexpected, wild, and violent as they had been, they had given me an irresistible impression of sorrow. The glimpse of the steamboat had for some reason filled those savages with unrestrained grief. The danger, if any, I expounded, was from our proximity to a great human passion let loose. Even extreme grief may ultimately vent itself in violence — but more generally takes the form of apathy. . . .

"You should have seen the pilgrims stare! They had no heart to grin, or even to revile me; but I believe they thought me gone mad — with fright, maybe. I delivered a regular lecture. My dear boys, it was no good bothering. Keep a look-out? Well, you may guess I watched the fog for the signs of lifting as a cat watches a mouse; but for anything else our eyes were of no more use to us than if we had been buried miles deep in a heap of cotton-wool. It felt like it too — choking, warm, stifling. Besides, all I said, though it sounded extravagant, was absolutely true to fact. What we afterwards alluded to as an attack was really an attempt at repulse. The action was very far from being aggressive — it was not even defensive, in the usual sense: it was undertaken under the stress of desperation, and in its essence was purely protective.

"It developed itself, I should say, two hours after the fog lifted, and its commencement was at a spot, roughly speaking, about a mile and a half below Kurtz's station. We had just floundered and flopped round a bend, when I saw an islet, a mere grassy hummock of bright green, in the middle of the stream. It was the only thing of the kind; but as we opened the reach more, I perceived it was the head of a long sandbank, or rather of a chain of shallow patches stretching down the middle of the river. They were discoloured, just awash, and the whole lot was seen just under the water, exactly as a man's backbone is seen running down the middle of his back under the skin. Now, as far as I did see, I could go to the right or to the left of this. I didn't know either channel, of course. The banks looked pretty well alike, the depth appeared the same; but as I had been informed the station was on the west side, I naturally headed for the western passage.

"No sooner had we fairly entered it than I became aware it was much narrower than I had supposed. To the left of us there was the long uninterrupted shoal, and to the right a high steep bank heavily overgrown with bushes. Above the bush the trees stood in serried ranks. The twigs overhung the current thickly, and from distance to distance a large limb of some tree projected rigidly over the stream. It was then well on in the afternoon, the face of the forest was gloomy, and a broad strip of shadow had already fallen on the water. In this shadow we steamed up — very slowly, as you may imagine. I sheered her well inshore — the water being deepest near the bank, as the sounding-pole informed me.

"One of my hungry and forbearing friends was sounding in the bows just below me. This steamboat was exactly like a decked scow. On the deck there were two little teak-wood houses, with doors and win-dows. The boiler was in the fore-end, and the machinery right astern. Over the whole there was a light roof, supported on stanchions. The funnel projected through that roof, and in front of the funnel a small cabin built of light planks served for a pilot-house. It contained a couch, two camp-stools, a loaded Martini-Henry leaning in one corner, a tiny table, and the steering-wheel. It had a wide door in front and a broad shutter at each side. All these were always thrown open, of course. I spent my days perched up there on the extreme fore-end of that roof, before the door. At night I slept, or tried to, on the couch. An athletic black belonging to some coast tribe, and educated by my poor prede-cessor, was the helmsman. He sported a pair of brass earrings, wore a blue cloth wrapper from the waist to the ankles, and thought all the

world of himself. He was the most unstable kind of fool I had ever seen.
He steered with no end of a swagger while you were by; but if he lost
sight of you, he became instantly the prey of an abject funk, and would
let that cripple of a steamboat get the upper hand of him in a minute.

"I was looking down at the sounding-pole, and feeling much annoyed to see at each try a little more of it stick out of that river, when I
saw my poleman give up the business suddenly, and stretch himself flat
on the deck, without even taking the trouble to haul his pole in. He
kept hold on it though, and it trailed in the water. At the same time the
fireman, whom I could also see below me, sat down abruptly before his
furnace and ducked his head. I was amazed. Then I had to look at the
river mighty quick, because there was a snag in the fairway. Sticks, little
sticks, were flying about — thick: they were whizzing before my nose,
dropping below me, striking behind me against my pilot-house. All this
time the river, the shore, the woods, were very quiet — perfectly quiet.
I could only hear the heavy splashing thump of the stern-wheel and the
patter of these things. We cleared the snag clumsily. Arrows, by Jove!
We were being shot at! I stepped in quickly to close the shutter on the
land-side. That fool-helmsman, his hands on the spokes, was lifting his
knees high, stamping his feet, champing his mouth, like a reined-in
horse. Confound him! And we were staggering within ten feet of the
bank. I had to lean right out to swing the heavy shutter, and I saw a
face amongst the leaves on the level with my own, looking at me very
fierce and steady; and then suddenly, as though a veil had been removed
from my eyes, I made out, deep in the tangled gloom, naked breasts,
arms, legs, glaring eyes — the bush was swarming with human limbs in
movement, glistening, of bronze colour. The twigs shook, swayed, and
rustled, the arrows flew out of them, and then the shutter came to.
'Steer her straight,' I said to the helmsman. He held his head rigid, face
forward; but his eyes rolled, he kept on lifting and setting down his feet
gently, his mouth foamed a little. 'Keep quiet!' I said in a fury. I might
just as well have ordered a tree not to sway in the wind. I darted out.
Below me there was a great scuffle of feet on the iron deck; confused
exclamations; a voice screamed, 'Can you turn back?' I caught sight of
a V-shaped ripple on the water ahead. What? Another snag! A fusillade
burst out under my feet. The pilgrims had opened with their Winchesters, and were simply squirting lead into that bush. A deuce of a lot
of smoke came up and drove slowly forward. I swore at it. Now I
couldn't see the ripple or the snag either. I stood in the doorway, peer-
ing, and the arrows came in swarms. They might have been poisoned,
but they looked as though they wouldn't kill a cat. The bush began to

howl. Our woodcutters raised a warlike whoop; the report of a rifle just at my back deafened me. I glanced over my shoulder, and the pilot-house was yet full of noise and smoke when I made a dash at the wheel. The fool-nigger had dropped everything, to throw the shutter open and let off that Martini-Henry. He stood before the wide opening, glaring, and I yelled at him to come back, while I straightened the sudden twist out of that steamboat. There was no room to turn even if I had wanted to, the snag was somewhere very near ahead in that confounded smoke, there was no time to lose, so I just crowded her into the bank — right into the bank, where I knew the water was deep.

"We tore slowly along the overhanging bushes in a whirl of broken twigs and flying leaves. The fusillade below stopped short, as I had foreseen it would when the squirts got empty. I threw my head back to a glinting whiz that traversed the pilot-house, in at one shutter-hole and out at the other. Looking past that mad helmsman, who was shaking the empty rifle and yelling at the shore, I saw vague forms of men running bent double, leaping, gliding, distinct, incomplete, evanescent. Something big appeared in the air before the shutter, the rifle went overboard, and the man stepped back swiftly, looked at me over his shoulder in an extraordinary, profound, familiar manner, and fell upon my feet. The side of his head hit the wheel twice, and the end of what appeared a long cane clattered round and knocked over a little camp-stool. It looked as though after wrenching that thing from somebody ashore he had lost his balance in the effort. The thin smoke had blown away, we were clear of the snag, and looking ahead I could see that in another hundred yards or so I would be free to sheer off, away from the bank; but my feet felt so very warm and wet that I had to look down. The man had rolled on his back and stared straight up at me; both his hands clutched that cane. It was the shaft of a spear that, either thrown or lunged through the opening, had caught him in the side just below the ribs; the blade had gone in out of sight, after making a frightful gash; my shoes were full; a pool of blood lay very still, gleaming dark-red under the wheel; his eyes shone with an amazing lustre. The fusillade burst out again. He looked at me anxiously, gripping the spear like something precious, with an air of being afraid I would try to take it away from him. I had to make an effort to free my eyes from his gaze and attend to the steering. With one hand I felt above my head for the line of the steam whistle, and jerked out screech after screech hurriedly. The tumult of angry and warlike yells was checked instantly, and then from the depths of the woods went out such a tremulous and prolonged wail of mournful fear and utter despair as may be imagined to

follow the flight of the last hope from the earth. There was a great com-
motion in the bush; the shower of arrows stopped, a few dropping
shots rang out sharply — then silence, in which the languid beat of the
stern-wheel came plainly to my ears. I put the helm hard a-starboard at
the moment when the pilgrim in pink pyjamas, very hot and agitated,
appeared in the doorway. 'The manager sends me ——' he began in an
official tone, and stopped short. 'Good God!' he said, glaring at the
wounded man.

"We two whites stood over him, and his lustrous and inquiring
glance enveloped us both. I declare it looked as though he would presently put to us some question in a understandable language; but he
died without uttering a sound, without moving a limb, without twitch-
ing a muscle. Only in the very last moment, as though in response to
some sign we could not see, to some whisper we could not hear, he
frowned heavily, and that frown gave to his black death-mask an incon-
ceivably sombre, brooding, and menacing expression. The lustre of inquiring glance faded swiftly into vacant glassiness. 'Can you steer?' I
asked the agent eagerly. He looked very dubious; but I made a grab at
his arm, and he understood at once I meant him to steer whether or no.
To tell you the truth, I was morbidly anxious to change my shoes and
socks. 'He is dead,' murmured the fellow, immensely impressed. 'No
doubt about it,' said I, tugging like mad at the shoe-laces. 'And by the
way, I suppose Mr. Kurtz is dead as well by this time.'

"For the moment that was the dominant thought. There was a
sense of extreme disappointment, as though I had found out I had been
striving after something altogether without a substance. I couldn't have
been more disgusted if I had travelled all this way for the sole purpose
of talking with Mr. Kurtz. Talking with . . . I flung one shoe overboard,
and became aware that that was exactly what I had been looking forward to — a talk with Kurtz. I made the strange discovery that I had
never imagined him as doing, you know, but as discoursing. I didn't say
to myself, 'Now I will never see him' or 'Now I will never shake him by
the hand,' but, 'Now I will never hear him.' The man presented himself
as a voice. Not of course that I did not connect him with some sort of
action. Hadn't I been told in all the tones of jealousy and admiration
that he had collected, bartered, swindled, or stolen more ivory than all
the other agents together? That was not the point. The point was in his
being a gifted creature, and that of all his gifts the one that stood out
preeminently, that carried with it a sense of real presence, was his ability
to talk, his words — the gift of expression, the bewildering, the illuminating, the most exalted and the most contemptible, the pulsating

stream of light, or the deceitful flow from the heart of an impenetrable darkness.

"The other shoe went flying unto the devil-god of that river. I thought, By Jove! it's all over. We are too late; he has vanished — the gift has vanished, by means of some spear, arrow, or club. I will never hear that chap speak after all — and my sorrow had a startling extravagance of emotion, even such as I had noticed in the howling sorrow of these savages in the bush. I couldn't have felt more of lonely desolation somehow, had I been robbed of a belief or had missed my destiny in life. . . . Why do you sigh in this beastly way, somebody? Absurd? Well, absurd. Good Lord! mustn't a man ever —— Here, give me some tobacco." . . .

There was a pause of profound stillness, then a match flared, and Marlow's lean face appeared, worn, hollow, with downward folds and dropped eyelids, with an aspect of concentrated attention; and as he took vigorous draws at his pipe, it seemed to retreat and advance out of the night in the regular flicker of the tiny flame. The match went out.

"Absurd!" he cried. "This is the worst of trying to tell . . . Here you all are, each moored with two good addresses, like a hulk with two anchors, a butcher round one corner, a policeman round another, excellent appetites, and temperature normal — you hear — normal from year's end to year's end. And you say, Absurd! Absurd be — exploded! Absurd! My dear boys, what can you expect from a man who out of sheer nervousness had just flung overboard a pair of new shoes? Now I think of it, it is amazing I did not shed tears. I am, upon the whole, proud of my fortitude. I was cut to the quick at the idea of having lost the inestimable privilege of listening to the gifted Kurtz. Of course I was wrong. The privilege was waiting for me. Oh yes, I heard more than enough. And I was right, too. A voice. He was very little more than a voice. And I heard — him — it — this voice — other voices — all of them were so little more than voices — and the memory of that time itself lingers around me, impalpable, like a dying vibration of one immense jabber, silly, atrocious, sordid, savage, or simply mean, without any kind of sense. Voices, voices — even the girl herself — now —— "

He went silent for a long time.

"I laid the ghost of his gifts at last with a lie," he began suddenly. "Girl! What? Did I mention a girl? Oh, she is out of it — completely. They — the women I mean — are out of it — should be out of it. We must help them to stay in that beautiful world of their own, lest ours gets worse. Oh, she had to be out of it. You should have heard the disinterred body of Mr. Kurtz saying, 'My Intended.' You would have

perceived directly then how completely she was out of it. And the lofty
frontal bone of Mr. Kurtz! They say the hair goes on growing sometimes, but this — ah — specimen was impressively bald. The wilderness
had patted him on the head, and, behold, it was like a ball — an ivory
ball; it had caressed him, and — lo! — he had withered; it had taken
him, loved him, embraced him, got into his veins, consumed his flesh,
and sealed his soul to its own by the inconceivable ceremonies of some
devilish initiation. He was its spoiled and pampered favourite. Ivory? I
should think so. Heaps of it, stacks of it. The old mud shanty was bursting with it. You would think there was not a single tusk left either above
or below the ground in the whole country. 'Mostly fossil,' the manager
had remarked disparagingly. It was no more fossil than I am; but they
call it fossil when it is dug up. It appears these niggers do bury the tusks
sometimes — but evidently they couldn't bury this parcel deep enough
to save the gifted Mr. Kurtz from his fate. We filled the steamboat with
it, and had to pile a lot on the deck. Thus he could see and enjoy as long
as he could see, because the appreciation of this favour had remained
with him to the last. You should have heard him say, 'My ivory.' Oh yes,
I heard him. 'My Intended, my ivory, my station, my river, my ——'
everything belonged to him. It made me hold my breath in expectation of hearing the wilderness burst into a prodigious peal of laughter
that would shake the fixed stars in their places. Everything belonged to
him — but that was a trifle. The thing was to know what he belonged
to, how many powers of darkness claimed him for their own. That was
the reflection that made you creepy all over. It was impossible — it was
not good for one either — trying to imagine. He had taken a high seat
amongst the devils of the land — I mean literally. You can't understand.
How could you? — with solid pavement under your feet, surrounded
by kind neighbours ready to cheer you or to fall on you, stepping deli-
cately between the butcher and the policeman, in the holy terror of
scandal and gallows and lunatic asylums — how can you imagine what
particular region of the first ages a man's untrammelled feet may take
him into by the way of solitude — utter solitude without a policeman — by the way of silence — utter silence, where no warning voice
of a kind neighbour can be heard whispering of public opinion? These
little things make all the great difference. When they are gone you must
fall back upon your own innate strength, upon your own capacity for
faithfulness. Of course you may be too much of a fool to go wrong —
too dull even to know you are being assaulted by the powers of darkness. I take it, no fool ever made a bargain for his soul with the devil:
the fool is too much of a fool, or the devil too much of a devil — I

don't know which. Or you may be such a thunderingly exalted creature
as to be altogether deaf and blind to anything but heavenly sights and
sounds. Then the earth for you is only a standing place — and whether
to be like this is your loss or your gain I won't pretend to say. But most
of us are neither one nor the other. The earth for us is a place to live in,
where we must put up with sights, with sounds, with smells, too, by
Jove! — breathe dead hippo, so to speak, and not be contaminated.
And there, don't you see? your strength comes in, the faith in your ability for the digging of unostentatious holes to bury the stuff in — your
power of devotion, not to yourself, but to an obscure, back-breaking
business. And that's difficult enough. Mind, I am not trying to excuse
or even explain — I am trying to account to myself for — for — Mr.
Kurtz — for the shade of Mr. Kurtz. This initiated wraith from the back
of Nowhere honoured me with its amazing confidence before it vanished altogether. This was because it could speak English to me. The
original Kurtz had been educated partly in England, and — as he was
good enough to say himself — his sympathies were in the right place.
His mother was half-English, his father was half-French. All Europe
contributed to the making of Kurtz; and by and by I learned that, most
appropriately, the International Society for the Suppression of Savage
Customs had entrusted him with the making of a report, for its future
guidance. And he had written it too. I've seen it. I've read it. It was eloquent, vibrating with eloquence, but too high-strung, I think. Seventeen pages of close writing he had found time for! But this must have
been before his — let us say — nerves went wrong, and caused him
to preside at certain midnight dances ending with unspeakable rites,
which — as far as I reluctantly gathered from what I heard at various
times — were offered up to him — do you understand? — to Mr. Kurtz
himself. But it was a beautiful piece of writing. The opening paragraph,
however, in the light of later information, strikes me now as ominous.
He began with the argument that we whites, from the point of development we had arrived at, 'must necessarily appear to them [savages] in
the nature of supernatural beings — we approach them with the might
as of a deity,' and so on, and so on. 'By the simple exercise of our will
we can exert a power for good practically unbounded,' etc. etc. From
that point he soared and took me with him. The peroration was magnificent, though difficult to remember, you know. It gave me the notion
of an exotic Immensity ruled by an august Benevolence. It made me
tingle with enthusiasm. This was the unbounded power of eloquence —
of words — of burning noble words. There were no practical hints to
interrupt the magic current of phrases, unless a kind of note at the foot

of the last page, scrawled evidently much later, in an unsteady hand, may be regarded as the exposition of a method. It was very simple, and at the end of that moving appeal to every altruistic sentiment it blazed at you, luminous and terrifying, like a flash of lightning in a serene sky: 'Exterminate all the brutes!' The curious part was that he had apparently forgotten all about that valuable postscriptum, because, later on, when he in a sense came to himself, he repeatedly entreated me to take good care of 'my pamphlet' (he called it), as it was sure to have in the future a good influence upon his career. I had full information about all these things, and, besides, as it turned out, I was to have the care of his memory. I've done enough for it to give me the indisputable right to lay it, if I choose, for an everlasting rest in the dust-bin of progress, amongst all the sweepings and, figuratively speaking, all the dead cats of civilisation. But then, you see, I can't choose. He won't be forgotten. Whatever he was, he was not common. He had the power to charm or frighten rudimentary souls into an aggravated witch-dance in his honour; he could also fill the small souls of the pilgrims with bitter misgivings: he had one devoted friend at least, and he had conquered one soul in the world that was neither rudimentary nor tainted with self-seeking. No; I can't forget him, though I am not prepared to affirm the fellow was exactly worth the life we lost in getting to him. I missed my late helmsman awfully — I missed him even while his body was still lying in the pilot-house. Perhaps you will think it passing strange this regret for a savage who was no more account than a grain of sand in a black Sahara. Well, don't you see, he had done something, he had steered; for months I had him at my back — a help — an instrument. It was a kind of partnership. He steered for me — I had to look after him, I worried about his deficiencies, and thus a subtle bond had been created, of which I only became aware when it was suddenly broken. And the intimate profundity of that look he gave me when he received his hurt remains to this day in my memory — like a claim of distant kinship affirmed in a supreme moment.

"Poor fool! If he had only left that shutter alone. He had no restraint, no restraint — just like Kurtz — a tree swayed by the wind. As soon as I had put on a dry pair of slippers, I dragged him out, after first jerking the spear out of his side, which operation I confess I performed with my eyes shut tight. His heels leaped together over the little doorstep; his shoulders were pressed to my breast; I hugged him from behind desperately. Oh! he was heavy, heavy; heavier than any man on earth, I should imagine. Then without more ado I tipped him overboard. The current snatched him as though he had been a wisp of grass, and I saw the body roll over twice before I lost sight of it for ever. All the pilgrims and the manager were then congregated on the awning-deck about the pilot-house, chattering at each other like a flock of excited magpies, and there was a scandalised murmur at my heartless promptitude. What they wanted to keep that body hanging about for I can't guess. Embalm it, maybe. But I had also heard another, and a very ominous, murmur on the deck below. My friends the wood-cutters were likewise scandalised, and with a better show of reason — though I admit that the reason itself was quite inadmissible. Oh, quite! I had made up my mind that if my late helmsman was to be eaten, the fishes alone should have him. He had been a very second-rate helmsman while alive, but now he was dead he might have become a first-class tempta-tion, and possibly cause some startling trouble. Besides, I was anxious to take the wheel, the man in pink pyjamas showing himself a hopeless duffer at the business.

"This I did directly the simple funeral was over. We were going half-speed, keeping right in the middle of the stream, and I listened to the talk about me. They had given up Kurtz, they had given up the station; Kurtz was dead, and the station had been burnt — and so on, and so on. The red-haired pilgrim was beside himself with the thought that at least poor Kurtz had been properly revenged. 'Say! We must have made a glorious slaughter of them in the bush. Eh? What do you think? Say?' He positively danced, the bloodthirsty little gingery beggar. And he had nearly fainted when he saw the wounded man! I could not help saying, 'You made a glorious lot of smoke, anyhow.' I had seen, from the way the tops of the bushes rustled and flew, that almost all the shots had gone too high. You can't hit anything unless you take aim and fire from the shoulder; but these chaps fired from the hip with their eyes shut. The retreat, I maintained — and I was right — was caused by the screeching of the steam-whistle. Upon this they forgot Kurtz, and began to howl at me with indignant protests.

"The manager stood by the wheel murmuring confidentially about the necessity of getting well away down the river before dark at all events, when I saw in the distance a clearing on the river-side and the outlines of some sort of building. 'What's this?' I asked. He clapped his hands in wonder. 'The station!' he cried. I edged in at once, still going half-speed.

"Through my glasses I saw the slope of a hill interspersed with rare trees and perfectly free from undergrowth. A long decaying building on the summit was half buried in the high grass; the large holes in the peaked roof gaped black from afar; the jungle and the woods made a background. There was no enclosure or fence of any kind; but there had been one apparently, for near the house half a dozen slim posts remained in a row, roughly trimmed, and with their upper ends ornamented with round carved balls. The rails, or whatever there had been between, had disappeared. Of course the forest surrounded all that. The river-bank was clear, and on the water side I saw a white man under a hat like a cart-wheel beckoning persistently with his whole arm. Examining the edge of the forest above and below, I was almost certain I could see movements — human forms gliding here and there. I steamed past prudently, then stopped the engines and let her drift down. The man on the shore began to shout, urging us to land. 'We have been attacked,' screamed the manager. 'I know — I know. It's all right,' yelled back the other, as cheerful as you please. 'Come along. It's all right. I am glad.'

"His aspect reminded me of something I had seen — something funny I had seen somewhere. As I manœuvred to get alongside, I was asking myself, 'What does this fellow look like?' Suddenly I got it. He looked like a harlequin. His clothes had been made of some stuff that was brown holland probably, but it was covered with patches all over, with bright patches, blue, red, and yellow — patches on the back, patches on the front, patches on elbows, on knees; coloured binding round his jacket, scarlet edging at the bottom of his trousers; and the sunshine made him look extremely gay and wonderfully neat withal, because you could see how beautifully all this patching had been done. A beardless, boyish face, very fair, no features to speak of, nose peeling, little blue eyes, smiles and frowns chasing each other over that open countenance like sunshine and shadow on a wind-swept plain. 'Look out, captain!' he cried; 'there's a snag lodged in here last night.' What! Another snag? I confess I swore shamefully. I had nearly holed my cripple, to finish off that charming trip. The harlequin on the bank turned his little pug-nose up to me. 'You English?' he asked, all smiles. 'Are you?' I shouted from the wheel. The smiles vanished, and he shook his head as if sorry for my disappointment. Then he brightened up. 'Never mind!' he cried encouragingly. 'Are we in time?' I asked. 'He is up there,' he replied, with a toss of the head up the hill, and becoming gloomy all of a sudden. His face was like the autumn sky, overcast one moment and bright the next.

"When the manager, escorted by the pilgrims, all of them armed to the teeth, had gone to the house, this chap came on board. 'I say, I don't like this. These natives are in the bush,' I said. He assured me earnestly it was all right. 'They are simple people,' he added; 'well, I am glad you came. It took me all my time to keep them off.' 'But you said it was all right,' I cried. 'Oh, they meant no harm,' he said; and as I stared he corrected himself, 'Not exactly.' Then vivaciously, 'My faith, your pilot-house wants a clean-up!' In the next breath he advised me to keep enough steam on the boiler to blow the whistle in case of any trouble. 'One good screech will do more for you than all your rifles. They are simple people,' he repeated. He rattled away at such a rate he quite overwhelmed me. He seemed to be trying to make up for lots of silence, and actually hinted, laughing, that such was the case. 'Don't you talk with Mr. Kurtz?' I said. 'You don't talk with that man — you listen to him,' he exclaimed with severe exaltation. 'But now ———' He waved his arm, and in the twinkling of an eye was in the uttermost depths of despondency. In a moment he came up again with a jump, possessed himself of both my hands, shook them continuously, while he gabbled: 'Brother sailor . . . honour . . . pleasure . . . delight . . . introduce myself . . . Russian . . . son of an arch-priest . . . Government of Tambov . . . What? Tobacco! English tobacco; the excellent English tobacco! Now, that's brotherly. Smoke? Where's a sailor that does not smoke?'

"The pipe soothed him, and gradually I made out he had run away from school, had gone to sea in a Russian ship; ran away again; served some time in English ships; was now reconciled with the arch-priest. He made a point of that. 'But when one is young one must see things, gather experience, ideas; enlarge the mind.' 'Here!' I interrupted. 'You can never tell! Here I met Mr. Kurtz,' he said, youthfully solemn and reproachful. I held my tongue after that. It appears he had persuaded a Dutch trading-house on the coast to fit him out with stores and goods, and had started for the interior with a light heart, and no more idea of what would happen to him than a baby. He had been wandering about that river for nearly two years alone, cut off from everybody and everything. 'I am not so young as I look. I am twenty-five,' he said. 'At first old Van Shuyten would tell me to go to the devil,' he narrated with keen enjoyment; 'but I stuck to him, and talked and talked, till at last he got afraid I would talk the hind-leg off his favourite dog, so he gave me some cheap things and a few guns, and told me he hoped he would never see my face again. Good old Dutchman, Van Shuyten. I sent him one small lot of ivory a year ago, so that he can't call me a little thief when I get back. I hope he got it. And for the rest, I don't care. I had some wood stacked for you. That was my old house. Did you see?'

"I gave him Towson's book. He made as though he would kiss me, but restrained himself. 'The only book I had left, and I thought I had lost it,' he said, looking at it ecstatically. 'So many accidents happen to

a man going about alone, you know. Canoes get upset sometimes —
and sometimes you've got to clear out so quick when the people get
angry.' He thumbed the pages. 'You made notes in Russian?' I asked.
He nodded. 'I thought they were written in cipher,' I said. He laughed,
then became serious. 'I had lots of trouble to keep these people off,' he
said. 'Did they want to kill you?' I asked. 'Oh no!' he cried, and checked
himself. 'Why did they attack us?' I pursued. He hesitated, then said
shamefacedly, 'They don't want him to go.' 'Don't they?' I said curiously. He nodded a nod full of mystery and wisdom. 'I tell you,' he
cried, 'this man has enlarged my mind.' He opened his arms wide, staring at me with his little blue eyes that were perfectly round."

III

"I looked at him, lost in astonishment. There he was before me, in
motley, as though he had absconded from a troupe of mimes, enthusiastic, fabulous. His very existence was improbable, inexplicable, and
altogether bewildering. He was an insoluble problem. It was inconceivable how he had existed, how he had succeeded in getting so far, how
he had managed to remain — why he did not instantly disappear. 'I
went a little farther,' he said, 'then still a little farther — till I had gone
so far that I don't know how I'll ever get back. Never mind. Plenty
time. I can manage. You take Kurtz away quick — quick — I tell you.'
The glamour of youth enveloped his parti-coloured rags, his destitu-
tion, his loneliness, the essential desolation of his futile wanderings. For
months — for years — his life hadn't been worth a day's purchase; and
there he was gallantly, thoughtlessly alive, to all appearance indestruc-
tible solely by the virtue of his few years and of his unreflecting audacity.
I was seduced into something like admiration — like envy. Glamour
urged him on, glamour kept him unscathed. He surely wanted nothing
from the wilderness but space to breathe in and to push on through.
His need was to exist, and to move onwards at the greatest possible risk,
and with a maximum of privation. If the absolutely pure, uncalculating,
unpractical spirit of adventure had ever ruled a human being, it ruled
this be-patched youth. I almost envied him the possession of this mod-
est and clear flame. It seemed to have consumed all thought of self so
completely, that, even while he was talking to you, you forgot that it
was he — the man before your eyes — who had gone through these
things. I did not envy him his devotion to Kurtz, though. He had not
meditated over it. It came to him, and he accepted it with a sort of

eager fatalism. I must say that to me it appeared about the most dangerous thing in every way he had come upon so far.

"They had come together unavoidably, like two ships becalmed
near each other, and lay rubbing sides at last. I suppose Kurtz wanted
an audience, because on a certain occasion, when encamped in the forest, they had talked all night, or more probably Kurtz had talked. 'We
talked of everything,' he said, quite transported at the recollection. 'I
forgot there was such a thing as sleep. The night did not seem to last an
hour. Everything! Everything! . . . Of love too.' 'Ah, he talked to you
of love!' I said, much amused. 'It isn't what you think,' he cried, almost
passionately. 'It was in general. He made me see things — things.'

"He threw his arms up. We were on deck at the time, and the head-
man of my wood-cutters, lounging near by, turned upon him his heavy
and glittering eyes. I looked around, and I don't know why, but I assure
you that never, never before, did this land, this river, this jungle, the
very arch of this blazing sky, appear to me so hopeless and so dark, so
impenetrable to human thought, so pitiless to human weakness. 'And,
ever since, you have been with him, of course?' I said.

"On the contrary. It appears their intercourse had been very much
broken by various causes. He had, as he informed me proudly, managed
to nurse Kurtz through two illnesses (he alluded to it as you would to
some risky feat), but as a rule Kurtz wandered alone, far in the depths
of the forest. 'Very often coming to this station, I had to wait days and
days before he would turn up,' he said. 'Ah, it was worth waiting for! —
sometimes.' 'What was he doing? exploring or what?' I asked. 'Oh yes,
of course'; he had discovered lots of villages, a lake too — he did not
know exactly in what direction; it was dangerous to inquire too much —
but mostly his expeditions had been for ivory. 'But he had no goods to
trade with by that time,' I objected. 'There's a good lot of cartridges
left even yet,' he answered, looking away. 'To speak plainly, he raided
the country,' I said. He nodded. 'Not alone, surely!' He muttered
something about the villages round that lake. 'Kurtz got the tribe to
follow him, did he?' I suggested. He fidgeted a little. 'They adored
him,' he said. The tone of these words was so extraordinary that I
looked at him searchingly. It was curious to see his mingled eagerness
and reluctance to speak of Kurtz. The man filled his life, occupied his
thoughts, swayed his emotions. 'What can you expect?' he burst out;
'he came to them with thunder and lightning, you know — and they
had never seen anything like it — and very terrible. He could be very
terrible. You can't judge Mr. Kurtz as you would an ordinary man. No,
no, no! Now — just to give you an idea — I don't mind telling you, he

wanted to shoot me too one day — but I don't judge him.' 'Shoot you!' I cried. 'What for?' 'Well, I had a small lot of ivory the chief of that village near my house gave me. You see I used to shoot game for them. Well, he wanted it, and wouldn't hear reason. He declared he would shoot me unless I gave him the ivory and then cleared out of the country, because he could do so, and had a fancy for it, and there was nothing on earth to prevent him killing whom he jolly well pleased. And it was true too. I gave him the ivory. What did I care! But I didn't clear out. No, no. I couldn't leave him. I had to be careful, of course, till we got friendly again for a time. He had his second illness then. Afterwards I had to keep out of the way; but I didn't mind. He was living for the most part in those villages on the lake. When he came down to the river, sometimes he would take to me, and sometimes it was better for me to be careful. This man suffered too much. He hated all this, and somehow he couldn't get away. When I had a chance I begged him to try and leave while there was time; I offered to go back with him. And he would say yes, and then he would remain; go off on another ivory hunt; disappear for weeks; forget himself amongst these people — forget himself — you know.' 'Why! he's mad,' I said. He protested indignantly. Mr. Kurtz couldn't be mad. If I had heard him talk, only two days ago, I wouldn't dare hint at such a thing. . . . I had taken up my binoculars while we talked, and was looking at the shore, sweeping the limit of the forest at each side and at the back of the house. The consciousness of there being people in that bush, so silent, so quiet — as silent and quiet as the ruined house on the hill — made me uneasy. There was no sign on the face of nature of this amazing tale that was not so much told as suggested to me in desolate exclamations, completed by shrugs, in interrupted phrases, in hints ending in deep sighs. The woods were unmoved, like a mask — heavy, like the closed door of a prison — they looked with their air of hidden knowledge, of patient expectation, of unapproachable silence. The Russian was explaining to me that it was only lately that Mr. Kurtz had come down to the river, bringing along with him all the fighting men of that lake tribe. He had been absent for several months — getting himself adored, I suppose — and had come down unexpectedly, with the intention to all appearance of making a raid either across the river or down stream. Evidently the appetite for more ivory had got the better of the — what shall I say? — less material aspirations. However, he had got much worse suddenly. 'I heard he was lying helpless, and so I came up — took my chance,' said the Russian. 'Oh, he is bad, very bad.' I directed my glass to the house. There were no signs of life, but there were the ruined roof, the long mud wall peeping above the grass, with three little square window-holes, no two of the same size; all this brought within reach of my hand, as it were. And then I made a brusque movement, and one of the remaining posts of that vanished fence leaped up in the field of my glass. You remember I told you I had been struck at the distance by certain attempts at ornamentation, rather remarkable in the ruinous aspect of the place. Now I had suddenly a nearer view, and its first result was to make me throw my head back as if before a blow. Then I went carefully from post to post with my glass, and I saw my mistake. These round knobs were not ornamental but symbolic; they were expressive and puzzling, striking and disturbing — food for thought and also for vultures if there had been any looking down from the sky; but at all events for such ants as were industrious enough to ascend the pole. They would have been even more impressive, those heads on the stakes, if their faces had not been turned to the house. Only one, the first I had made out, was facing my way. I was not so shocked as you may think. The start back I had given was really nothing but a movement of surprise. I had expected to see a knob of wood there, you know. I returned deliberately to the first I had seen — and there it was, black, dried, sunken, with closed eyelids — a head that seemed to sleep at the top of that pole, and, with the shrunken dry lips showing a narrow white line of the teeth, was smiling too, smiling continuously at some endless and jocose dream of that eternal slumber.

"I am not disclosing any trade secrets. In fact the manager said afterwards that Mr. Kurtz's methods had ruined the district. I have no opinion on that point, but I want you clearly to understand that there was nothing exactly profitable in these heads being there. They only showed that Mr. Kurtz lacked restraint in the gratification of his various lusts, that there was something wanting in him — some small matter which, when the pressing need arose, could not be found under his magnificent eloquence. Whether he knew of this deficiency himself I can't say. I think the knowledge came to him at last — only at the very last. But the wilderness had found him out early, and had taken on him a terrible vengeance for the fantastic invasion. I think it had whispered to him things about himself which he did not know, things of which he had no conception till he took counsel with this great solitude — and the whisper had proved irresistibly fascinating. It echoed loudly within him because he was hollow at the core. . . . I put down the glass, and the head that had appeared near enough to be spoken to seemed at once to have leaped away from me into inaccessible distance.

"The admirer of Mr. Kurtz was a bit crestfallen. In a hurried, indistinct voice he began to assure me he had not dared to take these — say, symbols — down. He was not afraid of the natives; they would not stir till Mr. Kurtz gave the word. His ascendancy was extraordinary. The camps of these people surrounded the place, and the chiefs came every day to see him. They would crawl . . . 'I don't want to know anything of the ceremonies used when approaching Mr. Kurtz,' I shouted. Curious, this feeling that came over me that such details would be more intolerable than those heads drying on the stakes under Mr. Kurtz's windows. After all, that was only a savage sight, while I seemed at one bound to have been transported into some lightless region of subtle horrors, where pure, uncomplicated savagery was a positive relief, being something that had a right to exist — obviously — in the sunshine. The young man looked at me with surprise. I suppose it did not occur to him that Mr. Kurtz was no idol of mine. He forgot I hadn't heard any of these splendid monologues on, what was it? on love, justice, conduct of life — or what not. If it had come to crawling before Mr. Kurtz, he crawled as much as the veriest savage of them all. I had no idea of the conditions, he said: these heads were the heads of rebels. I shocked him excessively by laughing. Rebels! What would be the next definition I was to hear? There had been enemies, criminals, workers — and these were rebels. Those rebellious heads looked very subdued to me on their sticks. 'You don't know how such a life tries a man like Kurtz,' cried Kurtz's last disciple. 'Well, and you?' I said. 'I! I! I am a simple man. I have no great thoughts. I want nothing from anybody. How can you compare me to . . . ?' His feelings were too much for speech, and suddenly he broke down. 'I don't understand,' he groaned. 'I've been doing my best to keep him alive, and that's enough. I had no hand in all this. I have no abilities. There hasn't been a drop of medicine or a mouthful of invalid food for months here. He was shamefully abandoned. A man like this, with such ideas. Shamefully! Shamefully! I — I — haven't slept for the last ten nights. . . .'

"His voice lost itself in the calm of the evening. The long shadows of the forest had slipped downhill while we talked, had gone far beyond the ruined hovel, beyond the symbolic row of stakes. All this was in the gloom, while we down there were yet in the sunshine, and the stretch of the river abreast of the clearing glittered in a still and dazzling splendour, with a murky and overshadowed bend above and below. Not a living soul was seen on the shore. The bushes did not rustle.

"Suddenly round the corner of the house a group of men appeared, as though they had come up from the ground. They waded waist-deep in the grass, in a compact body, bearing an improvised stretcher in their midst. Instantly, in the emptiness of the landscape, a cry arose whose shrillness pierced the still air like a sharp arrow flying straight to the very heart of the land; and, as if by enchantment, streams of human beings — of naked human beings — with spears in their hands, with bows, with shields, with wild glances and savage movements, were poured into the clearing by the dark-faced and pensive forest. The bushes shook, the grass swayed for a time, and then everything stood still in attentive immobility.

"'Now, if he does not say the right thing to them we are all done for,' said the Russian at my elbow. The knot of men with the stretcher had stopped too, half-way to the steamer, as if petrified. I saw the man on the stretcher sit up, lank and with an uplifted arm, above the shoulders of the bearers. 'Let us hope that the man who can talk so well of love in general will find some particular reason to spare us this time,' I said. I resented bitterly the absurd danger of our situation, as if to be at the mercy of that atrocious phantom had been a dishonouring necessity. I could not hear a sound, but through my glasses I saw the thin arm extended commandingly, the lower jaw moving, the eyes of that apparition shining darkly far in its bony head that nodded with grotesque jerks. Kurtz — Kurtz — that means 'short' in German — don't it? Well, the name was as true as everything else in his life — and death. He looked at least seven feet long. His covering had fallen off, and his body emerged from it pitiful and appalling as from a winding-sheet. I could see the cage of his ribs all astir, the bones of his arm waving. It was as though an animated image of death carved out of old ivory had been shaking its hand with menaces at a motionless crowd of men made of dark and glittering bronze. I saw him open his mouth wide — it gave him a weirdly voracious aspect, as though he had wanted to swallow all the air, all the earth, all the men before him. A deep voice reached me faintly. He must have been shouting. He fell back suddenly. The stretcher shook as the bearers staggered forward again, and almost at the same time I noticed that the crowd of savages was vanishing without any perceptible movement of retreat, as if the forest that had ejected these beings so suddenly had drawn them in again as the breath is drawn in a long aspiration.

"Some of the pilgrims behind the stretcher carried his arms — two shot-guns, a heavy rifle, and a light revolver-carbine — the thunderbolts of that pitiful Jupiter. The manager bent over him murmuring as he walked beside his head. They laid him down in one of the little cabins — just a room for a bed-place and a camp-stool or two, you

know. We had brought his belated correspondence, and a lot of torn
envelopes and open letters littered his bed. His hand roamed feebly
amongst these papers. I was struck by the fire of his eyes and the com-
posed languor of his expression. It was not so much the exhaustion of
disease. He did not seem in pain. This shadow looked satiated and
calm, as though for the moment it had had its fill of all the emotions.

"He rustled one of the letters, and looking straight in my face said,
'I am glad.' Somebody had been writing to him about me. These special recommendations were turning up again. The volume of tone he
emitted without effort, almost without the trouble of moving his lips,
amazed me. A voice! a voice! It was grave, profound, vibrating, while
the man did not seem capable of a whisper. However, he had enough
strength in him — factitious no doubt — to very nearly make an end of
us, as you shall hear directly.

"The manager appeared silently in the doorway; I stepped out at
once and he drew the curtain after me. The Russian, eyed curiously by
the pilgrims, was staring at the shore. I followed the direction of his
glance.

"Dark human shapes could be made out in the distance, flitting
indistinctly against the gloomy border of the forest, and near the river
two bronze figures, leaning on tall spears, stood in the sunlight under
fantastic head-dresses of spotted skins, warlike and still in statuesque
repose. And from right to left along the lighted shore moved a wild and
gorgeous apparition of a woman.

"She walked with measured steps, draped in striped and fringed
cloths, treading the earth proudly, with a slight jingle and flash of barbarous ornaments. She carried her head high; her hair was done in the
shape of a helmet; she had brass leggings to the knee, brass wire gauntlets to the elbow, a crimson spot on her tawny cheek, innumerable
necklaces of glass beads on her neck; bizarre things, charms, gifts of
witch-men, that hung about her, glittered and trembled at every step.
She must have had the value of several elephant tusks upon her. She was
savage and superb, wild-eyed and magnificent; there was something
ominous and stately in her deliberate progress. And in the hush that
had fallen suddenly upon the whole sorrowful land, the immense wilderness, the colossal body of the fecund and mysterious life seemed to
look at her, pensive, as though it has been looking at the image of its
own tenebrous and passionate soul.

"She came abreast of the steamer, stood still, and faced us. Her long
shadow fell to the water's edge. Her face had a tragic and fierce aspect
of wild sorrow and of dumb pain mingled with the fear of some strug-

gling, half-shaped resolve. She stood looking at us without a stir, and like the wilderness itself, with an air of brooding over an inscrutable purpose. A whole minute passed, and then she made a step forward. There was a low jingle, a glint of yellow metal, a sway of fringed draperies, and she stopped as if her heart had failed her. The young fellow by my side growled. The pilgrims murmured at my back. She looked at us all as if her life had depended upon the unswerving steadiness of her glance. Suddenly she opened her bared arms and threw them up rigid above her head, as though in an uncontrollable desire to touch the sky, and at the same time the swift shadows darted out on the earth, swept around on the river, gathering the steamer in a shadowy embrace. A formidable silence hung over the scene.

"She turned away slowly, walked on, following the bank, and passed into the bushes to the left. Once only her eyes gleamed back at us in the dusk of the thickets before she disappeared.

"'If she had offered to come aboard I really think I would have tried to shoot her,' said the man of patches nervously. 'I had been risking my life every day for the last fortnight to keep her out of the house. She got in one day and kicked up a row about those miserable rags I picked up in the storeroom to mend my clothes with. I wasn't decent. At least it must have been that, for she talked like a fury to Kurtz for an hour, pointing at me now and then. I don't understand the dialect of this tribe. Luckily for me, I fancy Kurtz felt too ill that day to care, or there would have been mischief. I don't understand. . . . No — it's too much for me. Ah, well, it's all over now.'

"At this moment I heard Kurtz's deep voice behind the curtain: 'Save me! — save the ivory, you mean. Don't tell me. Save *me*! Why, I've had to save you. You are interrupting my plans now. Sick! Sick! Not so sick as you would like to believe. Never mind. I'll carry my ideas out yet — I will return. I'll show you what can be done. You with your little peddling notions — you are interfering with me. I will return. I . . .'

"The manager came out. He did me the honour to take me under the arm and lead me aside. 'He is very low, very low,' he said. He considered it necessary to sigh, but neglected to be consistently sorrowful. 'We have done all we could for him — haven't we? But there is no disguising the fact, Mr. Kurtz has done more harm than good to the Company. He did not see the time was not ripe for vigorous action. Cautiously, cautiously — that's my principle. We must be cautious yet. The district is closed to us for a time. Deplorable! Upon the whole, the trade will suffer. I don't deny there is a remarkable quantity of ivory — mostly fossil. We must save it, at all events — but look how precarious the position is — and why? Because the method is unsound.' 'Do you,' said I, looking at the shore, 'call it "unsound method"?' 'Without doubt,' he exclaimed hotly. 'Don't you?' . . . 'No method at all,' I murmured after a while. 'Exactly,' he exulted. 'I anticipated this. Shows a complete want of judgment. It is my duty to point it out in the proper quarter.' 'Oh,' said I, 'that fellow — what's his name? — the brickmaker, will make a readable report for you.' He appeared confounded for a moment. It seemed to me I had never breathed an atmosphere so vile, and I turned mentally to Kurtz for relief — positively for relief. 'Nevertheless, I think Mr. Kurtz is a remarkable man,' I said with emphasis. He started, dropped on me a cold heavy glance, said very quietly, 'He *was*,' and turned his back on me. My hour of favour was over; I found myself lumped along with Kurtz as a partisan of methods for which the time was not ripe: I was unsound! Ah! but it was something to have at least a choice of nightmares.

"I had turned to the wilderness really, not to Mr. Kurtz, who, I was ready to admit, was as good as buried. And for a moment it seemed to me as if I also were buried in a vast grave full of unspeakable secrets. I felt an intolerable weight oppressing my breast, the smell of the damp earth, the unseen presence of victorious corruption, the darkness of an impenetrable night. . . . The Russian tapped me on the shoulder. I heard him mumbling and stammering something about 'brother seaman — couldn't conceal — knowledge of matters that would affect Mr. Kurtz's reputation.' I waited. For him evidently Mr. Kurtz was not in his grave; I suspect that for him Mr. Kurtz was one of the immortals. 'Well!' said I at last, 'speak out. As it happens, I am Mr. Kurtz's friend — in a way.'

"He stated with a good deal of formality that had we not been 'of the same profession,' he would have kept the matter to himself without regard to consequences. He suspected 'there was an active ill-will towards him on the part of these white men that ——' 'You are right,' I said, remembering a certain conversation I had overheard. 'The manager thinks you ought to be hanged.' He showed a concern at this intelligence which amused me at first. 'I had better get out of the way quietly,' he said earnestly. 'I can do no more for Kurtz now, and they would soon find some excuse. What's to stop them? There's a military post three hundred miles from here.' 'Well, upon my word,' said I, 'perhaps you had better go if you have any friends amongst the savages near by.' 'Plenty,' he said. 'They are simple people — and I want nothing, you know.' He stood biting his lip, then: 'I don't want any harm to happen to these whites here, but of course I was thinking of Mr. Kurtz's reputation — but you are a brother seaman and ——' 'All right,' said I, after a time. 'Mr. Kurtz's reputation is safe with me.' I did not know how truly I spoke.

"He informed me, lowering his voice, that it was Kurtz who had ordered the attack to be made on the steamer. 'He hated sometimes the idea of being taken away — and then again . . . But I don't understand these matters. I am a simple man. He thought it would scare you away — that you would give it up, thinking him dead. I could not stop him. Oh, I had an awful time of it this last month.' 'Very well,' I said. 'He is all right now.' 'Y-e-e-es,' he muttered, not very convinced apparently. 'Thanks,' said I; 'I shall keep my eyes open.' 'But quiet — eh?' he urged anxiously. 'It would be awful for his reputation if anybody here ——' I promised a complete discretion with great gravity. 'I have a canoe and three black fellows waiting not very far. I am off. Could you give me a few Martini-Henry cartridges?' I could, and did, with proper secrecy. He helped himself, with a wink at me, to a handful of my tobacco. 'Between sailors — you know — good English tobacco.' At the door of the pilot-house he turned round — 'I say, haven't you a pair of shoes you could spare?' He raised one leg. 'Look.' The soles were tied with knotted strings sandal-wise under his bare feet. I rooted out an old pair, at which he looked with admiration before tucking it under his left arm. One of his pockets (bright red) was bulging with cartridges, from the other (dark blue) peeped 'Towson's Inquiry,' etc. etc. He seemed to think himself excellently well equipped for a renewed encounter with the wilderness. 'Ah! I'll never, never meet such a man again. You ought to have heard him recite poetry — his own too it was, he told me. Poetry!' He rolled his eyes at the recollection of these delights. 'Oh, he enlarged my mind!' 'Good-bye,' said I. He shook hands and vanished in the night. Sometimes I ask myself whether I had ever really seen him — whether it was possible to meet such a phenomenon! . . .

"When I woke up shortly after midnight his warning came to my mind with its hint of danger that seemed, in the starred darkness, real enough to make me get up for the purpose of having a look round. On the hill a big fire burned, illuminating fitfully a crooked corner of the station-house. One of the agents with a picket of a few of our blacks, armed for the purpose, was keeping guard over the ivory; but deep within the forest, red gleams that wavered, that seemed to sink and rise from the ground amongst confused columnar shapes of intense blackness, showed the exact position of the camp where Mr. Kurtz's adorers were keeping their uneasy vigil. The monotonous beating of a big drum filled the air with muffled shocks and a lingering vibration. A steady droning sound of many men chanting each to himself some weird incantation came out from the black, flat wall of the woods as the humming of bees comes out of a hive, and had a strange narcotic effect upon my half-awake senses. I believe I dozed off leaning over the rail, till an abrupt burst of yells, an overwhelming outbreak of a pent-up and mysterious frenzy, woke me up in a bewildered wonder. It was cut short all at once, and the low droning went on with an effect of audible and soothing silence. I glanced casually into the little cabin. A light was burning within, but Mr. Kurtz was not there.

"I think I would have raised an outcry if I had believed my eyes. But I didn't believe them at first — the thing seemed so impossible. The fact is, I was completely unnerved by a sheer blank fright, pure abstract terror, unconnected with any distinct shape of physical danger. What made this emotion so overpowering was — how shall I define it? — the moral shock I received, as if something altogether monstrous, intolerable to thought and odious to the soul, had been thrust upon me unexpectedly. This lasted of course the merest fraction of a second, and then the usual sense of commonplace, deadly danger, the possibility of a sudden onslaught and massacre, or something of the kind, which I saw impending, was positively welcome and composing. It pacified me, in fact, so much, that I did not raise an alarm.

"There was an agent buttoned up inside an ulster and sleeping on a chair on deck within three feet of me. The yells had not awakened him; he snored very slightly; I left him to his slumbers and leaped ashore. I did not betray Mr. Kurtz — it was ordered I should never betray him — it was written I should be loyal to the nightmare of my choice. I was anxious to deal with this shadow by myself alone — and to this day I don't know why I was so jealous of sharing with anyone the peculiar blackness of that experience.

"As soon as I got on the bank I saw a trail — a broad trail through the grass. I remember the exultation with which I said to myself, 'He can't walk — he is crawling on all-fours — I've got him.' The grass was wet with dew. I strode rapidly with clenched fists. I fancy I had some vague notion of falling upon him and giving him a drubbing. I don't know. I had some imbecile thoughts. The knitting old woman with the cat obtruded herself upon my memory as a most improper person to be sitting at the other end of such an affair. I saw a row of pilgrims squirting lead in the air out of Winchesters held to the hip. I thought I would never get back to the steamer, and imagined myself living alone and unarmed in the woods to an advanced age. Such silly things — you know. And I remember I confounded the beat of the drum with the beating of my heart, and was pleased at its calm regularity.

"I kept to the track though — then stopped to listen. The night was very clear; a dark blue space, sparkling with dew and starlight, in which black things stood very still. I thought I could see a kind of motion ahead of me. I was strangely cocksure of everything that night. I actually left the track and ran in a wide semicircle (I verily believe chuckling to myself) so as to get in front of that stir, of that motion I had seen — if indeed I had seen anything. I was circumventing Kurtz as though it had been a boyish game.

"I came upon him, and, if he had not heard me coming, I would have fallen over him too, but he got up in time. He rose, unsteady, long, pale, indistinct, like a vapour exhaled by the earth, and swayed slightly, misty and silent before me; while at my back the fires loomed between the trees, and the murmur of many voices issued from the forest. I had cut him off cleverly; but when actually confronting him I seemed to come to my senses, I saw the danger in its right proportion. It was by no means over yet. Suppose he began to shout? Though he could hardly stand, there was still plenty of vigour in his voice. 'Go away — hide yourself,' he said, in that profound tone. It was very awful. I glanced back. We were within thirty yards from the nearest fire. A black figure stood up, strode on long black legs, waving long black arms, across the glow. It had horns — antelope horns, I think — on its head. Some sorcerer, some witch-man, no doubt: it looked fiend-like enough. 'Do you know what you are doing?' I whispered. 'Perfectly,' he answered, raising his voice for that single word: it sounded to me far off and yet loud, like a hail through a speaking-trumpet. If he makes a row we are lost, I thought to myself. This clearly was not a case for fisticuffs, even apart from the very natural aversion I had to beat that Shadow — this wandering and tormented thing. 'You will be lost,' I said — 'utterly lost.' One gets sometimes such a flash of inspiration, you know. I did say the right thing, though indeed he could not have been more irretrievably lost than he was at this very moment, when the foundations of our intimacy were being laid — to endure — to endure — even to the end — even beyond.

" 'I had immense plans,' he muttered irresolutely. 'Yes,' said I; 'but if you try to shout I'll smash your head with ——' There was not a stick or a stone near. 'I will throttle you for good,' I corrected myself. 'I was on the threshold of great things,' he pleaded, in a voice of longing, with a wistfulness of tone that made my blood run cold. 'And now for this stupid scoundrel ——' 'Your success in Europe is assured in any case,'

I affirmed steadily. I did not want to have the throttling of him, you understand — and indeed it would have been very little use for any practical purpose. I tried to break the spell — the heavy, mute spell of the wilderness — that seemed to draw him to its pitiless breast by the awakening of forgotten and brutal instincts, by the memory of gratified and monstrous passions. This alone, I was convinced, had driven him out to the edge of the forest, to the bush, towards the gleam of fires, the throb of drums, the drone of weird incantations; this alone had beguiled his unlawful soul beyond the bounds of permitted aspirations. And, don't you see, the terror of the position was not in being knocked on the head — though I had a very lively sense of that danger too — but in this, that I had to deal with a being to whom I could not appeal in the name of anything high or low. I had, even like the niggers, to invoke him — himself — his own exalted and incredible degradation. There was nothing either above or below him — and I knew it. He had kicked himself loose of the earth. Confound the man! he had kicked the very earth to pieces. He was alone, and I before him did not know whether I stood on the ground or floated in the air. I've been telling you what we said — repeating the phrases we pronounced — but what's the good? They were common everyday words — the familiar, vague sounds exchanged on every waking day of life. But what of that? They had behind them, to my mind, the terrific suggestiveness of words heard in dreams, of phrases spoken in nightmares. Soul! If anybody had ever struggled with a soul, I am the man. And I wasn't arguing with a lunatic either. Believe me or not his intelligence was perfectly clear — concentrated, it is true, upon himself with horrible intensity, yet clear; and therein was my only chance — barring, of course, the killing him there and then, which wasn't so good, on account of unavoidable noise. But his soul was mad. Being alone in the wilderness, it had looked within itself, and, by Heavens! I tell you, it had gone mad. I had — for my sins, I suppose, to go through the ordeal of looking into it myself. No eloquence could have been so withering to one's belief in mankind as his final burst of sincerity. He struggled with himself too. I saw it — I heard it. I saw the inconceivable mystery of a soul that knew no restraint, no faith, and no fear, yet struggling blindly with itself. I kept my head pretty well; but when I had him at last stretched on the couch, I wiped my forehead, while my legs shook under me as though I had carried half a ton on my back down that hill. And yet I had only supported him, his bony arm clasped round my neck — and he was not much heavier than a child.

"When next day we left at noon, the crowd, of whose presence behind the curtain of trees I had been acutely conscious all the time, flowed out of the woods again, filled the clearing, covered the slope with a mass of naked, breathing, quivering, bronze bodies. I steamed up a bit, then swung down-stream, and two thousand eyes followed the evolutions of the splashing, thumping, fierce river-demon beating the water with its terrible tail and breathing black smoke into the air. In front of the first rank, along the river, three men, plastered with bright red earth from head to foot, strutted to and fro restlessly. When we came abreast again, they faced the river, stamped their feet, nodded their horned heads, swayed their scarlet bodies; they shook towards the fierce river-demon a bunch of black feathers, a mangy skin with a pendent tail — something that looked like a dried gourd; they shouted periodically together strings of amazing words that resembled no sounds of human language; and the deep murmurs of the crowd, interrupted suddenly, were like the responses of some satanic litany.

"We had carried Kurtz into the pilot-house: there was more air there. Lying on the couch, he stared through the open shutter. There was an eddy in the mass of human bodies, and the woman with helmeted head and tawny cheeks rushed out to the very brink of the stream. She put out her hands, shouted something, and all that wild mob took up the shout in a roaring chorus of articulated, rapid, breathless utterance.

"'Do you understand this?' I asked.

"He kept on looking out past me with fiery, longing eyes, with a mingled expression of wistfulness and hate. He made no answer, but I saw a smile, a smile of indefinable meaning, appear on his colourless lips that a moment after twitched convulsively. 'Do I not?' he said slowly, gasping, as if the words had been torn out of him by a supernatural power.

"I pulled the string of the whistle, and I did this because I saw the pilgrims on deck getting out their rifles with an air of anticipating a jolly lark. At the sudden screech there was a movement of abject terror through that wedged mass of bodies. 'Don't! don't you frighten them away,' cried some one on deck disconsolately. I pulled the string time after time. They broke and ran, they leaped, they crouched, they swerved, they dodged the flying terror of the sound. The three red chaps had fallen flat, face down on the shore, as though they had been shot dead. Only the barbarous and superb woman did not so much as flinch, and stretched tragically her bare arms after us over the sombre and glittering river.

"And then that imbecile crowd down on the deck started their little fun, and I could see nothing more for smoke.

"The brown current ran swiftly out of the heart of darkness, bearing us down towards the sea with twice the speed of our upward progress; and Kurtz's life was running swiftly too, ebbing, ebbing out of his heart into the sea of inexorable time. The manager was very placid, he had no vital anxieties now, he took us both in with a comprehensive and satisfied glance: the 'affair' had come off as well as could be wished. I saw the time approaching when I would be left alone of the party of 'unsound method.' The pilgrims looked upon me with disfavour. I was, so to speak, numbered with the dead. It is strange how I accepted this unforeseen partnership, this choice of nightmares forced upon me in the tenebrous land invaded by these mean and greedy phantoms.

"Kurtz discoursed. A voice! a voice! It rang deep to the very last. It survived his strength to hide in the magnificent folds of eloquence the barren darkness of his heart. Oh, he struggled! he struggled! The wastes of his weary brain were haunted by shadowy images now — images of wealth and fame revolving obsequiously round his unextinguishable gift of noble and lofty expression. My Intended, my station, my career, my ideas — these were the subjects for the occasional utterances of elevated sentiments. The shade of the original Kurtz frequented the bedside of the hollow sham, whose fate it was to be buried presently in the mould of primeval earth. But both the diabolic love and the unearthly hate of the mysteries it had penetrated fought for the possession of that soul satiated with primitive emotions, avid of lying fame, of sham distinction, of all the appearances of success and power.

"Sometimes he was contemptibly childish. He desired to have kings meet him at railway stations on his return from some ghastly Nowhere, where he intended to accomplish great things. 'You show them you have in you something that is really profitable, and then there will be no limits to the recognition of your ability,' he would say. 'Of course you must take care of the motives — right motives — always.' The long reaches that were like one and the same reach, monotonous bends that were exactly alike, slipped past the steamer with their multitude of secular trees looking patiently after this grimy fragment of another world, the forerunner of change, of conquest, of trade, of massacres, of blessings. I looked ahead — piloting. 'Close the shutter,' said Kurtz suddenly one day; 'I can't bear to look at this.' I did so. There was a silence. 'Oh, but I will wring your heart yet!' he cried at the invisible wilderness.

"We broke down — as I had expected — and had to lie up for repairs at the head of an island. This delay was the first thing that shook

Kurtz's confidence. One morning he gave me a packet of papers and a photograph — the lot tied together with a shoe-string. 'Keep this for me,' he said. 'This noxious fool' (meaning the manager) 'is capable of prying into my boxes when I am not looking.' In the afternoon I saw him. He was lying on his back with closed eyes, and I withdrew quietly, but I heard him mutter, 'Live rightly, die, die . . .' I listened. There was nothing more. Was he rehearsing some speech in his sleep, or was it a fragment of a phrase from some newspaper article? He had been writing for the papers and meant to do so again, 'for the furthering of my ideas. It's a duty.'

"His was an impenetrable darkness. I looked at him as you peer down at a man who is lying at the bottom of a precipice where the sun never shines. But I had not much time to give him, because I was helping the engine-driver to take to pieces the leaky cylinders, to straighten a bent connecting-rod, and in other such matters. I lived in an infernal mess of rust, filings, nuts, bolts, spanners, hammers, ratchet-drills — things I abominate, because I don't get on with them. I tended the little forge we fortunately had aboard; I toiled wearily in a wretched scrap-heap — unless I had the shakes too bad to stand.

"One evening coming in with a candle I was startled to hear him say a little tremulously, 'I am lying here in the dark waiting for death.' The light was within a foot of his eyes. I forced myself to murmur, 'Oh, nonsense!' and stood over him as if transfixed.

"Anything approaching the change that came over his features I have never seen before, and hope never to see again. Oh, I wasn't touched. I was fascinated. It was as though a veil had been rent. I saw on that ivory face the expression of sombre pride, of ruthless power, of craven terror — of an intense and hopeless despair. Did he live his life again in every detail of desire, temptation, and surrender during that supreme moment of complete knowledge? He cried in a whisper at some image, at some vision — he cried out twice, a cry that was no more than a breath:

" 'The horror! The horror!'

"I blew the candle out and left the cabin. The pilgrims were dining in the mess-room, and I took my place opposite the manager, who lifted his eyes to give me a questioning glance, which I successfully ignored. He leaned back, serene, with that peculiar smile of his sealing the unexpressed depths of his meanness. A continuous shower of small flies steamed upon the lamp, upon the cloth, upon our hands and faces. Suddenly the manager's boy put his insolent black head in the doorway, and said in a tone of scathing contempt:

" 'Mistah Kurtz — he dead.'

"All the pilgrims rushed out to see. I remained, and went on with my dinner. I believe I was considered brutally callous. However, I did not eat much. There was a lamp in there — light, don't you know — and outside it was so beastly, beastly dark. I went no more near the remarkable man who had pronounced a judgment upon the adventures of his soul on this earth. The voice was gone. What else had been there? But I am of course aware that next day the pilgrims buried something in a muddy hole.

"And then they very nearly buried me.

"However, as you see, I did not go to join Kurtz there and then. I did not. I remained to dream the nightmare out to the end, and to show my loyalty to Kurtz once more. Destiny. My destiny! Droll thing life is — that mysterious arrangement of merciless logic for a futile purpose. The most you can hope from it is some knowledge of yourself — that comes too late — a crop of unextinguishable regrets. I have wrestled with death. It is the most unexciting contest you imagine. It takes place in an impalpable greyness, with nothing underfoot, with nothing around, without spectators, without clamour, without glory, without the great desire of victory, without the great fear of defeat, in a sickly atmosphere of tepid scepticism, without much belief in your own right, and still less in that of your adversary. If such is the form of ultimate wisdom, then life is a greater riddle than some of us think it to be. I was within a hair's-breadth of the last opportunity for pronouncement, and I found with humiliation that probably I would have nothing to say. This is the reason why I affirm that Kurtz was a remarkable man. He had something to say. He said it. Since I had peeped over the edge myself, I understand better the meaning of his stare, that could not see the flame of the candle, but was wide enough to embrace the whole universe, piercing enough to penetrate all the hearts that beat in the darkness. He had summed up — he had judged. 'The horror!' He was a remarkable man. After all, this was the expression of some sort of belief; it had candour, it had conviction, it had a vibrating note of revolt in its whisper, it had the appalling face of a glimpsed truth — the strange commingling of desire and hate. And it is not my own extremity I remember best — a vision of greyness without form filled with physical pain, and a careless contempt for the evanescence of all things — even of this pain itself. No! It is his extremity that I seem to have lived through. True, he had made that last stride, he had stepped over the edge, while I had been permitted to draw back my hesitating foot. And perhaps in this is the whole difference; perhaps all the wisdom, and all truth, and all sincerity, are just compressed into that inappreciable moment of time in which we step over the threshold of the invisible. Perhaps! I like to think my summing-up would not have been a word of careless contempt. Better his cry — much better. It was an affirmation, a moral victory paid for by innumerable defeats, by abominable terrors, by abominable satisfactions. But it was a victory! That is why I have remained loyal to Kurtz to the last, and even beyond, when a long time after I heard once more, not his own voice, but the echo of his magnificent eloquence thrown to me from a soul as translucently pure as a cliff of crystal.

"No, they did not bury me, though there is a period of time which I remember mistily, with a shuddering wonder, like a passage through some inconceivable world that had no hope in it and no desire. I found myself back in the sepulchral city resenting the sight of people hurrying through the streets to filch a little money from each other, to devour their infamous cookery, to gulp their unwholesome beer, to dream their insignificant and silly dreams. They trespassed upon my thoughts. They were intruders whose knowledge of life was to me an irritating pretence, because I felt so sure they could not possibly know the things I knew. Their bearing, which was simply the bearing of commonplace individuals going about their business in the assurance of perfect safety, was offensive to me like the outrageous flauntings of folly in the face of a danger it is unable to comprehend. I had no particular desire to enlighten them, but I had some difficulty in restraining myself from laughing in their faces, so full of stupid importance. I daresay I was not very well at that time. I tottered about the streets — there were various affairs to settle — grinning bitterly at perfectly respectable persons. I admit my behavior was inexcusable, but then my temperature was seldom normal in these days. My dear aunt's endeavours to 'nurse up my strength' seemed altogether beside the mark. It was not my strength that wanted nursing, it was my imagination that wanted soothing. I kept the bundle of papers given me by Kurtz, not knowing exactly what to do with it. His mother had died lately, watched over, as I was told, by his Intended. A clean-shaved man, with an official manner and wearing gold-rimmed spectacles, called on me one day and made inquiries, at first circuitous, afterwards suavely pressing, about what he was pleased to denominate certain 'documents.' I was not surprised, because I had had two rows with the manager on that subject out there. I had refused to give up the smallest scrap out of that package, and I took the same attitude with the spectacled man. He became darkly menacing at last, and with much heat argued that the Company had the right to every bit

of information about its 'territories.' And, said he, 'Mr. Kurtz's knowledge of unexplored regions must have been necessarily extensive and
peculiar — owing to his great abilities and to the deplorable circumstances in which he had been placed: therefore ——' I assured him Mr.
Kurtz's knowledge, however extensive, did not bear upon the problems
of commerce or administration. He invoked then the name of science.
'It would be an incalculable loss if,' etc. etc. I offered him the report of
the 'Suppression of Savage Customs,' with the postscriptum torn off.
He took it up eagerly, but ended by sniffing at it with an air of contempt. 'This is not what we had a right to expect,' he remarked. 'Expect
nothing else,' I said. 'There are only private letters.' He withdrew upon
some threat of legal proceedings, and I saw him no more; but another
fellow, calling himself Kurtz's cousin, appeared two days later, and was
anxious to hear all the details about his dear relative's last moments.
Incidentally he gave me to understand that Kurtz had been essentially
a great musician. 'There was the making of an immense success,' said
the man, who was an organist, I believe, with lank grey hair flowing
over a greasy coat-collar. I had no reason to doubt his statement; and
to this day I am unable to say what was Kurtz's profession, whether he
ever had any — which was the greatest of his talents. I had taken him
for a painter who wrote for the papers, or else for a journalist who could
paint — but even the cousin (who took snuff during the interview)
could not tell me what he had been — exactly. He was a universal
genius — on that point I agreed with the old chap, who thereupon
blew his nose noisily into a large cotton handkerchief and withdrew in
senile agitation, bearing off some family letters and memoranda without importance. Ultimately a journalist anxious to know something of
the fate of his 'dear colleague' turned up. This visitor informed me
Kurtz's proper sphere ought to have been politics 'on the popular side.'
He had furry straight eyebrows, bristly hair cropped short, an eyeglass
on a broad ribbon, and, becoming expansive, confessed his opinion
that Kurtz really couldn't write a bit — 'but Heavens! how that man
could talk! He electrified large meetings. He had faith — don't you
see? — he had the faith. He could get himself to believe anything —
anything. He would have been a splendid leader of an extreme party.'
'What party?' I asked. 'Any party,' answered the other. 'He was an —
an — extremist.' Did I not think so? I assented. Did I know, he asked,
with a sudden flash of curiosity, 'what it was that had induced him to go
out there?' 'Yes,' said I, and forthwith handed him the famous Report
for publication, if he thought fit. He glanced through it hurriedly,

mumbling all the time, judged 'it would do,' and took himself off with this plunder.

"Thus I was left at last with a slim packet of letters and the girl's portrait. She struck me as beautiful — I mean she had a beautiful expression. I know that the sunlight can be made to lie too, yet one felt that no manipulation of light and pose could have conveyed the delicate shade of truthfulness upon those features. She seemed ready to listen without mental reservation, without suspicion, without a thought for herself. I concluded I would go and give her back her portrait and those letters myself. Curiosity? Yes; and also some other feeling perhaps. All that had been Kurtz's had passed out of my hands: his soul, his body, his station, his plans, his ivory, his career. There remained only his memory and his Intended — and I wanted to give that up too to the past, in a way — to surrender personally all that remained of him with me to that oblivion which is the last word of our common fate. I don't defend myself. I had no clear perception of what it was I really wanted. Perhaps it was an impulse of unconscious loyalty, or the fulfillment of one of those ironic necessities that lurk in the facts of human existence. I don't know. I can't tell. But I went.

"I thought his memory was like the other memories of the dead that accumulate in every man's life — a vague impress on the brain of shadows that had fallen on it in their swift and final passage; but before the high and ponderous door, between the tall houses of a street as still and decorous as a well-kept alley in a cemetery, I had a vision of him on the stretcher, opening his mouth voraciously, as if to devour all the earth with all its mankind. He lived then before me; he lived as much as he had ever lived — a shadow insatiable of splendid appearances, of frightful realities; a shadow darker than the shadow of the night, and draped nobly in the folds of a gorgeous eloquence. The vision seemed to enter the house with me — the stretcher, the phantom-bearers, the wild crowd of obedient worshippers, the gloom of the forests, the glitter of the reach between the murky bends, the beat of the drum, regular and muffled like the beating of a heart — the heart of a conquering darkness. It was a moment of triumph for the wilderness, an invading and vengeful rush which, it seemed to me, I would have to keep back alone for the salvation of another soul. And the memory of what I had heard him say afar there, with the horned shapes stirring at my back, in the glow of fires, within the patient woods, those broken phrases came back to me, were heard again in their ominous and terrifying simplicity. I remembered his abject pleading, his abject threats, the colossal scale of his vile desires, the meanness, the torment, the tempestuous anguish of his soul. And later on I seemed to see his collected languid manner, when he said one day, 'This lot of ivory now is really mine. The Company did not pay for it. I collected it myself at a very great personal risk. I am afraid they will try to claim it as theirs though. H'm. It is a difficult case. What do you think I ought to do — resist? Eh? I want no more than justice.' . . . He wanted no more than justice — no more than justice. I rang the bell before a mahogany door on the first floor, and while I waited he seemed to stare at me out of the glassy panel — stare with that wide and immense stare embracing, condemning, loathing all the universe. I seemed to hear the whispered cry, 'The horror! The horror!'

"The dusk was falling. I had to wait in a lofty drawing-room with three long windows from floor to ceiling that were like three luminous and bedraped columns. The bent gilt legs and backs of the furniture shone in indistinct curves. The tall marble fireplace had a cold and monumental whiteness. A grand piano stood massively in a corner; with dark gleams on the flat surfaces like a sombre and polished sarcophagus. A high door opened — closed. I rose.

"She came forward, all in black, with a pale head, floating towards me in the dusk. She was in mourning. It was more than a year since his death, more than a year since the news came; she seemed as though she would remember and mourn for ever. She took both my hands in hers and murmured, 'I had heard you were coming.' I noticed she was not very young — I mean not girlish. She had a mature capacity for fidelity, for belief, for suffering. The room seemed to have grown darker, as if all the sad light of the cloudy evening had taken refuge on her forehead. This fair hair, this pale visage, this pure brow, seemed surrounded by an ashy halo from which the dark eyes looked out at me. Their glance was guileless, profound, confident, and trustful. She carried her sorrowful head as though she were proud of that sorrow, as though she would say, I — I alone know how to mourn for him as he deserves. But while we were still shaking hands, such a look of awful desolation came upon her face that I perceived she was one of those creatures that are not the play-things of Time. For her he had died only yesterday. And, by Jove! the impression was so powerful that for me too he seemed to have died only yesterday — nay, this very minute. I saw her and him in the same instant of time — his death and her sorrow — I saw her sorrow in the very moment of his death. Do you understand? I saw them together — I heard them together. She had said, with a deep catch of the breath, 'I have survived'; while my strained ears seemed to hear distinctly, mingled with her tone of despairing regret, the summing-up whisper of his eternal condemnation. I asked myself what I was doing there, with a sensation of panic in my heart as though I had blundered into a place of cruel and absurd mysteries not fit for a human being to behold. She motioned me to a chair. We sat down. I laid the packet gently on the little table, and she put her hand over it. . . . 'You knew him well,' she murmured, after a moment of mourning silence.

" 'Intimacy grows quickly out there,' I said. 'I knew him as well as it is possible for one man to know another.'

" 'And you admired him,' she said. 'It was impossible to know him and not to admire him. Was it?'

" 'He was a remarkable man,' I said unsteadily. Then before the appealing fixity of her gaze, that seemed to watch for more words on my lips, I went on, 'It was impossible not to ——'

" 'Love him,' she finished eagerly, silencing me into an appalled dumbness. 'How true! how true! But when you think that no one knew him so well as I! I had all his noble confidence. I knew him best.'

" 'You knew him best,' I repeated. And perhaps she did. But with every word spoken the room was growing darker, and only her forehead, smooth and white, remained illumined by the unextinguishable light of belief and love.

" 'You were his friend,' she went on. 'His friend,' she repeated, a little louder. 'You must have been, if he had given you this, and sent you to me. I feel I can speak to you — and oh! I must speak. I want you — you who have heard his last words — to know I have been worthy of him. . . . It is not pride. . . . Yes! I am proud to know I understood him better than anyone on earth — he told me so himself. And since his mother died I have had no one — no one — to — to ——'

"I listened. The darkness deepened. I was not even sure whether he had given me the right bundle. I rather suspect he wanted me to take care of another batch of his papers which, after his death, I saw the manager examining under the lamp. And the girl talked, easing her pain in the certitude of my sympathy; she talked as thirsty men drink. I had heard that her engagement with Kurtz had been disapproved by her people. He wasn't rich enough or something. And indeed I don't know whether he had not been a pauper all his life. He had given me some reason to infer that it was his impatience of comparative poverty that drove him out there.

" '. . . Who was not his friend who had heard him speak once?' she was saying. 'He drew men towards him by what was best in them.' She looked at me with intensity. 'It is the gift of the great,' she went on, and the sound of her low voice seemed to have the accompaniment of all the other sounds, full of mystery, desolation, and sorrow, I had ever heard — the ripple of the river, the soughing of the trees swayed by the wind, the murmurs of the crowds, the faint ring of incomprehensible words cried from afar, the whisper of a voice speaking from beyond the threshold of an eternal darkness. 'But you have heard him! You know!' she cried.

" 'Yes, I know,' I said with something like despair in my heart, but bowing my head before the faith that was in her, before that great and saving illusion that shone with an unearthly glow in the darkness, in the triumphant darkness from which I could not have defended her — from which I could not even defend myself.

" 'What a loss to me — to us!' — she corrected herself with beautiful generosity; then added in a murmur, 'To the world.' By the last gleams of twilight I could see the glitter of her eyes, full of tears — of tears that would not fall.

" 'I have been very happy — very fortunate — very proud,' she went on. 'Too fortunate. Too happy for a little while. And now I am unhappy for — for life.'

"She stood up; her fair hair seemed to catch all the remaining light in a glimmer of gold. I rose too.

" 'And of all this,' she went on mournfully, 'of all his promise, and of all his greatness, of his generous mind, of his noble heart, nothing remains — nothing but a memory. You and I ——'

" 'We shall always remember him,' I said hastily.

" 'No!' she cried. 'It is impossible that all this should be lost — that such a life should be sacrificed to leave nothing — but sorrow. You know what vast plans he had. I knew of them too — I could not perhaps understand — but others knew of them. Something must remain. His words, at least, have not died.'

" 'His words will remain,' I said.

" 'And his example,' she whispered to herself. 'Men looked up to him — his goodness shone in every act. His example ——'

" 'True,' I said; 'his example too. Yes, his example. I forgot that.'

" 'But I do not. I cannot — I cannot believe — not yet. I cannot believe that I shall never see him again, that nobody will see him again, never, never, never.'

"She put out her arms as if after a retreating figure, stretching them back and with clasped pale hands across the fading and narrow sheen of the window. Never see him! I saw him clearly enough then. I shall see this eloquent phantom as long as I live, and I shall see her too, a tragic and familiar Shade, resembling in this gesture another one, tragic also, and bedecked with powerless charms, stretching bare brown arms over the glitter of the infernal stream, the stream of darkness. She said suddenly very low, 'He died as he lived.'

"'His end,' said I, with dull anger stirring in me, 'was in every way worthy of his life.'

"'And I was not with him,' she murmured. My anger subsided before a feeling of infinite pity.

"'Everything that could be done ——' I mumbled.

"'Ah, but I believed in him more than anyone on earth — more than his own mother, more than — himself. He needed me! Me! I would have treasured every sigh, every word, every sign, every glance.'

"I felt like a chill grip on my chest. 'Don't,' I said, in a muffled voice.

"'Forgive me. I — I — have mourned so long in silence — in silence. . . . You were with him — to the last? I think of his loneliness. Nobody near to understand him as I would have understood. Perhaps no one to hear . . .'

"'To the very end,' I said shakily. 'I heard his very last words. . . .' I stopped in a fright.

"'Repeat them,' she murmured in a heartbroken tone. 'I want — I want — something — something — to — to live with.'

"I was on the point of crying at her, 'Don't you hear them?' The dusk was repeating them in a persistent whisper all around us, in a whisper that seemed to swell menacingly like the first whisper of a rising wind. 'The horror! The horror!'

"'His last word — to live with,' she insisted. 'Don't you understand I loved him — I loved him — I loved him!'

"I pulled myself together and spoke slowly.

"'The last word he pronounced was — your name.'

"I heard a light sigh and then my heart stood still, stopped dead short by an exulting and terrible cry, by the cry of inconceivable triumph and of unspeakable pain. 'I knew it — I was sure!' . . . She knew. She was sure. I heard her weeping; she had hidden her face in her hands. It seemed to me that the house would collapse before I could escape, that the heavens would fall upon my head. But nothing happened. The heavens do not fall for such a trifle. Would they have fallen, I wonder, if I had rendered Kurtz that justice which was his due? Hadn't he said he wanted only justice? But I couldn't. I could not tell her. It would have been too dark — too dark altogether. . . ."

Marlow ceased, and sat apart, indistinct and silent, in the pose of a meditating Buddha. Nobody moved for a time. "We have lost the first of the ebb," said the Director suddenly. I raised my head. The offing was barred by a black bank of clouds, and the tranquil waterway leading to the uttermost ends of the earth flowed sombre under an overcast sky — seemed to lead into the heart of an immense darkness.

PART TWO

Heart of Darkness in Cultural Context

Cultural Documents
and Illustrations

Kayla Walker Edin

INTRODUCTION

There are two ways to place *Heart of Darkness* within its cultural contexts. The first involves an examination of the cultural milieu in which Conrad wrote. Maps, pictures, letters, and book reviews contemporaneous with its publication are provided here in order to guide readers toward a more nuanced understanding of the novella as it appeared in its initial form. They are also meant to facilitate a deeper understanding of two important historical events that seem to underlie the action of the text: King Léopold of Belgium's monopoly of the ivory and rubber trade in the "Congo Free State" and the growing controversy and opposition in England to the harsh colonial techniques he employed in the process.

Documents reproduced here include an 1834 European map (p. 102 in this volume) of the kind that Conrad recalls seeing as a child, full of "blank spaces" where the heart of Africa — the Congo — lies. The map invites us to join the young Conrad in poring over incomplete maps like this one, and to hypothesize about their appeal. Did Conrad's own multiethnic heritage increase his fascination with places in the world that appeared to defy description or identification? Did his twenty-year career at sea represent an attempt to color in the "blank spaces" on a map, or rather an attempt to grapple with the gaps and occlusions —

blank spaces — in his own self-conception? The map of Africa that follows (p. 103) allows us to trace Conrad's journey into the Congo — on foot and by boat — in 1890. Excerpts of a report written by the Irish nationalist and British consul Roger Casement, whom Conrad met during his time in Africa, also appear in this volume. A piece of writing that starkly differs from Conrad's own, the "Casement Report" (p. 113) was instrumental in bringing international attention to the state of Congolese natives, and in facilitating the transfer of power in the region from Léopold to the Belgian government. Léopold's letter to *The Times* of London (p. 108) defending his colonial endeavors, as well as documentation collected by European missionaries and settlers as evidence against him, further situate Conrad's personal experiences and ruminations within a broader context of violent cultural and ideological division. Political cartoons published in England around this time provide a sense of the public outcry to which Léopold, Casement, and Conrad each felt compelled to respond in their own way. Pictures of native Congolese women provide both a context and a critique of Conrad's depiction of native women in *Heart of Darkness*.

The second way that we encounter the cultural contexts of *Heart of Darkness* is on our own, that is to say, by examining the cultural vantage point from which we assemble and view century-old materials. Readers today necessarily view the text through a twenty-first-century lens. It would be impossible (and counterproductive, anyway) to extract the text from the web of controversy and lively critical conversation that it has engendered over the past century. Indeed, its reception history now forms an important part of the novel. Anthropologists or postcolonial critics might encourage us to view the text as an artifact, an object that takes on a life of its own. To "see" it accurately, however, we must first gain awareness of how we as readers are situated in relation to the text and its contemporary context.

In the following pages, you will find excerpts of critical reviews from 1902 to the present. To contextualize these viewpoints, several documents are provided that offer clues about the cultural conditions surrounding the initial publication of *Heart of Darkness* in 1899 in *Blackwood's Edinburgh Magazine* (p. 122), a conservative monthly magazine that catered to a politically and socially conservative audience. Of course, the dissemination of *Heart of Darkness* did not end with *Blackwood's*. Its subsequent publication as a novella in 1902 made it available to a much wider audience. Critical reviews reproduced here exemplify the lively debate sparked by the text from its inception.

Reactions to Conrad's iconic work are hardly limited to critical reviews, critiques, and responses. For that reason, in the following pages, political cartoons and even a movie poster offer a sample of the many adaptations, critiques, and uses to which the novella has been put as its circulation has grown to encompass a global audience. This collection, however, is far from exhaustive. A simple Google search locates the presence of the title and/or memorable lines from the text in the titles of *National Geographic* articles and museum exhibits, video games and works of fiction, in feature films like *Apocalypse Now* (1979), and even in an episode of HBO's *Sex and the City*. As Charlotte York plans a traditional Jewish wedding to Harry Goldenblatt, she declares her intention to dance the hora, to which her wedding planner Anthony exclaims, "The hora! The hora!" riffing on Kurtz's final words to Marlow. From its inception to the present day, *Heart of Darkness* has inspired such wordplay in explorations of culture and gender, even as it continues to probe timeless questions about morality and bigotry, forcing readers to wrestle with this provocative text on their own terms.

Silverpoint etching of Joseph Conrad by Patrick Donovan, 1989.

From the collection of Ross Murfin.

MAPS OF AFRICA

Blank Map (1834)

Conrad was fascinated with maps throughout his life. In his late, auto-biographical retrospective entitled Some Reminiscences, *he recalls a formative incident in his childhood:*

> *It was in 1868, when I was nine years old or thereabouts, that while looking at a map of Africa of the time and putting my finger on the blank space then representing the unsolved mystery of the continent, I said to myself with absolute assurance and an amazing audacity which are no longer in my character now: "When I grow up I shall go there."*

*Twenty years later, Conrad traveled to Stanley Falls, the area on the map he had once imagined as "the blankest of blank spaces on the earth's figured surface" (*Reminiscences 41*). The "blank space" that Conrad put his finger on may be seen in the following map, made in 1834 by Carey, Lea, and Blanchard. A Chinese map of South Africa, believed to be the earliest map of Africa, dates back to 1389, more than a century before Western explorers and mapmakers reached the continent. Five centuries later, the European map of Africa inched toward its completion. By the time Conrad traveled there in 1890, the mapping was nearly complete.*

In some important ways, the "blank" map seems an apt metaphor for the ignorance that Europeans brought to the region, as well as the audacity

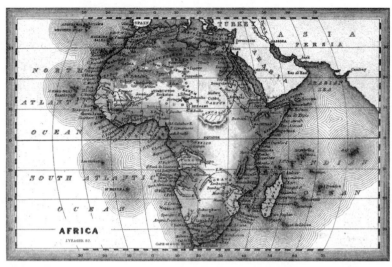

Blank Map.

Purchased from Vintage World Antique Maps and Prints, Wilton, CT. From the collection of Ross Murfin.

inherent in the mapping process (the designations of various landmarks with English names instead of their native counterparts is notable in this regard). They assumed, after all, that Africa was full of blank spaces, of voids that the paternal Europeans could fill with commerce and religious conversion. Heart of Darkness *was written as the catastrophic consequences of these assumptions were finally beginning to come to light.*

Map of Conrad's Congo Journey (1890)

Within thirty years after the young Joseph Conrad first dreamed of going to the unmapped, and therefore "blank," heart of Africa, European countries had aggressively colonized the continent. One American map of Africa copyrighted by Rand McNally in 1890 labels a tiny sliver of land northwest of the "Congo Free State" as "unexplored." By 1890 — the year of Conrad's arrival in the Congo — the so-called Free State was in fact the private domain of King Léopold II of Belgium. The following map offers a visual representation of Conrad's journey. After sailing to the Congo Free State, Conrad spent nearly a month in Matadi (where he met Roger

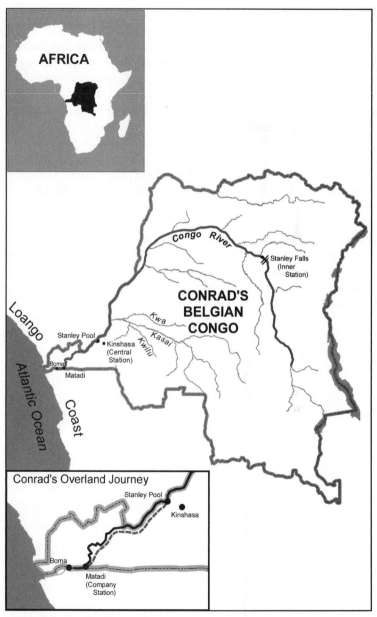

Map of Conrad's Congo Journey.

Cartography by Robert Foxworth.

Casement, the British consul who would become one of Léopold's harshest critics) before beginning the overland journey to Stanley Pool on foot. Thirty-six days later, he arrived in Kinshasa, only to learn that instead of captaining the Florida *as planned, he was to ship upriver not as a captain but as an ordinary sailor on the* Roi des Belges. *The four-week trip seems to have cured Conrad's zest for life at sea. He got out of his contract with the Société Anonyme Belge pour le Commerce du Haut-Congo and returned to Europe haunted by his experiences in the Congo.*

Years before his fellow traveler Casement penned an impassioned indictment against Léopold's policies in the Congo (the forty-plus pages became known as the "Casement Report": see pp. 113–15), Conrad felt compelled to write about what he'd seen. What resulted, however, was a very different kind of text, one that became a literary masterpiece as well as a valuable historical document. He drew heavily on his experiences when writing about Marlow's overland trek from the "Company Station" to the "Central Station" and subsequent career as a steamboat commander. Although Conrad never explicitly identifies the setting for Heart of Darkness, *the parallels between his own African experiences and Marlow's leave little room for doubt that it was the Congo.*

PHOTOGRAPHS OF AFRICAN WOMEN

From its earliest publication, Heart of Darkness *has provoked questions about the role and representation of women. From the 1903 unsigned review in the* Glasgow Evening News *(p. 125) in which the author argues that Conrad's oeuvre "has either ignored women, or at best made use of them as figures to fill a space in the background of his painting," to Gabrielle McIntire's 2002 article insisting that, despite their "near invisibility," women are nonetheless "an always-palpable presence in the background of the text" (pp. 330–44), the female characters in* Heart of Darkness *continue to fascinate readers. Such interest naturally leads to speculation about the "real" women in Africa who may have inspired Conrad's writing and to an examination of late-nineteenth-century photographs. Postcolonial critics rightly caution against attempting to discern the "truth" about citizens of colonized countries or continents by gazing through the lenses of their European occupiers. However, photographers contemporary with Conrad, like the German plantation owner and avid photographer Robert Visser (1860–1937), offer at least a glimpse of the native Congolese population that may inform our reading of gender in* Heart of Darkness. *Visser, by his own account one of the first Europeans to establish coffee and cocoa plantations in this region, managed several in the Congo from 1882 to 1904. It was during this period that the following photographs were taken (Adler and Stelzig 41).*

Postcard from the Africa album of the Visser family; women in photo
are portrayed as "untouched" by the influence of Europeans.

Dr. Christine Stelzig, Frankfurt am Main.

*Scholars like Katrin Adler and Christine Stelzig, who study and write
about Visser's photographs, acknowledge "the extent to which white photographers created a picture of 'exotic peoples' that was far more representative of a European clichéd point of view than of reality" (38). The same
could be (and has been) said of Conrad's depiction of native Africans.
Yet in several of Visser's photographs, like the ones reproduced here, he provides portraits of native women that differ dramatically from Conrad's
sensational depiction of Kurtz's African mistress. While Adler and Stelzig classify some of his work as "anthropological," other photographs seem
"respectful, personal, even tender" (46). In the postcard picture above,
Visser attempts to depict "natives" as untouched by European influence. In
the picture on page 107, he photographs his long-time partner (with whom
he had a son) and her family. Both photos provide a point of reference and
a point of contrast with Conrad's own, often conflicted portrayal of women
in* Heart of Darkness.

Visser's partner and her family.

Dr. Christine Stelzig, Frankfurt am Main.

LÉOPOLD II, KING OF BELGIUM

Letter to *The Times* of London (July 17, 1906)

King Léopold of Belgium never visited his "kingdom" in the Congo Free State, but he defended vigorously his treatment of the native population. As missionaries and explorers began to report instances of forced labor, mutilation, and murder, public opinion throughout Europe began to turn against him. After The Times *(London) published an editorial accusing him of abuses and atrocities, Léopold decided to respond. On July 17, 1906, he sent a letter to* The Times *containing 37 articles that characterized his actions as humanitarian and Christian in nature. The following excerpts provide a general flavor of his self-defense: he stresses the need for "order" and "security" in the Congo and warns against the native population's "laziness" and "propensity for lying." He insists that "the natives are not unhappy" and suggests that Belgian rule in the Congo is more popular than British rule is among its colonized African populations. As opposition from the international community grew and financial support for his undertakings declined, Léopold maintained his unapologetic stance. Nonetheless, in 1908, Belgium annexed his Congo Free State and renamed it the Belgian Congo. Léopold died the following year. A century after his death, Léopold continues to fascinate and repel historians, while the Belgian government continues to grapple with Léopold's legacy. Adam*

Hochschild's King Leopold's Ghost *(1998), a book written in the genre of "popular history" that characterizes the king as a tyrant, was a surprise best-seller that inspired a 2006 documentary by the same name. Translated into a dozen languages, its astonishing success suggests that Léopold's specter still haunts the imagination of an international audience. To that end, human rights organizations assert that Léopold's name belongs next to Hitler, Stalin, and other men whose names live on in infamy. The following document offers a rare glimpse into the rationale that may have inspired his notorious deeds, even as it seals his reputation.*

Sir,

2. [I]f my Government, when formulating the new Decrees relating to the Congo, has been especially mindful of the welfare of the natives, it has also had to be careful not to compromise the maintenance of order and internal security. This is at once a national and international calamity. . . .

3. There have been revolts in the Congo, but I believe these have been less numerous than in the British possessions, as, for example, Natal and Nigeria. The repressive methods to which we resort do not as a rule imply the use of artillery or cavalry. . . .

10. Native laziness must not be perpetuated; the negro must be made to shake off his idleness. If the native does not work, he will never rise above his present standard, but will continue to stain Central Africa with blood. Work is the only remedy for his woes, and in work lies the secret of his regeneration. . . .

15. The Sovereign does not possess a single share of the concessionary Companies nor of any other undertaking in the Congo; he does not derive any direct or indirect personal profit from them. The Congo is not exploited by its founder like a private enterprise. Not only does he not derive any personal profit whatsoever from the Congo, but he is the only Ruler of a State who has no civil list. . . .

19. Far from being a Royal robbery, as insinuated by the "Times," this "Domaine de la Couronne" is the employment by the Sovereign of certain property for purposes which are from the public benefit. This creation is in harmony with the views which I have always endeavored to put into practice during the whole of my reign. . . .

28. If my views and dealings are not well known in England, the real state of things in the Congo is still less well known. Certain persons seem only to be occupied in finding or inventing faults and crimes. The natives' well-known propensity for lying greatly facilitates their task. . . .

31. Before writing to you, I awaited the return from the Congo of Lieutenant-General Baron Wahis, Commander of the Army Division of Brussels. . . . He assures me that the natives are not unhappy in the Congo, and that their condition is improving, especially in that part of the territory which is exploited by the Government. . . .

33. General Wahis is of opinion that the Congo natives are not longing for a change of rulers. We have brought them into contact with civilization; we are beginning to educate them, we have preserved them from the abuse of alcohol, we have vaccinated them, we are making superhuman efforts to overcome the sleeping sickness, and we are creating numerous and rapid ways of communication. . . .

36. You may, perhaps, find my letter too long and too outspoken. I belong to an independent country, the institutions of which are the most liberal in existence. I have served this country in public office for fifty-five years without interruption. I have devoted my attention to Central Africa for twenty-six years, also uninterruptedly, animated with that Belgian sentiment which is neither bloodthirsty, despotic, nor unenlightened. . . .

I am, &c,

(Signed) Léopold

Etched portrait of King Léopold.

"My yearly income from the Congo is millions of guineas." Cartoon from Mark Twain's satirical *King Léopold's Soliloquy: A Defense of His Congo Rule*. Twain produced this pamphlet in 1905 in condemnation of Léopold's tyrannical rule over the Congo Free State. In it, Twain skewers the king, who wildly defends his own actions, claiming that the English are impossible to please.

Beinecke Rare Book and Manuscript Library, Yale University.

Documenting Abuse in the Congo Free State

Roger Casement

Report of the British Consul, Roger Casement, on the Administration of the Congo Free State (1904)

As eyewitness reports and photographs of atrocities occurring in King Léopold's Congo Free State proliferated, governments and citizens of other countries began to take notice. In 1885, several nations signed the Berlin Act, which charged the Congo government "to bind themselves to watch over the preservation of the native tribes and to care for their moral and material welfare." England was one of the signatories. Thus, the government sent British consul Roger Casement to the Congo Free State to investigate the accumulating reports of abuses against the native population. Casement's report was published in 1904. The full report runs forty pages long, with an additional twenty pages of individual statements gathered from victims and witnesses alike who report killings, mutilations, kidnappings, and beatings of men, women, and children by soldiers of Bula Madadi — the name used by the natives for the Congo administration of King Léopold. Copies of the report were sent to the Belgian government as

British Parliamentary Papers, 1904, LXII, Cd. 1933.

well as to the governments of countries that were signatories to the 1885 Berlin Act, including Germany, France, and Russia. As a result, international pressure to reform began to mount. The Congo administration was forced to investigate the atrocities documented by Casement, leading to the arrest and punishment of some white officials responsible for these acts.

In the selection that follows, Casement compares the sad state of the native population as he found it with the relative well-being he encountered only sixteen years prior. He concludes that the effects of European influence have been extremely detrimental on the indigenous people. Their systems of trade have been completely disrupted. Men and women alike are "summoned on the instant" to perform services for the Congo administration or "government" under threat of imprisonment or beating. He reports that even children are not immune from torture. In particular, he reports the case of a "young lad" whose "right hand was cut off at the wrist," a common practice among soldiers who were required to send proof that their bullets were used to kill natives. Often, they would simply maim their victims in order to provide an all-too-visible reminder that they were doing their jobs "well."

Casement's report was instrumental in bringing the troubling nature of European activity in the Congo Free State to light. With his endorsement and support, British journalist and shipping agent E. D. Morel founded the Congo Reform Association, which burgeoned into the first major human rights initiative in modern history. Other early voices of dissent included African American politician, historian, and Civil War veteran George Washington Williams, who was the first to publicize the plight of the Congolese. After meeting Léopold in 1889, he traveled to the Congo in 1890. His missive entitled "An Open Letter to His Serene Majesty Léopold II, King of the Belgians and Sovereign of the Independent State of Congo" is the earliest public indictment of Léopold's actions there. African American Presbyterian missionary William Henry Sheppard, who spent nearly twenty years living in the Congo, vigorously endeavored to publicize the atrocities he witnessed. Popular British author Sir Arthur Conan Doyle and American author Mark Twain lent their fame and literary talents to the cause as well.

I have the honor to submit my Report on my recent journey on the Upper Congo.

1. [T]he region visited was one of the most central in the Congo State. . . . Moreover, I was enabled by visiting this district, to contrast

its present state with the condition in which I had known it some sixteen years ago . . . and I was thus able to institute a comparison between a sate [*sic*] of affairs I had myself seen when the natives loved their own savage lives in anarchic and disorderly communities, uncontrolled by Europeans, and that created by more than a decade of very energetic European intervention . . . by Belgian officials in introducing their methods of rule over one of the most savage regions of Africa. . . .

6. The people have not easily accommodated themselves to the altered condition of life brought about by European government in their midst. Where formerly they were accustomed to take long voyages down to Stanley Pool to sell slaves, ivory, dried fish, or other local products . . . they find themselves today debarred from all such activity. . . . The open selling of slaves and the canoe convoys, which navigated the Upper Congo (River), have everywhere disappeared. . . .

7. [But] much that was not reprehensible in native life has disappeared along with it. The trade in ivory has today entirely passed from the hands of the natives of the Upper Congo. . . . Complaints as to the manner of exacting service are . . . frequent. . . . If the local official has to go on a sudden journey men are summoned on the instant to paddle his canoe, and a refusal entails imprisonment or a beating. If the Government plantation or the kitchen garden require weeding, a soldier will be sent to call in the women from some of the neighboring towns . . . ; to the women suddenly forced to leave their household tasks and to tramp off, hoe in hand, baby on back, with possibly a hungry and angry husband at home, the task is not a welcome one. During the course of these operations there had been much loss of life, accompanied, I fear, by a somewhat general mutilation of the dead, as proof that the soldiers had done their duty. . . .

12. Two cases (of mutilation) came to my actual notice while I was in the lake district. One, a young man, both of whose hands had been beaten off with the butt ends of rifles against a tree; the other a young lad of 11 or 12 years of age, whose right hand was cut off at the wrist. . . . I [*sic*] both these cases the Government soldiers had been accompanied by white officers whose names were given to me. Of six natives (one girl, three little boys, one youth, and one old woman) who had been mutilated in this way during the rubber regime, all except one were dead at the date of my visit.

Photographs of Mutilated Africans (1909)

In order to regulate and economize on bullets, King Léopold's Congo Free State required its soldiers to send hands of their native victims to the Congo administration as "proof" of death. The administration endeavored to prevent bullets from being wasted on hunting or sport; undaunted, the intrepid soldiers found a way around this rule. They cut off the hands of living adults and children, sent the hands to their superiors, and continued to use the bullets as they pleased. In his report to the British government in 1904 (see the preceding document, pp. 113–15), Roger Casement describes two young men, one "whose hands had been beaten off with the butt ends of rifles against a tree" and another "whose right hand was cut off at the wrist." According to Casement, this mutilation was widely practiced on girls, boys, elderly women, and men as well. Numerous photographs from this time period document this sordid practice. Citizen advocates and established authors joined Casement in documenting these

Congolese natives and rubber plantation workers whose hands have been cut off for failing to deliver enough caoutchouc (rubber).

The Granger Collection, New York.

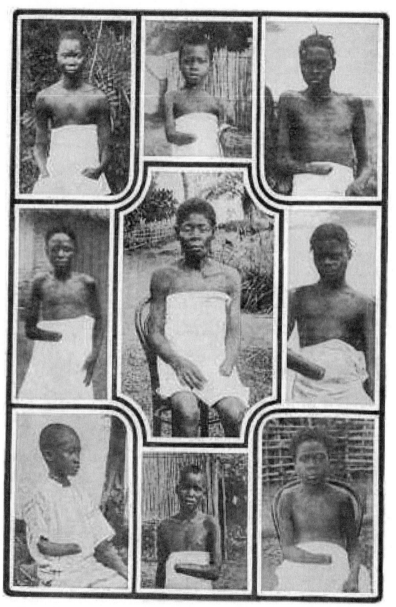

Collage of photos depicting victims, some of them children, of soldiers of King Léopold's Congo Free State.

From *The Crime of the Congo* by Arthur Conan Doyle.

horrific crimes, including Mark Twain, who wrote the satiric King Léopold's Soliloquy: A Defense of His Congo Rule *in 1905, and Arthur Conan Doyle, creator of Sherlock Holmes, who wrote an impassioned critique of colonialism entitled* The Crime of the Congo *in an astonishing eight days in 1909. The book provides graphic descriptions of violence against natives, as well as some photographs of the mutilations. Doyle later based one of his characters in* The Lost World *on Casement.*

HEART OF DARKNESS FROM A MULTI-MEDIA PERSPECTIVE

Punch Cartoons (1906 and 1980)

Punch, *a British weekly magazine that operated from 1841 to 1992 and from 1996 to 2002, was noted for its humor, satire, and pointed political commentary. Two political cartoons, published nearly a century apart, make particularly explicit statements about the issues central to* Heart of Darkness.

The first, published in 1906, depicts a strong African man being strangled by a snake. The coils of the snake dominate the picture; in lieu of fangs, the head of the snake sports a crown and the bearded face of King Léopold. The image is entitled "In the Rubber Coils." The caption reads, "Scene — The Congo 'Free' State." The juxtaposition of the word free with the image of entrapment calls the audience's attention to the irony of the situation that Conrad had written about just a few years earlier. Heart of Darkness *focuses on the ivory trade that flourished in the Congo, but rubber was an equally precious resource that European "settlers" and their intrepid leader King Léopold were intent on exploiting and importing. Both enterprises wreaked devastating effects on the African people who were "employed" in the process.*

In 1980, close to a century later, Punch *magazine published a second cartoon of interest to Conrad's readers. This time, a white man's body*

"In the Rubber Coils."

Mary Evans Picture Library/The Image Works.

dominates the scene. Instead of a snake coiled around him, helicopters hover over his head. His white skull protrudes from the page, perhaps meant to indicate his erudition. In his hand, he clutches a book with "Conrad" printed on the cover. Behind him, a man clutches the bars of a cage and stares straight ahead in horror at something invisible to the reader.

A cartoon depicts a scene evocative of 1979's *Apocalypse Now.*

Reproduced with permission of Punch Ltd., www.punch.co.uk

Although no caption is provided, the allusion to Francis Ford Coppola's film Apocalypse Now *(released the previous year in 1979) is clear. Like its earlier counterpart, the cartoon depicts the inadequacy of human judgment when pitted against imperial greed. Yet another interpretation suggests itself. Is the Kurtz figure, played by Marlon Brando (as depicted in the cartoon) using* Heart of Darkness *as a guidebook? Is Conrad's text complicit or even directive in imperial pursuits? If so, are the cartoons themselves involved in the imperialistic greed they endeavor to critique? Like the allusive yet elusive* Heart of Darkness, *the genre of the political cartoon entrusts its final interpretation to the judgment of its reader.*

Blackwood's Magazine: First Installment of *Heart of Darkness* (February 1899)

The copy of Heart of Darkness *that you hold in your hands today looks quite different than the text as it appeared to its original audience in 1899. In the nineteenth century, it became a common publishing practice to serialize texts in magazines or journals. In February 1899, the first installment of* Heart of Darkness *appeared in* Blackwood's Magazine, *and the rest of Conrad's text in two subsequent monthly issues. In 1902,* Heart of Darkness *was published in a single volume alongside two other short stories by Conrad:* Youth *and* The End of the Tether. *Edward Garnett's unsigned review in* Academy and Literature *on December 6, 1902, predicts that "These two will be more popular than the third" which he nonetheless calls a "most amazing" story.*

The publication history of Heart of Darkness *may have surprising implications for contemporary critical discussions of the novel. In the ongoing debate about whether* Heart of Darkness *sanctions or censures racism, critic William Atkinson suggests that the novella's original context may hold the answer. In his 2004 article "Bound in* Blackwood's: *The Imperialism of* Heart of Darkness *in Its Immediate Context," Atkinson notes that Conrad wrote a letter to William Blackwood stating that the subject of his African story was very much "of our time" (Conrad, qtd. by Atkinson 368)[1] and declaring his intention to write about "imperialism, specifically with King Léopold's colonial project in central Africa" (Atkinson 368). Atkinson classifies* Blackwood's *as a rather conservative magazine that catered to a conservative audience. The magazine "projected itself as weighty, considered, and above all realistic" (390). Thus, its audience would not have been conditioned to read* against *the text like contemporary critics tend to do. Atkinson concludes that* Heart of Darkness *"acknowledges the complexities of the imperial project, or human imperfections, and of the consequent dangers of being beyond the reins of civilized life. In doing so, it is fully a part of the moral and political discourse of* Blackwood's, *whose basic rule is that good imperialists are British and bad imperialists are not" (390).*

The image here shows the cover of the February 1899 edition of Blackwood's Magazine *in which the first installment of* Heart of Darkness *appeared. The document serves as a powerful reminder that we approach a very different text from the one that Conrad wrote over a century ago.*

[1]Atkinson, William. "Bound in *Blackwood's*: The Imperialism of *Heart of Darkness* in Its Immediate Context." *Twentieth Century Literature* 50.4 (2004): 368–93. Print.

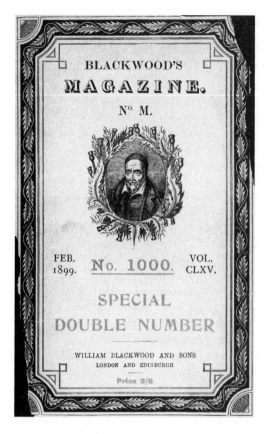

Cover of *Blackwood's Magazine*, 1899.

Conrad First, The Joseph Conrad Periodical Archive.

Critical editions of Heart of Darkness *like the one you hold in your hands often include pictures and critical analyses from the text's century-long reception history. Editorial assumptions about the text are always implicit in any publication. As "A Critical History" (pp. 137–62) elucidates, each decade in the text's history reveals a slightly different priority or critical question that readers attempt to answer by way of interpretation. Atkinson offers a powerful reminder that book historians and literary anthropologists might reiterate: the context of the text influences the way that audiences understand it. If* Heart of Darkness *as a text is always inscribed in some type of cultural context, how might this realization shape our understanding of the text's reception in 1899? Of its reception today?*

EDWARD GARNETT

Unsigned Review in *Academy and Literature* (December 6, 1902)

Edward Garnett's "unsigned review" of Heart of Darkness, *published in* Academy and Literature *on December 6, 1902, provides what Conrad himself seemed to feel was a most intelligent appreciation of his novella. In a letter to Garnett dated December 22, 1902, Conrad writes, "My dearest fellow you quite overcome me. And your brave attempt to grapple with the foggishness of* Heart of Darkness . . . , *to explain what I myself tried to shape blindfold, as it were, touched me profoundly" (p. 137). Garnett's analysis seems to anticipate certain kinds of psychoanalytic readings that were to proliferate around the text in the 1960s. In this excerpt from his early review, Garnett suggests that the "art" of the novella mirrors the "infinite shades of the white man's uneasy, disconcerted, and fantastic relations with the exploited barbarism of Africa." He states that Conrad provides a "masterly analysis of two Continents in conflict" with the kind of narrative prowess reminiscent of the great nineteenth-century writer and philosopher Fyodor Dostoevsky. Perhaps Garnett's only major misstep lies in his prediction that because of its complicated narrative structure,* Heart of Darkness *will prove to be the least popular of the three stories published in the single volume that he reviews. Initially, his forecast seemed accurate: early reviews tended to concentrate on* Youth *and* The End of the Tether. *Over time, however, the overwhelming staying power of* Heart of Darkness *has proved incontestable, suggesting that readers are drawn to, rather than repelled by, its artful complexity.*

Just as landscape art implies the artist catching the exact relation of a tree to the earth from which it springs, and of the earth to the sky, so the art of "Heart of Darkness" implies the catching of infinite shades of the white man's uneasy, disconcerted, and fantastic relations with the exploited barbarism of Africa; it implies the acutest analysis of the deterioration of the white man's *morale*, when he is let loose from European restraint, and planted down in the tropics as an "emissary of light" armed to the teeth, to make trade profits out of the "subject races." The weirdness, the brilliance, the psychological truth of this masterly analysis of two Continents in conflict, of the abysmal gulf between the

Sherry, Norman, ed. *Conrad: The Critical Heritage.* London: Routledge & Kegan Paul Ltd., 1973.

white man's system and the black man's comprehension of its results, is conveyed in a rapidly rushing narrative which calls for close attention on the reader's part. But the attention once surrendered, the pages of the narrative are as enthralling as the pages of Dostoevsky's *Crime and Punishment.* The stillness of the somber African forests, the glare of sunshine, the feeling of dawn, of noon, of night on the tropical rivers, the isolation of the unnerved, degenerating whites staring all day and every day at the Heart of Darkness which is alike meaningless and threatening to their own creed and conceptions of life, the helpless bewilderment of the unhappy savages in the grasp of their flabby and rapacious conquerors — all this is a page torn from the life of the Dark Continent — a page which has been hitherto carefully blurred and kept away from European eyes. There is no "intention" in the story, no *parti pris,* no prejudice one way or the other; it is simply a piece of art, fascinating and remorseless, and the artist is but intent on presenting his sensations in that sequence and arrangement whereby the meaning or the meaninglessness of the white man in uncivilized Africa can be felt in its really significant aspects.

ANONYMOUS

"Mr. Conrad's Philosophy," Unsigned Review in the *Glasgow Evening News* (April 30, 1903)

An anonymous review entitled "Mr. Conrad's Philosophy," published in the Glasgow Evening News *on April 30, 1903, attempts to address criticisms leveled at Conrad by disappointed readers who bemoan the lack of romance in his writings. Perhaps "seduced by hearsay praise into taking up one of Mr. Conrad's books," the reviewer tells us, readers "have laid it down with the disappointed remark that 'there is no love in it.'" The writer acknowledges that, throughout Conrad's oeuvre, he "has either ignored women, or at best made use of them as figures to fill a space in the background of his painting." However, the author argues that Conrad deals profoundly with "the relations of the sexes" precisely through this avoidance of the conventional love story. By rejecting the use of romantic tropes, Conrad comments profoundly on fundamental issues pertaining to both sexes by exploring the human condition more generally. In the excerpt that follows, the author maintains that* Heart of Darkness *reflects Conrad's*

Sherry, Norman, ed. *Conrad: The Critical Heritage.* London: Routledge & Kegan Paul Ltd., 1973.

personal philosophy about human individualism and "the essential lone-
liness of the human soul" that men and women alike confront when they
come "face to face with the universe," a universe that ultimately eludes
meaningful comprehension.

Feminist critics often analyze the places in Heart of Darkness *where*
Conrad occludes the feminine presence. This review anticipates the kinds
of feminist readings that critics like Bette London, Johanna Smith, and
Gabrielle McIntire will make many decades later. Like this early critic, they
suggest ways in which these omissions shadow the text and further its artis-
tic or political aims.

A writer of art so masterly, of understanding so sympathetically profound, is not to be held as limited in his outlook on life to a few odd
bits of abnormal experience gathered in out-of-the-way corners. And
it seems, to the present writer at least, that one must look for the explanation to something deeper in Mr. Conrad's philosophy of life. That
something which seems to lie at the bottom of all his writing is his
intensely individualistic regard. He has felt — possibly felt more than
perceived — the essential loneliness of the human soul, face to face with
the universe.

In all his writing one feels that his problem has been the revelation
of the soul wrestling with or sinking beneath its own weakness, the
elemental forces of Nature, or the mysterious force of circumstances —
struggling, yielding, suffering, but always solitary, individual, isolated.
It is not, indeed, that he bungles the relationship of his figures to each
other — he is too sure in his grip of character for that. It is that character is for him an essentially individual creation, separate from, comparatively untouched by ordinary human relationship.

For this reason it is, surely, that he avoids so constantly alike the
sexual factor and that social aspect of man which has so deeply modified the thought of the past century. While Zola, for example, always
tended to make his characters mere social types, representative of great
streams of tendency, Mr. Conrad, following rather the old mystics, pushes
towards the other extreme of regarding his types as self-pivoted units,
though, it is true, always with an aim less directly ethical and more
artistic than that of Zola.

It is here, one conjectures, that one is able to detect the underlying
tendency which directs his choice of subject to those simple sailor-folk,
those crude and primitive souls who are by circumstance and nature cut
off from all the complex inter-action of organised society, and therefore
nearer the purely individual problems of existence. Unhampered by the

superficial intricacy of social life, or the disturbing and fluctuating influences of sexual relations, he plunges into the inmost hearts of these beings, whose springs of action are so few and simple.

Apocalypse Now (1979)

Since the advent of television and film decades after its publication, Heart of Darkness *has permeated small and big screens alike. From off-hand allusions to Kurtz's final words in the HBO hit series of the 1990s* Sex and the City *to the full-scale adaptation by Nicholas Roeg broadcast by Turner Network Television in 1994 starring John Malkovich as Kurtz,* Heart of Darkness *provides filmmakers with an irresistible wealth of inspiration, as well as material for artistic expression of any number of contemporary concerns. Francis Ford Coppola's 1979 film* Apocalypse Now *is perhaps the most famous representation. Set in the context of the Vietnam War, it features a "Colonel Kurtz" (Marlon Brando) whom "Captain Willard" (Martin Sheen as a Marlow figure) must assassinate. The film pairs arresting visual imagery and a haunting soundtrack with music by the Doors and the Rolling Stones in an intertextual montage that captures the* Zeitgeist *of the 1970s.*

Such on-screen adaptations provide critics with fresh insights into the content and technique of Conrad's writings. In "The Hollow Heart of Hollywood: Apocalypse Now *and the New Sound Space," Thomas Elsaesser and Michael Wedle draw comparisons between the narrative "space" of the novella and the "sound space" and "figurative space" at work in* Apocalypse Now. *For instance, they compare Conrad's narrative frame — a first-person testimonial told to a captive audience within the text — with the "complex audiovisual texture of the opening of* Apocalypse Now *[that] serves as an apt prelude to the highly subjective mode of narration that will lead both Willard and the immediately disoriented viewer on a journey through psychological torment and violent horror" (162). Elsaesser and Wedle's work, which appears in* Conrad on Film *(1997) alongside a collection of essays analyzing Conrad's cinematic presence, testifies to the ongoing critical interest elicited by Conrad's currency in popular culture. The aesthetically arresting* Apocalypse Now, *in particular, demonstrates the applicability of Conrad's deeper themes to twentieth-century preoccupations and conflicts and suggests their relevance to present-day issues.*

Elsaesser, Thomas, and Michael Wedle. "The Hollow Heart of Hollywood: *Apocalypse Now* and the New Sound Space." *Conrad on Film*. Cambridge: Cambridge UP, 1997, 151–75.

Movie poster from *Apocalypse Now*, 1979.

Zoetrope/United Artists/The Kobal Collection.

In the movie poster, the disembodied face of a white man looms above the outlines of a Vietnamese landscape. The face is superimposed over a blackened sky, crowned with a setting sun that creates a kind of crooked halo. Helicopters fly across the sun away from the face, as if they are emerging from the man's forehead. Isolated in the upper-right-hand corner, the partially obscured face of a Vietnamese-looking Martin Sheen emerges from the shadows. The resulting palimpsest seems to evoke the same questions as the novella that inspired it: whose story is being told, and by whom? Does humankind dominate nature, or does nature eventually force humanity to succumb to its darkness? When two civilizations collide, can any human being transcend, much less control, the chaos that ensues?

CARYL PHILLIPS

"Was Joseph Conrad Really a Racist?" (2007): An Interview with Chinua Achebe

After the publication of his 1958 novel Things Fall Apart, *African poet and scholar Chinua Achebe rose to international fame. Since that time, Achebe's first (and most critically acclaimed) novel has been translated into more than fifty languages and is widely taught in schools and universities around the world. Born in Nigeria, Achebe was educated in English-speaking schools. He wrote* Things Fall Apart *out of a growing sense of frustration with the depiction of the nations and people of Africa by European writers, among them Joseph Conrad. Between 1971 and 1976, Achebe lectured at several universities in the United States. On February 18, 1975, he delivered a Chancellor's Lecture at the University of Massachusetts, Amherst, entitled "An Image of Africa" that attacked Joseph Conrad as a "bloody racist" and argued that* Heart of Darkness *is a deeply racist text.*

Achebe began this landmark critique by recounting his experience as a young visiting professor at a North American university. When he mentioned the topic of his class — African literature — to a student, the student remarked how "funny" it is — "he never had thought of Africa as having that kind of stuff, you know." Struck by the casual racism that surfaced in this chance conversation, Achebe began to ruminate on the invisible structures of oppression that continue to taint "Africa" in the

From Achebe, Chinua. "An Image of Africa." *The Massachusetts Review* 18.4 (Winter 1977): 782–94 and Caryl Phillips. *Philosophia Africana* 10.1 (2007): 59–66.

Chinua Achebe.

Don Hamerman.

*minds of even the most liberal Westerners, particularly those in the acad-
emy. Achebe argued that truly great artists must rise above contemporary
prejudices of their day in order to merit the label of genius so often ascribed
to Conrad. He challenged his audience to expose* Heart of Darkness *as
racist propaganda and to cast it out of the literary canon forever. In
subsequent published versions of his speech, Achebe made minor revisions.
Most notably, in his 1987 revision, he amended his description of Conrad
as a "bloody racist" to read "thoroughgoing racist" instead. Yet his message
remained consistent: no good can come from elevating* Heart of Darkness
to a place of honor in the academy.

*In 2007, Yale University English professor Caryl Phillips sat down
with Achebe to discuss his views. Phillips, an author and playwright born
in St. Kitts and raised in England, does not initially consider* Heart of
Darkness *to be a racist text. In the excerpt below, he gives Achebe a chance
to change his mind. The interview and article, which originally appeared
in* Philosophia Africana *in 2007, make reference to the revised 1987 version of "An Image of Africa."*

Caryl Phillips.

© Colin McPherson/
Corbis.

Chinua Achebe leans forward to make his point. He raises a gentle finger in the manner of a benevolent schoolmaster. "But you have to understand. Art is more than just good sentences; this is what makes this situation tragic. The man is a capable artist and as such I expect better from him. I mean, what is his point in that book? Art is not intended to put people down. If so, then art would ultimately discredit itself."

"The man would appear to be obsessed with 'that' word."

"Nigger."

Achebe nods.

Achebe has taught term-long university courses dedicated to this one slim volume first published in 1902.

As long ago as February 1975, while a visiting professor at the University of Massachusetts in Amherst, Achebe delivered a public lecture entitled "An Image of Africa: Racism in Conrad's *Heart of Darkness.*" The lecture has since come to be recognized as one of the most important and influential treatises in post-colonial literary discourse. However, the problem is, I disagree with Achebe's response to the novel, and have never viewed Conrad — as Achebe states in his lecture — as simply "a thoroughgoing racist." Yet at the same time, I hold Achebe in the highest possible esteem.

Those critics who have defended *Heart of Darkness* against charges of racism have often pointed to both the methodology of narration and Conrad's anti-colonial purpose. The narrator of the novel is Marlow, who is simply retelling a story that was told to him by a shadowy second figure. However, in his lecture Achebe makes it clear he is not fooled by this narrative gamesmanship or the claims of those who would argue that the complex polyphony of the storytelling is Conrad's way of trying to deliberately distance himself from the views of his characters.

Achebe has no problem with a novel that seeks to question both European ambivalence toward the colonizing mission and her own "system" of civilization. What he has a huge problem with is a novelist — in fact, an artist — who attempts to resolve these important questions by denying Africa and Africans their full and complex humanity.

I thought again of my own response to the novel. There are three remarkable journeys in *Heart of Darkness*. First, Marlow's actual journey up-river to Kurtz's inner station. Second, the larger journey that Marlow takes us on from civilized Europe, back to the beginning of creation when nature reigned, and then back to civilized Europe. And finally, the journey that Kurtz undergoes as he sinks down through the many levels of the self to a place where he discovers unlawful and repressed ambiguities of civilization.

In all three journeys, Conrad's restless narrative circles back on itself as though trapped in the complexity of the situation. The overarching question is, what happens when one group of people, supposedly more humane and civilized than another group, attempts to impose itself upon its "inferiors"? In such circumstances will there always be an individual who, removed from the shackles of "civilized" behavior, feels compelled to push at the margins of conventional "morality"? What happens to this one individual who imagines himself to be released from the moral order of society and therefore free to behave as "savagely" or as "decently" as he deems fit? How does this man respond to chaos?

Conrad uses colonization, and the trading intercourse that flourished in its wake, to explore these universal questions about man's capacity for evil. The end of European colonization has not rendered *Heart of Darkness* any less relevant, for Conrad was interested in the making of a modern world in which colonization was simply one facet.

The uprootedness of people, and their often disquieting encounter with the "other," is a constant theme in his work, and particularly so in this novel. Conrad's writing prepares us for a new world in which modern man has had to endure the psychic and physical pain of displacement and all the concomitant confusion of watching imagined concrete standards become mutable. Modern descriptions of twentieth-century famines, war, and genocide all seem to be eerily prefigured by Conrad, and *Heart of Darkness* abounds with passages that seem terrifyingly contemporary in their descriptive accuracy.

The novel purposes no program for dismantling European racism or imperialistic exploitation, and as a reader I have never had any desire to confuse it with an equal opportunity pamphlet. I have always believed that Conrad's only program is doubt; in this case, doubt about the supremacy of European humanity and the ability of this supposed humanity to maintain its imagined status beyond the high streets of Europe. However, I already sense I had better shore up my argument with something more resilient than this.

[Achebe]: Conrad didn't like black people. Great artists manage to be bigger than their times. In the case of Conrad you can actually show that there were people at the same time as him, and before him, who were not racists with regard to Africa.

Despite Achebe's compelling "evidence," I am still finding it difficult to dismiss this man and his short novel. Are we to throw all racists out of the canon? Are we, as Achebe suggests, to ignore the period in which novels are written and demand that the artist rise above the prejudices of his times?

"Chinua, I think Conrad offends you because he was a disrespectful visitor."

"I am an African. What interests me is what I learn in Conrad about myself. To use me as a symbol may be bright or clever, but if it reduces my humanity by the smallest fraction, I don't like it."

"Conrad does present Africans as having 'rudimentary' souls."

Achebe draws himself upright.

"Yes, you will notice that the European traders have 'tainted' souls, Marlow has a 'pure' soul, but I am to accept that mine is 'rudimentary'?" He shakes his head. "Towards the end of the nineteenth century, there was a very short-lived period of ambivalence about the certainty of this colonizing mission, and *Heart of Darkness* falls into this period. But you cannot compromise my humanity in order that you explore your own ambiguity. I cannot accept that. My humanity is not to be debated, nor is it to be used simply to illustrate European problems."

The realization hits me with force. I am not an African. Were I an African, I suspect I would feel the same way as my host. But I was raised in Europe, and although I have learned to reject the stereotypically reductive images of Africa and Africans, I am undeniably interested in the break-up of a European mind and the health of European civilization. I feel momentarily ashamed that I might have become caught up with this theme and subsequently overlooked how offensive this novel might be to a man such as Chinua Achebe and to millions of other Africans. Achebe is right; to the African reader, the price of Conrad's eloquent denunciation of colonization is the recycling of racist notions of the "dark" continent and her people. Those of us who are not from Africa may be prepared to pay this price, but this price is far too high for Achebe. However lofty Conrad's mission, he has, in keeping with times past and present, compromised African humanity in order to examine the European psyche.

PART THREE

Heart of Darkness: A Case Study in Contemporary Criticism

A Critical History of
Heart of Darkness

Ross C Murfin
Kayla Walker Edin

Heart of Darkness was published serially in *Blackwood's Magazine* in 1899. But it was not seriously reviewed until 1902, when it was reprinted in a hardcover volume entitled *Youth*. Even then, the other two works published in the collection, *Youth* and *The End of the Tether*, were received more favorably. In an unsigned 1902 review, Edward Garnett both explained and deplored the fact that *Heart of Darkness* was the least popular of the three tales. Calling it "too strong" a piece of "meat for the ordinary reader," he insisted that it was nonetheless "the high water mark" of Conrad's "talent," a "psychological masterpiece" relating "the sub-conscious life within us . . . to our conscious actions, feelings, and outlook." As such, Garnett concluded, it offers an "analysis of the deterioration of the white man's *morale*, when he is let loose from European restraint, and planted down in the tropics as an 'emissary of light' armed to the teeth, to make trade profits out of the 'subject races'" (Sherry 132–33). (An excerpt from this review is reproduced in Part Two of this edition; pp. 124–25.) Responding to Garnett in a personal letter, Conrad wrote: "My dearest fellow you quite overcome me. And your brave attempt to grapple with the foggishness of *Heart of Darkness* . . . , to explain what I myself tried to shape blindfold, as it were, touched me profoundly" (Karl and Davies 2:467–68).

The tone of Conrad's response is treacherously difficult to determine. But of this we can be sure: Garnett was right in declaring the novel to be about the immorality of whites in Africa. The idea behind *Heart of Darkness*, Conrad had written to William Blackwood one month before the first installment of the novel appeared in *Blackwood's Magazine*, "is the criminality of inefficiency and pure selfishness when tackling the civilizing work in Africa." This much, too, we can feel certain of: Conrad knew that the theme of his book was not obvious, and that serious readers like Garnett *would* have to reflect before being rewarded by the discovery of meaning. "The idea is so wrapped up in secondary notions," he had admitted in an 1899 letter to R. B. Cunninghame Graham, "that You — even You! — may miss it" (Karl and Davies 1:139–40, 157).

Blackwood's Magazine served a generally conservative readership. Critic William Atkinson, whose argument in his 2004 article "Bound in *Blackwood's*: The Imperialism of *Heart of Darkness* in Its Immediate Context" is explored more fully in Part Two (pp. 122–23), suggests that the novella's original publication context indicates an intention on Conrad's part to express conservative (that is to say, generally approving) views about imperialism (an argument that postcolonial writers and critics like Chinua Achebe would certainly endorse). Readers of *Blackwood's*, Atkinson argues, would neither be conditioned nor inclined to read "against" the text like literary critics are apt to do today. Given that Conrad knew his readership, we might wonder whether his letters concerning the "foggishnesss of *Heart of Darkness*" and his own inability "to explain" a work he supposedly "shape[d] blindfold" are disingenuous.

Conrad, of course, may simply have been trying to sound humble in these letters. Yet another possibility is that, when he says that "the idea" in the book is "so wrapped up in secondary notions" that even good readers can "miss it," he is suggesting that meaning inevitably lies beyond the details that point toward but also veil it in a work of novelistic art, that the idea of a work can only emerge as the product of a reader's experience of more immediate, if secondary details. "You must remember," Conrad goes on to say in the letter to Graham, "that I don't start with an abstract notion. I start with definite images and as their rendering is true some little effect is produced" (Karl and Davies 2:157–58).

Some early readers of Conrad, however, failed to find his images any more definite than his ideas. E. M. Forster, best known for his novel *A Passage to India* (1924), once wrote that, in Conrad's writings, "sentence after sentence discharges its smoke screen into our abashed eyes," and he went on to accuse the author of being "misty" at "the edges" as well as "in the middle" (138). Forster was not the only artist-critic who found Conrad a little too fuzzy. The poet John Masefield, later to become poet laureate, declared that there is "too much cobweb" in *Heart of Darkness*, that Conrad's style, in general, is neither "vigorous, direct, effective, like that of Mr. [Rudyard] Kipling," nor "clear and fresh like that of Mr. [Robert Louis] Stevenson" (Sherry 142).

Not all those who commented on style, though, found the novel notable for its lack of directness, precision, or clarity. A reviewer for the *Athenaeum* commented on Conrad's atmosphere but did so in order to praise, not fault, it. "He presents the atmosphere in which his characters move and act with singular fidelity, by means of watching and careful building in which the craftsman's methods are never obtrusive, and after turning . . . the last page of one of his books, we rise saturated by the very air they breathed" (Sherry 198). Still other reviewers were, as Garnett had been, silent on the subject of writing style. An anonymous reviewer writing in the *Manchester Guardian* found in *Heart of Darkness* not atmosphere at all but, instead, "a great expression of adventure and romance" (Sherry 134). Still another anonymous review, entitled "Mr. Conrad's Philosophy" and published in the *Glasgow Evening News* on April 30, 1903 (pp. 125–27), eschews questions of style to raise a second-order question about Conrad's apparent exclusion of the feminine gender from his fiction, a question the reviewer answers by saying that it served a greater purpose: to reflect Conrad's personal philosophy about human individualism and "the essential loneliness of the human soul" that men and women alike confront when they come "face to face" with a "universe" that ultimately eludes comprehension.

Was *Heart of Darkness* — is *Heart of Darkness* — a philosophical novel, an adventure tale, a political exposé? Or is it primarily an atmospheric work, and, if so, is the atmosphere so precisely evoked that we feel we breathe it, right alongside the characters? Or are Conrad's words like so much cobweb? The debate over these and other questions was intense during the decades that followed the publication of *Heart of Darkness*, and to a great extent, the various critical positions taken by reviewers in the first half of the twentieth century still guide us as we ask questions of the novel and arrive at interpretations of it. After all, no work is approached in a vacuum, and the interpretive history of a work is part of the context in which we read it. When we publish our views, even if we do so only in a comment to a few other readers of a particular work, we add to and alter slightly the language in which that work is and will be discussed. Those who follow are likely to locate their respective positions vis-à-vis our own.

Not surprisingly, then, when F. R. Leavis set out critically to assess *Heart of Darkness* fifty years after its serial publication, he praised strengths and attacked weaknesses in ways that had been prepared for him by previous critics. In his influential study of English fiction, *The Great Tradition*, Leavis begins by asserting that E. M. Forster was correct to fault Conrad for obscurity and a vaporous style. However, Leavis then insists that other critics were correct, too, in praising Conrad's ability to describe things and actions precisely, thereby creating an "overwhelming sinister and fantastic 'atmosphere'" (177). Leavis has it both ways by arguing that Conrad pictures places — such as the grove "greenish" with "gloom" in which Marlow stumbles upon diseased, starving Africans (p. 31) — with descriptions that can be terribly vivid. But the novelist becomes vague and foggy, according to Leavis, when he steps back to philosophize.

Part of the problem, Leavis concludes, is that Conrad tends to overburden philosophical passages with adjectives that obscure rather than describe. "There are places in *Heart of Darkness*," he points out, where Conrad has already "overworked" words like "'inscrutable,' 'inconceivable,' 'unspeakable.' . . . Yet still they recur." Quoting Conrad's sentence "It was the stillness of an implacable force brooding over an inscrutable intention" (p. 49), Leavis goes on to remark that Conrad's vocabulary often backfires, particularly when it tries to express a sense of profundity or horror. Conrad repeatedly uses words such as *inexpressible* and *incomprehensible*, Leavis hypothesizes, in order to "magnify" a "thrilled sense of the unspeakable potentialities of the human soul." But "the actual effect is not to magnify but rather to muffle" (Leavis 179).

Giving as an example the scene in which human heads are found mounted on posts surrounding Kurtz's house, Leavis praises the image, which he says tells us all we need to know, but faults Conrad for supplementing such images with what he calls the "adjectival and worse than supererogatory insistence on 'unspeakable rites,' 'unspeakable secrets,' 'monstrous passions.'" Conrad tries too hard, Leavis thinks, to "impose . . . a 'significance' that is merely an emotional insistence on the presence of what he can't produce. . . . He is intent on making a virtue out of not knowing what he means" (Leavis 180).

These are strong words coming from a critic who ranks Conrad as one of the four great novelists in a great tradition of British fiction. They are words, nonetheless, that express what other, earlier readers felt. More important, though, they are words that later critics have found useful. For what Leavis unwittingly gave to later critics was the language that, with revision, could be used to discuss not the flaws of *Heart of Darkness* but rather the special nature of the novel's greatness.

Albert J. Guerard, in his much-acclaimed 1958 study *Conrad the Novelist*, reaffirms but also drastically revises the views of *Heart of Darkness* afforded by Leavis. One way Guerard differs significantly from Leavis is in the attention he pays not to Kurtz but to Marlow. "F. R. Leavis," Guerard writes, "seems to regard him as a narrator only, providing a 'specific and concretely realized point of view' " (Guerard 38). Indeed, Marlow *was* to Leavis a mere agent, the character whose primary purpose in the narrative is to provide those "details and circumstances of the voyage" that make palpable the fantastic "atmosphere" Kurtz inhabits (Leavis 176). "But Marlow," Guerard asserts to the contrary, "is recounting a spiritual voyage of self-discovery," and it is that voyage and that discovery that should interest readers of *Heart of Darkness*. For Guerard the story is like a "powerful dream" in which Marlow meets up with his own, dark, passional nature. Marlow feels the excitement of what he calls the "wild and passionate uproar," finds himself fascinated by abominations, and, most important, meets a strange alter ego or double. The most important stage in Marlow's journey within, according to Guerard, is the one in which he comes to recognize his kinship with Kurtz, "a white man and sometimes idealist who had fully responded to the wilderness: a potential and fallen self. . . . At the climax Marlow follows Kurtz ashore, confounds the beat of the drum with the beating of his heart, . . . and brings [Kurtz] back to the ship. He returns to Europe a changed and more knowing man" (Guerard 39, 38).

By seeing the novel as a dream of self-discovery, Guerard not only expands upon what Edward Garnett said when he called *Heart of Darkness* a psychological masterpiece but also explains why the world has been so taken with this story that *is*, at least in some ways, fuzzy, smoky, misty, unclear. *Heart of Darkness* is ambiguous as a *dream* is ambiguous; it is powerful precisely to the extent that it is *not* precise. "If my summary [of the novel as a dream] has even a partial validity," Guerard concludes, "it should explain and to an extent justify some of the 'adjectival and worse than supererogatory insistence' to which F. R. Leavis . . . objects. I am willing to grant that the unspeakable rites and unspeakable secrets become wearisome, but the fact — at once literary and psychological — is that they must remain *unspoken*" (42). In other words, if *Heart of Darkness* were perfectly precise in its profoundest passages, it would not be dreamlike; more important, it could not seem like *our* dream. To say "murder" or "death" or "greed" or "lust," instead of using that more "misty" phrase "The horror" (p. 85) would be to distance most readers from that horror. Thus Guerard makes use of Leavis even while seeming to reject him. He turns a vocabulary of critical objection into a language of critical analysis, a language that may be used to explain just why *Heart of Darkness* is so haunting.

Thomas Moser, who in 1957 published an important study entitled *Joseph Conrad: Achievement and Decline*, begins with two ideas: that Conrad "is as great as F. R. Leavis believe[s] him to be, and as serious and subtle as . . . Albert J. Guerard" has shown him to be. It is Guerard, though, who seems to have influenced Moser most directly. "*Heart of Darkness*, 'The Secret Sharer,' and *Lord Jim* are all principally concerned with the theme of self-knowledge," Moser asserts, sounding like Guerard. "We must recognize our potential weaknesses, our plague spots, in order to achieve a perceptive, moral life" (Moser 1, 24).

Moser, however, does more than repeat Guerard's reading of the novel; like Guerard and Leavis before him, he bends and adapts a strong predecessor's language in order to make it useful in a new way. In stating that Conrad's early works show us that "we must recognize our plague spots," Moser has already developed an idea only latent in Guerard, namely, that Marlow in the jungle is like the reader in the text, that somehow Marlow's quest for self-knowledge must be doubled by our own. "It is difficult to discuss Conrad's technique without referring to its effect upon the reader," Moser writes, "for Conrad's masterly control of the reader's responses is one of the most significant results of his unorthodox methods. By holding back information and moving forward and backward in time, Conrad catches up and involves the reader in a moral situation, makes the reader's emotions follow a course analogous to that of the characters" (42).

In addition to expanding on Guerard's view of the novel as one of self-discovery, Moser develops a still older view of the novel: that it is a work critical of racist European imperialism. Unlike early reviewers, however, Moser sees the theme of anti-imperialism as being inseparable from the novel's imagery, and he discusses the connection to show that it was thematically useful to Conrad to create superficially confusing imagery. In *Heart of Darkness*, Moser points out, the usual pattern is reversed and "darkness means truth, whiteness means falsehood" (47). The reversal tells simultaneously a political truth about races in the Congo, a psychological truth about Marlow and all of us (the truth is within, therefore dark and obscure), and any number of moral truths (the trade in ivory is dark and dirty). One pair of colors can suggest all these different kinds of meanings, Moser adds, because *Heart of*

Darkness was written by "Conrad the artist," who happened also to be "Conrad the moralist, . . . Conrad the psychologist," and "Conrad the commentator on politics" (38).

Moser's reminder that Conrad was an *artist* was made time and time again by the New Critics, who dominated Anglo-American academic criticism in the middle decades of the twentieth century. The New Criticism — or formalism, as it is now usually called — was a reaction against the tendency to see poems and novels as products of the author's personal and historical experience. Formalists such as William K. Wimsatt warned against trying to discern an author's intention; our time as readers is better spent, they suggested, in describing the way the parts of the work interrelate to form beautiful artistic unities. Albert Guerard prepared the way for formalist readings of *Heart of Darkness* by focusing attention on Marlow — a tale-teller — and his narrative, rather than on its subjects: Africa, ivory, battle scenes, Kurtz. Guerard also showed a formalist tendency in believing that Conrad's dreamlike ambiguity may be part of the meaning, not just a fault of Conrad's that gets in the way of some other meaning that Conrad surely intended us to see.

Numerous critics writing since 1960 have paid attention to the artistic form or unity of *Heart of Darkness*. Leo Gurko reminds us that "the novel . . . begins and ends on a yawl, on the deck of which Marlow is telling his story to four men." The unity provided by that opening and closing scene, moreover, is reinforced by descriptions of the scene. ("The sea-reach of the Thames stretched before us like the beginning of an interminable waterway"; "the sea and the sky were welded together without a joint" [p. 17].) Together, Gurko argues, Conrad's images lead us to view nature as a continuum, to see the story as a continuum like nature, and to conclude that the "theme of all experience being one experience . . . underlies the story, and appears in several variations" (Gurko 148). Marlow's lie to the Intended, for instance, is like Europe's imperialistic dealings in Africa. "The lie, like the imperialism, is an evil thing." But both are "redeemed," according to Gurko, "by a benevolent and idealistic motivation" (151).

In taking this rather tolerant view of imperialism, and in suggesting that Conrad took such a view, Gurko differs from most later critics who have written on the subject. For instance, in *Conrad's Politics*, published in 1967, Avrom Fleishman insists that "In Africa as well as in the Indies, the disruptive effects of imperialism on native society were clear to Conrad" (89). Whereas previous critics had emphasized the breakdown of the mores of white men sent to the tropics armed and in search of profits, Fleishman discusses the moral decay of Africans once

Europeans have been loosed upon them. Several of Fleishman's predecessors had implied that *Heart of Darkness* tells how imperialism reduces
white emissaries from a civilized to a primitive state, leaving them no
better morally than the savages whom they exploit. Against this view,
Fleishman responds correctively. The natives unspeakably treated by a
degenerating Kurtz were not barbarians prone to committing unpro-
voked atrocities. Or, rather, they were not until Kurtz came among them
and prompted them "to organized warfare in order to obtain ivory for
export" (Fleishman 90).

Although he makes no mention of Fleishman's views, Bruce Johnson concurs with many of them in *Conrad's Models of Mind*, published
four years after *Conrad's Politics*. Like Fleishman, Johnson disagrees
with the notion that Conrad held tribal life in low esteem. And like
Gurko, to whom he several times refers, Johnson finds in *Heart of
Darkness* the view that nature is a unity, a continuum. Indeed, for Johnson, unity with nature is what the African natives have until "civilized"
whites — who do not have this unity — disrupt and destroy it. Conrad,
Johnson argues, held the Victorian view "that the savage is one with
nature, while the civilized white man has fallen — for better or worse —
from the primal unity" (Johnson 71). According to this view of Africans, the native "feels no sense of alienation" and, therefore, no "need
to create his own contingent values and sanctions." Europeans, who *do*
feel alienated from that "something great and invincible" we call nature,
do create such values and sanctions. The combination, as Johnson sees
it, can literally be deadly. The unalienated native tends "readily to accept
what presents itself convincingly," as if it had "divine sanction" (Johnson 72). An alienated European like Kurtz, who shapes rather than
accepts the world, exploits precisely this tendency. By presenting himself convincingly, Kurtz becomes a people's disruptive, destructive,
even murderous god.

In 1975, four years after the appearance of Johnson's important
study, two very different essays were published that have had an enormous influence on the way in which *Heart of Darkness* has been read
subsequently. One of these, by Frederick Crews, was a book chapter
entitled "Conrad's Uneasiness — and Ours." Rather than analyzing
Conrad's "models of mind," as Johnson had done, Crews applies *to*
Conrad's fiction psychoanalytic models developed by Sigmund Freud.
In doing so, he finds *Heart of Darkness* to be an expression of the Oedipus complex, which involves the repressed childhood wish to displace
the parent of the same sex and take his or her place in the affections of

the parent of the opposite sex. Crews suggests that if the plot of *Heart of Darkness* "were recounted to a psychoanalyst as a dream," Kurtz, "the exposed sinner," would be "an image of the father, accused of sexual 'rites' with the mother." Marlow, the "dreamer," would be an image of the son interrupting the "primal scene" by making his "journey" into "the maternal body" (56).

The other, very different 1975 essay that greatly influenced subsequent criticism was first given as a speech at the University of Massachusetts by Nigerian novelist Chinua Achebe. Achebe complains about Conrad's "need . . . to set Africa up as the foil of Europe," to "project" an "image of Africa as . . . the antithesis of Europe and therefore of civilization" (119–20). "What actually worries Conrad," Achebe claims, "is the lurking hint of kinship, of common ancestry," between the people living on the banks of the Thames and those living on the banks of the Congo (122). Anticipating the objection that it is only Marlow who is troubled by the sense of kinship, Achebe acknowledges that, through his "narrator behind a narrator" construction, Conrad has "set up layers of insulation between himself and the moral universe of his story." Achebe, however, believes that in the last analysis "Marlow seems to enjoy Conrad's complete confidence" (123). Why? Because "Conrad was a bloody racist" (124).

Achebe's "take" on Conrad, like that of Crews, is admittedly an extreme one, one that he reasserted as recently as 2007 in an interview with Caryl Phillips, a Yale University English professor (see pp. 129–34). The notion that *Heart of Darkness* is a racist work, like the notion that we should view Conrad's novella as a dream told by a patient named Charlie Marlow to his psychoanalyst, is one that many critics have already dismissed. And perhaps with good reason. The paragraphs that follow summarize the views of critics who have written compellingly about *Heart of Darkness* during the period 1980–2010. What you will find, as you learn about them, is that the ideas of Crews and Achebe have led to some interesting debates — debates in which critics have given us new reasons to accept and reject, select and choose between, modify and develop the claim that *Heart of Darkness* reveals repressed passions or racist attitudes. Thanks to Crews and Achebe, in other words, we now have a spectrum of ideas about fiction, psychology, and racial attitudes somewhere along which your own positions and options probably fit.

Since Crews published his now-famous chapter, a number of critics have read Conrad in terms of the Oedipus complex. As Catharine Rising notes in her book *Darkness at Heart: Fathers and Sons in Conrad* (1990), some of these interpreters view *Heart of Darkness* as Crews does, in terms of a sexual rivalry between Marlow (or Conrad) and his father. But others have viewed the story in terms of a more general oedipal rivalry, one involving an illustrious older man, a young man with mixed feelings about his elder, the death of the former, and the survival of the latter, who surpasses his father figure morally or artistically. (As psychoanalytic critic Joseph Dobrinsky has pointed out, Conrad's father, Apollo, was not only a political revolutionary but also a poet.)

A number of critics who wrote on *Heart of Darkness* in the 1980s and 1990s followed Crews's lead by applying psychological or psychoanalytic theory to *Heart of Darkness* but not by seeing Conrad's story as a manifestation of the Oedipus complex. Using Freud's notion that human beings are essentially double in nature — that all of us contain a rational, socialized self and a dark double, a repressed instinctual self — Donald M. Kartiganer viewed Kurtz as Marlow's "outlaw" alter ego in his 1985 article "Freud's Reading Process: The Divided Protagonist Narrative and the Case of the Wolf Man" (8). Betinna Knapp subsequently viewed *Heart of Darkness* not as a tale revealing Marlow's dark side but, rather, as one through which Conrad searched for *his* exiled "shadow" self, an identity consisting of "animal" traits he projects onto African blacks. Knapp's reading, rather than being Freudian, is based on the writings of Carl Gustav Jung, a psychoanalytic theorist who developed the concept that there is a collective human unconscious. According to Knapp's Jungian reading, Conrad's story of a journey to the heart of the African continent draws on "archaic levels of the human psyche," levels inhabited by "archetypal" images such as that of the waterway and those involving eating and being eaten (50).

One of the most interesting psychoanalytic readings, Barry Stampfl's "Marlow's Rhetoric of (Self-) Deception in *Heart of Darkness*" (1991), focuses less on images and symbols than on syntax. Using Freud's concept that repressed ideas sometimes are allowed to surface so long as they are negated, Stampfl examines "Marlow's negatives" (the oft-repeated word *impenetrable* would be an example") and related "belief qualifiers." (Marlow says of dying slaves that it was "as if" they were "overcome with a great weariness" [p. 32]; speaking of the Company, he says that "It was just as though I had been let into some conspiracy" [p. 25].) According to Stampfl, negative and highly qualified terms often give us insight into what Marlow knows down deep to be true (that the Congo *has* been penetrated — raped — by Europeans, that the African

slaves he sees *are* overcome by weariness). The knowledge that nega-
tions and belief qualifiers half cover up and half reveal is not so much
that of the id or the archaic unconscious as it is the knowledge of political evil, the reality that Marlow's imperialistic culture would rather not
acknowledge.

Stampfl is not the only critic writing since 1980 to take a modified
psychoanalytic approach to the broader cultural issues raised in *Heart
of Darkness*. (Indeed, Tony Brown does so in an essay published in
2000 and reprinted in this volume; see pp. 350–66.) In his book *Desire
and Its Discontents* (1991), Eugene Goodheart, like Stampfl, argues
that the "psychological aspect" and "political meanings" of Conrad's
tale are intertwined, since "politics itself may be read as enactment of
desire" (23). (For Goodheart, civilized reason and repressed passions
are not the opposites they seem to some Freudians; they come together
in the "'civilized' will to impose, to dominate, and control" [24]).
Other critics have used the vocabulary and insights of psychoanalysis
to examine not the global politics but the *gender* politics of *Heart of
Darkness*. Claire Kahane does so in a discussion of the scene in which
Marlow lies to the Intended by telling the pure and sheltered young
woman that the last thing Kurtz said ("The horror!") was her name.
Kahane finds in Marlow's lie a set of "Freudian switch-words"; a young
woman's name substitutes for "the horror," which "echoes its homonym 'whore,'" which, in turn, reveals a deep-seated "fear of and rage
at woman" (145).

The lie to the Intended has been a major focus of the growing number of feminist readings of *Heart of Darkness* that have appeared since
1980 (including the 2002 reading by Gabrielle McIntire that appears
in this volume; see pp. 330–44). For Nina Pelikan Straus ("The Exclusion of the Intended from Secret Sharing in *Heart of Darkness*" [1987]),
the scene of Marlow's famous lie is but the most memorable of many
that affect male and female readers differently, reminding the latter
that this is a tale "concerned with a kind of mainstream male experience" that has been "deliberately hidden" from the women inside the
text. Although not denying that "the sexism of Marlow and Kurtz"
may be "part of 'the horror' that Conrad intends to disclose," Straus
maintains that "the feminist reader's access" to Conrad's most famous
work is "especially problematic," a fact she uses to explain "decades
of nearly exclusive male commentary surrounding *Heart of Darkness*"
(123–24). Putting the problem succinctly, Straus at one point comments that "[f]or a woman reader" to "identify with Marlow" is to
"court self-degradation" (130).

In " 'Too Beautiful Altogether': Ideologies of Gender and Empire in *Heart of Darkness*" (pp. 189–204), Johanna M. Smith argues that "*Heart of Darkness* demonstrates the brutality in discourses of empire and gender" (p. 202). She approaches her eventual encounter with the scene in which Marlow lies to the Intended by arguing that Marlow's imperialistic ideology is fundamentally inseparable from his belief that women and men inhabit "separate spheres." And yet the Victorian ideology of separate spheres, Smith notes, "was under pressure in the late nineteenth century," as "the New Woman was becoming visible in the stores, offices, and streets," thus asserting her right to occupy several different spheres in society (p. 196). The text itself offers contradictions to Marlow's belief — contradictions he is quick to occlude and reframe. For instance, when Kurtz's dying words seem to him shamefully "feminine," Marlow quickly constructs the Intended as a potential site for male bonding, one where he can reconcile himself with Kurtz and the "masculine world" of imperialism by lying about Kurtz's final words, substituting the name of the Intended for the words Kurtz actually uttered.

Smith begins her argument with a definition of ideology as a set of shared assumptions that become "natural" cultural practices. Ideology is enacted through a shared "discourse" whose adherents speak and act on common assumptions. Never static, ideology always risks exposing itself as constructed. In *Heart of Darkness*, Smith suggests, Marlow's depictions of women, particularly those in which he "silences" them, signify sites of ideological disconnect, moments when the ideology and discourse of "separate spheres" expose their own fallibility. The African laundress, the African "savage mistress," and the two women at the Company office, all of whom Smith analyzes closely, never speak. Yet, the very absence of their speech draws our attention to the futility of Marlow's attempts to describe them — and to the fallacy inherent in his insistence that women occupy separate spheres, spheres apart from the masculine narrative he constructs and the masculine adventure it recounts. For instance, during his journey into the jungle, Marlow suddenly remembers the face of the elder of the two silent Company women; "her reappearance," Smith maintains, "dramatizes the futility of Marlow's attempt to separate the realm of domesticity from that of colonial adventure, the feminine sphere from the masculine" (p. 196). Admittedly, when Marlow encounters his aunt and Kurtz's Intended, both speak. However, Smith argues, Marlow frames their speech in ways that "shore up" both an ideology of separate spheres and the masculine imperialism that these separate spheres enable (p. 196).

In "Reading Race and Gender in Conrad's Dark Continent" (1989), Bette London implicitly agrees with Straus that *Heart of Darkness* is an off-putting tale for female, not to mention feminist, readers — and with Smith's view that the discourses of gender and empire are inseparable — that, in London's words, "gender and race" are "interlocking systems," not only in Conrad's text but also in the patriarchal ideology in which it is grounded. Onto Africa is projected "the 'dark continent'" of female sexuality, a sexuality and continent from which the novel's European women are excluded. But the same exclusion that renders the Intended something less than sexual renders her African counterpart something less than a woman. Referred to as a "wild and gorgeous apparition of a woman," she is little more than a symbol — of a sexuality that is dark and savage and of a dark savagery that is sexual. London thus takes the following view: "Dependent upon unexamined assumptions, themselves culturally suspect, the novel, in its representations of sex and gender, supports dubious cultural claims; it participates in and promotes a racial as well as gender ideology that the narrative represents as transparent and 'self-evident'" (238).

In arguing that *Heart of Darkness* reproduces and reinforces racist attitudes, London demonstrates that she is substantially in agreement with Achebe. She complains, however, that in "detailing the distortions mapped by the novel's registers of race, [Achebe] reads gender univocally." He does so in spite of the fact that "the very features that inform Achebe's racial critique . . . mark the novel's representations of women as well. For these other 'rudimentary souls,' denied even the distinction of a name (the aunt, the Intended), also speak only to convict themselves. . . . Similarly, the narrative's projection of Africa as . . . 'the antithesis of Europe' coincides with its construction of the feminine as the foil to masculinity" (239).

London is hardly alone in agreeing with Achebe's basic claim. Susan Blake, for instance, has reinforced Achebe's viewpoint in her oft-cited 1990 article "Racism and the Classics: Teaching *Heart of Darkness*." So has Benita Parry, who in *Conrad and Imperialism* (1983) argues that "although the resonances of white are rendered discordant [by *Heart of Darkness*], . . . black and dark do serve in the text as equivalences for the savage and unredeemed, the corrupt and degraded . . . the cruel and atrocious" (23). But the opposite position has also been taken, not only by European and North American critics like Mark Kinkead-Weeks but also by African and other critics speaking from the vantage point of the postcolonial world such as C. P. Sarvan, of the University of Zambia.

(Both Sarvan and Kinkead-Weeks take strong issue with Achebe's statement that Marlow enjoys "Conrad's complete confidence.")

Speaking of Achebe, the celebrated South American novelist Wilson Harris wrote in 1990, "I am convinced his judgment or dismissal of *Heart of Darkness* is a profoundly mistaken one" (161). Harris takes the view that Conrad's work is a forward-looking "frontier novel," a text that "stands upon a threshold of capacity" that Conrad "pointed" toward but "never attained" (162). That view is shared by Peter Nazareth, a Ugandan who reminds his audience that "Jane Austen's characters in *Mansfield Park* could live a luxurious life while the patriarch left for the colonies; Conrad actually takes us to the colonies to show us what happened there when the patriarch or his agents arrived and how his wealth at home came from brutal colonial action. Conrad was therefore a mental liberator" (221).

One critic who has staked out a more-or-less middle ground between Achebe and his most outspoken opponents is Patrick Brantlinger, whose "*Heart of Darkness*: Anti-Imperialism, Racism, or Impressionism?" is reprinted in this volume (pp. 303–24). Another is Sandya Shetty, who in a 1989 article entitled "*Heart of Darkness*: Out of Africa Some New Thing Never Comes" states that Achebe "is right on the mark" in suggesting that "Conrad's picture of Africa" is "an ideological construction rather than historical reality or pure artistic creation" (467). But she denies that Conrad paints as favorable a picture of Europe as Achebe suggests. In fact, she views Conrad as a critic of empire whose critique fails in ways that the theoretical writings of cultural critic Edward Said can help us understand. Shetty summarizes Said's argument this way: "The critic of empire who functions from within the dominant culture must find it well nigh impossible to venture far beyond the very ideological barriers which he purports to dissolve." Conrad fails to venture beyond or dissolve those barriers because, "rather than offering an alternative vocabulary for discussing racial and colonial politics," he relies heavily on "the language of the dominant culture which he intends to criticize" (462). Given that fact, Shetty argues that "it cannot . . . be surprising that Conrad's colonial works participate in the very ideology which they attempt to expose and destroy" (463).

Other critics have sidestepped the question of Conrad's racism, preferring to focus on whether Conrad was supportive of imperialism, an institution that depended on and reinforced racist attitudes. Hunt Hawkins, author of a series of articles on *Heart of Darkness* published between 1979 and 1992, has viewed the novel as a critique of Belgium's imperialist venture but its author as a man generally supportive of British imperialism and colonialism. (In *The Location of Culture* [1994], the postcolonial critic Homi K. Bhabha states that *Heart of Darkness* may be set in the Belgian Congo but "the power and presence of the English" permeates not only Marlow's discourse but also Conrad's [108].) In a 1991 article entitled "Exotic Nostalgia: Conrad and the New Imperialism," Chris Bongie suggests that Conrad's belief in and longing for community caused him to have ambivalent feelings about imperialism, which held out the (false) promise of worldwide community.

One of the more challenging treatments of this subject is to be found in Vincent P. Pecora's *Self and Form in Modern Narrative* (1989), which outlines the difficulties faced by a writer who wishes to critique an institution like imperialism from the outside. Imperialism contradicts itself in several ways (systematic oppression involving laissez-faire democracy, a grand scheme relying on small-scale entrepreneurs). As a further complication, any attempt to critique something as hegemonic — that is, generally accepted — as imperialism runs the risk of reinforcing the very ideology it intends to undermine, for the critique must rely on devices (such as irony) that can be overlooked and, therefore, that can and do backfire. Marlow's lie, according to Pecora, illustrates the difficulty Conrad faced, the double bind he was in: "an attempt to preserve" the "humanity his independence [from imperialism] requires," Marlow's "transgression" is also "a perfect preservation of imperialist rhetoric." That is to say, it does exactly what obfuscating imperialistic rhetoric does: it hides from the home folk what is being done in the colonies in the interests of empire and enlightenment (159).

Since 1990, the critical conversation about *Heart of Darkness* has shifted somewhat back to questions of form and style, even as passionate debate around the ethical dimensions of the text continues. The terms of the debate, however, have begun to move past binary oppositions involving European/African, Coloniser/Colonised, Racist/Nonracist categories into a more nuanced consideration of what it means to read, study, teach, and appreciate *Heart of Darkness* on its own terms.

In "Dedication to Hunger: The Anorexic Aesthetic" (1997), Leslie Heywood offers a cultural-critical and feminist interpretation of *Heart of Darkness* that builds on the unique work by Mark Anderson in "Anorexia and Modernism, or How I Learned to Diet In All Directions" (1988–1989). Anderson had argued that certain canonical, usually male-authored modernist texts are characterized by an "anorexic logic" and feature emaciated or anorexic men. These men "embody an ambiguity

of gender that would either deny sexual difference or fuse male and
female identities in a complex androgynous form" (qtd. by Heywood
353). In a text that makes explicit use of "body weight as a sign system"
(358), Heywood proposes that Marlow's emaciated frame inscribes
him in a "long historical tradition [that] equates ascetics and philosophical or religious sages" (359). In the course of his narration, Marlow consistently employs "anorexic tropes," often noting the body
weight of European and African characters alike (359). While Conrad
writes from within a late-nineteenth-century notion that "equated body
fat with corruption and laziness" (360), perhaps accounting for the fact
that many of the government officials Marlow meets along the way are
overweight, their appearance contrasts sharply (and perhaps contradic-
torily) with Marlow's description of Kurtz, who is described by Heywood as "an anorexic ideal of bodiless existence." When Kurtz dies, it
is the loss of his voice, not his physical presence, that Marlow purports
to miss the most (363).

   This "anorexic logic" suggests fascinating implications for Conrad's
female characters as well. Heywood cites the feminist analyses of both
Smith and Strauss, who had argued that the narrative arch of *Heart of
Darkness* is enabled by the exclusion of women and nonwhite characters. Heywood maintains that her anorexic logic paradigm can explain
this exclusion: "Marlow's attempt to attain and present a perspective
that would not be merely subjective and personal but transcendental,
claiming a privileged proximity to 'truth,' is part of the logic here called
'anorexic'" (365). Men like Marlow strive toward this transcendental
state by practicing restraint. In Western European discourse, lack of
restraint is often classified as "feminine"; by the same token, "feminine" is a criticism directed quite frequently at nonwhite populations.
Because women by definition cannot escape the feminization that
threatens Marlow and Kurtz at every turn, their racial identity and/or
body weight are quite beside the point: they "cannot function in the
anorexic sign system that by definition excludes them" (372). The
women in Marlow's story refuse to fulfill his expectations and thus defy
his explanations. Unable to be articulated in the terms of his master
narrative, they simply disappear from the text. By the same token, Marlow insistently assumes that his African shipmates are savage cannibals,
despite their emaciated frames and their apparent refusal to eat their
passengers.

   The fact that Conrad elicits a strong feminist response should in no
way suggest that feminist critics are united in reading *Heart of Darkness*
as a sexist text. Just as cultural and postcolonial critics have begun to

resist the binary designation of Conrad's novella as racist or nonracist, recent feminist critics have begun to suggest alternative approaches that open up, rather than foreclose, Conrad's unique depictions of gender. Contesting Smith's conclusion that Conrad "unwittingly participate[s]" in the patriarchal ideology of detachment, French critics Fawzia Afszal-Khan and Carole Stone, in their article entitled "Gender, Race, and Narrative Structure: A Reappraisal of Joseph Conrad's *Heart of Darkness*" (1997), suggest that, in some senses, the opposite is true: "the inherent ambiguities and contradictions in Marlow's narrative, in fact, the circularity and open-endedness of the narrative itself, as well as the high degree of self-consciousness of the narrative form, make it possible to interpret Conrad more favorably" (221). In short, they suggest that Conrad's narrative form assiduously avoids participation in patriarchal ideology by evading the closure and judgment that such an alignment would entail. This evasive quality shares characteristics with what Julia Kristeva calls *l'écriture féminine*: a "feminine" way of writing that is semiotic and unfixed. Stone and Afszal-Khan argue that Conrad's depiction of Kurtz's African mistress instantiates "the text's divided attitudes toward female power" as a source of fear and fascination for Conrad and Marlow alike (225). They suggest that Conrad's own position as "racial outsider" — a Polish emigrant in England — "contributed to his sensitivity to marginal and oppressed groups" (232), concluding by stressing the open-endedness of their own argument. Far from suggesting that Conrad's views are nonracist or nonsexist, they wish to suggest that he "may have seen into the horror of the 'heart of darkness' in more complex and ambiguous ways than a closed or univocal interpretation allows" (232). In this way, the form of their argument mirrors its content, exemplifying perhaps the type of *l'écriture féminine* that they argue Conrad's text exemplifies.

Over the past twenty years, as feminist criticism has become increasingly established and respected in academia, the discipline has expanded to encompass gender criticism or, more broadly, gender studies. Gender studies encompasses feminist as well as queer studies and grows out of the basic premise that "masculinity," like femininity, is constructed, problematic, and influential (thus meriting equally close analysis). Queer theory is a paradigm offering critics a chance to discern unspoken, often same-sex, desire within texts, particularly texts written within a homophobic cultural context. Andrew Michael Roberts's *Conrad and Masculinity* (2000) epitomizes this gender approach. Roberts traces Conrad's conflicted depiction of masculinity throughout his *oeuvre*. He examines the novella within the context of one of the most basic premises of the modernist movement: the tenuous relationship between language, truth, and reality. He builds on the general agreement of critics that "Conrad's fiction emphasizes the problematic nature of questions of what we can know, how we can know it and what degree of certainty is possible" (118). He purports that relatively little attention has been paid to the way that gender informs Conrad's treatment of knowledge in *Heart of Darkness*. Roberts maintains that women are either excluded from or particularly privy to various specific types of knowledge. Similarly, against the backdrop of a late-nineteenth-century culture that grew increasingly obsessed with defining heterosexual and homosexual identity, desire between men remains unspoken throughout the text. Roberts draws our attention to the multiple places where Marlow drops heavy hints about unspoken rites, rituals, and desires at the heart of his experience, and surmises the following:

> The case for a reading of 'Heart of Darkness' in terms of homosexual desire may be summarized as follows. It concerns a story told by one man to a group of men with whom he feels a close bond, a bond necessary for them to understand his story, although he nevertheless feels part of it cannot be communicated. His story concerns his growing fascination, disgust, and identification for another man, centered on his realization that this man has been involved in taboo practices about which the story-teller (Marlow) will not be specific. This realization creates, at least in the mind of the story-teller, an enduring intimacy with the other man, despite his death, an intimacy involving the sharing of a disgraceful yet exciting knowledge from which the dead man's fiancée must be protected. (134)

In the course of his analysis, Roberts draws on the work of three major theorists: Friedrich Nietzsche, Michel Foucault, and Eve Kosofsky Sedgwick. Foucault builds on Nietzsche's radical understanding of knowledge as something produced, and as a tool of power rather than as a neutral description of the world, by asking "what is at stake in the will to truth, in the will to utter this 'true' discourse, if not desire and power?" (qtd. by Roberts 120). Sedgwick adds a feminist corrective to this theoretical perspective by pointing out that, from the late nineteenth century on, major nodes of thought in twentieth-century Western culture were fixated on homosexual and heterosexual definitions of men. Thus, women were defined purely in terms of their relationships to men and masculine desire, and were treated as mere functionaries of exchange within a patriarchal power structure.

Building on these premises, Roberts suggests that "the epistemology of Conrad's work is explicable in terms of (social) structures of
male power and (psychic) structures of male desire" (l21), yet he avoids
reading the novella as "simply a concealed narrative of male homosexual desire." Rather, the text keeps multiple factors of "sexual knowledge and ignorance" in play (134). Operating within the predominant
discourses of power and gender, Conrad's novella represents women
either as entities ignorant of particular kinds of knowledge that men
may have access to, or as "symbols of a mysterious truth and objects of
a secret knowledge" separate from what men know and understand
(121). Roberts acknowledges that "Conrad's work does not always
uncritically reproduce such a discourse" (121). He suggests that readers are frequently invited to empathize with female characters as well as
male characters who temporarily occupy a "femininized" position. In
doing so, "the fiction offers some critical purchase on these structures
of exploitation without ever fully analyzing or stepping outside them"
(122). Still, Marlow's frequent allusions to "unspeakable" things seem
associated, according to Sedgwick, "with a homophobic discourse
which treats same-sex desire as something which cannot be spoken of."
Furthermore, in *Heart of Darkness*, "the technique also produces racist
effects, since Africa, African people, and women are drawn into this
symbolic black hole. The empty signifier is empty only in terms of the
story's symbolic self-understanding; ideologically, it has a history and a
meaning" (126).

A 2002 book titled *Approaches to Teaching Conrad's* Heart of Darkness *and* The Secret Sharer testifies both to the ongoing popularity of
the novella in classrooms (it may well be the single most frequently
taught text in American universities) and the caution with which teachers approach the work in light of a thirty-year history of objections to
its purported racism. Mark Eaton's essay entitled "Teaching *Heart of
Darkness* after New Historicism" offers ideas on how to approach the
text in light of critiques like Achebe's that purport to reveal Conrad and
Marlow's latent racism. Eaton notes that "[s]tudents are often quick to
excuse authors for almost any view, no matter how objectionable, on
the grounds that they lived in a less enlightened time. *Heart of Darkness*
can help direct students to a much more subtle understanding of how
ideology works, not in the older false-consciousness sense of blinding Conrad to what he should see, but in the post-Althusserian sense
of allowing him to see what he did" (59). Other contributors to the

volume address such topics as characterization, narrative form, and historical context. An entire section is most tellingly devoted to "Teaching the Controversies."

Achebe's 1975 declaration that Conrad was a "bloody racist" sparked a debate that continues to the present day. Lately, postcolonial cultural critics like Stephen Ross and Byron Caminero-Santangelo have expressed concern that this debate too often involves a "cultural binary" in which two viewpoints polarize based on a convenient relationship of "opposition" that may not in fact exist. In *Conrad and Empire* (2004), Ross chooses to deviate somewhat from the dominant postcolonial conversation by setting aside questions of whether *Heart of Darkness* is a racist text. Instead, he looks at Conrad's treatment of "Empire" in four of Conrad's major works, including *Heart of Darkness*, borrowing terminology from Michael Hardt and Antonio Negri's 2000 book entitled *Empire*. Hardt and Negri define *empire* as a "*decentered* and *deterritorializing* apparatus of rule that progressively incorporates the entire global realm within its open, expanding frontiers" (qtd. by Ross 9). Ross argues that Conrad's work anticipates this type of globalization and grapples with its implications. In particular, "empire" gives precedence to financial gain over governmental rule. In *Heart of Darkness*, Ross argues, Conrad "both depicts and critiques the profit-driven arbitrariness of incipient Empire as it bears upon and transforms the individual subject" through his descriptions of Kurtz and the Company (31). He analyzes the relationship between Kurtz and his "Intended" as exemplifying the way that Kurtz grapples with deferred desire and "the impingement of Imperial economic imperatives into the libidinal life of the subject" (42).

Joining Ross's endeavor to create an alternative discourse that sets aside certain polarizing binary oppositions, Caminero-Santangelo maintains in *African Fiction and Joseph Conrad: Reading Postcolonial Intertextuality* (2005) that readers should consider African literature not as a mere revisionary addendum to "the canon" of Western literature but as works in their own right that reflect the influence of Western canonical texts and writers even as they explore a wide range of historically specific ideologies. He suggests, for example, that we read *Heart of Darkness* alongside Nadine Gordimer's 1981 novel about apartheid in South Africa entitled *July's People* in order to examine the extent to which both Conrad and Gordimer disrupt certain colonial assumptions and norms, though to varying degrees: "Read together with *Heart of Darkness*, *July's People* makes clear that limitations imposed by social and political conditions necessarily result in Marlow's and, to a lesser extent, Conrad's inability to break from the colonial discourse of their time — despite their intermittent sense of the contradictions and silences in that discourse" (108). Caminero-Santangelo's analysis demonstrates the way that postcolonial critics in particular tend to read cross-textually, often placing noncanonical texts next to canonical ones in order to allow fresh interpretations to emerge and new voices to be heard.

The interest that *Heart of Darkness* evokes among postcolonial critics is rivaled perhaps only by new historicists, who find in the novella rich inspiration and room for analysis. New historicist arguments often proceed by way of honing in on a particular artifact, discourse, or historical event that shares its chronological point of origin with the text at hand. While critics of this method fear that anecdotal evidence might oversimplify certain dynamics of the text or the historical epoch in which it was written, Ivan Kreilkamp demonstrates one way in which this technique might be fruitfully brought to bear on certain questions of form and structure that have fascinated readers of *Heart of Darkness* for over a century. In *Voice and the Victorian Storyteller* (2005), Kreilkamp attempts to understand the narrative structure of *Heart of Darkness* by way of the artifact. In particular, Kreilkamp contextualizes the novella within the technology of the "phonograph" — a trope that modernist writers like James Joyce and T. S. Eliot later employ in *Ulysses* and *The Waste Land*, respectively — to illustrate the kind of fragmented ways in which these authors represent individual identity. Kreilkamp suggests that "*Heart of Darkness* travels away from an idealized scene of storytelling towards the disembodied voice of a circulating textuality" but stops short of assigning the label of *l'écriture féminine* that Stone and Afszal-Khan prescribe. Instead, Kreilkamp concludes that "ultimately the novel does not fully embrace such an understanding of language as anonymous and fragmentary circulation" (204). In this respect, Kreilkamp argues that the book "remains a Victorian novel, albeit one teetering at the verge of the twentieth century's new world of mechanized utterance" (204).

In *Modernism, Metaphysics, and Sexuality* (2006), Debrah Raschke places *Heart of Darkness* firmly within the camp of the modernist movement. Modernism arose from a crisis in knowledge and belief during a period of rapidly changing gender roles. Raschke argues that wherever a crisis in "truth" occurs within a modernist text, a crisis in gender occurs as well. Relying on Luce Irigaray's rereading of Western metaphysics, Raschke argues that "the shifting status of truth and the shifting status of women" that occupied late-nineteenth-century modernist thought are inextricably linked (9). She examines this phenomenon in landmark modernist works: E. M. Forster's *A Passage to India* and *Maurice*; D. H. Lawrence's *Women in Love*; Virginia Woolf's *A Room of One's Own* and *To the Lighthouse*; and of course, Conrad's *Heart of Darkness*. She argues that each of these texts "that explore a crisis in knowing also reveal a concomitant crisis in sexuality — a nascent awareness that metaphysic's authority depends on sexual definitions, that these definitions are not fixed truths. These shifts have implications for defining knowledge and other sacrosanct spaces" (10). In *Heart of Darkness*, Marlow struggles to maintain control over his shifting narrative, even as "[t]he very act of telling affirms and protects a homosocial community that demands observation of certain rules of narration (just as the Western metaphysical narratives have in their various reproductions produced the truth of the 'self-same,' which have invariably denied woman access)." She concludes that "just as women must be kept out of the mainstream of the tale" (Marlow assures his all-male audience that women are "out of it — completely" (p. 63) even though their presence underlies the text from beginning to end), so "they are kept out of Western metaphysics, modes of expression that threaten the masculine narrative [that] must be silenced as well" (87).

Like Kreilkamp and Raschke, Daniel Just, in his 2008 article entitled "Between Narrative Paradigms," attempts to place *Heart of Darkness* within its proper contemporary context. While Kreilkamp argues that the text belongs to the Victorian era, "marking the end of the Victorian mythology of the storyteller" even as it demonstrates "the resilience of that myth" (205), and Raschke classifies the novella as an incontrovertibly modernist text, Just suggests that neither category can contain *Heart of Darkness*. Expanding on the work of early-twentieth-century critics like Georg Lukács who see the "novella" as a genre indicative of "a transitory phrase between social periods and narrative paradigms" such as Victorianism, realism, or modernism, Just argues that the designation as a transitional text commonly assigned to Conrad's novella is much more complicated than critics have hitherto acknowledged. The dominant critical view that Conrad plays a significant role in shifting the Western narrative discourse from realism to modernism was first advanced by such critics as Fredric Jameson and Ian Watt, who see Conrad as the quintessential "herald of Modernism" (274). Just suggests that *Heart of Darkness* proves this shift was far from seamless. Instead of epitomizing the modernist "solution" to the shortcomings of representation in its literary predecessors, the novella exposes the problems that Modernism would have to address: "What Modernism had to patch over and dissolve in its stylistic experiments was precisely what *Heart of Darkness* tried to expose, namely, the speechlessness in the face of Western atrocities. Only by laying bare an empty abyss of language and not hiding one's inability to tell a story, Conrad believed, could one try to do justice to the negative effects of the narrow-minded and egocentric cultural values" (285). He credits Conrad's work for the modernist movement's prompt introduction in literature of "a new form for these values — a new form for the latest, modern type of individuality, as well as a new form for the novel as its privileged expression" (285).

In his 2008 article entitled "Beyond the Dialectic," Ihor Junyk reflects the trend of recent critics to seek out fresh terms of debate about the content and the structure of *Heart of Darkness* that allow readers to take the text in altogether new directions. Junyk uses Friedrich Hegel's theoretical model of "Master" and "Slave" to demonstrate places in the text where Conrad deviates from predominant Western ideas of aggression and subjection. In "Independence and Dependence of Self Consciousness: Lordship and Bondage," from *Phenomenology of Spirit*, Hegel suggests a model for violent interpersonal relations: the scene of recognition. When two subjects encounter each other, the conflict inevitably results in the victory of one over the other — the "Master" over the "Slave." Junyk suggests that two "encounters" in the text — Marlow's meetings with Kurtz and his meeting with the Intended — "end not in the globalization of one perspective to the detriment of the other — which is to say, in domination and incorporation of the other into the same — but in the affirmation of alterity, respect, and responsibility" (142). Junyk suggests that Conrad's paradigm is closer to that of Emmanuel Levinas, who suggests that a face-to-face encounter between two subjects "affirms both proximity and distance, negotiating connection and alterity" (145). Levinas's philosophical model provides Junyk with a way out of the "dialectical opposition" embedded in Western thought, not to mention the critical history of *Heart of Darkness*, and allows him to argue that "the dominion of violence and sameness by which Conrad imagines European imperialism is not unshakeable or inevitable" (156).

WORKS CITED

Achebe, Chinua. "An Image of Africa." *Massachusetts Review* 18 (1977): 782–94. Rpt. in *Joseph Conrad: Third World Perspectives*. Ed. Robert D. Hamner. Washington: Three Continents, 1990. Print. See pp. 119–29.

Afszal-Khan, Fawzia, and Carole Stone. "Gender, Race, and Narrative Structure: A Reappraisal of Joseph Conrad's *Heart of Darkness*." *Conradiana* 29.3 (1997): 221–34. Print.

Anderson, Mark. "Anorexia and Modernism, or How I Learned to Diet In All Directions." *Discourse: Journal for Theoretical Studies in Media and Culture* 11.1 (1988–1989): 28–41. Print.

Atkinson, William. "Bound in *Blackwood's*: The Imperialism of *Heart of Darkness* in Its Immediate Context." *Twentieth Century Literature* 50.4 (2004): 368–93. Print.

Bhabha, Homi K. *The Location of Culture*. London: Routledge, 1994. Print.

Blake, Susan L. "Racism and the Classics: Teaching *Heart of Darkness*." *Joseph Conrad: Third World Perspectives*. Ed. Robert D. Hamner. Washington: Three Continents, 1990. Print.

Bongie, Chris. "Exotic Nostalgia: Conrad and the New Imperialism." *Macropolitics of Nineteenth-Century Literature: Nationalism, Exoticism, Imperialism*. Ed. Jonathan Arac and Harriet Ritvo. Philadelphia: U of Pennsylvania P, 1991. Print.

Brantlinger, Patrick. "*Heart of Darkness*: Anti-Imperialism, Racism, or Impressionism?" *Criticism* 27 (1985): 363–85. Rev. and rpt. as "Epilogue: Kurtz's 'Darkness' and Conrad's *Heart of Darkness*" in Brantlinger, *Rule of Darkness: British Literature and Imperialism, 1830–1914*. Ithaca: Cornell UP, 1988. Print.

Caminero-Santangelo, Byron. *African Fiction and Joseph Conrad: Reading Postcolonial Intertextuality*. Albany: State U of New York P, 2005. Print.

Crews, Frederick. *Out of My System: Psychoanalysis, Ideology, and Critical Methodology*. Oxford: Oxford UP, 1975. Print.

Dobrinsky, Joseph. *The Artist in Conrad's Fiction: A Psycho-critical Study*. Ann Arbor: UMI Research Press, 1988 (Studies in Modern Literature, No. 92). Print.

Eaton, Mark. "Teaching *Heart of Darkness* after New Historicism." *Approaches to Teaching Conrad's* Heart of Darkness *and* The Secret Sharer. Eds. Hunt Hawkins and Brian W. Shaffer. New York: MLA, 2002. Print.

Fleishman, Avrom. *Conrad's Politics*. Baltimore: Johns Hopkins UP, 1967. Print.

Forster, E. M. *Abinger Harvest*. London: Edward Arnold, 1936. Print.

Goodheart, Eugene. *Desire and Its Discontents*. New York: Columbia UP, 1991. Print.

Guerard, Albert J. *Conrad the Novelist*. Cambridge: Harvard UP, 1958. Print.

Gurko, Leo. *Joseph Conrad: Giant in Exile*. New York: Macmillan, 1962. Print.

Harris, Wilson. "The Frontier on Which *Heart of Darkness* Stands." *Joseph Conrad: Third World Perspectives*. Ed. Robert D. Hamner. Washington: Three Continents, 1990. Print.

Hawkins, Hunt. "Conrad and the Psychology of Colonialism." *Conrad Revisited: Essays for the Eighties*. Ed. Ross C Murfin. Tuscaloosa: U of Alabama P, 1985. Print.

———. "Conrad's Critique of Imperialism in *Heart of Darkness*." *PMLA* 94 (1979): 286–99. Print.

———. "Conrad's *Heart of Darkness*: Politics and History." *Conradiana* 24 (1992): 207–17. Print.

Heywood, Leslie. "Dedication to Hunger: The Anorexic Aesthetic." *Modernism, Gender, and Culture: A Cultural Studies Approach*. Eds. Lisa Rado and William E. Cain. New York: Garland, 1997. 353–74. Print.

Johnson, Bruce. *Conrad's Models of Mind*. Minneapolis: U of Minnesota P, 1971. Print.

Junyk, Ihor. "Beyond the Dialectic: Conrad, Levinas, and the Scene of Recognition." *MFS: Modern Fiction Studies* 54.1 (2008): 140–59. Print.

Just, Daniel. "Between Narrative Paradigms: Joseph Conrad and the Shift from Realism to Modernism from a Genre Perspective." *English Studies: A Journal of English Language and Literature* 89.3 (2008): 273–86. Print.

Kahane, Claire. "Seduction and the Voice of the Text: *Heart of Darkness* and *The Good Soldier*." *Seduction and Theory: Readings of Gender, Representation, and Rhetoric*. Ed. Dianne Hunter. Urbana: U of Illinois P, 1989. Print.

Karl, Frederick R., and Laurence Davies, eds. The *Collected Letters of Joseph Conrad*. Cambridge: Cambridge UP, 1983. Print.

Kartiganer, Donald M. *The Psychoanalytic Study of Literature*. Hillsdale: Analytic, 1985. Print.

Knapp, Bettina. *Exile and the Writer: Exoteric and Esoteric Experiences: A Jungian Approach*. University Park: Pennsylvania State UP, 1991. Print.

Kreilkamp, Ivan. *Voice and the Victorian Storyteller*. Cambridge: Cambridge UP, 2005. Print.

Leavis, F. R. The *Great Tradition*. New York: New York UP, 1963. Print.

London, Bette. "Reading Race and Gender in Conrad's Dark Continent." *Criticism* 31 (1989): 235–52. Print.

Moser, Thomas. *Joseph Conrad: Achievement and Decline*. Cambridge: Harvard UP, 1957. Print.

Nazareth, Peter. "Out of Darkness: Conrad and Other Third World Writers." *Joseph Conrad: Third World Perspectives*. Ed. Robert D. Hamner. Washington: Three Continents, 1990. Print.

Parry, Benita. *Conrad and Imperialism*. London: Macmillan, 1983. Print.

Pecora, Vincent P. *Self and Form in Modern Narrative*. Baltimore: Johns Hopkins UP, 1989. Print.

Raschke, Debrah. *Modernism, Metaphysics, and Sexuality*. Selinsgrove: Susquehanna UP 2006. Print.

Rising, Catharine. *Darkness at Heart: Fathers and Sons in Conrad*. New York: Greenwood, 1990. Print.

Roberts, Andrew Michael. *Conrad and Masculinity*. New York: St. Martin's, 2000. Print.

Ross, Stephen. *Conrad and Empire*. Columbia: U of Missouri P, 2004. Print.

Sherry, Norman, ed. *Conrad: The Critical Heritage*. London: Routledge, 1973.

Shetty, Sandya, "*Heart of Darkness*: Out of Africa Some New Thing Never Comes." *Journal of Modern Literature* 15 (1989): 461–74. Print.

Stampfl, Barry. "Marlow's Rhetoric of (Self-) Deception in *Heart of Darkness*." *Modern Fiction Studies* 37 (1991): 183–96. Print.

Straus, Nina Pelikan. "The Exclusion of the Intended from Secret Sharing in Conrad's *Heart of Darkness*." *Novel: A Forum on Fiction* 20 (1987): 123–37. Print.

Feminist and Gender
Criticism and
Heart of Darkness

WHAT ARE FEMINIST AND
GENDER CRITICISM?

Among the most exciting and influential developments in the field
of literary studies, feminist and gender criticism participate in a broad
philosophical discourse that extends far beyond literature, far beyond
the arts in general. The critical *practices* of those who explore the representation of women and men in works by male or female, lesbian or
gay writers inevitably grow out of and contribute to a larger and more
generally applicable *theoretical* discussion of how gender and sexuality
are constantly shaped by and shaping institutional structures and attitudes, artifacts and behaviors.

Feminist criticism was accorded academic legitimacy in American
universities "around 1981," Jane Gallop claims in her book *Around
1981: Academic Feminist Literary Theory* (1992). With Gallop's title and
approximation in mind, Naomi Schor has since estimated that "around
1985, feminism began to give way to what has come to be called gender studies" (275). Some would argue that feminist criticism became
academically legitimate well before 1981. Others would take issue with
the notion that feminist criticism and women's studies have been giving
way to gender criticism and gender studies, and with the either/or distinction that such a claim implies. Taken together, however, Gallop and

Schor provide us with a useful fact — that of feminist criticism's historical precedence — and a chronological focus on the early to mid-1980s,
a period during which the feminist approach was unquestionably influential and during which new interests emerged, not all of which were
woman centered.

During the early 1980s, three discrete strains of feminist theory and
practice — commonly categorized as French, North American, and
British — seemed to be developing. French feminists tended to focus
their attention on language. Drawing on the ideas of the psychoanalytic
philosopher Jacques Lacan, they argued that language as we commonly
think of it — as public discourse — is decidedly phallocentric, privileging what is valued by the patriarchal culture. They also spoke of the
possibility of an alternative, feminine language and of *l'écriture féminine*: women's writing. Julia Kristeva, who is generally seen as a pioneer
of French feminist thought even though she dislikes the feminist label,
suggested that feminine language is associated with the maternal and
derived from the pre-oedipal fusion between mother and child. Like
Kristeva, Hélène Cixous and Luce Irigaray associated feminine writing
with the female body. Both drew an analogy between women's writing
and women's sexual pleasure, Irigaray arguing that just as a woman's
"*jouissance*" is more diffuse and complex than a man's unitary phallic
pleasure ("woman has sex organs just about everywhere"), so "feminine" language is more diffuse and less obviously coherent than its
"masculine" counterpart (*This Sex* 101–03).

Kristeva, who helped develop the concept of *l'écriture féminine*,
nonetheless urged caution in its use and advocacy. Feminine or feminist
writing that resists or refuses participation in "masculine" discourse,
she warned, risks political marginalization, relegation to the outskirts
(pun intended) of what is considered socially and politically significant.
Kristeva's concerns were not unfounded: the concept of *l'écriture féminine* did prove controversial, eliciting different kinds of criticism from
different kinds of feminist and gender critics. To some, the concept
appears to give writing a biological basis, thereby suggesting that there
is an *essential* femininity, and/or that women are *essentially* different
from men. To others, it seems to suggest that men can write as women,
so long as they abdicate authority, sense, and logic in favor of diffusive-
ness, playfulness, even nonsense.

While French feminists of the 1970s and early 1980s focused on
language and writing from a psychoanalytic perspective, North American critics generally practiced a different sort of criticism. Characterized

by close textual reading and historical scholarship, it generally took one of two forms. Critics like Kate Millett, Carolyn Heilbrun, and Judith Fetterley developed what Elaine Showalter called the "feminist critique" of "male constructed literary history" by closely examining canonical works by male writers, exposing the patriarchal ideology implicit in such works and arguing that traditions of systematic masculine dominance are indelibly inscribed in our literary tradition. Fetterley urged women to become "resisting readers" — to notice how biased most of the classic texts by male authors are in their language, subjects, and attitudes and to actively reject that bias as they read, thereby making reading a different, less "immasculating" experience. Meanwhile, another group of North American feminists, including Showalter, Sandra Gilbert, Susan Gubar, and Patricia Meyer Spacks, developed a different feminist critical model — one that Showalter referred to as "gynocriticism." These critics analyzed great books by women from a feminist perspective, discovered neglected or forgotten women writers, and attempted to recover women's culture and history, especially the history of women's communities that nurtured female creativity.

The North American endeavor to recover women's history — for example, by emphasizing that women developed their own strategies to gain power within their sphere — was seen by British feminists like Judith Newton and Deborah Rosenfelt as an endeavor that "mystifies" male oppression, disguising it as something that has created a special world of opportunities for women. More important from the British standpoint, the universalizing and "essentializing" tendencies of French theory and a great deal of North American practice disguised women's oppression by highlighting sexual difference, thereby seeming to suggest that the dominant system may be impervious to change. As for the North American critique of male stereotypes that denigrate women, British feminists maintained that it led to counterstereotypes of female virtue that ignore real differences of race, class, and culture among women.

By now, the French, North American, and British approaches have so thoroughly critiqued, influenced, and assimilated one another that the work of most Western practitioners is no longer easily identifiable along national boundary lines. Instead, it tends to be characterized according to whether the category of *woman* is the major focus in the exploration of gender and gender oppression or, alternatively, whether the interest in sexual difference encompasses an interest in other differences that also define identity. The latter paradigm encompasses the work of feminists of color, Third World (preferably called postcolonial) feminists, and lesbian feminists, many of whom have asked whether the universal category of woman constructed by certain French and North American predecessors is appropriate to describe women in minority groups or non-Western cultures.

These feminists stress that, while all women are female, they are something else as well (such as African American, lesbian, Muslim Pakistani). This "something else" is precisely what makes them — including their problems and their goals — different from other women. As Armit Wilson has pointed out, Asian women living in Great Britain are expected by their families and communities to preserve Asian cultural traditions; thus, the expression of personal identity through clothing involves a much more serious infraction of cultural rules than it does for a Western woman. Gloria Anzaldúa has spoken personally and eloquently about the experience of many women on the margins of Eurocentric North American culture. "I am a border woman," she writes in *Borderlands: La Frontera = The New Mestiza* (1987). "I grew up between two cultures, the Mexican (with a heavy Indian influence) and the Anglo. . . . Living on the borders and in margins, keeping intact one's shifting and multiple identity and integrity is like trying to swim in a new element, an 'alien' element" (i).

Instead of being divisive and isolating, this evolution of feminism into femin*isms* has fostered a more inclusive, global perspective. The era of recovering women's texts, especially texts by white Western women, has been succeeded by a new era in which the goal is to recover entire cultures of women. Two important figures of this new era are Trinh T. Minh-ha and Gayatri Spivak. Spivak, in works such as *In Other Worlds: Essays in Cultural Politics* (1987) and *Outside in the Teaching Machine* (1993), has shown how political independence (generally looked upon by metropolitan Westerners as a simple and beneficial historical and political reversal) has complex implications for "subaltern" or subproletarian women.

The understanding of woman not as a single, deterministic category but rather as the nexus of diverse experiences has led some white, Western, "majority" feminists like Jane Tompkins and Nancy K. Miller to advocate and practice "personal" or "autobiographical" criticism. Once reluctant to reveal themselves in their analyses for fear of being labeled idiosyncratic, impressionistic, and subjective by men, some feminists are now openly skeptical of the claims to reason, logic, and objectivity that male critics have made in the past. With the advent of more personal feminist critical styles has come a powerful new interest in women's autobiographical writings, manifested in essays such as "Authorizing the Autobiographical" by Shari Benstock, which first appeared in her influential collection *The Private Self: Theory and Practice of Women's Autobiographical Writings* (1988).

Some feminists have argued that traditional autobiography is a gendered, "masculinist" genre; its established conventions call for a lifeplot that turns on action, triumph through conflict, intellectual selfdiscovery, and often public renown. The body, reproduction, children, and intimate interpersonal relationships are generally well in the background and often absent. Arguing that the lived experiences of women and men differ — women's lives, for instance, are often characterized by interruption and deferral — Leigh Gilmore has developed a theory of women's self-representation in her book *Autobiographics: A Feminist Theory of Self-Representation.*

Autobiographics was published in 1994, well after the chronological divide that, according to Schor, separates the heyday of feminist criticism and the rise of gender studies. Does that mean that Gilmore's book is a feminist throwback? Is she practicing gender criticism instead, the use of the word *feminist* in her book's subtitle notwithstanding? Or are both of these questions overly reductive? As implied earlier, many knowledgeable commentators on the contemporary critical scene are skeptical of the feminist/gender distinction, arguing that feminist criticism is by definition gender criticism and pointing out that one critic whose work *everyone* associates with feminism (Julia Kristeva) has problems with the feminist label while another critic whose name is continually linked with the gender approach (Teresa de Lauretis) continues to refer to herself and her work as feminist.

Certainly, feminist and gender criticism are not polar opposites but, rather, exist along a continuum of attitudes toward sex and sexism, sexuality and gender, language and the literary canon. There are, however, a few distinctions to be made between those critics whose writings are inevitably identified as being toward one end of the continuum or the other.

One distinction is based on focus: as the word implies, *feminists* have concentrated their efforts on the study of women and women's issues. Gender criticism, by contrast, has not been woman centered. It has tended to view the male and female sexes — and the masculine and feminine genders — in terms of a complicated continuum, much as we are viewing feminist and gender criticism. Critics like Diane K. Lewis have raised the possibility that black women may be more like white men in terms of familial and economic roles, like black men in terms of their relationships with whites, and like white women in terms of their relationships with men. Lesbian gender critics have asked whether lesbian women are really more like straight women than they are like gay (or for that matter straight) men. That we refer to gay and lesbian studies as gender studies has led some to suggest that gender studies is a misnomer; after all, homosexuality is not a gender. This objection may easily be answered once we realize that one purpose of gender criticism is to criticize gender as we commonly conceive of it, to expose its insufficiency and inadequacy as a category.

Another distinction between feminist and gender criticism is based on the terms *gender* and *sex*. As de Lauretis suggests in *Technologies of Gender* (1987), feminists of the 1970s tended to equate gender with sex, gender difference with sexual difference. But that equation doesn't help us explain "the differences among women, . . . the differences *within women*." After positing that "we need a notion of gender that is not so bound up with sexual difference," de Lauretis provides just such a notion by arguing that "gender is not a property of bodies or something originally existent in human beings"; rather, it is "the product of various social technologies, such as cinema" (2). Gender is, in other words, a construct, an effect of language, culture, and its institutions. It is gender, not sex, that causes a weak old man to open a door for an athletic young woman. And it is gender, not sex, that may cause one young woman to expect old men to behave in this way, another to view this kind of behavior as chauvinistic and insulting, and still another to have mixed feelings (hence de Lauretis's phrase "differences *within women*") about "gentlemanly gallantry."

Still another related distinction between feminist and gender criticism is based on the essentialist views of many feminist critics and the constructionist views of many gender critics (both those who would call themselves feminists and those who would not). Stated simply and perhaps too reductively, the term *essentialist* refers to the view that women are essentially different from men. *Constructionist*, by contrast, refers to the view that most of those differences are characteristics not of the male and female sex (nature) but, rather, of the masculine and feminine genders (nurture). Because of its essentialist tendencies, "radical feminism," according to the influential gender critic Eve Kosofsky Sedgwick, "tends to deny that the meaning of gender or sexuality has ever significantly changed; and more damagingly, it can make future change appear impossible" (*Between Men* 13).

Most obviously essentialist would be those feminists who empha-
size the female body, its difference, and the manifold implications of
that difference. The equation made by some avant-garde French feminists between the female body and the *maternal* body has proved especially troubling to some gender critics, who worry that it may paradoxically play into the hands of extreme conservatives and fundamentalists
seeking to reestablish patriarchal family values. In her book *The Reproduction of Mothering* (1978), Nancy Chodorow, a sociologist of gender, admits that what we call "mothering" — not having or nursing
babies but mothering more broadly conceived — is commonly associated not just with the feminine gender but also with the female sex,
often considered nurturing by nature. But she critically interrogates the
common assumption that it is in women's nature or biological destiny
to "mother" in this broader sense, arguing that the separation of home
and workplace brought about by the development of capitalism and the
ensuing industrial revolution made mothering *appear* to be essentially a
woman's job in modern Western society.

If sex turns out to be gender where mothering is concerned, what
differences *are* grounded in sex — that is, nature? *Are* there *essential* differences between men and women — other than those that are purely
anatomical and anatomically determined (for example, a man can exclusively take on the job of feeding an infant milk, but he may not do so
from his own breast)? A growing number of gender critics would answer
the question in the negative. Sometimes referred to as "extreme constructionists" and "postfeminists," these critics have adopted the viewpoint of philosopher Judith Butler, who in her book *Gender Trouble*
(1990) predicts that "sex, by definition, will be shown to have been
gender all along" (8). As Naomi Schor explains their position, "there is
nothing outside or before culture, no nature that is not always and
already enculturated" (278).

Whereas a number of feminists celebrate women's difference, postfeminist gender critics would agree with Chodorow's statement that
men have an "investment in difference that women do not have" (Eisenstein and Jardine 14). They see difference as a symptom of oppression,
not a cause for celebration, and would abolish it by dismantling gender
categories and, ultimately, destroying gender itself. Since gender categories and distinctions are embedded in and perpetuated through language, gender critics like Monique Wittig have called for the wholesale transformation of language into a nonsexist, and nonheterosexist,
medium.

Language has proved the site of important debates between feminist and gender critics, essentialists and constructionists. Gender critics have taken issue with those French feminists who have spoken of a feminine language and writing and who have grounded differences in language and writing in the female body.[1] For much the same reason, they have disagreed with those French-influenced Anglo-American critics who, like Toril Moi and Nancy K. Miller, have posited an essential relationship between sexuality and textuality. (In an essentialist sense, such critics have suggested that when women write, they tend to break the rules of plausibility and verisimilitude that men have created to evaluate fiction.) Gender critics like Peggy Kamuf posit a relationship only between *gender* and textuality, between what most men and women *become* after they are born and the way in which they write. They are therefore less interested in the author's sexual "signature" — in whether the author was a woman writing — than in whether the author was (to borrow from Kamuf) "Writing like a Woman."

Feminists like Miller have suggested that no man could write the "female anger, desire, and selfhood" that Emily Brontë, for instance, inscribed in her poetry and in *Wuthering Heights* (*Subject* 72). In the view of gender critics, it is and has been possible for a man to write like a woman, a woman to write like a man. Shari Benstock, a noted feminist critic whose investigations into psychoanalytic and poststructuralist theory have led her increasingly to adopt the gender approach, poses the following question to herself in *Textualizing the Feminine* (1991): "Isn't it precisely 'the feminine' in Joyce's writings and Derrida's that carries me along?" (45). In an essay entitled "Unsexing Language: Pronomial Protest in Emily Dickinson's 'Lay this Laurel,'" Anna Shannon Elfenbein has argued that "like Walt Whitman, Emily Dickinson crossed the gender barrier in some remarkable poems," such as "We learned to like the Fire / By playing Glaciers — when a Boy —" (Berg et al. 215).

It is also possible, in the view of most gender critics, for women to read as men, men as women. The view that women can, and indeed have been forced to, read as men has been fairly noncontroversial. Everyone agrees that the literary canon is largely "androcentric" and

---

[1]Because feminist/gender studies, not unlike sex/gender, should be thought of as existing along a continuum of attitudes and not in terms of simple opposition, attempts to highlight the difference between feminist and gender criticism arc inevitably prone to reductive overgeneralization and occasional distortion. Here, for instance, French feminism is made out to be more monolithic than it actually is. Hélène Cixous has said that a few men (such as Jean Genet) have produced "feminine writing," although she suggests that these are exceptional men who have acknowledged their own bisexuality.

that writings by men have tended to "immasculate" women, forcing them to see the world from a masculine viewpoint. But the question of whether men can read as women has proved to be yet another issue dividing feminist and gender critics. Some feminists suggest that men and women have some essentially different reading strategies and outcomes, while gender critics maintain that such differences arise entirely out of social training and cultural norms. One interesting result of recent attention to gender and reading is Elizabeth A. Flynn's argument that women in fact make the best interpreters of imaginative literature. Based on a study of how male and female students read works of fiction, she concludes that women come up with more imaginative, open-ended readings of stories. Quite possibly the imputed hedging and tentativeness of women's speech, often seen by men as disadvantages, are transformed into useful interpretive strategies — receptivity combined with critical assessment of the text — in the act of reading (Flynn and Schweickart 286).

In singling out a catalyst of the gender approach, many historians of criticism have pointed to Michel Foucault. In his *History of Sexuality* (1976, tr. 1978), Foucault distinguished sexuality (that is, sexual behavior or practice) from sex, calling the former a "technology of sex." De Lauretis, who has deliberately developed her theory of gender "along the lines of . . . Foucault's theory of sexuality," explains his use of "technology" this way: "Sexuality, commonly thought to be a natural as well as a private matter, is in fact completely constructed in culture according to the political aims of the society's dominant class" (*Technologies* 2, 12). Foucault suggests that homosexuality as we now think of it was to a great extent an invention of the nineteenth century. In earlier periods there had been "acts of sodomy" and individuals who committed them, but the "sodomite" was, according to Foucault, "a temporary aberration," not the "species" he became with the advent of the modern concept of homosexuality (42–43). By historicizing sexuality, Foucault made it possible for his successors to consider the possibility that all of the categories and assumptions that currently come to mind when we think about sex, sexual difference, gender, and sexuality are social artifacts, the products of cultural discourses.

In explaining her reason for saying that feminism began to give way to gender studies "around 1985," Schor says that she chose that date "in part because it marks the publication of *Between Men*," a seminal book in which Eve Kosofsky Sedgwick "articulates the insights of feminist criticism onto those of gay-male studies, which had up to then pursued often parallel but separate courses (affirming the existence of a homosexual or female imagination, recovering lost traditions, decoding the cryptic discourse of works already in the canon by homosexual or feminist authors)" (276). Today, gay and lesbian criticism is so much a part of gender criticism that some people equate it with the gender approach, while others have begun to prefer the phrase "sexualities criticism" to "gender criticism."

Following Foucault's lead, some gay and lesbian gender critics have argued that the heterosexual/homosexual distinction is as much a cultural construct as is the masculine/feminine dichotomy. Arguing that sexuality is a continuum, not a fixed and static set of binary oppositions, a number of gay and lesbian critics have critiqued heterosexuality as a norm, arguing that it has been an enforced corollary and consequence of what Gayle Rubin has referred to as the "sex/gender system." (Those subscribing to this system assume that persons of the male sex should be masculine, that masculine men are attracted to women, and therefore that it is natural for masculine men to be attracted to women and unnatural for them to be attracted to men.) Lesbian gender critics have also taken issue with their feminist counterparts on the grounds that they proceed from fundamentally heterosexual and even heterosexist assumptions. Particularly offensive to lesbians like the poet-critic Adrienne Rich have been those feminists who, following Doris Lessing, have implied that to make the lesbian choice is to make a statement, to act out feminist hostility against men. Rich has called heterosexuality "a beachhead of male dominance" that, "like motherhood, needs to be recognized and studied as a political institution" ("Compulsory Heterosexuality" 143, 145).

If there is such a thing as reading like a woman and such a thing as reading like a man, how then do lesbians read? Are there gay and lesbian ways of reading? Many would say that there are. Rich, by reading Emily Dickinson's poetry as a lesbian — by not assuming that "heterosexual romance is the key to a woman's life and work" — has introduced us to a poet somewhat different from the one heterosexual critics have made familiar (*Lies* 158). As for gay reading, Wayne Koestenbaum has defined "the (male twentieth-century first world) gay reader" as one who "reads resistantly for inscriptions of his condition, for texts that will confirm a social and private identity founded on a desire for other men. . . . Reading becomes a hunt for histories that deliberately foreknow or unwittingly trace a desire felt not by author but by reader, who is most acute when searching for signs of himself" (Boone and Cadden 176–77).

Lesbian critics have produced a number of compelling reinterpretations, or in-scriptions, of works by authors as diverse as Emily Dickinson, Virginia Woolf, and Toni Morrison. As a result of these provocative readings, significant disagreements have arisen between straight and lesbian critics and among lesbian critics as well. Perhaps the most famous and interesting example of this kind of interpretive controversy involves the claim by Barbara Smith and Adrienne Rich that Morrison's novel *Sula* can be read as a lesbian text — and author Toni Morrison's counterclaim that it cannot.

Gay male critics have produced a body of readings no less revisionist and controversial, focusing on writers as staidly classic as Henry James and Wallace Stevens. In Melville's *Billy Budd* and *Moby-Dick*, Robert K. Martin suggests, a triangle of homosexual desire exists. In the latter novel, the hero must choose between a captain who represents "the imposition of the male on the female" and a "Dark Stranger" (Queequeg) who "offers the possibility of an alternate sexuality, one that is less dependent upon performance and conquest" (5).

Masculinity as a complex construct producing and reproducing a constellation of behaviors and goals, many of them destructive (like performance and conquest) and most of them injurious to women, has become the object of an unprecedented number of gender studies. A 1983 issue of *Feminist Review* contained an essay entitled "Anti-Porn: Soft Issue, Hard World," in which B. Ruby Rich suggested that the "legions of feminist men" who examine and deplore the effects of pornography on women might better "undertake the analysis that can tell us why men like porn (not, piously, why this or that exceptional man does *not*)" (Berg 185). The advent of gender criticism makes precisely that kind of analysis possible. Stephen H. Clark, who alludes to Rich's challenge, reads T. S. Eliot "as a man." Responding to "Eliot's implicit appeal to a specifically masculine audience — " 'You! hypocrite lecteur! — mon semblable, — mon *frère!*' " — Clark concludes that poems like "Sweeney Among the Nightingales" and "Gerontion," rather than offering what they are usually said to offer — "a social critique into which a misogynistic language accidentally seeps" — instead articulate a masculine "psychology of sexual fear and desired retaliation" (Berg et al. 173).

Some gender critics focusing on masculinity have analyzed "the anthropology of boyhood," a phrase coined by Mark Seltzer in an article in which he comparatively reads, among other things, Stephen Crane's *The Red Badge of Courage*, Jack London's *White Fang*, and the first *Boy Scouts of America* handbook (Boone and Cadden 150). Others have examined the fear men have that artistry is unmasculine, a guilty worry that surfaces perhaps most obviously in "The Custom-House," Hawthorne's lengthy preface to *The Scarlet Letter*. Still others have studied the representation in literature of subtly erotic disciple-patron relationships, relationships like the ones between Nick Carraway and Jay Gatsby, Charlie Marlow and Lord Jim, Doctor Watson and Sherlock Holmes, and any number of characters in Henry James's stories. Not all of these studies have focused on literary texts. Because the movies have played a primary role in gender construction during our lifetimes, gender critics have analyzed the dynamics of masculinity (vis-à-vis femininity and androgyny) in films from *Rebel Without a Cause* to *Tootsie* to last year's Academy Award nominees. One of the "social technologies" most influential in (re)constructing gender, film is one of the media in which today's sexual politics is most evident.

Necessary as it is, in an introduction such as this one, to define the difference between feminist and gender criticism, it is equally necessary to conclude by unmaking the distinction, at least partially. The two topics just discussed (film theory and so-called queer theory) give us grounds for undertaking that necessary deconstruction. The alliance I have been creating between gay and lesbian criticism on one hand and gender criticism on the other is complicated greatly by the fact that not all gay and lesbian critics are constructionists. Indeed, a number of them (Robert K. Martin included) share with many feminists the *essentialist* point of view; that is to say, they believe homosexuals and heterosexuals to be essentially different, different by nature, just as a number of feminists believe men and women to be different.

In film theory and criticism, feminist and gender critics have so influenced one another that their differences would be difficult to define based on any available criteria, including the ones outlined above. Cinema has been of special interest to feminists like Trinh T. Minh-ha (herself a filmmaker) and Spivak (whose critical eye has focused on movies including *My Beautiful Laundrette* and *Sammie and Rosie Get Laid*). Teresa de Lauretis, whose *Technologies of Gender* (1987) has proved influential in the area of gender studies, continues to publish film criticism consistent with earlier, unambiguously feminist works in which she argued that "the representation of woman as spectacle — body to be looked at, place of sexuality, and object of desire — so pervasive in our culture, finds in narrative cinema its most complex expression and widest circulation" (*Alice* 4).

Feminist film theory has developed alongside a feminist performance theory grounded in Joan Riviere's recently rediscovered essay
"Womanliness as a Masquerade" (1929), in which the author argues
that there is no femininity that is *not* masquerade. Marjorie Garber, a
contemporary cultural critic with an interest in gender, has analyzed the
constructed nature of femininity by focusing on men who have apparently achieved it — through the transvestism, transsexualism, and other
forms of "cross-dressing" evident in cultural productions from Shakespeare to Elvis, from "Little Red Riding Hood" to *La Cage aux Folles*.
The future of feminist and gender criticism, it would seem, is not one
of further bifurcation but one involving a refocusing on femininity,
masculinity, and related sexualities, not only as represented in poems,
novels, and films but also as manifested and developed in video, on
television, and along the almost infinite number of waystations rapidly
being developed on the information highways running through an
exponentially expanding cyberspace.

In the epigraph to Johanna M. Smith's essay "Too Beautiful Altogether," Hélène Cixous argues that, through history, men have seen
women as a " 'dark continent' to penetrate and to 'pacify.' " Smith accepts Cixous's metaphorical characterization of patriarchal subjugation
as geographical conquest, but she also significantly develops Cixous's
insight by suggesting that there is an actual (not just metaphorical) *link*
between the subjugation of women in Western society and the historical colonization of non-Western women *and* men by European powers.
The imperialist and patriarchal ideologies that have colluded to silence
and subjugate are of course reflected in a novel like Conrad's *Heart of
Darkness*, since works of literature inevitably reflect the dominant ideologies of the age in which they were written. But when seen from a
fresh critical perspective, an imaginative work by a visionary writer may
also be seen to reveal *contradictions* within ideologies, particularly
ideologies that are beginning to break down. (Both the imperialistic
ideology of civilizing through conquest and the patriarchal ideology of
"separate spheres" were "under pressure in the late nineteenth century," Smith points out.) We can see through the contradictions within
ideologies of gender and of empire, Smith suggests, when we see *Heart
of Darkness* through the lens of "feminist 'revision.' "
Approaching Marlow's narrative as the product of a moment both
in the history of imperialism and in the history of patriarchy, Smith
shows how patriarchal and imperialist ideologies guide the creation of

the novel's (minor) women characters, either causing them to remain silent (for if they spoke, they would surely condemn their oppressors, calling them what they are) or causing them to speak the myths men would have them speak.

Smith's essay affords an excellent example of the feminist approach because, at one point or another, it reflects the interests and practices of each of the now-traditional forms of feminist criticism. By beginning her essay with the admission that a man's novel about manly adventure may not seem important to the feminist enterprise, Smith reminds us of the priorities of American gynocritics, which were to recover and analyze literary works written by women. In her subsequent attention to the subject of silent women and women who speak but speak as men — as well as in her suggestion that feminist readers may hear Conrad's women speaking their mind through the "gaps" in Marlow's discourse — Smith shows an awareness of French feminist issues. Smith's analysis even more obviously exemplifies the feminist critique of a literary work by a man, in the way that it points out how Conrad, through Marlow, repeats a belief system that domesticates women, thereby subjugating them to a separate, secondary sphere.

But Smith's essay is far more than a *reprise* of traditional feminist approaches. It reflects the insights of contemporary, postcolonial feminism(s) in its sensitivity to matters of race, class, and nationality. (Smith shows that the gender construct defining the femininity of the story's dark-skinned native women is very different from the one defining the identity of Marlow's aunt or Kurtz's Intended.) "Too Beautiful Altogether" also reflects the thinking of most feminist gender critics insofar as it views the feminine not as an essential quality of *woman* but rather as a cultural construct, the several versions of which prescribe the identity of women, groups of women. In its final pages, Smith's essay even addresses the construct of masculinity, thereby reflecting the concerns of nonfeminist as well as feminist gender critics. "The ideology of separate spheres enables masculine imperialism," Smith argues. "By creating an alternative women's sphere 'lest ours get worse,' men can continue to confront their 'own true stuff' in their world. And the violence with which Marlow's lie sacrifices the Intended to this masculine world," Smith concludes, "indicates the strength of its homosocial bonds" (p. 201).

FEMINIST AND GENDER CRITICISM: A SELECTED BIBLIOGRAPHY

Feminist Criticism and Theory: General Texts

Belsey, Catherine, and Jane Moore, eds. *The Feminist Reader: Essays in Gender and the Politics of Literary Criticism.* 2d ed. Houndmills: Macmillan, 1997. Print. An anthology of feminist critical theory and practice.

Benstock, Shari. *Feminist Issues in Literary Scholarship.* Bloomington: Indiana UP, 1987. Print.

Conboy, Katie, Nadia Medina, and Sarah Stanbury, eds. *Writing on the Body: Female Embodiment and Feminist Theory.* New York: Columbia UP, 1997. Print.

de Lauretis, Teresa, ed. *Feminist Studies/Critical Studies.* Bloomington: Indiana UP, 1986. Print.

Eagleton, Mary, ed. *Feminist Literary Theory: A Reader.* 2d ed. Oxford: Blackwell, 1996. Print.

———. *Working with Feminist Criticism.* Cambridge: Blackwell, 1996. Print.

Eisenstein, Hester, and Alice Jardine, eds. *The Future of Difference.* Boston: G. K. Hall, 1980. Print.

Fuss, Diana. *Essentially Speaking: Feminist Nature and Difference.* New York: Routledge, 1989. Print.

Gallop, Jane. *Around 1981: Academic Feminist Literary Theory.* New York: Routledge, 1992. Print.

Heilbrun, Carolyn. *Toward a Recognition of Androgyny.* New York: Harper Colophon, 1973. Print.

hooks, bell. *Feminist Theory: From Margin to Center.* 2d ed. Cambridge: South End, 2000. Print.

Lovell, Terry, ed. *British Feminist Thought: A Reader.* Oxford: Basil Blackwell, 1990. Print.

Miller, Nancy K., ed. *The Poetics of Gender.* New York: Columbia UP, 1986. Print.

Millett, Kate. *Sexual Politics.* Garden City: Doubleday, 1970. Print.

Moi, Toril. *Sexual/Textual Politics: Feminist Literary Theory.* 2d ed. London: Routledge, 2002. Print.

Nicholson, L., ed. *The Second Wave: A Reader in Feminist Theory.* New York: Routledge, 1997. Print.

Plain, Gill, and Susan Sellers. *A History of Feminist Literary Criticism.* Cambridge: Cambridge UP, 2007. Print.

Robbins, Ruth. *Literary Feminisms*. New York: St. Martin's, 2000. Print.

Rooney, Ellen, ed. *The Cambridge Companion to Feminist Literary Theory*. Cambridge: Cambridge UP, 2006. Print.

Showalter, Elaine, ed. *The New Feminist Criticism: Essays on Women, Literature, and Theory*. New York: Pantheon, 1985. Print. See especially Showalter's "Toward a Feminist Poetics," 125–43, and Annette Kolodny's "Dancing Through the Minefield: Some Observations on the Theory, Practice, and Politics of a Feminist Literary Criticism," 144–67.

Stimpson, Catharine R. "Feminist Criticism." *Redrawing the Boundaries: The Transformation of English and American Literary Studies*. Eds. Stephen Greenblatt and Giles Gunn. New York: MLA, 1992. 251–70. Print.

Warhol, Robyn R., and Diane Price Herndl, eds. *Feminisms: An Anthology of Literary Theory and Criticism*. Rev. ed. New Brunswick: Rutgers UP, 1997. Print.

Warhol-Down, Robyn, and Diane Price Herndl, eds. *Feminisms Redux: An Anthology of Literary Theory and Criticism*. New Brunswick: Rutgers UP, 2009. Print.

French Feminist Theory

Beauvoir, Simone de. *The Second Sex*. Trans. and ed. H. M. Parshley. New York: Bantam, 1961. Print.

Cavallaro, Dani. *French Feminist Theory: An Introduction*. London: Continuum, 2003. Print.

Cixous, Hélène. "The Laugh of the Medusa." Trans. Keith Cohen and Paula Cohen. *Signs* 1 (1976): 875–93. Print.

Cixous, Hélène, and Catherine Clement. *The Newly Born Woman*. Trans. Betsy Wing. Minneapolis: U of Minnesota P, 1986. Print.

Irigaray, Luce. *This Sex Which Is Not One*. Trans. Catherine Porter. Ithaca: Cornell UP, 1985. Print.

Kristeva, Julia. *Desire in Language: A Semiotic Approach to Literature and Art*. Ed. Leon S. Roudiez. Trans. Thomas Gora, Alice Jardine, and Leon S. Roudiez. New York: Columbia UP, 1980. Print.

Marks, Elaine, and Isabelle de Courtivron, eds. *New French Feminisms: An Anthology*. Amherst: U of Massachusetts P, 1980. Print.

Moi, Toril, ed. *French Feminist Thought: A Reader*. Oxford: Basil Blackwell, 1987. Print.

Women's Writing and Creativity

Berg, Temma F., et al., eds. *Engendering the Word: Feminist Essays in Psychosexual Poetics.* Urbana: U of Illinois P, 1989. Print. See especially the essays by Anna Shannon Elfenbein, B. Ruby Rich, and Stephen Clark.

Castle, Terry. *Boss Ladies, Watch Out!: Essays on Women, Sex, and Writing.* New York: Routledge, 2002. Print.

Gilbert, Sandra M., and Susan Gubar. *The Madwoman in the Attic: The Woman Writer and the Nineteenth-Century Literary Imagination.* New Haven: Yale UP, 1979. Print.

Jacobus, Mary, ed. *Women Writing and Writing about Women.* New York: Barnes, 1979. Print.

Miller, Nancy K. *Subject to Change: Reading Feminist Writing.* New York: Columbia UP, 1988. Print.

Mills, Sara. *Feminist Stylistics.* London: Routledge, 1995. Print.

Poovey, Mary. *The Proper Lady and the Woman Writer: Ideology as Style in the Works of Mary Wollstonecraft, Mary Shelley, and Jane Austen.* Chicago: U of Chicago P, 1984. Print.

Showalter, Elaine. *A Literature of Their Own: British Women Novelists from Brontë to Lessing.* Princeton: Princeton UP, 1977. Print.

Warren, Joyce W., and Margaret Dickie, eds. *Challenging Boundaries: Gender and Periodization.* Athens: U of Georgia P, 2000. Print.

Gender Criticism and Theory:
General Texts, Studies

Benstock, Shari. *Textualizing the Feminine: Essays on the Limits of Genre.* Norman: U of Oklahoma P, 1991. Print.

Boone, Joseph A., and Michael Cadden, eds. *Engendering Men: The Question of Male Feminist Criticism.* New York: Routledge, 1990. Print. See especially the essays by Wayne Koestenbaum and Mark Seltzer.

Butler, Judith. *Gender Trouble: Feminism and the Subversion of Identity.* New York: Routledge, 1990. Print. For a new introduction by the author, see the 1999 edition.

Chodorow, Nancy. *The Reproduction of Mothering: Psychoanalysis and the Sociology of Gender.* Updated ed. Berkeley: U of California P, 1999. Print.

de Lauretis, Teresa. *Technologies of Gender: Essays on Theory, Film, and Fiction.* Bloomington: Indiana UP, 1987. Print.

Flood, Michael. *The Men's Bibliography: A Comprehensive Bibliography of Writing on Men, Masculinities, Gender, and Sexualities.* 19th ed. Canberra: 2008. *The Men's Bibliography.* Web. 21 January 2010.

Foucault, Michel. *The History of Sexuality.* Trans. Robert Hurley. Vol. 1. New York: Pantheon, 1978. Print.

Garber, Marjorie. *Vested Interests: Cross-Dressing and Cultural Anxiety.* New York: Routledge, 1992. Print.

Goodman, Lizbeth. *Literature and Gender.* London: Routledge, 1996. Print.

Halberstam, Judith. *Female Masculinity.* Durham: Duke UP, 1998. Print.

hooks, bell. *We Real Cool: Black Men and Masculinity.* London: Routledge, 2004. Print.

Kamuf, Peggy. "Writing Like a Woman." *Women and Language in Literature and Society.* New York: Praeger, 1980. 284–99. Print.

Poovey, Mary. *Uneven Developments: The Ideological Work of Gender in Mid-Victorian England.* Chicago: U of Chicago P, 1988. Print.

Riviere, Joan. "Womanliness as a Masquerade." 1929. Rpt. in *Formations of Fantasy.* Eds. Victor Burgin, James Donald, and Cora Kaplan. London: Methuen, 1986. 35–44. Print.

Rubin, Gayle. "The Traffic in Women: Notes on the 'Political Economy' of Sex." *Toward an Anthropology of Women.* Ed. Rayna R. Reiter. New York: Monthly Review, 1975. 157–210. Print.

Schor, Naomi. "Feminist and Gender Studies." *Introduction to Scholarship in Modern Languages and Literatures.* Ed. Joseph Gibaldi. New York: MLA, 1992. 262–87. Print.

Sedgwick, Eve Kosofsky. *Between Men: English Literature and Male Homosocial Desire.* New York: Columbia UP, 1988. Print.

———. "Gender Criticism." *Redrawing the Boundaries: The Transformation of English and American Literary Studies.* Eds. Stephen Greenblatt and Giles Gunn. New York: MLA, 1992. 271–302. Print.

Gay and Lesbian Criticism/Sexualities Criticism

Abelove, Henry, Michèle Aina Barale, and David Halperin, eds. *The Lesbian and Gay Reader.* New York: Routledge, 1993. Print. Contains Gayle Rubin's essay "Thinking Sex: Notes for a Radical Theory of the Politics of Sexuality." 3–44.

de Lauretis, Teresa. *Technologies of Gender: Essays on Theory, Film, and Fiction.* Bloomington: Indiana UP, 1987. Print.

Dollimore, Jonathan. *Sexual Dissidence: Augustine to Wilde, Freud to Foucault.* Oxford: Clarendon, 1991. Print.

Edelman, Lee. *Homographesis: Essays in Gay Literary and Cultural Theory.* New York: Routledge, 1994. Print.

Haggerty, George E., and Bonnie Zimmerman. *Professions of Desire: Lesbian and Gay Studies in Literature.* New York: MLA, 1995. Print.

Halperin, David M. *One Hundred Years of Homosexuality and Other Essays on Greek Love.* New York: Routledge, 1990. Print.

Kollar, Veronika. *Lesbian Discourses: Images of a Community.* New York: Routledge, 2008. Print.

Munt, Sally, ed. *New Lesbian Criticism: Literary and Cultural Readings.* New York: Harvester Wheatsheaf, 1992. Print.

Raitt, Suzanne. *Volcanos and Pearl Divers: Essays in Lesbian Feminist Studies.* London: Onlywomen P, 1995. Print.

Rich, Adrienne. "Compulsory Heterosexuality and Lesbian Existence." *Signs* 5 (Summer 1980): 631–60. Print.

Stimpson, Catharine R. "Zero Degree Deviancy: The Lesbian Novel in English." *Critical Inquiry* 8 (1981): 363–79. Print.

Wittig, Monique. *The Straight Mind and Other Essays.* Boston: Beacon, 1992. Print. See especially "One Is Not Born a Woman," 9–20, and "The Mark of Gender," 76–89.

Queer Theory

Beemyn, Brett, and Mickey Eliason, eds. *Queer Studies: A Lesbian, Gay, Bisexual, and Transgender Anthology.* New York: New York UP, 1996. Print.

Butler, Judith. *Bodies That Matter: On the Discursive Limits of "Sex."* New York: Routledge, 1993. Print.

Corber, Robert, ed. *Queer Studies: An Interdisciplinary Reader.* Malden, MA: Blackwell, 2003. Print.

de Lauretis, Teresa. "Queer Theory: Lesbian and Gay Sexualities." *differences* 3.2 (1991) (special issue). Print.

Duberman, Martin, ed. *Queer Representations: Reading Lives, Reading Cultures.* New York: New York UP, 1997. Print.

Halberstam, Judith. *In a Queer Time and Place: Transgender Bodies, Subcultural Lives.* New York: New York UP, 2005. Print.

Jagose, Annamarie. *Queer Theory.* New York: New York UP, 1996. Print.

Sedgwick, Eve Kosofsky. *Epistemology of the Closet.* Berkeley: U of California P, 1991. Print.

———. *Tendencies.* Durham: Duke UP, 1993. Print.

Sinfield, Alan. *Cultural Politics — Queer Reading*. 2d ed. London: Routledge, 2005. Print.

Sullivan, Nikki. *A Critical Introduction to Queer Theory*. Edinburgh: Edinburgh UP, 2003. Print.

Valocchi, Stephen, and Robert J. Corber, eds. *Queer Studies: An Interdisciplinary Reader*. Malden: Blackwell, 2003. Print.

Intersections within Feminist and Gender Studies

Case, Sue-Ellen. *Feminist and Queer Performance: Critical Strategies*. Basingstoke: Palgrave Macmillan, 2009. Print.

Giffney, Noreen. "Denormatizing Queer Theory: More Than (Simply) Lesbian and Gay Studies." *Feminist Theory* 5.1 (2004): 73–78.

Green, Adam I. "Gay but Not Queer: Toward a Post-Queer Sexuality Studies." *Theory and Society* 31 (2002): 521–45. Print.

Harris, Laura Alexandra. "Queer Black Feminism: The Pleasure Principle." *Feminist Review* 54 (Autumn 1996): 3–30. Print.

Lovaas, Karen E., et al., eds. *LGBT Studies and Queer Theory: New Conflicts, Collaborations, and Contested Terrain*. Binghamton: Harrington Park, 2006. Print.

Piontek, Thomas. *Queering Gay and Lesbian Studies*. Urbana: U of Illinois P, 2006. Print.

Richardson, Diane, et al., eds. *Intersections Between Feminist and Queer Theory*. Houndmills: Palgrave Macmillan, 2006. Print.

Weed, Elizabeth, and Naomi Schor, eds. *Feminism Meets Queer Theory*. Indianapolis: Indiana UP, 1997. Print.

Wilchins, Riki. *Queer Theory, Gender Theory: An Instant Primer*. Los Angeles: Alyson, 2004. Print.

Intersections with Film Theory

Aaron, Michele, ed. *New Queer Cinema*. New Brunswick: Rutgers UP, 2004. Print. See especially B. Ruby Rich's essay "New Queer Cinema."

Carson, Diane, Janice R. Welsch, and Linda Dittmar, eds. *Multiple Voices in Feminist Film Criticism*. Minneapolis: U of Minnesota P, 1994. Print.

de Lauretis, Teresa. *Alice Doesn't: Feminism, Semiotics, Cinema*. Bloomington: Indiana UP, 1986. Print.

Desai, Jigna. *Beyond Bollywood: The Cultural Politics of South Asian Diasporic Film*. New York: Routledge, 2004. Print.

Dyer, Richard. *Now You See It: Studies in Lesbian and Gay Film.* 2d ed. London: Routledge, 2003.

Erens, Patricia, ed. *Issues in Feminist Film Criticism.* Bloomington: Indiana UP, 1990. Print.

Griffiths, Robin. *Queer Cinema in Europe.* Bristol: Intellect, 2008. Print.

McHugh, Kathleen, and Vivian Sobchack, eds. "Beyond the Gaze: Recent Approaches to Film Feminisms." *Signs* 30.1 (Autumn 2004) (special issue). Print.

Modleski, Tania. *Feminism without Women: Culture and Criticism in a "Postfeminist" Age.* New York: Routledge, 1991. Print.

Mulvey, Laura. *Visual and Other Pleasures.* 2d ed. Houndmills: Palgrave Macmillan, 2009. Print.

Penley, Constance. *Feminism and Film Theory.* New York: Routledge, 1988. Print.

William, David Foster. *Queer Issues in Contemporary Latin American Cinema.* Austin: U of Texas P, 2003. Print.

Intersections with Race, Class, and Nationality

Anzaldúa, Gloria. *Borderlands: La Frontera = The New Mestiza.* 2d ed. San Francisco: Aunt Lute, 1999. Print.

Castillo, Debra A. *Talking Back: Toward a Latin American Feminist Literary Criticism.* Ithaca: Cornell UP, 1992. Print.

Christian, Barbara. *Black Feminist Criticism: Perspectives on Black Women Writers.* New York: Pergamon, 1985. Print.

———. *New Black Feminist Criticism, 1985–2000.* Urbana: U of Illinois P, 2007. Print.

Feldman, Yael S. *No Room of Their Own: Gender and Nation in Israeli Women's Fiction.* New York: Columbia UP, 1999. Print.

Higonnet, Margaret, ed. *Borderwork: Feminist Engagements with Comparative Literature.* Ithaca: Cornell UP, 1994. Print.

Hill Collins, Patricia, ed. *Black Feminist Thought: Knowledge, Consciousness, and the Politics of Empowerment.* 2d ed. New York: Routledge, 2000. Print.

———. *Black Sexual Politics: African Americans, Gender, and the New Racism.* New York: Routledge, 2005. Print.

hooks, bell. *Ain't I a Woman?: Black Women and Feminism.* Boston: South End, 1981. Print.

Hubbard, Dolan. *Recovered Writers/Recovered Texts: Race, Class, and Gender in Black Women's Literature.* Knoxville: U of Tennessee P, 1997. Print.

James, Joy, and T. Denean Sharpley-Whiting, eds. *The Black Feminist Reader.* Malden: Blackwell, 2000. Print. See especially Part 1, "Literary Theory."

Johnson, Barbara. *The Feminist Difference: Literature, Psychoanalysis, Race, and Gender.* Cambridge: Harvard UP, 1998. Print.

Johnson, E. Patrick, and Mae G. Henderson, eds., *Black Queer Studies: A Critical Anthology.* Durham: Duke UP, 2005. Print.

Mohanty, Chandra Talpade, Ann Russo, and Lourdes Torres, eds. *Third World Women and the Politics of Feminism.* Bloomington: Indiana UP, 1991. Print.

Moraga, Cherríe, and Gloria Anzaldúa. *This Bridge Called My Back: Writings by Radical Women of Color.* New York: Kitchen Table, 1981. Print.

Newton, Judith, and Deborah Rosenfelt, eds. *Feminist Criticism and Social Change: Sex, Class and Race in Literature and Culture.* New York: Methuen, 1985. Print.

Robinson, Lillian S. *Sex, Class, and Culture.* Bloomington: Indiana UP, 1978. Print.

Smith, Barbara. *The Truth That Never Hurts: Writings on Race, Gender, and Freedom.* New Brunswick: Rutgers UP, 1998. Print. See especially "Toward a Black Feminist Criticism."

Spivak, Gayatri Chakravorty. *In Other Worlds: Essays in Cultural Politics.* New York: Methuen, 1987. Print.

Wilson, Amrit. *Finding a Voice: Asian Women in Britain.* London: Virago, 1978. Print.

Intersections with Postcolonial Theory and Criticism

Azim, Firdous. *The Colonial Rise of the Novel.* London: Routledge, 1993. Print.

Emberley, Julia. *Thresholds of Difference: Feminist Critique, Native Women's Writings, Postcolonial Theory.* Toronto: U of Toronto P, 1993. Print.

Hawley, John C., ed. *Postcolonial and Queer Theories: Intersections and Essays.* Westport: Greenwood, 2001. Print.

Lewis, Reina, and Sara Mills, eds. *Feminist Postcolonial Theory: A Reader.* Edinburgh: Edinburgh UP, 2003. Print.

Mills, Sara. *Gender and Colonial Space.* Manchester: Manchester UP, 2005. Print.

Sharpe, Jenny. *Allegories of Empire: The Figure of the Woman in the Colonial Text.* Minneapolis: U of Minnesota P, 1993. Print.

Spivak, Gayatri Chakravorty. *Outside in the Teaching Machine.* New York: Routledge, 1993. Print.

Minh-ha, Trinh T. *Woman, Native, Other: Writing Postcoloniality and Feminism.* Bloomington: Indiana UP, 1989. Print.

Yeğenoğlu, Meyda. *Colonial Fantasies: Towards a Feminist Reading of Orientalism.* Cambridge: Cambridge UP, 1998. Print.

Intersections with Other Critical Perspectives

Armour, Ellen T. *Deconstruction, Feminist Theology, and the Problem of Difference: Subverting the Race/Gender Divide.* Chicago: U of Chicago P, 1999. Print.

Armstrong, Nancy, ed. *Literature as Women's History I. Genre* 19–20 (1986–87) (special issue). Print.

Deutscher, Penelope. *Yielding Gender: Feminism, Deconstruction, and the History of Philosophy.* London: Routledge, 1997. Print.

Elam, Diane. *Feminism and Deconstruction.* London: Routledge, 1994. Print.

"Feminism and Deconstruction." *Feminist Studies* 14 (1988) (special issue). Print.

Floyd, Kevin. *The Reification of Desire: Toward a Queer Marxism.* Minneapolis: U of Minnesota P, 2009. Print.

Flynn, Elizabeth A., and Patrocinio P. Schweickart, eds. *Gender and Reading: Essays on Readers, Texts, and Contexts.* Baltimore: Johns Hopkins UP, 1986. Print.

Gaard, Greta, and Patrick D. Murphy, eds. *Ecofeminist Literary Criticism: Theory, Interpretation, Pedagogy.* Urbana: U of Illinois P, 1998. Print.

Gamer, Shirley Nelson. *The (M)other Tongue: Essays in Feminist Psychoanalytic Interpretation.* Ithaca: Cornell UP, 1985. Print.

Hall, Donald E. *Reading Sexualities: Hermeneutic Theory and the Future of Queer Studies.* London: Routledge, 2009. Print.

Higonnet, Margaret, and Joan Templeton, eds. *Reconfigured Spheres: Feminist Explorations of Literary Space.* Amherst: U of Massachusetts P, 1994. Print.

Hohne, Karen, and Helen Wussow, eds. *A Dialogue of Voices: Feminist Literary Theory and Bakhtin.* Minneapolis: U of Minnesota P, 1994. Print.

Holland, Nancy J., ed. *Feminist Interpretations of Jacques Derrida.* University Park: Pennsylvania State UP, 1997. Print.

Howard, Jean. "The New Historicism in Renaissance Studies." *English Literary Renaissance* 16 (1986): 13–43. Print.

Landry, Donna, and Gerald Maclean. *Materialist Feminisms*. Cambridge: Blackwell, 1993. Print.

Newton, Judith. *Starting Over: Feminism and the Politics of Cultural Critique*. Ann Arbor: U of Michigan P, 1994. Print.

Self-Representation and Personal Criticism

Benstock, Shari, ed. *The Private Self: Theory and Practice of Women's Autobiographical Writings*. Chapel Hill: U of North Carolina P, 1988. Print.

Gallop, Jane. *Anecdotal Theory*. Durham: Duke UP, 2002. Print.

Gilmore, Leigh. *Autobiographics: A Feminist Theory of Self-Representation*. Ithaca: Cornell UP, 1994. Print.

Miller, Nancy K. *But Enough about Me: Why We Read Other People's Lives*. New York: Columbia UP, 2002. Print.

———. *Getting Personal: Feminist Occasions and Other Autobiographical Acts*. New York: Routledge, 1991. Print.

Prosser, Jay. *Second Skins: The Body Narratives of Transsexuality*. New York: Columbia UP, 1998. Print. A study of transsexual autobiography.

Rich, Adrienne. *On Lies, Secrets, and Silence: Selected Prose, 1966–1979*. New York: Norton, 1979. Print.

Swindells, Julia, ed. *The Uses of Autobiography*. London: Taylor & Francis, 1995. Print.

Feminist and Gender Readings

Bedant, Lauren. *The Female Complaint: On the Unfinished Business of Sentimentality in American Culture*. Durham: Duke UP, 2008. Print.

Brown, Anne E., and Marjanne E. Goozé, eds. *International Women's Writing: New Landscapes of Identity*. Westport: Greenwood, 1995. Print.

Bruder, Helen P., ed. *Women Reading William Blake*. New York: Palgrave Macmillan, 2007. Print.

Claridge, Laura, and Elizabeth Langland, eds. *Out of Bounds: Male Writing and Gender(ed) Criticism*. Amherst: U of Massachusetts P, 1980. Print.

Fetterley, Judith. *The Resisting Reader: A Feminist Approach to American Fiction*. Bloomington: Indiana UP, 1978. Print.

Ghosh, Bishnupriya, and Brinda Bose, eds. *Interventions: Feminist Dialogues on Third World Women's Literature and Film*. New York: Garland, 1997. Print.

Michie, Elsie. *Outside the Pale: Cultural Exclusion, Gender Difference, and the Victorian Writer.* Ithaca: Cornell UP, 1993. Print.

Orr, Elaine Neil. *Subject to Negotiation: Reading Feminist Criticism and American Women's Fictions.* Charlottesville: UP of Virginia, 1997. Print.

Straus, Barrie Ruth, ed. "Skirting the Texts: Feminisms' Re-reading of Medieval and Renaissance Texts: A Special Issue on Feminism, Theory, and Medieval and Renaissance Texts." *Exemplaria* 4.1 (Spring 1992) (special issue). Print.

Gay, Lesbian, and Queer Readings

Breen, Margaret Sönser. *Narratives of Queer Desire: Deserts of the Heart.* Basingstoke: Palgrave Macmillan, 2009. Print.

Bristow, Joseph, ed. *Sexual Sameness: Textual Differences in Lesbian and Gay Writing.* New York: Routledge, 1992. Print.

Craft, Christopher. *Another Kind of Love: Male Homosexual Desire in English Discourse, 1850–1920.* Berkeley: U of California P, 1994. Print.

Creech, James. *Closet Writing/Gay Reading: The Case of Melville's Pierre.* Chicago: U of Chicago P, 1993. Print.

Flannery, Denis. *On Sibling Love, Queer Attachment and American Writing.* Aldershot: Ashgate, 2007. Print.

Galvin, Mary E. *Queer Poetics: Five Modernist Women Writers.* Westport: Greenwood, 1999. Print.

Hoffman, Warren. *The Passing Game: Queering Jewish American Culture.* Syracuse: Syracuse UP, 2009. Print.

Lilly, Mark, ed. *Lesbian and Gay Writing: An Anthology of Critical Essays.* Philadelphia: Temple UP, 1990. Print.

Martin, Robert K. *Hero, Captain, and Stranger: Male Friendship, Social Critique, and Literary Form in the Sea Novels of Herman Melville.* Chapel Hill: U of North Carolina P, 1986. Print.

Packard, Chris. *Queer Cowboys and Other Erotic Male Friendships in Nineteenth-Century American Literature.* New York: Palgrave Macmillan, 2005. Print.

Samuels, Robert. *Hitchcock's Bi-Textuality: Lacan, Feminisms, and Queer Theory.* Albany: State U of New York P, 1998.

Sedgwick, Eve Kosofsky, ed. "Queerer Than Fiction." *Studies in the Novel* 28.3 (Fall 1996) (special issue). Print.

Traub, Valerie. *Desire and Anxiety: Circulations of Sexuality in Shakespearean Drama.* London: Routledge, 1992. Print.

Feminist and Gender Approaches
to *Heart of Darkness*

Bergenholtz, Rita A. "Conrad's *Heart of Darkness*." *The Explicator* 53 (1995): 102–06. Print.

Bode, Rita. " 'They . . . Should Be Out of It.': The Women of *Heart of Darkness*." *Conradiana* 26 (1994): 20–34. Print.

Hyland, Peter. "The Little Woman in *Heart of Darkness*." *Conradiana* 20 (1988): 3–11. Print.

Kaplan, Carola M. "Women's Caring and Men's Secret Sharing: Constructions of Gender and Sexuality in 'Heart of Darkness' and 'The Secret Sharer.' " Eds. Hunt Hawkins and Brian W. Shaffer. *Approaches to Teaching Conrad's "Heart of Darkness" and "The Secret Sharer."* New York: MLA, 2003. Print.

London, Bette. "Reading Race and Gender in Conrad's Dark Continent." *Criticism* 31 (1989): 235–52. Print.

Mongia, Padmini. "Empire, Narrative and the Feminine in *Lord Jim* and *Heart of Darkness*." Eds. Keith Carabine, Owen Knowles, and Wiesław Krajka. Boulder: East European Monographs, 1993. Print.

Nadelhaft, Ruth. "A Feminist Perspective on *Heart of Darkness*." *Joseph Conrad's Heart of Darkness*. Ed. D. C. R. A. Goonetilleke. London: Routledge, 2007. 92–100. Print.

Roberts, Andrew Michael. "Epistemology, Modernity and Masculinity." *Conrad and Masculinity*. Houndmills: Macmillan, 2000. 118–37. Print.

Robbins, Ruth. "Reading the Boys' Own Stories: *The Strange Case of Dr. Jekyll and Mr. Hyde, The Picture of Dorian Gray* and *Heart of Darkness*." *Literary Feminisms*. New York: St. Martin's, 2000. 217–41. Print.

Ruppel, Richard. "Male Intimacy in Conrad's Tales of Adventure: *The Nigger of the 'Narcissus'* and *Heart of Darkness*." *Homosexuality in the Life and Work of Joseph Conrad*. New York: Routledge, 2008. 22–40. Print.

Schneider, Lissa. *Conrad's Narratives of Difference; Not Exactly Tales for Boys*. New York: Routledge, 1993. Print. See chapter 1, "Iconography and the Feminine Ideal: Torches, Blindfolds, and the 'True Light of Femininity' in *Heart of Darkness, Lord Jim, The Rescue,* and 'The Return,' " 9–32, and chapter 4, "Politics in the House: Genre, Narrative, and the Domestic Drama in *The Secret Agent, Heart of Darkness,* and *Lord Jim*," 91–120.

Straus, Nina Pelikan. "The Exclusion of the Intended from Secret
    Sharing in Conrad's *Heart of Darkness.*" *Novel: A Forum on
    Fiction* 20 (1987): 123–37. Print.
Sullivan, Zohreh T. "Enclosure, Darkness, and the Body: Conrad's
    Landscape." *Centennial Review* 25 (1981): 59–79. Print.

A FEMINIST AND GENDER PERSPECTIVE

JOHANNA M. SMITH

"Too Beautiful Altogether": Ideologies of Gender and Empire in *Heart of Darkness*

> . . . what [men] have said so far, for the most part, stems from
> the opposition activity/passivity, from the power relation between
> a fantasized obligatory virility meant to invade, to colonize, and
> the consequential phantasm of woman as a "dark continent" to
> penetrate and to "pacify."
>
> –HÉLÈNE CIXOUS, "The Laugh of the Medusa"

A story about manly adventure narrated and written by men, *Heart of Darkness* might seem an unpropitious subject for feminist criticism. As my epigraph suggests, however, two colonizing ideologies operate in Conrad's story, and a feminist reading can interrogate these interrelated ideologies of gender and empire. To do such a reading is to engage in a feminist critique of ideology, for "feminist thinking is really *re*thinking, an examination of the way certain assumptions about women and the female character enter into the fundamental assumptions that organize all our thinking" (Jehlen 189). Such rethinking about *Heart of Darkness* reveals collusive imperatives of empire and gender: Marlow's narrative aims to "colonize" and "pacify" both savage darkness and women. By silencing the native[1] laundress and symbolizing the equally silent savage woman and the Company women, Marlow reconstructs his experience of the darkness they stand for. The story's two speaking

[1]The terms "savage" and "native" belong in quotation marks, to indicate their ideological valence. I have decided against this typographical awkwardness, but I ask the reader to remember the imperialist presuppositions behind these words.

European women, Marlow's aunt and Kurtz's Intended, perform a similar function. By restricting unsatisfactory feminine versions of imperialist ideology to them, Marlow is able to create his own masculine version to keep the darkness at bay.

In what follows I use "ideology" in two senses, to mean not only a conscious system of meaning, either imposed or willingly adopted, but also the unconscious grounding of individual experience. In the first sense, ideology refers to the processes whereby "meaning is produced, challenged, reproduced, transformed" (Barrett 73). An ideology works to construct a unified and consensual meaning for contradictory experiences and perceptions, by mystifying or disguising such contradictions. Ideologies often achieve this mystification by disguising customary social systems as natural relations; cultural systems in which one nation or gender is dominant over another, for instance, are represented as the natural order. It is through this guise of "the natural" that the second sense of ideology operates. Because we take for granted what is "natural," an ideology becomes the unexamined ground of experience, "the very condition of our experience of the world" (Belsey 5). Thus internalized, ideology becomes cultural practice, the way we live. Because it *is* practice, however, it does not remain static. As our experiences and formulations of what is "natural" shift, ideology must continually be "renewed, recreated, defended, and modified" (Williams 112). And in the course of such modifications, an ideology's contradictions may become visible.

To specify how ideological contradictions become visible in a literary text, the concept of discourse is helpful. A discourse is "a domain of language-use" (Belsey 5), a specific mode of speaking, writing, and thinking that includes certain shared assumptions. But a discourse is not simply a system of signs with a fixed content and modes of representation; rather it is a set of practices that "*construct* the objects of which they speak" (Humphries 108; emphasis added). In this sense, an ideology may be "*inscribed in* discourse" (Belsey 5); an ideology of gender or empire, for instance, is written into a term like "feminine" or "savage." Now, a literary text creates its own discourse, but this discourse is not independent of others, for "the language of ideology" (Belsey 107) is the literary text's "raw material." And like ideologies, discourses are "not natural and inevitable" (During 35) but "historical, provisional and open to change." Hence a literary text can "indicate the bounds within which particular meanings are constructed and negotiated in a given social formation" (Barrett 81). And if that social formation and its ideologies are in the process of modification, a text's literary and ideological discourses may contradict themselves and each other. Such contradictions may open gaps in the literary text that show ideology to be not "natural" but constructed, not fixed but shifting, not seamless but split.

To illustrate such gaps in *Heart of Darkness*'s ideology of empire, I turn to the clash of discourses first in a text by Kurtz and then in Marlow's response to it. Kurtz's report to the International Society for the Suppression of Savage Customs opens with a discourse of empire that mystifies conquest as humanitarianism: "'By the simple exercise of our will we can exert a power for good practically unbounded'" (p. 65). If conquest of the other is thus represented ideologically as "a power for good," then "the simple exercise of our will" in the suppression of savage customs is legitimated. As I have noted, however, dominant ideologies are not as monolithic or stable as Kurtz's sentence would like to imply. Under stress, an ideology may be brought out of the realm of the "natural" or unexamined; thus demystified, its contradictions become visible. The "New Imperialism" of the late nineteenth century, what Conrad calls "the new gang — the gang of virtue" (p. 40), was under precisely this kind of stress, a pressure to justify itself as "the transformation of an enlightened despotism into an even more luminous paternalism" (Bongie 275). That pressure splits Kurtz's text, so that a gap appears between his early advocacy of the "new gang" and the end of his report, "scrawled evidently much later": "'Exterminate all the brutes!'" (p. 66). This clash of discourses reveals the contradiction between the brutality of conquest and the mystifying "power for good" of imperialist ideology.

Marlow's response to Kurtz's report dramatizes additional contradictions. He admits to "tingl[ing] with enthusiasm" for the "unbounded power of eloquence" in Kurtz's "moving appeal to every altruistic sentiment," but he vacillates about the report's conclusion: at one moment it is "terrifying," at another it is "that valuable postscriptum" (pp. 65–66). The irony of the latter phrase functions here, as irony does throughout his narrative, as "evasion" (Klein 114); it enables him to tell, as if he were detached from its purpose, a story that affirms the ideologies on which his culture operates. Thus Marlow embodies "the uneasy position of the intellectual, unable to support fully, or challenge directly, the interests of the dominant class" (Glenn 253). Specifically, Marlow's ironic detachment intends to evade what is hinted by the gap between his two responses to the conclusion of Kurtz's report: his investment in the Company's imperialist project, his seduction by Kurtz's eloquence. If we approach such gaps in Marlow's discourse with feminist "re-vision" (Rich 35) — the act of "entering an old text from a new critical direction" — we can see the contradictions that his ideological discourses of empire and gender work to mystify. I begin with his representations of the native laundress, the savage woman, and the Company women.

The early episode involving the Company's chief accountant and his native laundress clarifies both the Company's imperialist-masculinist brutality and Marlow's collusion in it. Just prior to meeting the accountant, Marlow encounters a chain gang and its black overseer whose glance of complicity "seemed to take me into partnership" (p. 30) in "the great cause." This form of the "cause" momentarily undermines Marlow's masculinity; unlike the "strong, lusty, red-eyed devils" of conquest that "drove men — men, I tell you," this form is "flabby, pretending, weak-eyed." The accountant whom Marlow then meets is similarly feminized; sporting an "elegance of get-up" (pp. 31–32) that makes him look like "a hairdresser's dummy," he is an effeminate professional rather than a "strong, lusty" conqueror. Yet Marlow respects the "apple-pie order" of the accountant's books, especially in contrast with the surrounding "muddle" of "dusty niggers" and such. And his reaction to the man's "get-up" is ironic yet appreciative; the accountant had "verily accomplished something" by keeping up his appearance, and his clean shirts are "achievements of character" that demonstrate his "backbone." Irony here enables Marlow to displace an appalling "flabby" imperialism with the accountant's comic "backbone."

That irony also mystifies Marlow's complicity in such "achievements of character" by occluding the laundress who provides the backbone's starch. The accountant tells Marlow that he has been "teaching one of the native women" to launder his shirts (p. 33); but, he adds, " 'It was difficult. She had a distaste for the work.' " This representation of his "teaching" overcoming her "distaste" mystifies the Company man's oppression of an African woman, and here Marlow shows his collusion in the accountant's masculinism. Ideologies of empire and gender both operate in his account of this episode, but only the first is mocked; hence a gap opens in the text between the imperial oppression visible to Marlow when it sends native *men* to the grove of death, and the masculine oppression that remains invisible to him because it seems "natural" that a native woman should do a white man's laundry. In this gap the laundress becomes vividly present by virtue of her absence; here she, rather than Marlow or the accountant, might speak of her "distaste for the work."

*   *   *

That the laundress is silenced indicates Marlow's power, as the masculine narrator of *his* story, to conceal not only her story but those of the other silent women in *Heart of Darkness*. If we turn to his representation of the savage woman, we can see the purposes this silencing serves. Like Kurtz's eloquence in support of imperialism, Marlow's narrative is a mystification of power relations that shows that "[men] want to keep woman in the place of mystery, consign her to mystery, as they say 'keep her in her place, keep her at a distance' " (Cixous 49). As Marlow uses the savage woman to symbolize the enigma of the jungle, his ideological project is to distance and control both mysteries.

The savage woman who appears as Kurtz is being carried onto Marlow's ship is "the nexus where the discourses of imperialism and patriarchy coincide" (Mongia 146–47). As Marlow constructs her, she is the dark continent of both the African jungle and female sexuality. "A wild and gorgeous apparition of a woman" (p. 76), she is "savage and superb, wild-eyed and magnificent," "ominous and stately." When she appears,

> the immense wilderness, the colossal body of the fecund and mysterious life seemed to look at her, pensive, as though it had been looking at the image of its own tenebrous and passionate soul. (p. 76)

In this symbology Marlow distances the woman's body by conflating her with the jungle: as the jungle takes on a body, the woman becomes the "image" of the jungle's "soul."[2] By symbolizing the woman and personifying the jungle, Marlow works to contain and control both; thus stylized and immobilized, a complex of potentially dangerous forces becomes "pensive" and nonthreatening.

Once the woman moves toward the ship, however, those forces again become threatening, and Marlow again works to contain them. As she approaches the ship, "looking at us . . . like the wilderness itself" (p. 77) and "brooding over an inscrutable purpose," she represents for Marlow a menacing jungle sexuality. He has already described the jungle's absorption of Kurtz as sexual cannibalism: "it had taken him,

---

[2]In criticism as well as literature, such symbolizing is "particularly sinister" for women (Robinson 7); Jungian "pronouncements about The Masculine and The Feminine," for example, tend to perpetuate "specious generalizations" about both men's and women's psyches. Although Sullivan's reading of the story is Jungian, she points to the ideological uses of such generalizations when she notes that the savage woman, like the Intended, is "recognized, suppressed and rejected" in the service of masculinist and imperialist aims (79).

loved him, embraced him, got into his veins, consumed his flesh"
(p. 64). As that earlier moment had "feminize[d] the relation between
the adventurer and topography" (Mongia 139), so too does the savage
woman's "brooding" approach to the ship. She throws up her arms "as
though in an uncontrollable desire to touch the sky" (p. 77), and at this
moment shadows of the jungle "gather the steamer into a shadowy
embrace." In this gesture of appropriation by the woman/jungle, "the
boundaries of masculinity — knowledge, restraint, and order — are
under siege" (Mongia 141). Even if the content of her gesture is not
sexuality but the "wild sorrow" and "dumb pain" Marlow sees in her
face, this too threatens the boundaries of masculine restraint, for Marlow has already (over)responded to a similar loss of Kurtz. In his earlier
fear that Kurtz was dead, the "startling extravagance" of his sorrow was
"even such as I had noticed in the howling sorrow of these savages"
(p. 63). And his backpedaling from grief in that scene indicated his
masculine view that "unrestrained grief should be left to the natives and
the women" (Staten 723). Faced in the savage woman with not only
the threat of sexuality but also the allure of grief, Marlow contains both
with his stylized representation of a woman reaching for the sky, the
unattainable.

As Marlow turns the savage woman's body into a symbol of the
jungle, this process serves both masculinist and imperialist ends. It is
an effort to defuse and control the power and sexuality both of the
woman who "tread[s] the earth proudly" (p. 76) and of that "fecund"
earth itself. As an ideology of gender works to distance and conquer
the savage woman's body, so an ideology of empire works to distance
and conquer the mysterious life of the jungle. And Marlow successfully
silences the savage woman; like the native laundress, she does not speak
in his narrative. Like the laundress's silence, however, this one creates a
gap in the text, a sign of ideological stress that makes visible the fragility
of such containment. Such a gap thus reveals "the truth which ideology
represses, its own existence as ideology itself" (Belsey 63).

Further instances of ideology *as* ideology appear when we re-vision
Marlow's representation of the savage woman's adornments. After
detailing the "barbarous ornaments" she wears (p. 76), he concludes
that "[s]he must have had the value of several elephant tusks on her."
The woman's body is here commodified, to become merely the thing
on which "value" is displayed. Although Marlow notes that her hair is
shaped like a helmet and that she wears leggings and gauntlets, he dismisses these martial signs as "charms" that have meaning only as proto-
ivory. And although he relays the Russian's report that the woman

"'talk[s] like a fury'" (p. 77), he does not record her speech. If we reverse Marlow's emphasis and concentrate on the woman's military ornaments and vehement talk, they suggest that she might not be the conventionally feminine (sexually and emotionally dependent on Kurtz) or conventionally native (economically dependent on the ivory trade) figure constructed by Marlow's ideological narrative. She might be a woman warrior whose gestures and speech, remaining unreadable, give her the power that her "*formidable* silence" indicates (emphasis added). If such an interpretation demystifies Marlow's, however, it also runs the risk of forgetting that the savage woman is finally "an inaccessible blankness circumscribed by an interpretable text" (Spivak 264). In other words, to presume to speak for an Other is to follow Marlow's strategy, to produce a representation as ideologically grounded as his.

I have already noted the utility of men's efforts to keep women a mystery, to "'keep her in her place, keep her at a distance'" (Cixous 49). Marlow's third such effort to mask his collusion in imperialism appears in his distancing representation of the two women he encounters at the Company's Brussels office. The mystery of these two women is overdetermined by Marlow's relentless symbolizing. His insistence on their knitting links them with the three Fates of Greek and Roman mythology, who weave the thread of life and thus control human destiny. Furthermore, when Marlow describes the elder knitter "pilot[ing]" (p. 25) young men into the Company, the verb connects her with Charon, the pilot who ferries the dead across the Styx into Hades. These representations are part of the narrative retrospection intended to protect Marlow from the realization his narrative revives, that in this office he had contracted himself to the Company and to its imperialist "conspiracy." Hence he displaces the responsibility for his decision onto the younger woman "introducing, introducing continuously [young men] to the unknown," and onto the elder woman, "uncanny and fateful" in her "unconcerned wisdom." Marlow crossed the boundary between the self and the other, between individual adventure and Company conspiracy, once he stepped through the office door; hence he attempts to distance the troubling aspects of his decision behind the apparently solid boundary of gender difference.

Yet this maneuver is only momentarily successful, for the elder woman returns into Marlow's narrative. As he begins his journey into the jungle to retrieve Kurtz, this woman "obtruded herself upon my memory" (p. 80), breached the boundary established by his displacement. Her reappearance serves as a double signal that Marlow's effort to distance the Other — the women of the Company and the troubling imperialism he transferred to them — was bound to fail. When the elder Company woman intrudes in the shape of "the knitting old woman with the cat," the uneasiness Marlow displaced now returns with greater strength for its repression. This silent figure of civilized domesticity only *seems* incongruous in the jungle; her reappearance dramatizes the futility of Marlow's attempt to separate the realm of domesticity from that of colonial adventure, the feminine sphere from the masculine.

Like the ideology of imperialism, the ideology of separate, gendered spheres was under pressure in the late nineteenth century. Single and financially independent, the New Woman was becoming visible in the stores, offices, and streets of Europe and even in the dark continent; Mary Kingsley was one of several women travelers in Africa. Yet *Heart of Darkness* clings to the older ideology of separate spheres, in an effort to resolve the contradictions of Marlow's position vis-à-vis Kurtz. Marlow's experience of Kurtz places him in a "feminine predicament," a situation of perceived physical and/or social powerlessness (Klein 102–06). On the one hand, Marlow is seduced by the "unbounded power of eloquence" in Kurtz's imperialist ideology; on the other hand, he is also drawn to Kurtz's final summation, " 'The horror! The horror!' " (p. 85), because it too is "the expression of some sort of belief" (p. 86). Marlow attempts to escape this feminine predicament by his representations of his aunt and the Intended. Through them he constructs a feminine world of "idea"-belief to stand alongside the masculine world of Kurtz's "horror"-belief; located in separate spheres, these contradictory ideologies can coexist. And so that Marlow can stabilize his masculinity by confronting feminine ideologies of empire, the two European women are not silenced. By mocking the lack of imperial experience that their words convey, he can represent his own experience as a manly encounter with truth; through their echoes of the case Kurtz made for imperialism, he can reverse the powerlessness evinced in his response to Kurtz's eloquence. Marlow's construction of these women dramatizes the point of his story, its manful effort to shore up an ideology of imperialism with an ideology of separate spheres.

The belief that will later be grounded in the aunt and the Intended first emerges in Marlow's preface to his narrative.

> The conquest of the earth, which mostly means the taking it away from those who have a different complexion or slightly flatter noses than ourselves, is not a pretty thing when you look into it

too much. What redeems it is the idea only . . . not a sentimental pretence but an idea, and an unselfish belief in the idea —
something you can set up, and bow down before, and offer a
sacrifice to. . . . (p. 21)

Although this credo precedes the story Marlow tells his hearers, it is
important to remember that he has already "looked into" such a "conquest of the earth." Recuperating that experience requires an ideology
whereby an ugly exercise of power ("Exterminate all the brutes!") is
redeemed by an idea. Like his irony, Marlow's belief in the "idea"
behind imperialism is a retrospective attempt to mask his complicity
in the Company's imperialism. But Marlow's statement displays all the
contradictions he intends it to suppress: between the reality and the
idea of conquest, between an idea and a "sentimental pretence" (how
would one tell the difference?), between an "unselfish belief" and a
self-serving hypocrisy. After these framing sentences, Marlow "broke
off" before beginning his tale; this gap reveals the contradiction between
his need for an imperialist "idea" and his experience of the horror, a
contradiction he attempts to resolve by constructing the feminine
sphere of his aunt and the Intended.

Marlow's representations of his aunt perform several functions in
his narrative. He first mentions her in connection with his difficulties in
getting hired by the Company. After his own efforts and those of his
male relatives fail, his aunt, who believes in "the glorious idea" behind
the Company (p. 23), successfully intercedes for him. His condescend-
ing construction of her, as "a dear enthusiastic soul" who was "determined to make no end of fuss," intends to disguise the failure of his
own "fuss." Marlow's next comment on this transaction displays a
"class-based ambivalence" (Glenn 248) toward "bourgeois women col-
laborating in and acting as apologists for" ventures like the Company.
When he admits that "would you believe it? — I tried the women.
I, Charlie Marlow, set the women to work — to get a job. Heavens!"
(p. 23), his jocularity implies that no woman could have influence in
such masculine matters, and thus that the world of experience is and
should be a man's world.

During Marlow's farewell visit to his aunt, he uses her feminine lack
of experience and debased imperialist rhetoric to construct the "sentimental pretence" that can be distinguished from "an idea" and then
rejected. Like her room, which "most soothingly looked just as you
would expect a lady's drawing-room to look" (p. 26), her "emissary of
light" school of imperialism is represented as bourgeois and feminine.

She quotes Scripture "brightly" (in other words, she is uncritically devout); she is "carried off her feet" by "rot" and "humbug" (unlike Marlow, who knows a sentimental pretence when he sees one). And her "glorious idea" of his work — " 'weaning those ignorant millions from their horrid ways' " — is womanly idealism, whereas his response — "the Company was run for profit" — is manly realism.

But his aunt's belief in "weaning those ignorant millions" is not unambiguously feminine: it is a variant of the masculine imperialism in Kurtz's "exert[ing] a power for good practically unbounded." Why, then, do these words from Kurtz have "the unbounded power of eloquence" for Marlow, at least initially, whereas he dismisses his aunt's similar vision out of hand? To answer this question, we must examine a central passage in which Marlow equates truth with the masculine recognition of "fact." Commenting on one of his aunt's "bright" remarks, Marlow says:

> It's queer how out of touch with truth women are. They live in a world of their own, and there had never been anything like it, and never can be. It is too beautiful altogether, and if they were to set it up it would go to pieces before the first sunset. Some confounded fact we men have been living contentedly with ever since the day of creation would start up and knock the whole thing over. (p. 27)

Here it is assumed ("It's queer" — that is, strange but true) that all women (extrapolating from one woman) are out of touch with "truth," which is identified with masculine "fact." It follows that the nonfactual "world of their own" that women inhabit is "too beautiful" to exist; in the man's world "there had never been anything like it, and never can be." It also follows that "truth" can be experienced only in the masculine sphere. This is the burden of Marlow's description of native rites and his response to them. These rites display "truth stripped of its cloak" (p. 51); if they "were man enough," Marlow tells his male hearers, they would admit their response to such truth, as he did; in fact, to "meet that truth with his own true stuff" one must be "as much of a man" as the natives.

To this exclusively masculine sphere of experience and truth, Marlow then adds the capacity for belief. He first defines a man's "true stuff" as "inborn strength" (p. 51); he then distinguishes this inborn strength from "principles," which are mere "acquisitions, clothes, pretty rags"; and he concludes that true manly stuff is finally "a deliberate belief." By equating "a man's true stuff" with both his "inborn strength" and his "deliberate belief," Marlow constructs stuff/strength/ belief as "inborn" in men, natural to them. Even though a man's belief is acquired ("deliberate"), it is made to seem different in kind from principles, that "acquisition" with a whiff of the feminine ("pretty rags"). Belief, then, becomes a fully masculine activity: it inheres naturally in men and surfaces through manly experience. While his aunt is not "man enough" to experience savagery so as to come to "truth" and "deliberate belief," both Kurtz and Marlow are. The aunt's feminine version of imperialism is thus a "sentimental pretence" because, unlike Kurtz's "idea," it is not — and by definition cannot be — validated by experience. Through this process of mystification, Marlow has produced an ideological defense of masculine belief. Filtered through his manly experience of truth, belief in the imperialist "idea" can now be used to redeem a reality that is "not pretty."

To fully recuperate Kurtzian imperialism from the taint of a "too beautiful" feminine ideology, however, Marlow must cope with a "confounded fact": that Kurtz's own final recognition of "the horror" belies the "idea" that redeems conquest. As Marlow puts this difficulty, "No eloquence could have been so withering to one's belief in mankind as his final burst of sincerity" (p. 82). Here the contradiction between the eloquence of imperialism and the brutality of its exercise, which Marlow had earlier read in Kurtz's report, directly enters his experience. Kurtz's initial "eloquence" now stands in stark contrast to his final "sincerity," and this sincerity threatens to wither the "belief in mankind" that legitimates imperialism for Marlow. If this new voice were to drown out Kurtz's earlier eloquence, then belief in the "idea" would become impossible and Marlow's experience would become what he fears it to be: "one immense jabber . . . without any kind of sense." And even as Marlow attempts to belittle Kurtz as "very little more than a voice," he remains troubled by "voices, voices — even the girl herself — now — " (p. 63).

The placing of this first mention of Kurtz's Intended indicates the uses Marlow will make of her. The reference marks a "long" silence in Marlow's narrative, a gap after he reveals his fear of "jabber" and before he states the "deliberate belief" he has now invested in the Intended.

> Oh, she is out of it — completely. They — the women I mean — are out of it — should be out of it. We must help them to stay in that beautiful world of their own, lest ours gets worse. Oh, she had to be out of it. (p. 63)

That an ideology of separate spheres enables masculine imperialism could hardly be more clearly stated. Where Marlow had earlier dismissed this woman's world as "too beautiful altogether," its ideality is now essential: carefully kept "out of it," separated from "our" world of experience, the feminine sphere of "idea" will prevent the masculine sphere of "fact" from deteriorating. Marlow's speech thus suggests how "the masculine production of feminine identity works in the interests of the dominant ideology" (London 238). Specifically, it suggests his need to construct a "beautiful world" around the Intended. There he can order the cacophony of "voices, voices" — Kurtz's "eloquence," his "sincerity," and the Intended's "echo of his magnificent eloquence" (p. 87) — by setting her speech off against the others. And there he can contain Kurtzian imperialism, by embodying in the Intended an "unselfish belief" in the now purified "idea."

Like all the women in this story, then, the Intended is Marlow's construct. As he had earlier commodified the savage woman's body, he now reduces the Intended to a "pure brow" (p. 90) "illumined by the unextinguishable light of belief and love" (p. 91). He locates in her a "beautiful generosity" (p. 92) and "a mature capacity for fidelity, for belief, for suffering" (p. 90) — in short, the "unselfish belief" he requires. Most important, her faith in the power of Kurtzian eloquence enables Marlow to contain and transform that eloquence. "Bowing [his] head before the faith that was in her, before that great and saving illusion" (p. 92), Marlow removes the threat of eloquence from the sphere of his own experience and translates it into her "out of it" world. A faith in Kurtz's eloquence would have been a delusion in the man's sphere where it was contradicted by Kurtz's belief in the horror. In the Intended's feminine sphere, however, it becomes the "great and saving illusion" with which Marlow orders the "jabber" that would otherwise destroy his belief in the "idea." As Marlow bows before her faith, then, he fulfills his ideological project of creating the redeeming idea — "something you can set up, and bow down before, and offer a sacrifice to" (p. 21). While he appears to be bowing to *her*, he is in fact idolizing his own "idea" — the "something" he has "set up" in her.

To complete his posture of belief, however, Marlow must "offer a sacrifice," and who better than the Intended with her "capacity for suffering"? Hence his lie, telling her that Kurtz's last words were her name. It is true that Marlow feels he has sacrificed *himself*: even though he "hate[s], detest[s], and can't bear a lie" (p. 42), he tells this one out of his "infinite pity" for her suffering (p. 93). But if Marlow conceives himself as a "heroic deliverer" (Straus 129) rescuing the Intended from grief, with his "chivalric" lie he is in fact "underscoring an ideology that defines a protective lie as a moral act" when performed by a man. And surely the particular lie Marlow chooses is meant to satisfy his "dull anger" (p. 93) with the Intended's naïveté and her insistence that he give her something "to live with." He and his audience — and the reader — know that by substituting the Intended's name for "the horror" he equates the two; her ignorance of this equation becomes a punishing humiliation. Further intimations of assault are the setting — a "place of cruel and absurd mysteries" (p. 91) — and her responding to the lie with "an exulting and terrible cry" (p. 93) of "unspeakable pain" and "inconceivable triumph." With these four obfuscatory adjectives, Marlow suggests that he has sacrificed the Intended to her own "saving illusion," a suggestion that justifies his act: the pain he intended to inflict is validated (like the rape victim, she asked for it) by the accompanying triumph (and she liked it).[3]

Marlow's lie also functions to stabilize both the feminine sphere of "saving illusion" and the masculine sphere of "confounded fact." The lie protects the "beautiful world" of women that now enshrines his "deliberate belief"; because Marlow *knows* it is a lie, however, the world in which men experience the truth of horror continues to stand. Thus "Marlow brings truth to men by . . . bringing falsehood to women" (Straus 130). When he states that telling the Intended the truth would have been "too dark altogether" (p. 93), the echo of "too beautiful altogether" reverberates with this defensive rationale for cordoning off the woman's world. By creating an alternative women's sphere "lest ours gets worse," men can continue to confront their "own true stuff" in their world. And the violence with which Marlow's lie sacrifices the Intended to this masculine world indicates the strength of its homosocial bonds. As he successfully competes with the Intended for "the status of Kurtz's most enduring conquest" (London 245), the pain he inflicts on her dramatizes how women are used "to deny, distort, and censor men's passionate love for one another" (Straus 134). And not only women: Marlow's description of his helmsman's death becomes "a

---

[3]Staten (736–39) argues that Marlow functions as Kurtz's emissary, thereby fulfilling the latter's sadistic project of forcing the Intended into the total mourning that will confirm his existence. While Staten gives full value to the Intended's cry, his reading nonetheless shares in Marlow's commodification of her: Staten's tendency to reduce her to a cry is not unlike Marlow's tendency to reduce her to a function of himself.

supreme moment of male bonding" with his hearers (London 248), and his similar reductions of native men to conduits of narrative "delineate the common ground Marlow and his audience occupy" as white men (London 249). Thus, although Marlow consistently browbeats and insults his audience — and, by extension, Conrad's — finally the white bourgeois male reader is included in Marlow's "voice of cultural authority." With all these techniques of "artistic force" (Fogel 20) — the lie to the Intended, Marlow's offhand uses of the word "nigger," Conrad's "insistent, domineering" style (Fogel 21) — *Heart of Darkness* demonstrates the brutality in discourses of empire and gender.

I conclude with the issues raised by Conrad's style, for they are useful entries into recent critical re-visions of *Heart of Darkness*'s ideological discourses. In 1978, the Nigerian novelist Chinua Achebe termed Conrad "a bloody racist" (9), in part because of the stylistic "trickery" (4) with which he purported to describe Africa and Africans but in fact dehumanized them. Like Patrick Brantlinger's essay in this volume, essays by Benita Parry, Sandya Shetty, and Reynold Humphries analyze the extent to which Conrad's imperialist discourse "functions to hide the expansionism" of the Western bourgeoisie (Humphries 114) and to "naturalize its presence in the Third World." For André Brink, Conrad's stylistic obfuscations suggest that a "ready-made, conventional, eurocentric, male language" (4) is inadequate to "give literary substance to Africa"; as this language breaks down into jabber, "Woman" (5) becomes "the ground of meaning" in *Heart of Darkness*. Brink here replicates Conrad's gender ideology; in contrast, one feminist reading attributes the novel's "density and inaccessibility" not to the breakdown of its masculine language but to its "extremely masculine historical referentiality" (Straus 124), and another analyzes how the text enacts "the construction of the white male speaking subject as narrative authority" (London 239). Where John McClure and Patrick Parrinder analyze Conrad's dependence on conventions of the popular fiction that glorified imperial adventure, Padmini Mongia focuses on how such conventions construct African and European women as sites where anxieties of gender as well as empire are played out. In my feminist reading of *Heart of Darkness*, I too have tried to show the utility for imperialist ideology of a gender ideology that constructs a feminine sphere as "too beautiful altogether."

WORKS CITED

Achebe, Chinua. "An Image of Africa." *Research in African Literature* 9.1 (Spring 1978): 1–15.

Barrett, Michèle. "Ideology and the Cultural Production of Gender." *Feminist Criticism and Social Change: Sex, Class and Race in Literature and Culture.* Ed. Judith Newton and Deborah Rosenfelt. New York: Methuen, 1985. 65–85.

Belsey, Catherine. *Critical Practice.* London: Methuen, 1980.

Bongie, Chris. "Exotic Nostalgia: Conrad and the New Imperialism." *Macropolitics of Nineteenth-Century Literature: Nationalism, Exoticism, Imperialism.* Ed. Jonathan Arac and Harriet Ritvo. Philadelphia: U of Pennsylvania P, 1991. 268–85.

Brink, André. "Woman and Language in Darkest Africa: The Quest for Articulation in Two Postcolonial Novels." *Literator* 13.1 (Apr. 1992): 1–14.

Cixous, Hélène. "Castration or Decapitation?" Trans. Annette Kuhn. *Signs* 7 (1981): 41–55.

During, Simon. "Postmodernism or Post-Colonialism Today." *Textual Practice* 1.1 (Spring 1987): 32–47.

Fogel, Aaron. *Coercion to Speak: Conrad's Poetics of Dialogue.* Cambridge: Harvard UP, 1985. Print.

Glenn, Ian. "Conrad's *Heart of Darkness*: A Sociological Reading." *Literature and History* 13.2 (Autumn 1987): 238–56.

Humphries, Reynold. "The Discourse of Colonialism: Its Meaning and Relevance for Conrad's Fiction." *Conradiana* 21.2 (Summer 1989): 107–33.

Jehlen, Myra. "Archimedes and the Paradox of Feminist Criticism." *Feminist Theory: A Critique of Ideology.* Ed. Nannerl O. Keohane et al. Chicago: U of Chicago P, 1972. 189–215.

Klein, Karen. "The Feminine Predicament in Conrad's *Nostromo*." *Brandeis Essays in Literature.* Ed. John Hazel Smith. Waltham: Brandeis University English and American Literature Department, 1983. 101–16.

London, Bette. "Reading Race and Gender in Conrad's Dark Continent." *Criticism* 31.3 (Summer 1989): 235–52.

McClure, John A. "Late Imperial Romance." *Raritan* 10.4 (Spring 1991): 111–30.

Mongia, Padmini. "Empire, Narrative, and the Feminine in *Lord Jim* and *Heart of Darkness*." *Contexts for Conrad.* Ed. Keith Carabine et al. Boulder: East European Monographs, 1993. 135–50.

Parrinder, Patrick. "*Heart of Darkness*: Geography as Apocalypse." *Fin de Siècle/Fin du Globe: Fears and Fantasies of the Late Nineteenth Century*. Ed. John Stokes. Houndmills: Macmillan, 1992. 85–102.

Parry, Benita. *Conrad and Imperialism: Ideological Boundaries and Visionary Frontiers*. London: Macmillan, 1983.

Rich, Adrienne. "When We Dead Awaken: Writing as Re-Vision." *On Lies, Secrets and Silence: Selected Prose, 1966–1978*. New York: Norton, 1979. 33–49.

Robinson, Lillian S. *Sex, Class, and Culture*. New York: Methuen, 1978.

Shetty, Sandya. "*Heart of Darkness*: Out of Africa Some New Thing Rarely Comes." *Journal of Modern Literature* 15.4 (Spring 1989): 461–74.

Spivak, Gayatri Chakravorty. "Three Women's Texts and a Critique of Imperialism." *"Race," Writing, and Difference*. Ed. Henry Louis Gates, Jr. Chicago: U of Chicago P, 1985. 262–80.

Staten, Henry. "Conrad's Mortal Word." *Critical Inquiry* 12.4 (1986): 720–40.

Straus, Nina Pelikan. "The Exclusion of the Intended from Secret Sharing in Conrad's *Heart of Darkness*." *Novel: A Forum on Fiction* 20 (1987): 123–37.

Sullivan, Zohreh T. "Enclosure, Darkness, and the Body: Conrad's Landscape." *Centennial Review* 25 (1981): 59–79.

Williams, Raymond. *Marxism and Literature*. Oxford: Oxford UP, 1978.

Deconstruction
and
Heart of Darkness

WHAT IS DECONSTRUCTION?

Deconstruction has a reputation for being the most complex and forbidding of contemporary critical approaches to literature, but in fact almost all of us have, at one time, either deconstructed a text or badly wanted to deconstruct one. Sometimes when we hear a lecturer effectively marshal evidence to show that a book means primarily one thing, we long to interrupt and ask what he or she would make of other, conveniently overlooked passages that seem to contradict the lecturer's thesis. Sometimes, after reading a provocative critical article that *almost* convinces us that a familiar work means the opposite of what we assumed it meant, we may wish to make an equally convincing case for our former reading of the text. We may not think that the poem or novel in question better supports our interpretation, but we may recognize that the text can be used to support *both* readings. And sometimes we simply want to make that point: texts can be used to support seemingly irreconcilable positions.

To reach this conclusion is to feel the deconstructive itch. J. Hillis Miller, the preeminent American deconstructor, puts it this way: "Deconstruction is not a dismantling of the structure of a text, but a demonstration that it has already dismantled itself. Its apparently solid ground is no rock but thin air" ("Stevens' Rock" 341). To deconstruct a text isn't to show that all the high old themes aren't there to be found in it. Rather, it is to show that a text — not unlike DNA with its double helix — can have intertwined, opposite "discourses" — strands of narrative, threads of meaning.

Ultimately, of course, deconstruction refers to a larger and more complex enterprise than the practice of demonstrating that a text can have contradictory meanings. The term refers to a way of reading texts practiced by critics who have been influenced by the writings of the French philosopher Jacques Derrida. It is important to gain some understanding of Derrida's project and of the historical backgrounds of his work before reading the deconstruction that follows, let alone attempting to deconstruct a text.

Derrida, a philosopher of language who coined the term *deconstruction*, argues that we tend to think and express our thoughts in terms of opposites. Something is black but not white, masculine and therefore not feminine, a cause rather than an effect, and so forth. These mutually exclusive pairs or dichotomies are too numerous to list but would include beginning/end, conscious/unconscious, presence/absence, and speech/writing. If we think hard about these dichotomies, Derrida suggests, we will realize that they are not simply oppositions; they are also hierarchies in miniature. In other words, they contain one term that our culture views as being superior and one term viewed as negative or inferior. Sometimes the superior term seems only subtly superior (*speech, cause*), but at other times we know immediately which term is culturally preferable (*presence, beginning*, and *consciousness* are easy choices). But the hierarchy always exists.

Of particular interest to Derrida, perhaps because it involves the language in which all the other dichotomies are expressed, is the hierarchical opposition "speech/writing." Derrida argues that the "privileging" of speech, that is, the tendency to regard speech in positive terms and writing in negative terms, cannot be disentangled from the privileging of presence. (Postcards are written by absent friends; we read Plato because he cannot speak from beyond the grave.) Furthermore, according to Derrida, the tendency to privilege both speech and presence is part of the Western tradition of *logocentrism*, the belief that in some ideal beginning were creative *spoken* words, such as "Let there be light," spoken by an ideal, *present* God.[1] According to logocentric

---

[1]Derrida sometimes uses the word *phallogocentrism* to indicate that there is "a certain indissociability" between logocentrism and the "phallocentrism" (Derrida, *Acts* 57) of a culture whose God created light, the world, and man before creating woman — from Adam's rib. "Phallocentrism" is another name for patriarchy. The role that deconstruction has played in feminist analysis will be discussed later.

tradition, these words can now be represented only in unoriginal speech or writing (such as the written phrase in quotation marks above). Derrida doesn't seek to reverse the hierarchized opposition between speech and writing, or presence and absence, or early and late, for to do so would be to fall into a trap of perpetuating the same forms of thought and expression that he seeks to deconstruct. Rather, his goal is to erase the boundary between oppositions such as speech and writing, and to do so in such a way as to throw the order and values implied by the opposition into question.

Returning to the theories of Ferdinand de Saussure, who invented the modern science of linguistics, Derrida reminds us that the association of speech with present, obvious, and ideal meaning — and writing with absent, merely pictured, and therefore less reliable meaning — is suspect, to say the least. As Saussure demonstrated, words are *not* the things they name and, indeed, they are only arbitrarily associated with those things. A word, like any sign, is what Derrida has called a "deferred presence"; that is to say, "the signified concept is never present in itself," and "every concept is necessarily . . . inscribed in a chain or system, within which it refers to another and to other concepts" ("Différance" 138, 140). Neither spoken nor written words have present, positive, identifiable attributes themselves. They have meaning only by virtue of their difference from other words (*red, read, reed*) and, at the same time, their contextual relationship to those words. Take *read* as an example. To know whether it is the present or past tense of the verb — whether it rhymes with *red* or *reed* — we need to see it in relation to some other words (for example, *yesterday*).

Because the meanings of words lie in the differences between them and in the differences between them and the things they name, Derrida suggests that all language is constituted by *différance*, a word he has coined that puns on two French words meaning "to differ" and "to defer": words are the deferred presences of the things they "mean," and their meaning is grounded in difference. Derrida, by the way, changes the *e* in the French word *différence* to an *a* in his neologism *différance*; the change, which can be seen in writing but cannot be heard in spoken French, is itself a playful, witty challenge to the notion that writing is inferior or "fallen" speech.

In *Dissemination* (1972) and *De la grammatologie* [*Of Grammatology*] (1967), Derrida begins to redefine writing by deconstructing some old definitions. In *Dissemination*, he traces logocentrism back to Plato, who in the *Phaedrus* has Socrates condemn writing and who, in all the great dialogues, powerfully postulates that metaphysical longing for origins and ideals that permeates Western thought. "What Derrida does in his reading of Plato," Barbara Johnson points out in her translator's introduction to *Dissemination*, "is to unfold dimensions of Plato's *text* that work against the grain of (Plato's own) Platonism" (xxiv). Remember: that is what deconstruction does, according to Miller; it shows a text dismantling itself.

In *Of Grammatology*, Derrida turns to the *Confessions* of Jean-Jacques Rousseau and exposes a grain running against the grain. Rousseau — who has often been seen as another great Western idealist and believer in innocent, noble origins — on one hand condemned writing as mere representation, a corruption of the more natural, childlike, direct, and therefore undevious speech. On the other hand, Rousseau acknowledged his own tendency to lose self-presence and blurt out exactly the wrong thing in public. He confesses that, by writing at a distance from his audience, he often expressed himself better: "If I were present, one would never know what I was worth," Rousseau admitted (Derrida, *Of Grammatology* 142). Thus, Derrida shows that one strand of Rousseau's discourse made writing seem a secondary, even treacherous supplement, while another made it seem necessary to communication.

Have Derrida's deconstructions of *Confessions* and the *Phaedrus* explained these texts, interpreted them, opened them up and shown us what they mean? Not in any traditional sense. Derrida would say that anyone attempting to find a single, homogeneous or universal meaning in a text is simply imprisoned by the structure of thought that would oppose two readings and declare one to be right and not wrong, correct rather than incorrect. In fact, any work of literature that we interpret defies the laws of Western logic, the laws of opposition and noncontradiction. From deconstruction's point of view, texts don't say "A and not B." They say "A and not-A." "Instead of a simple 'either/or' structure," Johnson explains, "deconstruction attempts to elaborate a discourse that says *neither* 'either/or' *nor* 'both/and' nor even 'neither/nor,' while at the same time not totally abandoning these logics either. The word deconstruction is meant to undermine the either/or logic of the opposition 'construction/destruction.' Deconstruction is both, it is neither, and it reveals the way in which both construction and destruction are themselves not what they appear to be" (Johnson, *World* 12–13).

Although its ultimate aim may be to criticize Western idealism and logic, deconstruction began as a response to structuralism and to formalism, another structure-oriented theory of reading. Using Saussure's theory as Derrida was to do later, European structuralists attempted to create a *semiology*, or science of signs, that would give humankind at once a scientific and a holistic way of studying the world and its human inhabitants. Roland Barthes, a structuralist who later shifted toward poststructuralism, hoped to recover literary language from the isolation in which it had been studied and to show that the laws that govern it govern all signs, from road signs to articles of clothing. Claude Lévi-Strauss, a structural anthropologist who studied everything from village structure to the structure of myths, found in myths what he called *mythemes*, or building blocks, such as basic plot elements. Recognizing that the same mythemes occur in similar myths from different cultures, he suggested that all myths may be elements of one great myth being written by the collective human mind.

Derrida did not believe that structuralists had the concepts that would someday explain the laws governing human signification and thus provide the key to understanding the form and meaning of everything from an African village to Greek myth to Rousseau's *Confessions*. In his view, the scientific search by structural anthropologists for what unifies humankind amounts to a new version of the old search for the lost ideal, whether that ideal be Plato's bright realm of the Idea or the Paradise of Genesis or Rousseau's unspoiled Nature. As for the structuralist belief that texts have "centers" of meaning, in Derrida's view that derives from the logocentric belief that there is a reading of the text that accords with "the book as seen by God." Jonathan Culler, who thus translates a difficult phrase from Derrida's *L'Écriture et la différence* [*Writing and Difference*] (1967) in his book *Structuralist Poetics* (1975), goes on to explain what Derrida objects to in structuralist literary criticism:

> [When] one speaks of the structure of a literary work, one does so from a certain vantage point: one starts with notions of the meaning or effects of a poem and tries to identify the structures responsible for those effects. Possible configurations or patterns that make no contribution are rejected as irrelevant. That is to say, an intuitive understanding of the poem functions as the "centre" . . . : it is both a starting point and a limiting principle. (244)

Deconstruction calls into question assumptions made about literature by formalist, as well as by structuralist, critics. Formalism, or the New Criticism as it was once commonly called, assumes a work of literature to be a freestanding, self-contained object, its meanings found in the complex network of relations that constitute its parts (images, sounds, rhythms, allusions, and so on). To be sure, deconstruction is somewhat like formalism in several ways. Both formalism and deconstruction are text-oriented approaches whose practitioners pay a great deal of attention to rhetorical *tropes* (forms of figurative language including allegory, symbol, metaphor, and metonymy). And formalists, long before deconstructors, discovered counterpatterns of meaning in the same text. Formalists find ambiguity: deconstructors find undecidability. On close inspection, however, the formalist understanding of rhetorical tropes or figures is quite different from that of deconstruction, and undecidability turns out to be different from the ambiguity formalists find in texts.

Formalists, who associated literary with figurative language, made qualitative distinctions between types of figures of speech; for instance, they valued symbols and metaphors over metonyms. (A metonym is a term standing for something with which it is commonly associated or contiguous; we use metonymy when we say we had "the cold plate" for lunch.) From the formalist perspective, metaphors and symbols are less arbitrary figures than metonyms and thus rank more highly in the hierarchy of tropes: a metaphor ("I'm feeling blue") supposedly involves a special, intrinsic, nonarbitrary relationship between its two terms (the feeling of melancholy and the color blue); a symbol ("the river of life") allegedly involves a unique fusion of image and idea.

From the perspective of deconstruction, however, these distinctions are suspect. In "The Rhetoric of Temporality" Paul de Man deconstructs the distinction between symbol and allegory; elsewhere, he, Derrida, and Miller have similarly questioned the metaphor/metonymy distinction, arguing that all figuration is a process of linguistic substitution. In the case of a metaphor (or symbol), they claim, we have forgotten what juxtaposition or contiguity gave rise to the association that now seems mysteriously special. Derrida, in "White Mythology," and de Man, in "Theory of Metaphor in Rousseau's Second Discourse," have also challenged the priority of literal over figurative language, and Miller has gone so far as to deny the validity of the literal/figurative distinction, arguing that all words are figures because all language involves *catachresis*, "the violent, forced, or abusive importation of a term from another realm to name something which has no proper name" (Miller, *Ariadne* 21).

The difference between the formalist concept of literary ambiguity and the deconstructive concept of undecidability is as significant as the gap between formalist and deconstructive understandings of figurative language. Undecidability, as de Man came to define it, is a complex notion easily misunderstood. There is a tendency to assume it refers to readers who, when forced to decide between two or more equally plausible and conflicting readings, throw up their hands and decide that the choice can't be made. But undecidability in fact debunks this whole notion of reading as a decision-making process carried out on texts by readers. To say we are forced to choose or decide, or that we are unable to do so, is to locate the problem of undecidability falsely within ourselves, rather than recognizing that it is an intrinsic feature of the text.

Undecidability is thus different from ambiguity, as understood by formalists. Formalists believed that a complete understanding of a literary work is possible, an understanding in which ambiguities will be resolved objectively by the reader, even if only in the sense that they will be shown to have definite, meaningful functions. Deconstructors do not share that belief. They do not accept the formalist view that a work of literary art is demonstrably unified from beginning to end, in one certain way, or that it is organized around a single center that ultimately can be identified and defined. Neither do they accept the concept of irony as simply saying one thing and meaning another thing that will be understood with certainty by the reader. As a result, deconstructors tend to see texts as more radically heterogeneous than do formalists. The formalist critic ultimately makes sense of ambiguity; undecidability, by contrast, is never reduced, let alone mastered by deconstructive reading, although the incompatible possibilities between which it is impossible to decide can be identified with certainty.

For critics practicing deconstruction, a literary text is neither a sphere with a center nor an unbroken line with a definite beginning and end. In fact, many assumptions about the nature of texts have been put in question by deconstruction, which in Derrida's words "dislocates the borders, the framing of texts, everything which should preserve their immanence and make possible an internal reading or merely reading in the classical sense of the term" ("Some Statements" 86). A text consists of words inscribed in and inextricable from the myriad discourses that inform it; from the point of view of deconstruction, the boundaries between any given text and that larger text we call language are always shifting.

It was that larger text that Derrida was referring to when he made his famous statement *"there is nothing outside the text"* (*Grammatology* 158). To understand what Derrida meant by that statement, consider the following: we know the world through language, and the acts and practices that constitute that "real world" (the events of September 11, 2001, the decision to marry) are inseparable from the discourses out of which they arise and as open to interpretation as any work of literature.

Once we understand deconstruction's view of the literary text — as words that are part of and that resonate with an immense linguistic structure in which we live and move and have our being — we are in a better position to understand why deconstructors reach points in their readings at which they reveal, but cannot decide between, incompatible interpretive possibilities. A text is not a unique, hermetically sealed space. Perpetually open to being seen in the light of new contexts, any given text has the potential to be different each time it is read. Furthermore, as Miller has shown in *Ariadne's Thread: Story Lines* (1992), the various "terms" and "famil[ies] of terms" we use in performing our readings invariably affect the results. Whether we choose to focus on a novel's characters or its realism, for instance, leads us to different views of the same text. "No one thread," Miller asserts, "can be followed to a central point where it provides a means of overseeing, controlling, and understanding the whole" (21).

Complicating matters still further is the fact that the individual words making up narratives — the words out of which we make our mental picture of a character or place — usually have several (and often have conflicting) meanings due to the complex histories of their usage. (If your professor tells the class that you have written a "fulsome report" and you look up the word *fulsome* in a contemporary dictionary, you will learn that it can mean either "elaborate" or "offensive"; if, for some reason, you don't know what *offensive* means, you will find out that it can equally well describe your favorite quarterback and a racist joke.) "Each word," as Miller puts it, "inheres in a labyrinth of branching interverbal relationships"; often there are "forks in the etymological line leading to bifurcated or trifurcated roots." Deconstructors often turn to etymology, not to help them decide whether a statement means this or that, but rather as a way of revealing the coincidence of several meanings in the same text. "The effect of etymological retracing," Miller writes, "is not to ground the work solidly but to render it unstable, equivocal, wavering, groundless" (*Ariadne* 19).

Deconstruction is not really interpretation, the act of choosing between or among possible meanings. Derrida has glossed de Man's statement that "there is no need to deconstruct Rousseau" by saying that "this was another way of saying: there is always already deconstruction, at work *in* works, especially *literary* works. It cannot be applied, after the fact and from outside, as a technical instrument. Texts deconstruct *themselves* by themselves" (Derrida, *Memoires* 123). If deconstruction is not interpretation, then what is it? Deconstruction may be defined as reading, as long as reading is defined as de Man defined it — as a process involving moments of what he called *aporia* or terminal uncertainty, and as an act performed with full knowledge of the fact that all texts are ultimately unreadable (if reading means reducing a text to a single, homogeneous meaning). Miller explains unreadability by saying that although there are moments of great lucidity in reading, each "lucidity will in principle contain its own blind spot requiring a further elucidation and exposure of error, and so on, ad infinitum. . . . One should not underestimate, however, the productive illumination produced as one moves through these various stages of reading" (*Ethics* 42, 44).

Miller's point is important because, in a sense, it deconstructs or erases the boundary between the readings of deconstructors and the interpretations of more traditional critics. It suggests that all kinds of critics have had their moments of lucidity; it also suggests that critics practicing deconstruction know that their *own* insights — even their insights into what is or isn't contradictory, undecidable, or unreadable in a text — are hardly the last word. As Art Berman writes, "In *Blindness and Insight* de Man demonstrates that the apparently well-reasoned arguments of literary critics contain contradiction at their core; yet there is no alternative path to insight. . . . The readers of criticism recognize the blindness of their predecessors, reorganize it, and thereby gain both the insight of the critics and a knowledge of the contradiction that brings forth insight. Each reader, of course, has his own blindness; and the criticism of criticism is not a matter of rectifying someone else's mistakes" (Berman 239–40).

When de Man spoke of the resistance to theory he referred generally to the antitheoretical bias in literary studies. But he might as well have been speaking specifically of the resistance to deconstruction, as expressed not only in academic books and journals but also in popular magazines such as *Newsweek*. Attacks on deconstruction became more common and more personal some four years after de Man's death in 1983. That was the year that a Belgian scholar working on a doctoral thesis discovered ninety-two articles that de Man had written during World War II for the Brussels newspaper *Le Soir*, a widely read French-language daily that had fallen under Nazi control during the German occupation of Belgium. Ultimately, one hundred and seventy articles by de Man were found in *Le Soir*; another ten were discovered in *Het*

Vlaamsche Land, a collaborationist newspaper published in Flemish. These writings, which date from 1941 (when de Man was twenty-one years old), ceased to appear before 1943, by which time it had become clear to most Belgians that Jews were being shipped to death camps such as Auschwitz.

De Man's wartime journalism consists mainly, but not entirely, of inoffensive literary pieces. In one article de Man takes Germany's triumph in World War II as a given, places the German people at the center of Western civilization, and foresees a mystical era involving suffering but also faith, exaltation, and rapture. In another article, entitled "*Les Juifs dans la littérature actuelle*" ["Jews in Present-day Literature"], de Man scoffs at the notion that Jewish writers have significantly influenced the literature of his day and, worse, considers the merits of creating a separate Jewish colony that would be isolated from Europe.

No one who had known de Man since his immigration to the United States in 1948 had found him to be illiberal or anti-Semitic. Furthermore, de Man had spent his career in the United States demystifying or, as he would have said, "debunking" the kind of ideological assumptions (about the relationship between aesthetics and national cultures) that lie behind his most offensive Belgian newspaper writings. The critic who in *The Resistance to Theory* (1986) argued that literature must not become "a substitute for theology, ethics, etc." (de Man 24) had either changed radically since writing of the magical integrity and wholeness of the German nation and its culture or had not deeply believed what he had written as a young journalist.

These points have been made in various ways by de Man's former friends and colleagues. Geoffrey Hartman has said that de Man's later work, the work we associate with deconstruction, "looks like a belated, but still powerful, act of conscience" (26–31). Derrida, who like Hartman is a Jew, has read carefully de Man's wartime discourse, showing it to be "split, disjointed, engaged in incessant conflicts" (Hamacher, Hertz, and Keenan 135). "On the one hand," Derrida finds "*unpardonable*" de Man's suggestion that a separate Jewish colony be set up; "on the other hand," he notes that of the four writers de Man praises in the same article (André Gide, Franz Kafka, D. H. Lawrence, and Ernest Hemingway), not one was German, one (Kafka) *was* Jewish, and all four "represent everything that Nazism . . . would have liked to extirpate from history and the great tradition" (Hamacher, Hertz, and Keenan 145).

While friends asserted that some of de Man's statements were unpardonable, deconstruction's severest critics tried to use a young

man's sometimes deplorable statements as evidence that a whole critical movement was somehow morally as well as intellectually flawed. As
Andrej Warminski summed it up, "the 'discovery' of the 1941–42 writings is being used to perpetuate the old myths about so-called 'deconstruction'" (Hamacher, Hertz, and Keenan 389). Knowing what some
of those myths are — and why, in fact, they *are* myths — aids our
understanding in an indirect, contrapuntal way that is in keeping with
the spirit of deconstruction.

In his book *The Ethics of Reading* (1987), Miller refutes two notions
commonly repeated by deconstruction's detractors. One is the idea that
deconstructors believe a text means nothing in the sense that it means
whatever the playful reader *wants* it to mean. The other is the idea that
deconstruction is "immoral" insofar as it refuses to view literature in
the way it has traditionally been viewed, namely, "as the foundation
and embodiment, the means of preserving and transmitting, the basic
humanistic values of our culture" (9). Responding to the first notion,
Miller points out that neither Derrida nor de Man "has ever asserted
the freedom of the reader to make the text mean anything he or she
wants it to mean. Each has in fact asserted the reverse" (10). As for the
second notion — that deconstructors are guilty of shirking an ethical
responsibility because their purpose is not to (re)discover and (re)assert
the transcendent and timeless values contained in great books — Miller
argues that "this line of thought" rests "on a basic misunderstanding of
the way the ethical moment enters into the act of reading" (9). That
"ethical moment," Miller goes on to argue, "is not a matter of response
to a thematic content asserting this or that idea about morality. It is a
much more fundamental 'I must' responding to the language of literature in itself. . . . Deconstruction is nothing more or less than good
reading as such" (9–10). Reading itself, in other words, is an act that
leads to further ethical acts, decisions, and behaviors in a real world
involving relations to other people and to society at large. For these, the
reader must take responsibility, as for any other ethical act.

A third commonly voiced objection to deconstruction is to its playfulness, to the evident pleasure its practitioners take in teasing out all
the contradictory interpretive possibilities generated by the words in a
text, their complex etymologies and contexts, and their potential to be
read figuratively or even ironically. Certainly, playfulness and pleasure
are aspects of deconstruction. In his book *The Post Card* (1987), Derrida specifically associates deconstruction with pleasure; in an interview
published in a collection of his essays entitled *Acts of Literature* (1992),
he speculates that "it is perhaps this *jouissance* which most irritates the

all-out adversaries of deconstruction" (56). But such adversaries mis-read deconstruction's "*jouissance*," its pleasurable playfulness. Whereas they see it as evidence that deconstructors view texts as tightly enclosed fields on which they can play delightfully useless little word games, Derrida has said that the "subtle and intense pleasure" of deconstruc-tion arises from the "dismantl[ing]" of repressive assumptions, repre-sentations, and ideas — in short, from the "lifting of repression" (*Acts* 56–57). As Gregory S. Jay explains in his book *America the Scrivener: Deconstruction and the Subject of Literary History* (1990), "Deconstruc-tion has been not only a matter of reversing binary oppositions but also a matter of disabling the hierarchy of values they enable and of speculat-ing on alternative modes of knowing and of acting" (xii).

Far from viewing literature as a word-playground, Derrida, in Derek Attridge's words, "emphasizes . . . literature as an institution," one "not given in nature or the brain but brought into being by processes that are social, legal, and political, and that can be mapped historically and geographically" (*Acts* 23). By thus characterizing Derrida's empha-sis, Attridge counters the commonest of the charges that have been leveled at deconstructors, namely, that they divorce literary texts from historical, political, and legal institutions.

In *Memoires for Paul de Man* (1986), Derrida argues that, where history is concerned, "deconstructive discourses" have pointedly and effectively questioned "the classical assurances of history, the genealogi-cal narrative, and periodizations of all sorts" (15) — in other words, the tendency of historians to view the past as the source of (lost) truth and value, to look for explanations in origins, and to view as unified epochs (for example, the Victorian period, 1837–1901) what are in fact com-plex and heterogenous times in history. As for politics, Derrida points out that de Man invariably "says something about institutional struc-tures and the political stakes of hermeneutic conflicts," which is to say that de Man's commentaries acknowledge that conflicting interpreta-tions reflect and are reflected in the politics of institutions (such as the North American university).

In addition to history and politics, the law has been a subject on which deconstruction has had much to say of late. In an essay on Franz Kafka's story "Before the Law," Derrida has shown that for Kafka the law as such exists but can never be confronted by those who would do so and fulfill its commands. Miller has pointed out that the law "may only be confronted in its delegates or representatives or by its effects on us or others" (*Ethics* 20). What or where, then, is the law itself? The law's presence, Miller suggests, is continually deferred by narrative, that is, writing about or on the law which constantly reinterprets the law in the attempt to reveal what it really is and means. This very act of (re)interpretation, however, serves to "defer" or distance the law even further from the case at hand, since the (re)interpretation takes precedence (and assumes prominence) over the law itself. (As Miller defines it, narrative would include everything from a Victorian novel that promises to reveal moral law to the opinion of a Supreme Court justice regarding the constitutionality of a given action, however different these two documents are in the conventions they follow and the uses to which they are put.) Miller likens the law to a promise, "the validity of [which] does not lie in itself but in its future fulfillment," and to a story "divided against itself" that in the end "leaves its readers . . . still in expectation" (*Ethics* 33).

Because the facts about deconstruction are very different from the myth of its playful irreverence and irrelevance, a number of contemporary thinkers have found it useful to adapt and apply deconstruction in their work. For instance, a deconstructive theology has been developed. Architects have designed and built buildings grounded, as it were, in deconstructive architectural theory. In the area of law, the Critical Legal Studies movement has, in Christopher Norris's words, effectively used "deconstructive thinking" of the kind de Man used in analyzing Rousseau's *Social Contract* "to point up the blind spots, conflicts, and antinomies that plague the discourse of received legal wisdom." Critical legal theorists have debunked "the formalist view of law," that is, the "view which holds law to be a system of neutral precepts and principles," showing instead how the law "gives rise to various disabling contradictions," such as "the problematic distinction between 'private' and 'public' domains." They have turned deconstruction into "a sophisticated means of making the point that all legal discourse is performative in character, i.e., designed to secure assent through its rhetorical power to convince or persuade" (Norris, *Deconstruction and the Interests* 17). Courtroom persuasion, Gerald Lopez has argued in a 1989 article in the *Michigan Law Review*, consists of storytelling as much as argument (Clayton 13).

In the field of literary studies, the influence of deconstruction may be seen in the work of critics ostensibly taking some other, more political approach. Barbara Johnson has put deconstruction to work for the feminist cause. She and Shoshana Felman have argued that chief among those binary oppositions "based on repression of differences *within* entities" is the opposition man/woman (Johnson, *Critical* x). In a reading of the "undecidability" of "femininity" in Balzac's story "The Girl with the Golden Eyes," Felman puts it this way: "the rhetorical hierarchiza-tion of the . . . opposition between the sexes is . . . such that woman's *difference* is suppressed, being totally subsumed by the reference of the feminine to masculine identity" ("Rereading" 25).

Elsewhere, Johnson, Felman, and Gayatri Spivak have combined Derrida's theories with the psychoanalytic theory of Jacques Lacan to analyze the way in which gender and sexuality are ultimately textual, grounded in language and rhetoric. In an essay on Edmund Wilson's reading of Henry James's story *The Turn of the Screw*, Felman has treated sexuality as a form of rhetoric that can be deconstructed, shown to contain contradictions and ambiguities that more traditional readings of sexuality have masked. Gay and lesbian critics have seen the positive implications of this kind of analysis, hence Eve Kosofsky Sedgwick's admission in the early pages of her book *Epistemology of the Closet* (1990): "One main strand of argument in this book is deconstructive, in a fairly specific sense. The analytic move it makes is to demonstrate that categories presented in a culture as symmetrical binary opposi-tions . . . actually subsist in a more unsettled and dynamic tacit rela-tion" (9–10).

In telling "The Story of Deconstruction" in his book on contempo-rary American literature and theory, Jay Clayton assesses the current status of this unique approach. Although he notes how frequently deconstructive critics have been cited for their lack of political engage-ment, he concludes that deconstruction, "a movement accused of for-malism and arid intellectualism, participates in the political turn of con-temporary culture" (34). He suggests that what began as theory in the late 1960s and 1970s has, over time, developed into a method employed by critics taking a wide range of approaches to literature — ethnic, fem-inist, new historicist, Marxist — in addition to critics outside of literary studies per se who are involved in such areas as Critical Legal Studies and Critical Race Theory, which seeks to "sustain a complementary relationship between the deconstructive energies of Critical Legal Stud-ies and the constructive energies of civil rights activism" (58).

Clayton cites the work of Edward Said as a case in point. Through 1975, the year that his *Beginnings: Intention and Method* was published, Said was employing a form of deconstructive criticism that, in Clayton's words, emphasized the "power" of texts "to initiate projects in the real world" (45–46). Said became identified with cultural and postcolonial criticism, however, beginning in 1978 with the publication of his book *Orientalism*, in which he deconstructs the East/West, Orient/Occident opposition. Said argues that Eastern and Middle Eastern peoples have for centuries been stereotyped by the Western discourses of "orientalism," a textuality that in no way reflects the diversity and differences that exist among the peoples it claims to represent. According to Said, that stereotyping not only facilitated the colonization of vast areas of the globe by the so-called West but also still governs, to a great extent, relations with the Arab and the so-called Eastern world. The expansion of Said's field of vision to include not just literary texts but international relations is powerfully indicative of the expanding role that deconstruction currently plays in developing contemporary understandings of politics and culture, as well as in active attempts to intervene in these fields.

The purpose of deconstruction, Miller has written, is to show "the existence in literature of structures of language which contradict the law of non-contradiction." Why find the grain that runs against the grain? To restore what Miller has called "the strangeness of literature," to reveal the "capacity of each work to surprise the reader," to demonstrate that "literature continually exceeds any formula or theory with which the critic is prepared to encompass it" (*Fiction* 5).

In the essay that follows, Miller does all these things, including admitting that his own reading is "exceeded" by *Heart of Darkness.* In the last paragraph of his essay, he confesses his own complicity as a demystifying commentator: "I have attempted," he writes, "to perform an act of generic classification, with all the covert violence and unreason of that act, since no work is wholly commensurate with the boundaries of any genre" (p. 244).

The generic classification Miller refers to is his attempt to classify *Heart of Darkness* as an apocalypse and the apocalypse as an extended parable. (Whereas a parable is a little allegorical story designed to reveal some moral truth, an apocalypse is a highly figurative book of revelation or prophecy.) Of course, as a poststructuralist writing in opposition to the tradition of Western metaphysics, Miller classifies parables and apocalypses as genres that only *seem* to reveal spectral truths, be they the Bright Ideal or the Heart of Darkness. Miller deconstructs Jesus' parable of the sower to show how it is against itself; what its words reveal, Miller contends, is that if you need them then you cannot understand them. Miller also deconstructs Conrad's parable about the two kinds of stories, the parable of the "nut and the moonlit haze." (You will recall the contrast made between the "yarns of seamen . . . , the whole meaning of which" lies inside like a nut in a shell, and Marlow's stories, the meaning of which is said to lie "outside, enveloping the tale," which brings "it out only as a glow brings out a haze" [pp. 19–20].) The narrator's distinction begins to unravel, the more Miller discusses it — and the more he discusses the story Marlow actually tells.

What Miller is really unraveling, of course, is a set of hierarchized, binary oppositions between kinds of texts. By questioning the privileged status of apocalypses, parables, and Marlow's stories, he is erasing numerous boundaries: between the Bible and literature, high forms of narrative and low, and, ultimately, between literature and criticism. (He sets himself and us in the same line of "guilty witnesses" that includes the narrator, whose witness of Marlow perpetuates what Marlow witnessed, and Marlow himself.) And, of course, Miller is deconstructing the metaphor/metonymy opposition. Parables, apocalypses, and allegories are shown to be like metaphors; in strange ways, they can supposedly highlight invisible things with which they are, supposedly, fundamentally and inevitably involved. They supposedly allow us to experience, in the present, such things as Timeless Truth, the End, or the Beginning. In fact, Miller's reading contends, parables and apocalypses cannot reveal metaphysical secrets because, like all signs, they are metonyms, no more intrinsically involved with ultimate truths than the cold plate we order is with the plate, than the mist around the moon is with the sun's reflected light.

Conrad's distinctions, Miller shows, are "made in terms of figures," and even these figures, by an "unavoidable necessity," have to have other, different, supplemental figures to explain them. (Marlow's tales bring out meaning *as* a glow brings out a haze, *in the likeness* of one of these misty halos. . . .) To highlight the figurative nature of language, as Miller does throughout his reading of *Heart of Darkness*, is a typical poststructuralist move. Equally typical, though, is Miller's wondering whether all these figures of figures, supplements to supplements, necessarily carry us further away from Marlow's experience and its meaning. Like the fellows on the *Nellie*, who are said by Marlow to "see more than I could," for "you see me," figures "see" — and show — us more than a sailor like Marlow could possibly have experienced (p. 15).

Implicit in all of Miller's critical procedures, of course, is the poststructuralist assumption that *Heart of Darkness* defies the logic of noncontradiction. Like anything written — and the "apocalypse is after all a written not an oral genre" — *Heart of Darkness* says both "A" and "not-A." Its figures both illuminate their own workings and undermine them; it promises to reveal something and then shows us that that something (pure darkness) is what cannot be seen or shown, except as an absence. An ironic text, it is founded, Miller says, on unreason and is "indeterminate or undecidable in meaning."

The unfolding of indeterminacies requires an unusual style, one that Miller deploys adeptly in *"Heart of Darkness* Revisited." "I begin with three questions," Miller begins. (Are there three? Are they answered or even answerable?) "I shall approach an answer . . . by [a] . . . roundabout way" (p. 231). To write is to defer, just as to read the book of Revelation is to know what has not yet entered human experience. Miller's argument defers many central questions while drawing us close, in the process, to the workings of Conrad's text.

DECONSTRUCTION: A SELECTED BIBLIOGRAPHY

Deconstruction: General Texts

Arac, Jonathan, Wlad Godzich, and Wallace Martin, eds. *The Yale Critics: Deconstruction in America.* Minneapolis: U of Minnesota P, 1983. Print. See especially the essays by Bové, Godzich, Pease, and Corngold.

Bennington, Geoffrey. *Legislations: The Politics of Deconstruction.* London: Verso, 1994. Print.

Bloom, Harold, et al. *Deconstruction and Criticism.* New York: Seabury, 1979. Print. Includes essays by Bloom, Paul de Man, Jacques Derrida, Geoffrey Hartman, and J. Hillis Miller.

Butler, Christopher. *Interpretation, Deconstruction, and Ideology: An Introduction to Some Current Issues in Literary Theory.* Oxford: Oxford UP, 1984. Print.

Caputo, John D., ed./auth. *Deconstruction in a Nutshell: A Conversation with Jacques Derrida.* New York: Fordham UP, 1996. Print.

Caruth, Cathy, and Deborah Esch, eds. *Critical Encounters: Reference and Responsibility in Deconstructive Writing.* New Brunswick: Rutgers UP, 1995. Print.

Clayton, Jay. "The Story of Deconstruction." *The Pleasures of Babel: Contemporary American Literature and Theory.* New York: Oxford UP, 1993. 32–60. Print.

Critchley, Simon. *The Ethics of Deconstruction: Derrida and Levinas.* Oxford, UK, and Cambridge, MA: Blackwell, 1992, 2nd ed. Edinburgh: Edinburgh UP, 1999. Print.

Culler, Jonathan, ed. *Deconstruction: Critical Concepts in Literary and Cultural Studies*. London: Routledge, 2003. Print. Four-volume anthology of essays on deconstruction.

———. *On Deconstruction: Theory and Criticism After Structuralism*. Ithaca: Cornell UP, 1982. Print. The 25th anniversary (2007) edition contains an updated preface and bibliography.

Esch, Deborah. "Deconstruction." *Redrawing the Boundaries: The Transformation of English and American Literary Studies*. Eds. Stephen Greenblatt and Giles Gunn. New York: MLA, 1992. 374–91. Print.

Feminist Studies 14 (1988). Print. Special issue on deconstruction and feminism.

Gasché, Rodolphe. "Deconstruction as Criticism." *Glyph* 6 (1979): 177–215. Print.

Jay, Gregory S. *America the Scrivener: Deconstruction and the Subject of Literary History*. Ithaca: Cornell UP, 1990. Print.

Johnson, Barbara. *The Wake of Deconstruction*. Oxford: Blackwell, 1994. Print.

Kamuf, Peggy. *Book of Addresses*. Stanford: Stanford UP, 2005. Print.

Leitch, Vincent B. *Deconstructive Criticism: An Advanced Introduction*. New York: Columbia UP, 1983. Print.

Loesberg, Jonathan. *Aestheticism and Deconstruction: Pater, Derrida, and de Man*. Princeton: Princeton UP, 1991. Print.

McQuillan, Martin, ed. *Deconstruction: A Reader*. Edinburgh: Edinburgh UP, 2000. Print.

Melville, Stephen. *Philosophy Beside Itself: On Deconstruction and Modernism*. Minneapolis: U of Minnesota P, 1986. Print.

Norris, Christopher. *Deconstruction and the Interests of Theory*. Norman: U of Oklahoma P, 1989. Print.

———. *Deconstruction: Theory and Practice*. London: Methuen, 1982. Rev. ed. London: Routledge, 1991; 3d ed. London: Routledge, 2002. Print. The 1991 edition contains an afterword not in the original edition; the 2002 edition contains a new postscript and recommended reading in addition to the earlier bibliographies.

Norris, Christopher. *Deconstruction and the "Unfinished Project of Modernity."* New York: Routledge, 2000. Print.

Powell, Jim, and Joe Lee. *Deconstruction for Beginners*. Danbury: For Beginners, 2007. Print. An introductory approach using a graphic format.

Rapaport, Herman. *The Theory Mess: Deconstruction in Eclipse*. New York: Columbia UP, 2001. Print.

Royle, Nicholas. *Deconstructions: A User's Guide*. Hampshire: Palgrave, 2000. Print.

Stocker, Barry. *Routledge Philosophy Guidebook to Derrida on Deconstruction*. London: Routledge, 2006. Print.

Taylor, Mark C. *Deconstruction in Context: Literature and Philosophy*. Chicago: U of Chicago Press, 1986. Print.

Willis, Ika, and Martin McQuillan, eds. *The Origins of Deconstruction*. New York: Palgrave Macmillan, 2009. Print.

Wills, David. *Matchbook: Essays in Deconstruction*. Stanford: Stanford UP, 2005. Print.

Zima, Peter. *Deconstruction and Critical Theory*. Trans. Rainer Emig. London: Continuum, 2002. Print.

Works by or about de Man, Derrida, and Miller

Bennington, Geoffrey. *Interrupting Derrida*. London: Routledge, 2000. Print.

———, and Jacques Derrida. *Jacques Derrida*. Chicago: U of Chicago P, 1993. Print.

Cohen, Tom, ed. *Jacques Derrida and the Humanities: A Critical Reader*. Cambridge: Cambridge UP, 2001. Print.

———, et al., eds. *Material Events: Paul de Man and the Afterlife of Theory*. Minneapolis: U of Minnesota P, 2001. Print.

de Man, Paul. *Aesthetic Ideology*. Ed. Andrzej Warminski. Minneapolis: U of Minnesota P, 1996. Print. Published posthumously.

———. *Allegories of Reading*. New Haven: Yale UP, 1979. Print. See especially ch. 1, "Semiology and Rhetoric," and ch. 7, "Metaphor (*Second Discourse*)."

———. *Blindness and Insight*. New York: Oxford UP, 1971. Rev. ed. Minneapolis: U of Minnesota P, 1983. Print. The 1983 edition contains important essays not included in the original edition.

———. *Critical Writings, 1953–1978*. Ed. Lindsay Waters. Minneapolis: U of Minnesota P, 1989. Print.

———. "Phenomenality and Materiality in Kant." *Hermeneutics: Questions and Prospects*. Eds. Gary Shapiro and Alan Sica. Amherst: U of Massachusetts P, 1984. 121–44. Print.

———. *The Resistance to Theory*. Minneapolis: U of Minnesota P, 1986. Print.

————. *The Rhetoric of Romanticism.* New York: Columbia UP, 1984. Print.

————. "The Rhetoric of Temporality." In *Blindness and Insight.* Print.

————. *Romanticism and Contemporary Culture.* Eds. E. S. Burt, Kevin Newmarkj, and Andrzej Wasminski. Baltimore: Johns Hopkins UP, 1993. Print.

————. "Theory of Metaphor in Rousseau's Second Discourse." *Studies in Romanticism* (1973): 475–98. Print.

————. *Wartime Journalism, 1939–1943.* Eds. Werner Hamacher, Neil Hertz, and Thomas Keenan. Lincoln: U of Nebraska P, 1988. Print.

Derrida, Jacques. *Acts of Literature.* Ed. Derek Attridge. New York: Routledge, 1992. Print.

————. *A Derrida Reader: Between the Blinds.* Ed. Peggy Kamuf. New York: Columbia UP, 1991. Print.

————. "Différance." *Speech and Phenomena.* Trans. David B. Allison. Evanston: Northwestern UP, 1973. Print.

————. *Dissemination.* Trans. Barbara Johnson. Chicago: U of Chicago P, 1981. Print. See especially the "Translator's Introduction," which provides a useful point of entry into this work and others by Derrida.

————. "Force of Law: The 'Mystical Foundation of Authority.'" Trans. Mary Quaintance. *Deconstruction and the Possibility of Justice.* Eds. Drucilla Cornell et al. New York: Routledge, 1992. 3–67. Print.

————. *Given Time: I. Counterfeit Money.* Trans. Peggy Kamuf. Chicago: U of Chicago P, 1992. Print.

————. *Jacques Derrida: Basic Writings.* Ed. Barry Stocker. London: Routledge, 2007. Print. An anthology of Derrida's work.

————. *Margins of Philosophy.* Trans. Alan Bass. Chicago: U of Chicago P, 1982. Print. Contains the essay "White Mythology: Metaphor in the Text of Philosophy."

————. *Mémoires: For Paul de Man.* Trans. Cecile Lindsay, Jonathan Culler, and Eduardo Cadava. New York: Columbia UP, 1986. Print.

————. *Negotiations: Interventions and Interviews, 1971–2001.* Stanford: Stanford UP, 2002. Print.

————. *On the Name.* Ed. Thomas Dutoit. Stanford: Stanford UP, 1995. Print.

————. *Of Grammatology.* Trans. Gayatri C. Spivak. Baltimore: Johns Hopkins UP, 1976. Print.

———. "Passions." *Derrida: A Critical Reader.* Ed. David Wood. Cambridge: Basil Blackwell, 1992. Print.

———. *Positions.* Trans. Alan Bass. Chicago: U of Chicago P, 1981. Print. Three interviews with Derrida.

———. *The Post Card: From Socrates to Freud and Beyond.* Trans. with intro. Alan Bass. Chicago: U of Chicago P, 1987. Print.

———. *Signéponge/Signsponge.* New York: Columbia UP, 1984. Print.

———. "Some Statements and Truisms about Neo-logisms, Newisms, Postisms, and Other Small Seisisms." *The States of "Theory."* New York: Columbia UP, 1990. 63–94. Print.

———. *Sovereignties in Question: The Poetics of Paul Celan.* New York: Fordham UP, 2005. Print.

———. *Specters of Marx.* Trans. Peggy Kamuf. New York: Routledge, 1994. Print.

———. *Writing and Difference.* Trans. Alan Bass. Chicago: U of Chicago P, 1978. Print.

Dick, Kirby, and Amy Ziering Kofman, directors. *Derrida.* New York: Zeitgeist Video, 2003. DVD. A documentary on Derrida.

Direk, Zeynep, and Leonard Lawlor, eds. *Jacques Derrida.* London: Routledge, 2002. Print. Three-volume anthology of essays on Derrida.

Gasché, Rodolphe. *Inventions of Difference: On Jacques Derrida.* Cambridge: Harvard UP, 1994. Print.

———. *The Tain of the Mirror: Derrida and the Philosophy of Reflection.* Cambridge: Harvard UP, 1986. Print.

———. *Views and Interviews: On "Deconstruction" in America.* Aurora: Davies Group, 2007. Print.

———. *The Wild Card of Reading: On Paul de Man.* Cambridge: Harvard UP, 1998. Print.

Glendinning, Simon, and Robert Eaglestone, eds. *Derrida's Legacies: Literature and Philosophy.* London: Routledge, 2008. Print.

Hamacher, Werner, Neil Hertz, and Thomas Keenan. *Responses: On Paul de Man's Wartime Journalism.* Lincoln: U of Nebraska P, 1989. Print.

Hartman, Geoffrey. "Blindness and Insight: Paul de Man, Fascism, and Deconstruction." *The New Republic* (7 Mar. 1988): 26–31. Print.

———. *Saving the Text.* Baltimore: Johns Hopkins UP, 1981. Print.

Kates, Joshua. *Essential History: Jacques Derrida and the Development of Deconstruction.* Evanston: Northwestern UP, 1995. Print.

————. *Fielding Derrida: Philosophy, Literary Criticism, History, and the Work of Deconstruction.* New York: Fordham UP, 2008. Print.

Krapp, Peter. "Bibliography of Publications by Jacques Derrida." *Derrida: Online.* 13 December 2009. Web. 17 January 2010. <http://hydra.humanities.uci.edu/derrida/jdind.html>. An online compilation of texts and interviews by Derrida from 1962 to 2007.

Krupnick, Mark, ed. *Displacement: Derrida and After.* Bloomington: Indiana UP, 1987. Print.

McQuillan, Martin. *Paul de Man.* London: Routledge, 2001. Print.

Miller, J. Hillis. *Ariadne's Thread: Story Lines.* New Haven: Yale UP, 1992. Print.

————. *The Ethics of Reading: Kant, de Man, Eliot, Trollope, James, and Benjamin.* New York: Columbia UP, 1987. Print.

————. *Fiction and Repetition: Seven English Novels.* Cambridge: Harvard UP, 1982. Print.

————. *Hawthorne and History: Defacing It.* Cambridge: Basil Blackwell, 1991. Print. Contains a bibliography of Miller's work through 1990.

————. *Illustration.* Cambridge: Harvard UP, 1992. Print.

————. *The J. Hillis Miller Reader.* Ed. Julian Wolfreys. Stanford: Stanford UP, 2005. Print.

————. *The Linguistic Moment: From Wordsworth to Stevens.* Princeton: Princeton UP, 1985. Print.

————. *Literature as Conduct: Speech Acts in Henry James.* New York: Fordham UP, 2005. Print.

————. *On Literature.* London: Routledge, 2002. Print.

————. *Others.* Princeton: Princeton UP, 2001. Print.

————. *Reading Narrative.* Norman: U of Oklahoma P, 1998. Print.

————. *Speech Acts in Literature.* Stanford: Stanford UP, 2001. Print.

————. "Stevens' Rock and Criticism as Cure." *Georgia Review* 30 (1976): 3–31, 330–48. Print.

————. *Theory Now and Then.* Durham: Duke UP, 1991. Print.

————. *Topographies.* Stanford: Stanford UP, 1995. Print.

————. *Versions of Pygmalion.* Cambridge: Harvard UP, 1990. Print.

Miller, J. Hillis, and Manuel Asensi. *Black Holes/J. Hillis Miller; or, Boustrophedonic Reading.* Stanford: Stanford UP, 1999. Print. Two texts in one book, set on facing pages: Miller's analysis of the contemporary research university in the West and Asensi's interpretation of Miller's work.

Naas, Michael. *Taking on the Tradition: Jacques Derrida and the Legacies of Deconstruction.* Stanford: Stanford UP, 2003. Print.

Norris, Christopher. *Paul de Man, Deconstruction, and the Critique of Aesthetic Ideology.* New York: Routledge, 1988. Print.

Rorty, Richard. "Philosophy as a Kind of Writing: An Essay on Derrida." *New Literary History* 10 (1978): 141–60. Print.

Royle, Nicholas. *Jacques Derrida.* London: Routledge, 2003. Print.

Thomas, Michael, ed. *The Reception of Derrida: Translation and Transformation.* New York: Palgrave Macmillan, 2006. Print.

Waters, Lindsey, and Wlad Godzich, eds. *Reading de Man Reading.* Minneapolis: U of Minnesota P, 1989. Print.

Deconstruction and Its Applications

Armour, Ellen T. *Deconstruction, Feminist Theology, and the Problem of Difference: Subverting the Race/Gender Divide.* Chicago: U of Chicago P, 1999. Print.

Beardsworth, Richard. *Derrida and the Political.* London: Routledge, 1996. Print.

Brunette, Peter, and David Wills, eds. *Deconstruction and the Visual Arts: Art, Media, Architecture.* Cambridge: Cambridge UP, 1994. Print.

Caputo, John D. *What Would Jesus Deconstruct?: The Good News of Postmodernism for the Church.* Grand Rapids: Baker Academic, 2007. Print.

Cornell, Drucilla, Michael Rosenfeld, and David Gray Carlson, eds. *Deconstruction and the Possibility of Justice.* New York: Routledge, 1992. Print.

Elam, Diane. *Feminism and Deconstruction: Ms. en Abyme.* New York: Routledge, 1994. Print.

Felman, Shoshana. "Rereading Femininity." *Yale French Studies* 62 (1981): 19–44. Print.

Haverkamp, Anselm, ed. *Deconstruction Is/In America: A New Sense of the Political.* New York: New York UP, 1995. Print.

Holland, Nancy J., ed. *Feminist Interpretations of Jacques Derrida.* University Park: Pennsylvania State UP, 1997. Print.

Johnson, Philip, and Mark Wigley. *Deconstructivist Architecture.* Boston: Little, Brown, 1988. Print.

McQuillan, Martin, ed. *Deconstruction Reading Politics.* Basingstoke: Palgrave Macmillan, 2008. Print.

———, ed. *The Politics of Deconstruction: Jacques Derrida and the Other of Philosophy.* London: Pluto, 2007. Print.

Mouffe, Chantal, ed. *Deconstruction and Pragmatism.* London: Routledge, 1996. Print. Centered on a debate between Jacques Derrida and Richard Rorty on deconstruction and pragmatism, with context provided by Simon Critchley and Ernesto Laclau.

Nancy, Jean-Luc. *Dis-Enclosure: The Deconstruction of Christianity.* Trans. Bettina Bergo, Gabriel Malenfant, and Michael B. Smith. New York: Fordham UP, 2008. Print.

Papadakis, Andreas, Andrew Benjamin, and Catherine Cook, eds. *Deconstruction: Omnibus Volume.* New York: Rizzoli, 1989. Print.

Peters, Michael, and Gert Biesta. *Derrida, Deconstruction, and the Politics of Pedagogy.* New York: Lang, 2009. Print.

Plotnitsky, Arkady. *Complementarity: Anti-Epistemology After Bohr and Derrida.* Durham: Duke UP, 1994. Print.

Sallis, John, ed. *Deconstruction and Philosophy: The Texts of Jacques Derrida.* Chicago: U of Chicago P, 1987. Print.

Syrotinski, Michael. *Deconstruction and the Postcolonial: At the Limits of Theory.* Liverpool: Liverpool UP, 2007. Print.

Taylor, Mark. *Deconstructing Theology.* New York: Crossroad, 1982. Print.

Wheeler, Samuel C. *Deconstruction as Analytic Philosophy.* Stanford: Stanford UP, 2000. Print.

Wigley, Mark. *The Architecture of Deconstruction: Derrida's Haunt.* Cambridge: MIT P, 1993. Print.

Wihl, Gary. *The Contingency of Theory: Pragmatism, Expressivism, and Deconstruction.* New Haven: Yale UP, 1994. Print.

Wood, David. *Deconstruction of Time.* Atlantic Highlands: Humanities P International, 1989. Print.

Critiques of Deconstruction

Abrams, M. H. "The Deconstructive Angel." *Critical Inquiry* 3 (1977): 425–38. Print.

Ellis, John M. *Against Deconstruction.* Princeton: Princeton UP, 1989. Print.

Lehman, David. *Signs of the Times: Deconstruction and the Fall of Paul de Man.* New York: Poseidon, 1991. Print.

Further Reading on Deconstruction and Poststructuralism

Barthes, Roland. *S/Z*. Trans. Richard Miller. New York: Hill, 1974. Print. In this influential work, Barthes turns from a structuralist to a poststructuralist approach.

Benstock, Shari. *Textualizing the Feminine: On the Limits of Genre*. Norman: U of Oklahoma P, 1991. Print.

Berman, Art. *From the New Criticism to Deconstruction: The Reception of Structuralism and Post-Structuralism*. Urbana: U of Illinois P, 1988. Print.

Cohen, Tom. *Anti-Mimesis: From Plato to Hitchcock*. Cambridge: Cambridge UP, 1994. Print.

Culler, Jonathan. *Structuralist Poetics: Structuralism, Linguistics, and the Study of Literature*. Ithaca: Cornell UP, 1975. Print. See especially ch. 10, " 'Beyond' Structuralism: *Tel Quel*."

Felperin, Howard. *Beyond Deconstruction: The Uses and Abuses of Literary Theory*. Oxford: Oxford UP, 1985. Print.

Harari, Josué, ed. *Textual Strategies: Perspectives in Post-Structuralist Criticism*. Ithaca: Cornell UP, 1979. Print.

Johnson, Barbara. *A World of Difference*. Baltimore: Johns Hopkins UP, 1987. Print. Includes a preface addressing the de Man controversy, "A Note on the Wartime Writings of Paul de Man."

Leitch, Vincent B. *Cultural Criticism, Literary Theory, Poststructuralism*. New York: Columbia UP, 1982. Print.

McQuillan, Martin, ed. *Deconstruction After 9/11*. New York: Routledge, 2008. Print.

Sedgwick, Eve Kosofsky. *Epistemology of the Closet*. Berkeley: U of California P, 1990. Print.

Srajek, Martin. *In the Margins of Deconstruction: Jewish Conceptions of Ethics in Emmanuel Levinas and Jacques Derrida*. Dordrecht: Kluwer Acad., 1998. Print.

Ulmer, Gregory. *Applied Grammatology: Post(e) Pedagogy from Jacques Derrida to Joseph Beuys*. Baltimore: Johns Hopkins UP, 1985. Print.

———. *Teletheory: Grammatology in the Age of Video*. New York: Routledge, 1989. Print.

Deconstructive Readings

Atkins, G. Douglas. *Quests of Difference: Reading Pope's Poems*. Lexington: UP of Kentucky, 1986. Print.

Byrne, Eleanor, and Martin McQuillan. *Deconstructing Disney.* London: Pluto, 1999. Print.

Chase, Cynthia. "The Decomposition of the Elephants: Double-Reading *Daniel Deronda.*" *PMLA* 93 (1978): 215–27. Print.

Felperin, Howard. *The Uses of the Canon: Elizabethan Literature and Contemporary Theory.* Oxford: Clarendon, 1990. Print.

Flores, Ralph. *The Rhetoric of Doubtful Authority: Deconstructive Readings of Self-Questioning Narratives, St. Augustine to Faulkner.* Ithaca: Cornell UP, 1984. Print.

Jacobs, Carol. "The (Too) Good Soldier: 'A Real Story.'" *Glyph* 3 (1978): 32–51. Print.

Johnson, Barbara. "Anthropomorphism in Lyric and Law." *Yale Journal of Law and the Humanities* 10 (1998): 549–74. Print.

———. *The Critical Difference: Essays in the Contemporary Rhetoric of Reading.* Baltimore: Johns Hopkins UP, 1980. Print.

———. "Muteness Envy." *The Feminist Difference: Literature, Psychoanalysis, Race, and Gender.* Cambridge: Harvard UP, 1998. 129–53. Print.

Spivak, Gayatri. "Sex and History in *The Prelude* (1805): Books Nine to Thirteen." *Texas Studies in Language and Literature* 23 (1981): 324–60. Print.

Sussman, Henry. "The Deconstructionist as Politician: Melville's *The Confidence Man.*" *Glyph* 4 (1978): 32–56. Print.

Deconstructive and Poststructuralist Approaches to Conrad and *Heart of Darkness*

Bonney, William. *Thorns and Arabesques: Contexts for Conrad's Fiction.* Baltimore: Johns Hopkins UP, 1980. Print.

Brooks, Peter. "An Unreadable Report: Conrad's *Heart of Darkness.*" *Reading for the Plot: Design and Intention in Narrative.* New York: Knopf, 1984. Print.

Mansell, Darrell. "Trying to Bring Literature Back Alive: The Ivory in Joseph Conrad's *Heart of Darkness.*" *Criticism* 33 (1991): 205–15. Print.

Miller, J. Hillis. "Joseph Conrad: Should We Read *Heart of Darkness?*" *Others.* Princeton: Princeton UP, 2001. 104–36. Print.

Pecora, Vincent. "The Sounding Empire: Conrad's *Heart of Darkness.*" *Self and Form in Modern Narrative.* Baltimore: Johns Hopkins UP, 1989. Print.

Wolfreys, Julian. "Heart? of Darkness? Reading in the Dark with J. Hillis Miller and Joseph Conrad." *Deconstruction — Derrida.* New York: St. Martin's Press, 1998. Print.

A DECONSTRUCTIVE PERSPECTIVE

J. HILLIS MILLER

Heart of Darkness Revisited

I begin with three questions: Is it a senseless accident, a result of the crude misinterpretation or gross transformation of the mass media that the cinematic version of *Heart of Darkness* is called *Apocalypse Now*, or is there already something apocalyptic about Conrad's novel in itself? What are the distinctive features of an apocalyptic text? How would we know when we had one in hand?

I shall approach an answer to these questions by the somewhat roundabout way of an assertion that if *Heart of Darkness* is perhaps only problematically apocalyptic, there can be no doubt that it is parabolic. The distinctive feature of a parable, whether sacred or secular, is the use of a realistic story, a story in one way or another based firmly on what Marx calls man's "real conditions of life, and his relations with his kind," to express another reality or truth not otherwise expressible (Marx 476). When the disciples ask Jesus why he speaks to the multitudes in parables, he answers, "Therefore speak I to them in parables: because they seeing see not; and hearing they hear not, neither do they understand" (Matthew 13:13). A little later Matthew tells the reader that "without a parable spake he not unto them: That it might be fulfilled which was spoken by the prophet, saying, I will open my mouth in parables; I will utter things which have been kept secret from the foundation of the world" (Matthew 13:34–35). Those things which have been kept secret from the foundation of the world will not be revealed until they have been spoken in parable, that is, in terms which the multitude who lack spiritual seeing and hearing nevertheless see and hear, namely, the everyday details of their lives of fishing, farming, and domestic economy.

Conrad's story is a parable, in part, because it is grounded firmly in the details of real experience. Biographers such as Ian Watt, Frederick Karl, and Norman Sherry tell us all that is likely to be learned of Conrad's actual experience in the Congo, as well as of the historical originals of Kurtz, the particolored harlequin-garbed Russian, and other characters in the novel. If parables are characteristically grounded in representations of realistic or historical truth, *Heart of Darkness* admirably fulfills this requirement of parable. But it fills another requirement, too. Conrad's novel is a parable because, although it is based on what Marx called "real conditions," its narrator attempts through his tale to reveal some as-yet-unseen reality.

Unlike allegory, which tries to shed light on the past or even on our origins, parable tends to be oriented toward the future, toward last things, toward the mysteries of the kingdom of heaven and how to get there. Parable tends to express what Paul at the end of Romans, in echo of Matthew, calls "the revelation of the mystery, which was kept secret since the world began, but now is made manifest" (Romans 16:25–26). Parable, as we can now see, has at least one thing in common with apocalypse: it too is an act of unveiling that which has never been seen or known before. Apocalypse *means* unveiling; an apocalypse is a narrative unveiling or revelation. The last book of the Bible is the paradigmatic example of apocalypse in our tradition, though it is by no means the only example. The book of Revelation seeks to unveil a mystery of the future, namely, what will happen at time's ending.

My contention, then, is that *Heart of Darkness* fits, in its own way, the definitions of both parable and apocalypse, and that much illumination is shed on it by interpreting it in the light of these generic classifications. As Marlow says of his experience in the heart of darkness: "It was sombre enough too — . . . not very clear either. No, not very clear. And yet it seemed to throw a kind of light" (p. 22). A narrative that sheds light, that penetrates darkness, that clarifies and illuminates — this is one definition of that mode of discourse called parabolic or apocalyptic, but it might also serve to define the work of criticism or interpretation. All criticism claims to be enlightenment or *Aufklärung*.

How, though, does a story enlighten or clarify: in what ways may narratives illuminate or unveil? Conrad's narrator distinguishes between two different ways in which a narrative may be related to its meaning:

> The yarns of seamen have a direct simplicity, the whole meaning of which lies within the shell of a cracked nut. But Marlow was not typical (if his propensity to spin yarns be excepted), and to him the meaning of an episode was not inside like a kernel but outside [Ms: outside in the unseen], enveloping the tale which brought it out only as a glow brings out a haze, in the likeness of one of these misty halos that sometimes are made visible by the spectral illumination of moonshine. (pp. 19–20)

The narrator here employs two figures to describe two kinds of stories: simple tales and parables. Through the two figures, moreover, Conrad attempts to present the different ways in which these two kinds of narration relate to their meanings.

The meanings of the stories of most seamen, says the narrator, are inside the narration like the kernel of a cracked nut. I take it the narrator means the meanings of such stories are easily expressed, detachable from the stories and open to paraphrase in other terms, as when one draws an obvious moral: "Crime doesn't pay," or "Honesty is the best policy," or "The truth will out," or "Love conquers all." The figure of the cracked nut suggests that the story itself, its characters and narrative details, are the inedible shell which must be removed and discarded so the meaning of the story may be assimilated. This relation of the story to its meaning is a particular version of the relation of container to thing contained. The substitution of contained for container, in this case meaning for story, is one version of that figure called in classical rhetoric *synecdoche*, but this is a metonymic rather than a metaphorical synecdoche.[1] The meaning is adjacent to the story, contained within it as nut within shell, but the meaning has no intrinsic similarity or kinship to the story. Its relation to the story that contains it is purely contingent. The one happens to touch the other, as shell surrounds nut, as bottle its liquid contents, or as shrine-case its iconic image.

It is far otherwise with Marlow's stories. Their meaning — like the meaning of a parable — is outside, not in. It envelops the tale rather than being enveloped by it. The relation of container and thing contained is reversed. The meaning now contains the tale. Moreover, perhaps because of that enveloping containment, or perhaps for more obscure reasons, the relation of the tale to its meaning is no longer that of dissimilarity and contingency. The tale is the necessary agency of the bringing into the open or revelation of that particular meaning. It is not so much that the meaning is like the tale. It is not. But the tale is in preordained correspondence to or in resonance with the meaning. The tale magically brings the "unseen" meaning out and makes it visible.

Conrad has the narrator express this subtle concept of parabolic narration according to the parabolic "likeness" of a certain atmospheric phenomenon. "Likeness" is a homonym of the German *Gleichnis*, which is itself a term for parable. The meaning of a parable appears in the "spectral" likeness of the story that reveals it, or rather, it appears in the likeness of an exterior light surrounding the story, just as the

---

[1] In metaphorical synecdoche a part of something is used to signify the whole: "I see a sail" means "I see a ship." A metonymic synecdoche is one in which the signifying part is really only something contiguous with the thing signified, not intrinsic to it; "the bottle" is a metonymic synecdoche for liquor, since glass cannot really be part of liquor in the way a sail is part of a ship.

narrator's theory of parable appears not as such but in the "likeness" of the figure he proposes. Thus, the figure does double duty, both as a figure for the way Marlow's stories express their meaning and as a figure for itself, so to speak; that is, as a figure for its own mode of working. This is according to a mind-twisting torsion of the figure back on itself that is a regular feature of such figuration, parables of parable, or stories about storytelling. The figure both illuminates its own workings and at the same time obscures or undermines it, since a figure of a figure is an absurdity, or, as Wallace Stevens puts it, there is no such thing as a metaphor of a metaphor. What was the figurative vehicle of the first metaphor automatically becomes the literal tenor of the second metaphor.[2]

Let us look more closely at the exact terms of the metaphor Conrad's narrator proposes. To Marlow, the narrator says, "the meaning of an episode was not inside like a kernel but outside, enveloping the tale which brought it out only as a glow brings out a haze, in the likeness of one of these spectral illuminations of moonshine." The first simile here ("as a glow") is doubled by a second, similitude of a similitude ("in the likeness of . . ."). The "haze" is there all around on a dark night, but, like the meaning of one of Marlow's tales, it is invisible, inaudible, intangible in itself, like the darkness, or like that "something great and invincible" Marlow is aware of in the African wilderness, something "like evil or truth, waiting patiently for the passing away of this fantastic invasion" (p. 38). The haze, too, is like the climactic name for that truth, the enveloping meaning of the tale: "the horror," those last words of Kurtz that seem all around in the gathering darkness when Marlow makes his visit to Kurtz's Intended and tells his lie. "The dusk," Marlow says, "was repeating them in a persistent whisper all around us, in a whisper that seemed to swell menacingly like the first whisper of a rising wind. 'The horror! The horror!'" (p. 85).

The working of Conrad's figure is much more complex than perhaps it at first appears, both in itself and in the context of the fine grain of the texture of language in *Heart of Darkness* as a whole, as well as in the context of the traditional complex of figures, narrative motifs, and concepts to which it somewhat obscurely alludes. The atmospheric phenomenon that Conrad uses as the vehicle of his parabolic metaphor

---

[2]The "vehicle" of a figurative expression is the term used to refer to something else; the "tenor" is the person, thing, or concept referred to by the vehicle. In the metaphorical synecdoche used as an example in footnote 1 on p. 233, "sail" is the vehicle, "ship" the tenor; in the metonymic synecdoche, "bottle" is the vehicle, "liquor" the tenor. If you say you feel blue to mean you feel sad, "blue" is the vehicle, "sadness" the tenor.

is a perfectly real one, universally experienced. It is as referential and as widely known as the facts of farming Jesus uses in the parable of the sower. If you sow your seed on stony ground it will not be likely to sprout. An otherwise invisible mist or haze at night will show up as a halo around the moon. As in the case of Jesus' parable of the sower, Conrad uses his realistic and almost universally known facts as the means of expressing indirectly another truth less visible and less widely known, just as the narrative of *Heart of Darkness* as a whole is based on the facts of history and on the facts of Conrad's life but uses these to express something transhistorical and transpersonal, the evasive and elusive "truth" underlying both historical and personal experience.

Both Jesus' parable of the sower and Conrad's parable of the moonshine in the mist, curiously enough, have to do with their own efficacy — that is, with the efficacy of parable. Both are posited on their own necessary failure. Jesus' parable of the sower will give more only to those who already have and will take away from those who have not even what they have. If you can understand the parable you do not need it. If you need it you cannot possibly understand it. You are stony ground on which the seed of the word falls unavailing. Your eyes and ears are closed, even though the function of parables is to open the eyes and ears of the multitude to the mysteries of the kingdom of heaven. In the same way, Conrad, in a famous passage in the preface to *The Nigger of the "Narcissus,"* tells his readers, "My task which I am trying to achieve is, by the power of the written word, to make you hear, to make you feel — it is, before all, to make you *see*." No reader of Conrad can doubt that he means to make the reader see not only the vivid facts of the story he tells but the evasive truth behind them, of which they are the obscure revelation, what Conrad calls, a bit beyond the famous phrase from the preface just quoted, "that glimpse of truth for which you have forgotten to ask." To see the facts, out there in the sunlight, is also to see the dark truth that lies behind them. All Conrad's work turns on this double paradox: first the paradox of the two senses of seeing, seeing as physical vision and seeing as seeing through, as penetrating to or unveiling the hidden invisible truth, and second the paradox of seeing the darkness in terms of the light. Nor can the careful reader of Conrad doubt that in Conrad's case too, as in the case of the Jesus of the parable of the sower, the goal of tearing the veil of familiarity from the world and making us *see* cannot be accomplished. If we see the darkness already, we do not need *Heart of Darkness*. If we do not see it, reading *Heart of Darkness* or even hearing Marlow tell it will not help us. We shall remain among those who "seeing see not; and hearing they hear not, neither do they understand." Marlow makes this clear in an extraordinary passage in *Heart of Darkness*, one of those places in which the reader is returned to the primary scene of narration on board the *Nellie*. Marlow is explaining the first lie he told for Kurtz, his prevarication misleading the bricklayer at the Central Station into believing he (Marlow) has great power back home:

> "I became in an instant as much of a pretence as the rest of the bewitched pilgrims. This simply because I had a notion it somehow would be of help to that Kurtz whom at the time I did not see — you understand. He was just a word for me. I did not see the man in the name any more than you do. Do you see him? Do you see the story? Do you see anything? It seems to me I am trying to tell you a dream — making a vain attempt, because no relation of a dream can convey the dream-sensation, that commingling of absurdity, surprise, and bewilderment in a tremor of struggling revolt, that notion of being captured by the incredible which is of the very essence of dreams. . . ."
>
> He was silent for a while.
>
> ". . . No, it is impossible; it is impossible to convey the life-sensation of any given epoch of one's existence — that which makes its truth, its meaning — its subtle and penetrating essence. It is impossible. We live, as we dream — alone. . . ."
>
> He paused again as if reflecting, then added:
>
> "Of course in this you fellows see more than I could then. You see me, whom you know. . . ."
>
> It had become so pitch dark that we listeners could hardly see one another. For a long time already he, sitting apart, had been no more to us than a voice. There was not a word from anybody. The others might have been asleep, but I was awake. I listened, I listened on the watch for the sentence, for the word, that would give me the clue to the faint uneasiness inspired by this narrative that seemed to shape itself without human lips in the heavy night-air of the river. (p. 42)

The denial of the possibility of making the reader see by means of literature is made here through a series of moves, each one ironically going beyond and undermining the one before. When this passage is set against the one about the moonshine, the two together bring out into the open, like a halo in the mist, the way *Heart of Darkness* is posited on the impossibility of achieving its goal of revelation, or, to put this another way, the way it is a revelation of the impossibility of revelation.

In Conrad's parable of the moonshine, the moon shines already with reflected and secondary light. Its light is reflected from the primary light of that sun which is almost never mentioned as such in *Heart of Darkness*. The sun is only present in the glitter of its reflection from this or that object, for example, the surface of that river which, like the white place of the unexplored Congo on the map, fascinates Marlow like a snake. In one passage it is moonlight, already reflected light, which is reflected again from the river: "The moon had spread over everything a thin layer of silver — over the rank grass, over the mud, upon the wall of matted vegetation standing higher than the wall of a temple, over the great river I could see through a sombre gap glittering, glittering, as it flowed broadly by without a murmur" (p. 41). In the case of the parable of the moonshine too that halo brought out in the mist is twice-reflected light. The story, according to Conrad's analogy, the facts that may be named and seen, is the moonlight, while the halo brought out around the moon by the reflection of the moonlight from the diffused, otherwise invisible droplets of the mist, is the meaning of the tale, or rather, the meaning of the tale is the darkness that is made visible by that halo of twice-reflected light. But of course the halo does nothing of the sort. It only makes visible more light. What can be seen is only what can be seen. In the end this is always only more light, direct or reflected. The darkness is in principle invisible and remains invisible. All that can be said is that the halo gives the spectator indirect knowledge that the darkness is there. The glow brings out the haze, the story brings out its meaning, by magically generating knowledge that something is there, the haze in one case, the meaning of the story, inarticulate and impossible to be articulated, in any direct way at least, in the other. The expression of the meaning of the story is never the plain statement of that meaning but is always no more than a parabolic "likeness" of the meaning, as the haze is brought out "in the likeness of one of those misty halos that sometimes are made visible by the spectral illumination of moonshine."

In the passage in which Marlow makes explicit his sense of the impossibility of his enterprise, he says to his auditors on the *Nellie* first that he did not see Kurtz in his name any more than they do. The auditors of any story are forced to see everything of the story "in its name," since a story is made of nothing but names and their adjacent words. There is nothing to see literally in any story except the words on the page, the movement of the lips of the teller. Unlike Marlow, his listeners never have a chance to see or experience directly the man behind the name. The reader, if he or she happens at this moment to think of it (and the passage is clearly an invitation to such thinking, an invocation of it), is in exactly the same situation as that of Marlow's auditors, only

worse. When Marlow appeals to his auditors, Conrad is by a kind of
ventriloquism appealing to his readers: "Do you see him? Do you see
the story? Do you see anything? It seems to me I am trying to tell you
a dream — making a vain attempt." Conrad speaks through Marlow to
us. The reader too can reach the truth behind the story only through
names, never through any direct perception or experience. In the reader's case it is not even names proffered by a living man before him, only
names coldly and impersonally printed on the pages of the book he
holds in his hand. Even if the reader goes behind the fiction to the historical reality on which it is based, as Ian Watt and others have done,
he or she will only confront more words on more pages — Conrad's
letters or the historical records of the conquest and exploitation of the
Congo. The situation of the auditors, even of a living speaker, Marlow
says, is scarcely better, since what a story must convey through names
and other words is not the fact but the "life-sensation" behind the
fact "which makes its truth, its meaning — its subtle and penetrating
essence." This is once more the halo around the moon, the meaning
enveloping the tale. This meaning is as impossible to convey by way of
the life-facts that may be named as the "dream-sensation" is able to be
conveyed through a relation of the bare facts of the dream. Anyone
knows this who has ever tried to tell another person his dream and
has found how lame and flat, or how laughable, it sounds, since "no
relation of a dream can convey the dream-sensation." According to
Marlow's metaphor or proportional analogy: as the facts of a dream are
to the dream-sensation, so the facts of a life are to the life-sensation.
Conrad makes an absolute distinction between experience and the
interpretation of written or spoken signs. The sensation may only be
experienced directly and may by no means, oral or written, be commu-
nicated to another: "We live, as we dream, alone."

Nevertheless, Marlow tells his auditors, they have one direct or
experiential access to the truth enveloping the story: "You fellows
see more than I could then. You see me, whom you know." There is a
double irony in this. To see the man who has had the experience is to
have an avenue to the experience for which the man speaks, to which he
bears witness. Marlow's auditors see more than he could then — that is,
before his actual encounter with Kurtz. Ironically, the witness cannot
bear witness for himself. He cannot see himself or cannot see through
himself or by means of himself, in spite of, or in contradiction of,
Conrad's (or Marlow's) assertion a few paragraphs later that work is
"the chance to find yourself. Your own reality — for yourself, not for
others — what no other man can ever know. They can only see the

mere show, and never can tell what it really means" (p. 44). Though each man can only experience his own reality, his own truth, the paradox involved here seems to run, he can only experience it through another or by means of another as witness to a truth deeper in, behind the other. Marlow's auditors can only learn indirectly, through Marlow, whom they see. They therefore know more than he did. Marlow could only learn through Kurtz, when he finally encountered him face to face. The reader of *Heart of Darkness* learns through the relation of the primary narrator, who learned through Marlow, who learned through Kurtz. This proliferating relay of witnesses, one behind another, each revealing another truth further in which turns out to be only another witness, corresponds to the narrative form of *Heart of Darkness.* The novel is a sequence of episodes, each structured according to the model of appearances, signs, which are also obstacles or veils. Each veil must be lifted to reveal a truth behind which always turns out to be another episode, another witness, another veil to be lifted in its turn. Each such episode is a "fact dazzling, to be seen, like the foam on the depths of the sea, like a ripple on an unfathomable enigma" (p. 57), the fact for example that though the cannibal Africans on Marlow's steamer were starving, they did not eat the white men. But behind each enigmatic fact is only another fact. The relay of witness behind witness behind witness, voice behind voice behind voice, each speaking in ventriloquism through the one next farther out, is a characteristic of the genre of the apocalypse. In the book of Revelation, God speaks through Jesus, who speaks through a messenger angel, who speaks through John of Patmos, who speaks to us.

There is another reason beyond the necessities of revelation for this structure. The truth behind the last witness, behind Kurtz for example in *Heart of Darkness,* is, no one can doubt it, death, "the horror"; or, to put this another way, "death" is another name for what Kurtz names "the horror." No man can confront that truth face to face and survive. Death or the horror can only be experienced indirectly, by way of the face and voice of another. The relay of witnesses both reveals death and, luckily, hides it. As Marlow says, "the inner truth is hidden — luckily, luckily" (p. 49). This is another regular feature of the genre of the apocalypse. The word "apocalypse" means "unveiling," "revelation," but what the apocalypse unveils is not the truth of the end of the world it announces, but the act of unveiling. The unveiling unveils unveiling. It leaves its readers, auditors, witnesses, as far as ever from the always "not quite yet" of the imminent revelation — luckily. Marlow says it was not his own near-death on the way home down the river, "not my own extremity I remember best," but Kurtz's "extremity that I seem to have lived through." Then he adds, "True, he had made that last stride, he had stepped over the edge, while I had been permitted to draw back my hesitating foot. And perhaps in this is the whole difference; perhaps all the wisdom, and all truth, and all sincerity, are just compressed into that inappreciable moment of time in which we step over the threshold of the invisible. Perhaps!" (pp. 86–87). Marlow, like Orpheus returning without Eurydice from the land of the dead, comes back to civilization with nothing, nothing to bear witness to, nothing to reveal by the process of unveiling that makes up the whole of the narration of *Heart of Darkness*. Marlow did not go far enough into the darkness, but if he had, like Kurtz he could not have come back. All the reader gets is Marlow's report of Kurtz's last words, that and a description of the look on Kurtz's face: "It was as though a veil had been rent. I saw on that ivory face the expression of sombre pride, of ruthless power, of craven terror — of an intense and hopeless despair" (p. 85).

I have suggested that there are two ironies in what Marlow says when he breaks his narration to address his auditors directly. The first irony is the fact that the auditors see more than Marlow did because they see Marlow, whom they know; the second is that we readers of the novel see no living witness. (By Marlow's own account that is not enough. Seeing only happens by direct experience, and no act of reading is direct experience. The book's claim to give the reader access to the dark truth behind appearance is withdrawn by the terms in which it is proffered.) But there is, in fact, a third irony in this relay of ironies behind ironies in that Marlow's auditors of course do not see Marlow either. It is too dark. They hear only his disembodied voice. "It had become so pitch dark," says the narrator, "that we listeners could hardly see one another. For a long time already he, sitting apart, had been no more to us than a voice." Marlow's narrative does not seem to be spoken by a living incarnate witness, there before his auditors in the flesh. It is a "narrative that seemed to shape itself without human lips in the heavy night-air of the river." This voice can be linked to no individual speaker or writer as the ultimate source of its messages, not to Marlow, nor to Kurtz, nor to the first narrator, nor even to Conrad himself. The voice is spoken by no one to no one. It always comes from another, from the other of any identifiable speaker or writer. It traverses all these voices as what speaks through them. It gives them authority and at the same time dispossesses them, deprives them of authority, since they only speak with the delegated authority of another. As Marlow says of the voice of Kurtz and of all the other voices, they are what remain as a dying unanimous and anonymous drone or clang that exceeds any single identifiable voice and in the end is spoken by no one: "A voice. He was very little more than a voice. And I heard him — it — this voice — other voices — all of them were so little more than voices — and the memory of that time itself lingers around me, impalpable, like a dying vibration of one immense jabber, silly, atrocious, sordid, savage, or simply mean, without any kind of sense. Voices, voices — . . ." (p. 63).

For the reader, too, *Heart of Darkness* lingers in the mind or memory chiefly as a cacophony of dissonant voices. It is as though the story were spoken or written not by an identifiable narrator but directly by the darkness itself, just as Kurtz's last words seem whispered by the circumambient dusky air when Marlow makes his visit to Kurtz's Intended, and just as Kurtz himself presents himself to Marlow as a voice, a voice which exceeds Kurtz and seems to speak from beyond him: "Kurtz discoursed. A voice! a voice! It rang deep to the very last. It survived his strength to hide in the magnificent folds of eloquence the barren darkness of his heart" (p. 84). Kurtz has "the gift of expression, the bewildering, the illuminating, the most exalted and the most contemptible, the pulsating stream of light, or the deceitful flow from the heart of an impenetrable darkness" (pp. 62–63). Kurtz has intended to use his eloquence as a means of "wringing the heart of the wilderness," but "the wilderness had found him out early, and had taken on him a terrible vengeance for the fantastic invasion" (p. 73). The direction of the flow of language reverses. It flows from the darkness instead of toward it. Kurtz is "hollow at the core" (p. 73), and so the wilderness can speak through him, use him so to speak as a ventriloquist's dummy through which its terrible messages may be broadcast to the world: "Exterminate all the brutes!" "The horror!" (pp. 66, 85). The speaker to is spoken through. Kurtz's disembodied voice, or the voice behind voice behind voice of the narrators, or that "roaring chorus of articulated, rapid, breathless utterance" (p. 83) shouted by the natives on the bank, when Kurtz is taken on board the steamer — these are in the end no more direct a testimony of the truth than the words on the page as Conrad wrote them. The absence of a visible speaker of Marlow's words and the emphasis on the way Kurtz is a disembodied voice function as indirect expressions of the fact that *Heart of Darkness* itself is words without person, words which cannot be traced back to any single personality. This is once more confirmation of my claim that *Heart of Darkness* belongs to the genre of the parabolic apocalypse. The apocalypse is after all a written not an oral genre, and, as Jacques Derrida has pointed out, one characteristic of an apocalypse is that it turns on the invitation or "Come" spoken or written always by someone other than the one who seems to utter or write it.[3]

A full exploration of the way *Heart of Darkness* is an apocalypse would need to be put under the multiple aegis of the converging figures of irony, antithesis, catachresis, synecdoche, aletheia, and personification. Irony is a name for the pervasive tone of Marlow's narration, which undercuts as it affirms. Antithesis identifies the division of what is presented in the story in terms of seemingly firm oppositions that always ultimately break down. Catachresis is the proper name for a parabolic revelation of the darkness by means of visible figures that do not substitute for any possible literal expression of that darkness. Synecdoche is the name for the questionable relation of similarity between the visible sign, the skin of the surface, the foam on the sea, and what lies behind it, the pulsating heart of darkness, the black depths of the sea. Unveiling or *aletheia* labels that endless process of apocalyptic revelation that never quite comes off. The revelation is always future. Personification, finally, is a name for the consistent presentation of the darkness as some kind of living creature with a heart, ultimately as a woman who unmans all those male questors who try to dominate her. This pervasive personification is most dramatically embodied in the native woman, Kurtz's mistress: "the immense wilderness, the colossal body of the fecund and mysterious life seemed to look at her, pensive, as though it had been looking at the image of its own tenebrous and passionate soul" (p. 76).

Heart of Darkness is perhaps most explicitly apocalyptic in announcing the end, the end of Western civilization, or of Western imperialism, the reversal of idealism into savagery. As is always the case with apocalypses, the end is announced as something always imminent, never quite yet. Apocalypse is never now. The novel sets women, who are out of it, against men, who can live with the facts and have a belief to protect them against the darkness. Men can breathe dead hippo and not be contaminated. Male practicality and idealism reverse, however. They turn into their opposites because they are hollow at the core. They are vulnerable to the horror. They *are* the horror. The idealistic suppression of savage customs becomes, "Exterminate all the brutes!" Male idealism is the same thing as the extermination of the brutes. The suppression of savage customs is the extermination of the brutes. This is not

[3]See Jacques Derrida, "D'un ton apocalyptique adopté naguère en philosophie," in *Les Fins de l'homme*, ed. Phillippe Lacoue-Labarthe and Jean-Luc Nancy (Paris: Flammarion, 1981), 445–79, especially p. 468ff. The essay has been translated by John P. Learey, Jr., and published in the 1982 number of *Seineia* (62–97).

just word play but actual fact, as the history of the white man's conquest of the world has abundantly demonstrated. This conquest means
the end of the brutes, but it means also, in Conrad's view of history, the
end of Western civilization, with its ideals of progress, enlightenment,
and reason, its goal of carrying the torch of civilization into the wilderness and wringing the heart of the darkness. Or it is the imminence of
that end which has never quite come as long as there is someone to
speak or write of it.

I claim to have demonstrated that *Heart of Darkness* is not only
parabolic but also apocalyptic. It fits that strange genre of the apocalyptic text, the sort of text that promises an ultimate revelation without
giving it, and says always "Come" and "Wait." But there is an extra
twist given to the paradigmatic form of the apocalypse in *Heart of
Darkness*. The *Aufklärung* or enlightenment in this case is of the fact
that the darkness can never be enlightened. The darkness enters into
every gesture of enlightenment to enfeeble it, to hollow it out, to corrupt it and thereby to turn its reason into unreason, its pretense of
shedding light into more darkness. Marlow as narrator is in complicity
with this reversal in the act of identifying it in others. He too claims,
like the characteristic writer of an apocalypse, to know something no
one else knows and to be qualified on that basis to judge and enlighten
them. "I found myself back in the sepulchral city," says Marlow of his
return from the Congo,

> resenting the sight of people hurrying through the streets to filch a
> little money from each other, to devour their infamous cookery, to
> gulp their unwholesome beer, to dream their insignificant and silly
> dreams. They trespassed upon my thoughts. They were intruders
> whose knowledge of life was to me an irritating pretence, because I
> felt so sure they could not possibly know the things I knew. (p. 87)

The consistent tone of Marlow's narration is ironical. Irony is truth-
telling or a means of truth-telling, of unveiling. At the same time it is a
defense against the truth. This doubleness makes it, though it seems so
coolly reasonable, another mode of unreason, the unreason of a fundamental undecidability. If irony is a defense, it is also inadvertently a
means of participation. Though Marlow says, "I have a voice too, and
for good or evil mine is the speech that cannot be silenced" (p. 51), as
though his speaking were a cloak against the darkness, he too, in speaking ironically, becomes, like Kurtz, one of those speaking tubes or relay
stations through whom the darkness speaks. As theorists of irony from
Friedrich Schlegel and Soren Kierkegaard to Paul de Man have argued,

irony is the one trope that cannot be mastered or used as an instrument of mastery. An ironic statement is essentially indeterminate or undecidable in meaning. The man who attempts to say one thing while clearly meaning another ends up by saying the first thing too, in spite of himself. One irony leads to another. The ironies proliferate into a great crowd of little conflicting ironies. It is impossible to know in just what tone of voice one should read one of Marlow's sardonic ironies. Each is uttered simultaneously in innumerable conflicting tones going all the way from the lightest and most comical to the darkest, most somber and tragic. It is impossible to decide exactly which quality of voice should be allowed to predominate over the others. Try reading aloud the passage cited above and you will see this. Marlow's tone and meaning are indeterminate; his description of the clamor of native voices on the shore or of the murmur of all those voices he remembers from that time in his life also functions as an appropriate displaced description of his own discourse. Marlow's irony makes his speech in its own way another version of that multiple cacophonous and deceitful voice flowing from the heart of darkness, "a complaining clamour, modulated in savage discords," or a "tumultuous and mournful uproar," another version of that "one immense jabber, silly, atrocious, sordid, savage, or simply mean, without any kind of sense," not a voice, but voices (pp. 55, 63). In this inextricable tangle of voices and voices speaking within voices, Marlow's narration fulfills, no doubt without deliberate intent on Conrad's part, one of the primary laws of the genre of the apocalypse.

The final fold in this folding in of complicities in these ambiguous acts of unveiling is my own complicity as demystifying commentator. Behind or before Marlow is Conrad, and before or behind him stands the reader or critic. My commentary unveils a lack of decisive unveiling in *Heart of Darkness.* I have attempted to perform an act of generic classification, with all the covert violence and unreason of that act, since no work is wholly commensurate with the boundaries of any genre. By unveiling the lack of unveiling in *Heart of Darkness*, I have become another witness in my turn, as much guilty as any other in the line of witnesses of covering over while claiming to illuminate. My *Aufklärung* too has been of the continuing impenetrability of Conrad's *Heart of Darkness.*

WORK CITED

Marx, Karl. "Manifesto of the Communist Party." *The Marx-Engels Reader.* Ed. Robert C. Tucker. New York: Norton, 1978.

The New Historicism
and
Heart of Darkness

WHAT IS THE NEW HISTORICISM?

The title of Brook Thomas's *The New Historicism and Other Old-Fashioned Topics* (1991) is telling. Whenever an emergent theory, movement, method, approach, or group gets labeled with the adjective "new," trouble is bound to ensue, for what is new today is either established, old, or forgotten tomorrow. Few of you will have heard of the band called "The New Kids on the Block." New Age book shops and jewelry may seem "old hat" by the time this introduction is published. The New Criticism, or formalism, is just about the oldest approach to literature and literary study currently being practiced. The new historicism, by contrast, is *not* as old-fashioned as formalism, but it is hardly new, either. The term *new* eventually and inevitably requires some explanation. In the case of the new historicism, the best explanation is historical.

Although a number of influential critics working between 1920 and 1950 wrote about literature from a psychoanalytic perspective, the majority took what might generally be referred to as the historical approach. With the advent of the New Criticism, however, historically oriented critics almost seemed to disappear from the face of the earth. The dominant New Critics, or formalists, tended to treat literary works as if they were self-contained, self-referential objects. Rather than basing their interpretations on parallels between the text and historical contexts (such as the author's life or stated intentions in writing the work), these critics concentrated on the relationships *within* the text that give it its form and meaning. During the heyday of the New Criticism, concern about the interplay between literature and history virtually disappeared from literary discourse. In its place was a concern about intratextual repetition, particularly of images or symbols but also of rhythms and sound effects.

About 1970 the New Criticism came under attack by reader-response critics (who believe that the meaning of a work is not inherent in its internal form but rather is cooperatively produced by the reader and the text) and poststructuralists (who, following the philosophy of Jacques Derrida, argue that texts are inevitably self-contradictory and that we can find form in them only by ignoring or suppressing conflicting details or elements). In retrospect it is clear that, their outspoken opposition to the New Criticism notwithstanding, the reader-response critics and poststructuralists of the 1970s were very much *like* their formalist predecessors in two important respects: for the most part, they ignored the world beyond the text and its reader, and, for the most part, they ignored the historical contexts within which literary works are written and read.

Jerome McGann first articulated this retrospective insight in 1985, writing that "a text-only approach has been so vigorously promoted during the last thirty-five years that most historical critics have been driven from the field, and have raised the flag of their surrender by yielding the title 'critic,' and accepting the title 'scholar' for themselves" (*Inflections* 17). Most, but not all. The American Marxist Fredric Jameson had begun his 1981 book *The Political Unconscious* with the following two-word challenge: "Always historicize!" (9). Beginning about 1980, a form of historical criticism practiced by Louis Montrose and Stephen Greenblatt had transformed the field of Renaissance studies and begun to influence the study of American and English Romantic literature as well. And by the mid-1980s, Brook Thomas was working on an essay in which he suggests that classroom discussions of Keats's "Ode on a Grecian Urn" might begin with questions such as the following: Where would Keats have seen such an urn? How did a Grecian urn end up in a museum in England? Some very important historical and political realities, Thomas suggests, lie behind and inform Keats's definitions of art, truth, beauty, the past, and timelessness.

When McGann lamented the surrender of "most historical critics," he no doubt realized what is now clear to everyone involved in the study of literature. Those who had *not* yet surrendered — had not yet "yield[ed] the title 'critic'" to the formalist, reader-response, and post-structuralist "victors" — were armed with powerful new arguments and intent on winning back long-lost ground. Indeed, at about the same time that McGann was deploring the near-complete dominance of critics advocating the text-only approach, Herbert Lindenberger was sounding a more hopeful note: "It comes as something of a surprise," he wrote in 1984, "to find that history is making a powerful comeback" ("New History" 16).

We now know that history was indeed making a powerful comeback in the 1980s, although the word is misleading if it causes us to imagine that the historical criticism being practiced in the 1980s by Greenblatt and Montrose, McGann and Thomas, was the same as the historical criticism that had been practiced in the 1930s and 1940s. Indeed, if the word *new* still serves any useful purpose in defining the historical criticism of today, it is in distinguishing it from the old historicism. The new historicism is informed by the poststructuralist and reader-response theory of the 1970s, plus the thinking of feminist, cultural, and Marxist critics whose work was also "new" in the 1980s. New historicist critics are less fact- and event-oriented than historical critics used to be, perhaps because they have come to wonder whether the truth about what really happened can ever be purely and objectively known. They are less likely to see history as linear and progressive, as something developing toward the present or the future ("teleological"), and they are also less likely to think of it in terms of specific eras, each with a definite, persistent, and consistent *Zeitgeist* ("spirit of the times"). Consequently, they are unlikely to suggest that a literary text has a single or easily identifiable historical context.

New historicist critics also tend to define the discipline of history more broadly than it was defined before the advent of formalism. They view history as a social science and the social sciences as being properly historical. In *Historical Studies and Literary Criticism* (1985), McGann speaks of the need to make "sociohistorical" subjects and methods central to literary studies; in *The Beauty of Inflections: Literary Investigations in Historical Method and Theory* (1985), he links sociology and the future of historical criticism. "A sociological poetics," he writes, "must be recognized not only as relevant to the analysis of poetry, but in fact as central to the analysis" (62). Lindenberger cites anthropology as particularly useful in the new historical analysis of literature, especially anthropology as practiced by Victor Turner and Clifford Geertz.

Geertz, who has related theatrical traditions in nineteenth-century Bali to forms of political organization that developed during the same period, has influenced some of the most important critics writing the new kind of historical criticism. Due in large part to Geertz's anthropological influence, new historicists such as Greenblatt have asserted that literature is not a sphere apart or distinct from the history that is relevant to it. That is what the old criticism tended to do: present the background information you needed to know before you could fully appreciate the separate world of art. The new historicists have used what Geertz would call "thick description" to blur distinctions, not only between history and the other social sciences but also between background and foreground, historical and literary materials, political and poetical events. They have erased the old boundary line dividing historical and literary materials, showing that the production of one of Shakespeare's historical plays was a political act and historical event, while at the same time showing that the coronation of Elizabeth I was carried out with the same care for staging and symbol lavished on works of dramatic art.

In addition to breaking down barriers that separate literature and history, history and the social sciences, new historicists have reminded us that it is treacherously difficult to reconstruct the past as it really was, rather than as we have been conditioned by our own place and time to believe that it was. And they know that the job is utterly impossible for those who are unaware of that difficulty and insensitive to the bent or bias of their own historical vantage point. Historical criticism must be "conscious of its status as interpretation," Greenblatt has written (*Renaissance* 4). McGann obviously concurs, writing that "historical criticism can no longer make any part of [its] sweeping picture unselfconsciously, or treat any of its details in an untheorized way" (*Studies* 11).

Unselfconsciously and *untheorized* are the key words in McGann's statement. When new historicist critics of literature describe a historical change, they are highly conscious of, and even likely to discuss, the *theory* of historical change that informs their account. They know that the changes they happen to see and describe are the ones that their theory of change allows or helps them to see and describe. And they know, too, that their theory of change is historically determined. They seek to minimize the distortion inherent in their perceptions and representations by admitting that they see through preconceived notions; in other words, they learn to reveal the color of the lenses in the glasses that they wear.

Nearly everyone who wrote on the new historicism during the 1980s cited the importance of the late Michel Foucault. A French philosophical historian who liked to think of himself as an archaeologist of human knowledge, Foucault brought together incidents and phenomena from areas of inquiry and orders of life that we normally regard as being unconnected. As much as anyone, he encouraged the new historicist critic of literature to redefine the boundaries of historical inquiry.

Foucault's views of history were influenced by the philosopher Friedrich Nietzsche's concept of a *wirkliche* ("real" or "true") history that is neither melioristic (that is, "getting better all the time") nor metaphysical. Like Nietzsche, Foucault didn't see history in terms of a continuous development toward the present. Neither did he view it as an abstraction, idea, or ideal, as something that began "In the beginning" and that will come to THE END, a moment of definite closure, a Day of Judgment. In his own words, Foucault "abandoned [the old history's] attempts to understand events in terms of . . . some great evolutionary process" (*Discipline and Punish* 129). He warned a new generation of historians to be aware of the fact that investigators are themselves "situated." It is difficult, he reminded them, to see present cultural practices critically from within them, and because of the same cultural practices, it is extremely difficult to enter bygone ages. In *Discipline and Punish: The Birth of the Prison* (1975), Foucault admitted that his own interest in the past was fueled by a passion to write the history of the present.

Like Marx, Foucault saw history in terms of power, but his view of power probably owed more to Nietzsche than to Marx. Foucault seldom viewed power as a repressive force. He certainly did not view it as a tool of conspiracy used by one specific individual or institution against another. Rather, power represents a whole web or complex of forces; it is that which produces what happens. Not even a tyrannical aristocrat simply wields power, for the aristocrat is himself formed and empowered by a network of discourses and practices that constitute power. Viewed by Foucault, power is "positive and productive," not "repressive" and "prohibitive" (Smart 63). Furthermore, no historical event, according to Foucault, has a single cause; rather, it is intricately connected with a vast web of economic, social, and political factors.

A brief sketch of one of Foucault's major works may help clarify some of his ideas. *Discipline and Punish* begins with a shocking but accurate description of the public drawing and quartering of a Frenchman who had botched his attempt to assassinate King Louis XV in 1757. Foucault proceeds by describing rules governing the daily life of modern Parisian felons. What happened to torture, to punishment as public spectacle? he asks. What complex network of forces made it disappear? In working toward a picture of this "power," Foucault turns up many interesting puzzle pieces, such as the fact that in the early years of the nineteenth century, crowds would sometimes identify with the prisoner and treat the executioner as if *he* were the guilty party. But Foucault sets forth a related reason for keeping prisoners alive, moving punishment indoors, and changing discipline from physical torture into mental rehabilitation: colonization. In this historical period, people were needed to establish colonies and trade, and prisoners could be used for that purpose. Also, because these were politically unsettled times, governments needed infiltrators and informers. Who better to fill those roles than prisoners pardoned or released early for showing a willingness to be rehabilitated? As for rehabilitation itself, Foucault compares it to the old form of punishment, which began with a torturer extracting a confession. In more modern, "reasonable" times, psychologists probe the minds of prisoners with a scientific rigor that Foucault sees as a different kind of torture, a kind that our modern perspective does not allow us to see as such.

Thus, a change took place, but perhaps not as great a change as we generally assume. It may have been for the better or for the worse; the point is that agents of power didn't make the change because mankind is evolving and, therefore, more prone to perform good-hearted deeds. Rather, different objectives arose, including those of a new class of doctors and scientists bent on studying aberrant examples of the human mind. And where do we stand vis-à-vis the history Foucault tells? We are implicated by it, for the evolution of discipline as punishment into the study of the human mind includes the evolution of the "disciplines" as we now understand that word, including the discipline of history, the discipline of literary study, and now a discipline that is neither and both, a form of historical criticism that from the vantage point of the 1980s looked "new."

Foucault's type of analysis has been practiced by a number of literary critics at the vanguard of the back-to-history movement. One of them is Greenblatt, who along with Montrose was to a great extent responsible for transforming Renaissance studies in the early 1980s and revitalizing historical criticism in the process. Greenblatt follows Foucault's lead in interpreting literary devices as if they were continuous with all other representational devices in a culture; he therefore turns to scholars in other fields in order to better understand the workings of literature. "We wall off literary symbolism from the symbolic structures operative elsewhere," he writes, "as if art alone were a human creation, as if humans themselves were not, in Clifford Geertz's phrase, cultural artifacts" (*Renaissance* 4).

Greenblatt's name, more than anyone else's, is synonymous with the new historicism; his essay entitled "Invisible Bullets" (1981) has been said by Patrick Brantlinger to be "perhaps the most frequently cited example of New Historicist work" ("Cultural Studies" 45). An English professor at the University of California, Berkeley — the early academic home of the new historicism — Greenblatt was a founding editor of *Representations*, a journal published by the University of California Press that is still considered today to be *the* mouthpiece of the new historicism.

In *Learning to Curse* (1990), Greenblatt cites as central to his own intellectual development his decision to interrupt his literary education at Yale University by accepting a Fulbright fellowship to study in England at Cambridge University. There he came under the influence of the great Marxist cultural critic Raymond Williams, who made Greenblatt realize how much — and what — was missing from his Yale education. "In Williams' lectures," Greenblatt writes, "all that had been carefully excluded from the literary criticism in which I had been trained — who controlled access to the printing press, who owned the land and the factories, whose voices were being repressed as well as represented in literary texts, what social strategies were being served by the aesthetic values we constructed — came pressing back in upon the act of interpretation" (2).

Greenblatt returned to the United States determined not to exclude such matters from his own literary investigations. Blending what he had learned from Williams with poststructuralist thought about the indeterminacy or "undecidability" of meaning, he eventually developed a critical method that he now calls "cultural poetics." More tentative and less overtly political than cultural criticism, it involves what Thomas calls "the technique of montage. Starting with the analysis of a particular historical event, it cuts to the analysis of a particular literary text. The point is not to show that the literary text reflects the historical event but to create a field of energy between the two so that we come to see the event as a social text and the literary text as a social event" ("New Literary Historicism" 490). Alluding to deconstructor Jacques Derrida's assertion that "there is nothing outside the text," Montrose explains that the goal of this new historicist criticism is to show the "historicity of texts and the textuality of history" (Veeser, *The New Historicism* 20).

The relationship between the cultural poetics practiced by a number of new historicists and the cultural criticism associated with Marxism is important, not only because of the proximity of the two approaches but also because one must recognize the differences between the two to understand the new historicism. Still very much a part of the contemporary critical scene, cultural criticism (sometimes called "cultural studies" or "cultural critique") nonetheless involves several tendencies more compatible with the old historicism than with the thinking of new historicists such as Greenblatt. These include the tendency to believe that history is driven by economics; that it is determinable even as it determines the lives of individuals; and that it is progressive, its dialectic one that will bring about justice and equality.

Greenblatt does not privilege economics in his analyses and views individuals as agents possessing considerable productive power. (He says that "the work of art is the product of a negotiation between a creator or class of creators . . . and the institutions and practices of a society" [*Learning* 158]: he also acknowledges that artistic productions are "intensely marked by the private obsessions of individuals," however much they may result from "collective negotiation and exchange" [*Negotiations* vii].) His optimism about the individual, however, should not be confused with optimism about either history's direction or any historian's capacity to foretell it. Like a work of art, a work of history is the negotiated product of a private creator and the public practices of a given society.

This does not mean that Greenblatt does not discern historical change, or that he is uninterested in describing it. Indeed, in works from *Renaissance Self-Fashioning* (1980) to *Shakespearean Negotiations* (1988), he has written about Renaissance changes in the development of both literary characters and real people. But his view of change — like his view of the individual — is more Foucauldian than Marxist. That is to say, it is not melioristic or teleological. And, like Foucault, Greenblatt is careful to point out that any one change is connected with a host of others, no one of which may simply be identified as cause or effect, progressive or regressive, repressive or enabling.

Not all of the critics trying to lead students of literature back to history are as Foucauldian as Greenblatt. Some even owe more to Marx than to Foucault. Others, like Thomas, have clearly been more influenced by Walter Benjamin, best known for essays such as "Theses on the Philosophy of History" and "The Work of Art in the Age of Mechanical Reproduction." Still others — McGann, for example — have followed the lead of Soviet critic M. M. Bakhtin, who viewed literary works in terms of discourses and dialogues between the official, legitimate voices of a society and other, more challenging or critical voices echoing popular or traditional culture. In the "polyphonic" writings of Rabelais, for instance, Bakhtin found that the profane language of Carnival and other popular festivals offsets and parodies the "legitimate" discourses representing the outlook of the king, church, and socially powerful intellectuals of the day.

Moreover, there are other reasons not to consider Foucault the single or even central influence on the new historicism. First, he critiqued the old-style historicism to such an extent that he ended up being antihistorical, or at least ahistorical, in the view of a number of new historicists. Second, his commitment to a radical remapping of the relations of power and influence, cause and effect, may have led him to adopt too cavalier an attitude toward chronology and facts. Finally, the very act of identifying and labeling *any* primary influence goes against the grain of the new historicism. Its practitioners have sought to "decenter" the study of literature, not only by overlapping it with historical studies (broadly defined to include anthropology and sociology) but also by struggling to see history from a decentered perspective. That struggle has involved recognizing (1) that the historian's cultural and historical position may not afford the best purview of a given set of events and (2) that events seldom have any single or central cause. In keeping with these principles, it may be appropriate to acknowledge Foucault as just one of several powerful, interactive intellectual forces rather than to declare him the single, master influence.

Throughout the 1980s it seemed to many that the ongoing debates about the sources of the new historicist movement, the importance of Marx or Foucault, Walter Benjamin or Mikhail Bakhtin, and the exact locations of all the complex boundaries between the new historicism and other "isms" (Marxism and poststructuralism, to name only two) were historically contingent functions of the new historicism's *newness*. In the initial stages of their development, new intellectual movements are difficult to outline clearly because, like partially developed photographic images, they are themselves fuzzy and lacking in definition. They respond to disparate influences and include thinkers who represent a wide range of backgrounds; like movements that are disintegrating, they inevitably include a broad spectrum of opinions and positions.

From the vantage point of the 1990s, however, it seems that the inchoate quality of the new historicism is characteristic rather than a function of newness. The boundaries around the new historicism remain fuzzy, not because it hasn't reached its full maturity but because, if it is to live up to its name, it must always be subject to revision and redefinition as historical circumstances change. The fact that so many critics we label new historicist are working right at the border of Marxist, poststructuralist, cultural, postcolonial, feminist, and now even a new form of reader-response (or at least reader-oriented) criticism is evidence of the new historicism's multiple interests and motivations, rather than of its embryonic state.

New historicists themselves advocate and even stress the need to perpetually redefine categories and boundaries — whether they be disciplinary, generic, national, or racial — not because definitions are unimportant but because they are historically constructed and thus subject to revision. If new historicists like Thomas and reader-oriented critics like Steven Mailloux and Peter Rabinowitz seem to spend most of their time talking over the low wall separating their respective fields, then maybe the wall is in the wrong place. As Catherine Gallagher has suggested, the boundary between new historicists and feminists studying "people and phenomena that once seemed insignificant, indeed outside of history: women, criminals, the insane" often turns out to be shifting or even nonexistent (Veeser, *The New Historicism* 43).

If the fact that new historicists all seem to be working on the border of another school should not be viewed as a symptom of the new historicism's newness (or disintegration), neither should it be viewed as evidence that new historicists are intellectual loners or divisive outriders who enjoy talking over walls to people in other fields but who share no common views among themselves. Greenblatt, McGann, and Thomas all started with the assumption that works of literature are simultaneously influenced by and influencing reality, broadly defined. Whatever their disagreements, they share a belief in referentiality — a belief that literature refers to and is referred to by things outside itself— stronger than that found in the works of formalist, poststructuralist, and even reader-response critics. They believe with Greenblatt that the "central concerns" of criticism "should prevent it from permanently sealing off one type of discourse from another or decisively separating works of art from the minds and lives of their creators and their audiences" (*Renaissance* 5).

McGann, in his introduction to *Historical Studies and Literary Criticism*, turns referentiality into a rallying cry:

> What will not be found in these essays . . . is the assumption, so common in text-centered studies of every type, that literary works are self-enclosed verbal constructs, or looped intertextual fields of autonomous signifiers and signifieds. In these essays, the question of referentiality is once again brought to the fore. (3)

In "Keats and the Historical Method in Literary Criticism," he suggests a set of basic, scholarly procedures to be followed by those who have rallied to the cry. These procedures, which he claims are "practical derivatives of the Bakhtin school," assume that historicist critics will study a literary work's "point of origin" by studying biography and bibliography. The critic must then consider the expressed intentions of the author, because, if printed, these intentions have also modified the developing history of the work. Next, the new historicist must learn the history of the work's reception, as that body of opinion has become part of the platform on which we are situated when we study the work at our own particular "point of reception." Finally, McGann urges the new historicist critic to point toward the future, toward his or her *own* audience, defining for its members the aims and limits of the critical project and injecting the analysis with a degree of self-consciousness that alone can give it credibility (*Inflections* 62).

In his introduction to a collection of new historical writings on *The New Historicism* (1989), H. Aram Veeser stresses the unity among new historicists, not by focusing on common critical procedures but, rather, by outlining five "key assumptions" that "continually reappear and bind together the avowed practitioners and even some of their critics":

1. that every expressive act is embedded in a network of material practices;
2. that every act of unmasking, critique, and opposition uses the tools it condemns and risks falling prey to the practice it exposes;
3. that literary and non-literary texts circulate inseparably;
4. that no discourse, imaginative or archival, gives access to un-changing truths nor expresses inalterable human nature;
5. finally, . . . that a critical method and a language adequate to describe culture under capitalism participate in the economy they describe. (xi)

These same assumptions are shared by a group of historians practicing what is now commonly referred to as "the new cultural history." Influenced by *Annales*-school historians in France, post-Althusserian Marxists, and Foucault, these historians share with their new historicist counterparts not only many of the same influences and assumptions but also the following: an interest in anthropological and sociological subjects and methods; a creative way of weaving stories and anecdotes about the past into revealing thick descriptions; a tendency to focus on nontraditional, noncanonical subjects and relations (historian Thomas Laqueur is best known for *Making Sex: Body and Gender from the Greeks to Freud* [1990]); and some of the same journals and projects.

Thus, in addition to being significantly unified by their own interests, assumptions, and procedures, new historicist literary critics have participated in a broader, interdisciplinary movement toward unification virtually unprecedented within and across academic disciplines. Their tendency to work along disciplinary borderlines, far from being evidence of their factious or fractious tendencies, has been precisely what has allowed them to engage historians in a conversation certain to revolutionize the way in which we understand the past, present, and future.

In the essay that follows, Brook Thomas begins by claiming that if we are to catch a glimpse of the hazy truths that *Heart of Darkness* has to offer, we are going to have to approach Conrad's work with a renewed willingness to read historically. After all, the epigraph to his essay shows Conrad thought of fiction as history. Thomas begins his approach by providing a kind of history *of* history, by reminding us that, during the nineteenth century, history tended to be seen as an organic development toward the present. Consequently, the discontinuities of history were overlooked or, at least, glossed over by historians who all the while believed that they were describing the past as it really was.

Thomas critiques the old history not only to avoid its pitfalls but also because he sees Conrad as a kind of prototype of the new historicist, as a writer who, though in some ways biased in the ways of his culture, was nonetheless effective at debunking the melioristic historicism of his own age. Thomas uses "counter-memory," a phrase of Foucault's, to describe Conrad's picture of Kurtz, a man who gives the lie to meliorism by showing how the most "civilized" of Europeans can also be subhuman in savagery. In Thomas's view, Conrad anticipated the new historicism, too, by not choosing to try to tell how it was in the Congo via an objective-sounding, third-person, omniscient narrative. Even though Conrad had himself been there, he chose to tell his story indirectly, through an idiosyncratic, first-person narrator, Marlow, whose narrative is in turn relayed by another narrator who presumably has not even been to Africa. This elaborate structure makes us aware of structure *as* structure; thus, the novel doesn't pretend to offer us a perfectly clear, uncluttered, unbiased, perfectly natural view of the facts of the past.

Thomas, of course, is a newer historicist than Conrad; we can see this by the characteristics of his own text. The text praises Nietzsche, who helped decenter Western historical narrative, which had tended to assume that Western, idealist values were central and definitive and to judge the past of other cultures accordingly. Thomas also makes use of biographical and bibliographical information and, especially, of Conrad's own writings about his works. Those nonfiction writings, because they have shaped the critical reception of the fiction, must be attended to by the new historicist, in whose view the history of a work includes the work's point of origin, its point of reception, and even its future relationship with its audience. Finally, Thomas is not only familiar with but also adept at using the insights of avant-garde schools of criticism that have flourished since the demise of the old history. And yet, even as he uses them, he distances himself from them by situating them historically.

But Thomas can ill afford to historically situate and critically account for everyone and everything — from Conrad to reader-response criticism to the deconstructive readings of J. Hillis Miller — except himself. Were he to do so he would fall into the old trap in which the historical critic fails because he fails to admit his own historical limitations and consequent capacity for failure. Thomas implicitly does the former and explicitly admits the latter. "There is no guarantee that we will penetrate to the . . . heart of *Heart of Darkness*," Thomas writes (p. 266). There is, in its place, only the conviction that the heart of Conrad's novel can only be approached by the critic who practices sociohistorical criticism.

THE NEW HISTORICISM:
A SELECTED BIBLIOGRAPHY

The New Historicism: General Texts

Belsey, Catherine. "Historicizing New Historicism." *Presentist Shakespeares*. Eds. Hugh Grady and Terence Hawkes. London: Routledge, 2007. 27–45. Print.

Colebrook, Claire. *New Literary Histories: New Historicism and Contemporary Criticism*. Manchester: Manchester UP, 1997. Print.

Cox, Jeffrey N., and Larry J. Reynolds, eds. *New Historical Literary Study: Essays on Reproducing Texts, Representing History*. Princeton: Princeton UP, 1993. Print.

Fluck, Winfried, ed. "The Historical and Political Turn in Literary Studies." *REAL: Yearbook of Research in English and American Literature* 11 (1995) (special issue). Print.

Hens-Piazza, Gina. *New Historicism*. Minneapolis: Fortress, 2002. Print.

Howard, Jean. "The New Historicism in Renaissance Studies." *English Literary Renaissance* 16 (1986): 13–43. Print.

Lindenberger, Herbert. *The History in Literature: On Value, Genre, Institutions*. New York: Columbia UP, 1990. Print.

———. "Toward a New History in Literary Study." *Profession: Selected Articles from the Bulletins of the Association of Departments of English and the Association of the Departments of Foreign Languages*. New York: MLA, 1984. 16–23. Print.

Liu, Alan. "The Power of Formalism: The New Historicism." *English Literary History* 56 (1989): 721–71. Print.

McGann, Jerome. *The Beauty of Inflections: Literary Investigations in Historical Method and Theory*. Oxford: Clarendon–Oxford UP, 1985. Print.

———. *Historical Studies and Literary Criticism*. Madison: U of Wisconsin P, 1985. Print. See especially the introduction and the essays in "Historical Methods and Literary Interpretations" and "Biographical Contexts and the Critical Object."

Montrose, Louis A. "New Historicisms." *Redrawing the Boundaries: The Transformation of English and American Literary Studies*. Eds. Stephen Greenblatt and Giles Gunn. New York: MLA, 1992. 392–418. Print.

———. "Renaissance Literary Studies and the Subject of History." *English Literary Renaissance* 16 (1986): 5–12. Print.

Simpson, David. "Literary Criticism and the Return to 'History.'"
    Critical Inquiry 14 (1998): 721–47. Print.

Thomas, Brook. *The New Historicism and Other Old-Fashioned Topics.*
    Princeton: Princeton UP, 1991. Print.

———. "The New Literary Historicism." *A Companion to American
    Thought.* Eds. Richard Wightman Fox and James T. Klappenberg.
    New York: Basil Blackwell, 1995. Print.

Veeser, H. Aram, ed. *The New Historicism.* New York: Routledge,
    1989. Print. See especially Veeser's introduction; Louis Mon-
    trose's "Professing the Renaissance"; and Catherine Gallagher's
    "Marxism and the New Historicism."

———, ed. *The New Historicism Reader.* London: Routledge, 1993.
    Print.

Winn, James A. "An Old Historian Looks at the New Historicism."
    Comparative Studies in Society and History 35 (1993): 859–70.
    Print.

Works by or about Greenblatt

Greenblatt, Stephen J. *Hamlet in Purgatory.* Princeton: Princeton UP,
    2001.

———. *Learning to Curse: Essays in Early Modern Culture.* New York:
    Routledge, 1990.

———. *Marvelous Possessions: The Wonder of the New World.* Chicago:
    U of Chicago P, 1991.

———. *Renaissance Self-Fashioning from More to Shakespeare.* Chicago:
    U of Chicago P, 1980. See chapter 1 and the chapter on *Othello*
    titled "The Improvisation of Power."

———. *Shakespearean Negotiations: The Circulation of Social Energy
    in Renaissance England.* Berkeley: U of California P, 1988. See
    especially "The Circulation of Social Energy" and "Invisible
    Bullets."

———. "The Wicked Son." *Bookwire.* Web. 17 January 2010.
    <http://www.bookwire.com/bookwire/bbr/reviews/june2001/
    GREENBLATTInterview.htm>. Interview with Harvey Blume on
    Greenblatt's book *Practicing New Historicism,* coauthored with
    Catherine Gallagher, and other topics.

———. *Will in the World: How Shakespeare Became Shakespeare.* New
    York: Norton, 2004. Print.

Payne, Michael, ed. *The Greenblatt Reader.* Malden: Blackwell, 2005.
    Print.

Pieters, Jürgen. *Moments of Negotiation: The New Historicism of Stephen Greenblatt*. Amsterdam: Amsterdam UP, 2002. Print.

Robson, Mark. *Stephen Greenblatt*. London: Routledge, 2008. Print.

Cultural Materialism/Cultural Studies and New Historicism

Bertens, Hans. "Literature and Culture: The New Historicism and Cultural Materialism." *Literary Theory: The Basics*. 1st and 2d ed. London: Routledge, 2001, 2008. Print. See ch. 7, 135–53, in the 2008 edition.

Brannigan, John. *New Historicism and Cultural Materialism*. New York: St. Martin's, 1998. Print.

Brantlinger, Patrick. "Cultural Studies vs. the New Historicism." *English Studies/Cultural Studies: Institutionalizing Dissent*. Eds. Isaiah Smithson and Nancy Ruff. Urbana: U of Illinois P, 1994. 43–58. Print.

Felperin, Howard. *The Uses of the Canon: Elizabethan Literature and Contemporary Theory*. Oxford: Clarendon, 1990. Print. See ch. 8, "'Cultural Poetics' vs. 'Cultural Materialism': The Two New Historicisms in Renaissance Studies."

Hawthorn, Jeremy. *Cunning Passages: New Historicism, Cultural Materialism and Marxism in the Contemporary Literary Debate*. London: Arnold, 1996. Print.

Kiernan, Ryan, ed. *New Historicism and Cultural Materialism: A Reader*. London: Arnold, 1996. Print.

Representations. Print. This quarterly journal, published by the University of California Press, regularly publishes new historicist and cultural studies.

Wilson, Scott. *Cultural Materialism*. Cambridge: Blackwell, 1995. Print.

Critiques of the New Historicism

Dimock, Wai-chee. "Feminism, New Historicism, and the Reader." *American Literature* 63 (1991): 601–22. Print.

LaCapra, Dominick. *Soundings in Critical Theory*. Ithaca: Cornell UP, 1989. Print.

Newton, Judith. "History as Usual?: Feminism and the 'New Historicism.'" *Cultural Critique* 9 (1988): 87–121. Print.

Porter, Carolyn. "Are We Being Historical Yet?" *South Atlantic Quarterly* 87 (1988): 743–86. Print.

Foucault and His Influence

Dreyfus, Hubert L., and Paul Rabinow. *Michel Foucault: Beyond Structuralism and Hermeneutics.* Chicago: U of Chicago P, 1983. Print.

Foucault, Michel. *The Archaeology of Knowledge.* Trans. A. M. Sheridan Smith. New York: Harper, 1972. Print.

———. *Discipline and Punish: The Birth of the Prison.* Trans. Alan Sheridan. New York: Pantheon, 1978. Print.

———. *The Essential Foucault: Selections from Essential Works of Foucault, 1954–1984.* Eds. Paul Rabinow and Nikolas Rose. New York: New Press, 2003. Print. A one-volume anthology of Foucault's writings.

———. *The History of Sexuality.* Vol. 1. Trans. Robert Hurley. New York: Pantheon, 1978. Print.

———. *Language, Counter-Memory, Practice.* Ed. Donald F. Bouchard. Trans. Donald F. Bouchard and Sherry Simon. Ithaca: Cornell UP, 1977. Print.

———. *The Order of Things: An Archaeology of the Human Sciences.* New York: Vintage, 1973. Print.

———. *Politics, Philosophy, Culture.* Ed. Lawrence D. Kritzman. Trans. Alan Sheridan et al. New York: Routledge, 1988. Print.

———. *Power/Knowledge.* Ed. Colin Gordon. Trans. Colin Gordon et al. New York: Pantheon, 1980. Print.

———. *Technologies of the Self.* Eds. Luther H. Martin, Huck Gutman, and Patrick H. Hutton. Amherst: U of Massachusetts P, 1988. Print.

Gutting, Gary. *Foucault: A Very Short Introduction.* Oxford: Oxford UP, 2005. Print. An introduction for beginners to Foucault's work.

Lentricchia, Frank. "Foucault's Legacy: A New Historicism?" *The New Historicism.* Ed. H. Aram Veeser. New York: Routledge, 1989. Print.

Sheridan, Alan. *Michel Foucault: The Will to Truth.* New York: Tavistock, 1980. Print.

Smart, Barry. *Michel Foucault.* New York: Tavistock, 1985. Print.

Other Writers and Works of Interest to the New Historicism

Bakhtin, M. M. *The Dialogic Imagination: Four Essays.* Ed. Michael Holquist. Trans. Caryl Emerson. Austin: U of Texas P, 1981. Print. Includes a helpful introduction by Holquist.

Benjamin, Walter. "The Work of Art in the Age of Mechanical Reproduction." *Illuminations*. Ed. Hannah Arendt. Trans. Harry Zohn. New York: Harcourt, 1968. Print.

de Certeau, Michel. *The Practice of Everyday Life*. Trans. Steven F. Rendall. Berkeley: U of California P, 1984. Print.

Fried, Michael. *Absorption and Theatricality: Painting and Beholder in the Works of Diderot*. Berkeley: U of California P, 1980. Print.

Geertz, Clifford. *The Interpretation of Cultures*. New York: Basic, 1973. Print.

———. *Negara: The Theatre State in Nineteenth-Century Bali*. Princeton: Princeton UP, 1980. Print.

Goffman, Irving. *Frame Analysis*. New York: Harper, 1974. Print.

Jameson, Frederic. *The Political Unconscious*. Ithaca: Cornell UP, 1981. Print.

Koselleck, Reinhart. *Futures Past*. Trans. Keith Tribe. Cambridge: MIT P, 1985. Print.

Laqueur, Thomas Walter. *Making Sex: Body and Gender from the Greeks to Freud*. Cambridge: Harvard UP, 1990. Print.

Ryle, Gilbert. "The Thinking of Thoughts: What is 'Le Penseur' Doing?" *Collected Papers* 2. London: Hutchinson, 1971. 480–96. Print.

Said, Edward. *Orientalism*. New York: Columbia UP, 1978. Print.

Turner, Victor. *The Ritual Process: Structure and Anti-Structure*. Chicago: Aldine, 1969. Print.

White, Hayden. "The Historical Text as Literary Artifact." "The Structure of Historical Narrative," *CLIO* 3 (1974): 277–304. Print.

Williams, Raymond. *The Long Revolution*. New York: Columbia UP, 1961. Print.

———. *Problems in Materialism and Culture*. London: Verso, 1980. Print.

Young, Robert. *White Mythologies: Writing History and the West*. New York: Routledge, 1990. Print.

Further Reading on the New Historicism

Cohen, Ralph, ed. "New Historicisms, New Histories, and Others." *New Literary History: A Journal of Theory and Interpretation* 21 (1990) (special issue). Print.

Liu, Alan. *Local Transcendence: Essays on Postmodern Historicism and the Database*. Chicago: U of Chicago P, 2008. Print.

Michaels, Walter Benn. "The Victims of New Historicism." *Modern Language Quarterly* 54 (1993): 111–20. Print.

Mullaney, Steven. "After the New Historicism." *Alternative Shakespeares* 2. Ed. Terence Hawkes. London: Routledge, 1996. 17–37. Print.

Scala, Elizabeth, ed. "The Ends of Historicism: Medieval English Literary Study in the New Century." *Texas Studies in Literature and Language* 44 (2002) (special issue). Print.

Thomas, Brook. "The Historical Necessity for — and Difficulties with — New Historical Analysis in Introductory Courses." *College English* 49 (1987): 509–22. Print.

———. "Walter Benn Michaels and the New Historicism: Where's the Difference?" *Boundary 2* 18 (1991): 118–59. Print.

Wayne, Don E. "Power, Politics, and the Shakespearean Text: Recent Criticism in England and the United States." *Shakespeare Reproduced: The Text in History and Ideology.* Eds. Jean Howard and Marion O'Connor. New York: Methuen, 1987. 47–67. Print.

Wilson, Richard, and Richard Dutton, eds. *New Historicism & Renaissance Drama.* London: Longman, 1992. Print.

New Historicist Readings

Bercovitch, Sacvan. *The Rites of Assent: Transformations in the Symbolic Construction of America.* New York: Routledge, 1993. Print.

Brown, Gillian. *Domestic Individualism: Imagining Self in Nineteenth-Century America.* Berkeley: U of California P, 1990. Print.

Dollimore, Jonathan. *Radical Tragedy: Religion, Ideology and Power in the Drama of Shakespeare and His Contemporaries.* Brighton: Harvester, 1984. Print.

Dollimore, Jonathan, and Alan Sinfield, eds. *Political Shakespeare: New Essays in Cultural Materialism.* Manchester: Manchester UP, 1985. Print. This volume occupies the borderline between new historicist and cultural criticism. See especially the essays by Dollimore, Greenblatt, and Tennenhouse.

Gallagher, Catherine. *The Industrial Reformation of English Fiction.* Chicago: U of Chicago P, 1985. Print.

Gallagher, Catherine, and Stephen Greenblatt. *Practicing New Historicism.* Chicago: U of Chicago P, 2000. Print.

Goldberg, Jonathan. *James I and the Politics of Literature.* Baltimore: Johns Hopkins UP, 1983. Print.

Hanson, Philip. *This Side of Despair: How the Movies and American Life Intersected During the Great Depression*. Madison: Fairleigh Dickinson UP, 2008. Print.

Howard, Jean E., and Marion F. O'Connor, eds. *Shakespeare Reproduced: The Text in History and Ideology*. London: Methuen, 1987. Print.

Jardine, Lisa. *Reading Shakespeare Historically*. London: Routledge, 1996. Print.

Jurca, Catherine. *White Diaspora: The Suburb and the Twentieth-Century American Novel*. Princeton: Princeton UP, 2001. Print.

Liu, Alan. *Wordsworth: The Sense of History*. Stanford: Stanford UP, 1989. Print.

Madrigal, José A., ed. *New Historicism and the Comedia: Poetics, Politics and Practice*. Boulder: Soc. of Spanish and Spanish-American Studies, 1997. Print.

Marcus, Leah. *Puzzling Shakespeare: Local Reading and Its Discontents*. Berkeley: U of California P, 1988. Print.

McGann, Jerome. *The Romantic Ideology*. Chicago: U of Chicago P, 1983. Print.

Michaels, Walter Benn. *The Gold Standard and the Logic of Naturalism: American Literature at the Turn of the Century*. Berkeley: U of California P, 1987. Print.

Montrose, Louis Adrian. *The Purpose of Playing: Shakespeare and the Cultural Politics of the Elizabethan Theatre*. Chicago: U of Chicago P, 1996. Print.

———. " 'Shaping Fantasies': Figurations of Gender and Power in Elizabethan Culture." *Representations* 2 (1983): 61–94. Print. One of the most influential early new historicist essays.

———. *The Subject of Elizabeth: Authority, Gender, and Representation*. Chicago: U of Chicago P, 2006. Print.

Mullaney, Steven. *The Place of the Stage: License, Play, and Power in Renaissance England*. Chicago: U of Chicago P, 1987. Print.

The New Historicism: Studies in Cultural Poetics. Vols. 1–36. Berkeley: U of California P, 1988–1997. Print. Series edited by Stephen Greenblatt. See, for example, Catherine Gallagher's *Nobody's Story: The Vanishing Acts of Women Writers in the Marketplace, 1670–1920* (1994); Steven Justice's *Writing and Rebellion: England in 1381* (1994); and Daniel Boyarin's *Carnal Israel: Reading Sex in Talmudic Culture* (1993).

North, Michael. *The Dialect of Modernism: Race, Language, and Twentieth-Century Literature*. Oxford: Oxford UP, 1994. Print.

Orgel, Stephen. *The Authentic Shakespeare, and Other Problems of the Early Modern Stage.* New York: Routledge, 2002. Print.

———. *The Illusion of Power: Political Theater in the English Renaissance.* Berkeley: U of California P, 1975. Print.

Palmer, William J. *Dickens and New Historicism.* New York: St. Martin's, 1997. Print.

Sinfield, Alan. *Literature, Politics and Culture in Postwar Britain.* Berkeley: U of California P, 1989. Print.

Tennenhouse, Leonard. *Power on Display: The Politics of Shakespeare's Genres.* New York: Methuen, 1986. Print.

Thomas, Brook. *Civic Myths: A Law-and-Literature Approach to Citizenship.* Chapel Hill: UNC P, 1997. Print.

Tompkins, Jane. *Sensational Designs: The Cultural Work of American Fiction, 1790–1860.* New York: Oxford UP, 1985. Print.

New Historicist and Other Historical Approaches to *Heart of Darkness*

Brannigan, John. " 'On the Edge of a Black and Incomprehensible Frenzy': A New Historicist Reading of *Heart of Darkness.*" *New Historicism and Cultural Materialism.* New York: St. Martin's, 1998. 133–54. Print.

Brantlinger, Patrick. "*Heart of Darkness*: Anti-Imperialism, Racism, or Impressionism?" *Criticism* 27 (1985): 363–85. Print.

Dryden, Linda. "The Vexed Question of Humanity in *Heart of Darkness*: A Historicist Reading." *Joseph Conrad's Heart of Darkness.* Ed. D. C. R. A. Goonetilleke. London: Routledge, 2007. 83–91. Print.

Glenn, Ian. "Conrad's *Heart of Darkness*: A Sociological Reading." *Literature and History* 13 (1987): 238–56. Print.

Hawkins, Hunt. "Conrad and the Psychology of Colonialism." *Conrad Revisited: Essays for the Eighties.* Ed. Ross C Murfin. University: U of Alabama P, 1985. Print.

———. "Conrad's *Heart of Darkness*: Politics and History." *Conradiana* 24 (1992): 207–17. Print.

Humphries, Reynold. "The Discourse of Colonialism: Its Meaning and Relevance for Conrad's Fiction." *Conradiana* 21 (1989): 107–33. Print.

Parry, Benita. *Conrad and Imperialism.* London: Macmillan, 1983. Print.

A NEW HISTORICIST PERSPECTIVE

BROOK THOMAS

Preserving and Keeping Order
by Killing Time in *Heart of Darkness*

Fiction is history, human history, or it is nothing. But it is also
more than that; it stands on firmer ground, being based on the
reality of forms and the observation of social phenomena,
whereas history is based on documents, and the reading of print
and handwriting — on second-hand impression. Thus fiction is
nearer truth. But let that pass. A historian may be an artist too,
and a novelist is a historian, the preserver, the keeper, the
expounder, of human experience.

–JOSEPH CONRAD, *Notes on Life and Letters*

We can start, contrary to current critical practices, with some old-
fashioned generalizations about the history of ideas. And, when we
journey, as we must, to more specificity about Conrad's story there is
no guarantee that we will penetrate to the essential Truth — or non-
Truth — lying at the heart of *Heart of Darkness*; certainly not in a story
informing us that for Marlow "the meaning of an episode was not inside
like a kernel but outside, enveloping the tale which brought it out only
as a glow brings out a haze, in the likeness of one of these misty halos
that sometimes are made visible by the spectral illumination of moonshine" (p. 20). But we may be able to come closer to a truth that we
can glimpse only if we read historically the narrative that Conrad weaves
in his role as a historian of human experience.

1

The century that preceded the 1899 publication of *Heart of Darkness* was the great century of historiography; that is to say, the one in
which history sought to become a science. The eighteenth century's
emphasis on natural, universal laws that governed human society did not
suddenly vanish, but it was superseded by an emphasis on the organic
development of peoples and nations, developments that became the
object of study for the new science of history. In medieval times events
in history had been seen as *exempla*: as illustrations of moral laws or
truths. Relying on the sense of time that allowed anticipations of Chris-

tianity to be read into the ancient world and the Old Testament, historians in the Middle Ages had placed an event in the past on the same temporal plane as the present. Past and present events were interchangeable, capable of being interpreted to exhibit a moral truth to guide behavior. With the advent of a self-consciously modern age in the Renaissance, this sense of time began to alter.

Defining itself as a distinct epoch that had broken with that which came before, the Renaissance produced thinkers who, increasingly, considered events in the present to be different in kind from events in the past. Events were unique to the epochs in which they occurred. History no longer merely took place *in* time, it also took place *through* time; that is, history became temporalized. As a result, the passage of time gave each generation a novel perspective on the past. Past events were no longer so easily interpreted to be timeless *exempla*. Instead, they needed to be continually reinterpreted from the standpoint of a new present. To enter the Renaissance, Reinhart Koselleck writes in *Futures Past* (1985), is to enter the *Neuzeit*, the age of "new time."

By the eighteenth century this sense of history's temporality was widely held. Goethe, for instance, felt that it was self-evident that each generation had to rewrite world history. Nonetheless, eighteenth-century histories still stressed the universality of history. This stress on universal history continued to link history to moral philosophy, since history was often used to illustrate natural laws and the natural rights of man. The rise of the science of history was an attempt to break even this connection with moral philosophy. As the great spokesman of nineteenth-century historiography Leopold von Ranke wrote, his task was not to judge the past or to instruct the present for the profit of future ages, but "to show only what actually happened (*wie es eigentlich gewesen*)" (Bann 10). To accomplish this goal, Ranke emphasized the difference between primary and secondary sources. A history that wanted accurately to relate the past needed to rely on primary sources — documents actually produced in the period — not secondary ones — documents recording another period's interpretation of the past.

From our twentieth-century perspective Ranke's goal to tell only what actually happened sometimes seems naive. For instance, the attempt to reconstruct the past on the basis of primary source material seems to neglect the very real difficulties that arise in giving the past representation. As we are continually reminded by literary critics today, no history can possibly relate the past as it really was because our histories will always be influenced by our present perspective. Furthermore, histories are written in language; the rhetoric the historian adopts shapes and determines his representation of the past. This critical commonplace of today is in turn indebted to the insights of people like Conrad who, in the passage I quote at the start of this essay, reminds us that the documents that Ranke called "primary" sources merely give the historian a "second-hand impression" of an age. One of the concerns of this essay is to understand historically why Conrad felt that "the reality of forms and observation of social phenomena" in his fiction produce more truthful histories than those of most historians.

At least part of the reason is the crisis in historicism that occurred in the late nineteenth and early twentieth centuries. If historicism rested on the belief that the historian could objectively reconstruct the past, the ultimate truth it delivered seemed to be the impossibility of discovering the truth. Feeling that their task was to relive an era as sympathetically as possible by blotting out everything they knew about the latter course of history, historians came to see that all beliefs were historically contingent, including the belief in scientific objectivity. If this awareness came dangerously close to what Friedrich Meinecke called "the bottomless pit of relativism," it was tolerated because historicism retained a faith in progress (Iggers 175). Nineteenth-century histories might demonstrate that beliefs were historically contingent, but many adopted a teleological narrative structure: in other words, one that assumed that history had a design or purpose and that whatever was becoming was right. Values changed, but they were always appropriate to their age, and they progressed and developed over time. Even this faith, however, was undermined by the way historicism linked its histories to the emergence of individual nations. As each nation's history emerged, it became clear that not all narratives of progress could be right. If academic dispute did not bring this point home, World War I did.

But even before the destruction of the war, many Europeans had lost faith in the values that gave coherence to the historicist project. Increasingly, the attempt to give an objective description of the past gave way to modern subjectivist philosophies. As J. Hillis Miller summarizes, "Historicism does not mean merely an awareness of the contradictory diversity of cultures and attitudes. The ancient world had that. The modern historical sense means rather the loss of faith in the possibility of ever discovering the right and true culture, the right and true philosophy or religion" (*Disappearance* 10).

2

Miller's passage is an excellent one to place Conrad's fiction in the context of the history of ideas. By having Kurtz, who embodies Europe's most noble ideals, recognize the horror at the heart of darkness, Conrad brings us face to face with the disillusionment that many twentieth-century thinkers continue to confront, although much of the culture operates by trying to forget it. Marlow embodies this double perspective. On the one hand, back in Europe Marlow tries to forget Kurtz, "to surrender personally all that remained of him with me to that oblivion which is the last word of our common fate" (p. 89). On the other, Marlow cannot will Kurtz's memory away. For him and the reader it serves as what the French historian Michel Foucault has called a "counter-memory," a memory that disrupts the narrative of enlightened progress that official European culture tried to tell about its history. Unable completely to repress this counter-memory when he visits Kurtz's Intended, whose forehead, as the room grows darker, "remained illumined by the unextinguishable light of belief and love" (p. 91), Marlow refuses to destroy her illusions and tells her that the last word Kurtz had uttered was her name, thus linking this woman and all she stands for with "the horror." Official memory of light and counter-memory of darkness are in Conrad's narrative inextricably connected, even though the official memory's ascendancy depends upon the lies that repress the counter-memory.

In a world in which the truth that Marlow tells about civilized Europe is expressed through a lie, it is no wonder that Conrad claimed that fiction is nearer to truth than history. The way Conrad's art approaches the truth is not by stating it but by reminding us of the lie that accompanies every effort to name the truth. Art is closer to truth only in so far as it carries within it the counter-memory that its efforts to express the truth repress, just as the ivory keys of the grand piano that Marlow sees as he waits to greet the Intended become an emblem for the exploitation that Europe's high culture tried to cover up. Embodying the structural relationship between what is said and what is left unsaid, Conrad's story proves to be truer than history, not in its explicit statements but in its forms.

For instance, Conrad does not offer an omniscient narrative perspective that knows and states how it really was. Instead, he constructs a story in which his perspective gives way to a narrator's, that gives way to Marlow's, that gives way to Kurtz's. If this perspective does not tell us the truth, there is a certain truth in the formal techniques that illustrate the impossibility of directly stating the truth. Similarly, the linear narrative of nineteenth-century historicism, in which we move progressively toward a fuller understanding, is replaced by a narrative that concludes with a lie. Even so, there is a certain truth in the way the story unfolds, moving forward and backward in time, its narrative flow interrupted by Marlow's addresses to his audience and his own psychological avoidance of the actual encounter with Kurtz, who is mentioned early in the story but is not met until pages later.

To enter the world of *Heart of Darkness* is, in other words, to enter the world of modern fiction, a world in which authors' technical innovations responded to the loss of faith described by Miller as the "modern historical sense." But if the crisis in historicism helps place *Heart of Darkness* in context, the story also places the context in context. For Conrad's narrative about a European's journey to the heart of Africa helps us see the extent to which the crisis in late-nineteenth-century European thought was related to Europe's contact with what some recent critics, following Jacques Lacan's revision of Hegel, have come to call "the Other." It is probably no accident that the most important British modernist novelists are situated in positions on the borders of mainstream British culture that force them to encounter "the Other." Perhaps no other writer in the twentieth century achieved a mastery over the English language to match James Joyce. But Joyce was in an important sense a colonial writer, an Irish Catholic who spent his life in self-imposed exile on the Continent and who considered English an acquired tongue. An exiled Pole, Conrad quite literally wrote in an acquired language. D. H. Lawrence meanwhile came from a working-class family in the Midlands, carrying an accent that marked his difference from those producing "proper" English arts and letters. Only Virginia Woolf and E. M. Forster could be considered insiders. And Woolf, as a woman, occupied her own border country, while Forster's greatest work, *A Passage to India*, is about the encounter between East and West. Indeed, Europe's encounter with the non-European, so poignantly portrayed by Conrad in *Heart of Darkness*, played a part in one of the most important aspects of modern thought: Europe's discovery of "the Other" within itself.

As early as the late eighteenth century, Europeans had been forced to alter their view of a universal history centered in Europe. Paradoxically, this alteration resulted from the very imperialistic, overseas expansion that drew its ideological justification from the belief that reason, progress, and enlightenment emanated from the West. Brought into contact with such various cultures, Europeans found it impossible to retain belief in one universal culture. Instead, there were many cultures, each with its own history. Recognition of non-European cultures did not mean the abandonment of a Eurocentric perspective. Quite the contrary. Nineteenth-century historicism was adept at absorbing all cultures into a Eurocentric history. Nonetheless, the very presence of "the Other" within those histories heightened the possibility that their narratives would be "decentered." The crisis in historicism can be linked to this decentering, a decentering made possible, ironically, by the success of the West's imperialism.

One of the most important expressions of the decentering of Western narratives of progress and rationality is found in the work of the German philosopher Friedrich Nietzsche, who died the year after Conrad's story appeared. Nietzsche has had a strong influence on recent poststructuralist thought. It is, I think, no accident that two essays cited as starting points for poststructuralism contain explicit critiques of Eurocentrism. One is Paul de Man's "Crisis in Criticism" (1967), which emphasizes the blindness of the philosopher Edmund Husserl to non-Western cultures. The other is Jacques Derrida's "Structure, Sign, and Play in the Discourse of the Human Sciences" (1966), which points out that even the noble efforts to understand non-European cultures by the structuralist anthropologist Claude Lévi-Strauss inevitably adopt a Western perspective. Offering a theory that assures us that the desire for the presence of the truth is inevitably an unfulfilled desire, poststructuralism can productively analyze the world Conrad presents in *Heart of Darkness.* It can also serve as a sort of new faith, albeit a negative one, for critics like Miller trying to cope with the loss of confidence in the Eurocentric view that is dramatized by Conrad's narrative. In turn, Conrad's narrative helps locate the historical situation that created the conditions for the formation of post-structuralist thought.

This reciprocal relation between *Heart of Darkness* and poststructuralism also holds for another approach that proves so fruitful in reading Conrad's story: psychoanalysis. Albert J. Guerard's use of Sigmund Freud to describe *Heart of Darkness* as "A Journey Within" remains one of the most important pieces of Conrad criticism. Certainly, a powerful aspect of Conrad's story is the economy by which his tale about a physical journey into the darkness of Africa becomes a story about a psychological journey into the darkness of the human unconscious. But it is not only the case that psychoanalysis can be used to illuminate Conrad's narrative. Freud's narrative about the human psyche is also illuminated *by* narratives like Conrad's about what happens when a rational Westerner journeys into Africa. While it is commonplace to consider psychoanalysis a new scientific theory, one that provides a universal account of the structure of the human mind, an examination of Freud's metaphors suggests that we might consider psychoanalysis a historical event as well, one partly enabled by Western narratives about encounters with "the Other."

There are numerous similarities between Freud's narrative about the unconscious and Conrad's narrative about the European encounter with the non-European. Trying to describe the "wild and gorgeous apparition" (p. 76) of the African woman trying to protect Kurtz, Marlow tells his audience, "She stood looking at us without a stir, and like the wilderness itself, with an air of brooding over an inscrutable purpose" (p. 77). Freud, in a famous passage, compares female sexuality to the dark continent of Africa. For both of these Western males the otherness of female sexuality is described in terms of the otherness of the African continent. Just as in Freud's theory the unconscious eludes representation and rational understanding, so in Conrad's narrative Africa eludes all attempts of the Western mind — especially a male mind — to understand it. In this context we can better appreciate Marlow's description of himself as a young boy staring, as did Conrad, at the "many blank spaces" on the map of the world. Vowing some day to visit those unexplored regions, he finds, by the time he sets out on his journey, that what had once been "a blank space of delightful mystery — a white patch for a boy to dream gloriously over" — had become "a place of darkness" (p. 22). Finally recognized by the West, those unexplored, blank spots on the globe known as Africa were represented as darkness, the same metaphor psychoanalysis uses to represent the unexplored areas of the mind.

The way *Heart of Darkness* helps us analyze some of the critical approaches we use to analyze it proves very satisfying for our classical sense of balance. Having arrived at this symmetrical formulation, however, we should not rest too comfortably, because it raises a problem. To merge critical approaches and text is to risk the disappearance of the encounter with "the Other," which seemed of such historical significance. Just as in Conrad's story what seems to be an encounter with another turns out to be an encounter with the self — so that Marlow's encounter with Kurtz really becomes an encounter with himself and readers' encounters with Marlow transform into encounters with themselves — so in some critical schools today even the otherness of the story we are reading is denied. Although we can hold a material object in our hand with *Heart of Darkness* written on the title page and the words Conrad wrote printed on the pages to follow, we are told that what we call the text is in fact the product of our interpretations.

Ironically, then, a project that seems intent on decentering a Eurocentric point of view turns out to be the most Eurocentric of all. For just as Conrad's story can be read, not as a story about Africa, but actually as a story about Europe, so the decentering set in motion by Europe's encounter with "the Other" can be read as a statement about European thought, not about that which is foreign to it. Thinking we are encountering something outside of ourselves or Western culture, we end up merely discovering "the Other" within ourselves, a discovery that could be described as the most imperialistic of all, since what was once thought to be truly different is now absorbed into a system that accounts for its own decentering. In the meantime, "the Other" seems to be of interest only in so far as it can help the West in its task of self-definition.

3

If Conrad's narrative is one of the most effective expressions of the encounter between self and "Other," between the European and non-European, our task is not to affirm the truth of his narrative but to interrogate it. And what needs interrogation is Conrad's representation of the non-European. Why, we need to ask, in this narrative about Europe's encounter with Africa are Africans reduced to the mere function of providing us a spectral illumination about Europe? To answer that question we can turn to a passage in which Marlow describes the Africans:

> The earth seemed unearthly. We are accustomed to look upon the shackled form of a conquered monster, but there — there you could look at a thing monstrous and free. It was unearthly, and the men were — No, they were not inhuman. Well, you know, that was the worst of it — this suspicion of their not being inhuman. It would come slowly to one. They howled and leaped, and spun, and made horrid faces; but what thrilled you was just the thought of their humanity — like yours — the thought of your remote kinship with this wild and passionate uproar. Ugly. Yes, it was ugly enough; but if you were man enough you would admit to yourself that there was in you just the faintest trace of a response to the terrible frankness of that noise, a dim suspicion of there being a meaning in it which you — you so remote from the night of first ages — could comprehend. And why not? The mind of

man is capable of anything — because everything is in it, all the
past as well as all the future. What was there after all? Joy, fear,
sorrow, devotion, valour, rage — who can tell? — but truth —
truth stripped of its cloak of time. (p. 51)

Starting the paragraph with the paradox that the earth seemed
unearthly, Marlow sets up the expectation that the human beings inhab-
iting that unearthly earth will be inhuman, an expectation easy to arouse
because it would confirm his listeners' racial prejudices. But Conrad's
narrative disrupts such commonplace prejudices. The horror of the
story is not that the Africans are a deviant form of humanity, but that
the monster is also within the Europeans who consider themselves
superior. Thus, the passage suggests a number of ironic reversals. On
the one hand, the African continent is a shackled and conquered monster. On the other, it is the European conquerors who are conquered,
as their ruthless and violent imperialism unleashes their latent savagery,
making them more monstrous than those they profess to civilize.
Whereas the West has a tradition of believing that to make the unknown
known it has to be brought under control, Marlow suggests that what
allows Westerners to understand Africans is loss of control. Released
from the constraints of civilization, Europeans can feel a kinship with
those people who on the surface seem so different. Understanding
of the non-Western can occur, therefore, only when the West is conquered by the very people it feels it is conquering. True courage, a
courage in Marlow's world reserved for men (". . . but if you were man
enough . . ."), comes in admitting the possibility of being conquered
by "the Other," an "Other" that exists all along within the European.

One of the most obvious reasons why Westerners do not immediately recognize "the African" within themselves is the physical difference between races. But for Marlow physical differences, such as skin
color, are a surface deception. The real otherness is not physical but
temporal. When Westerners travel to Africa, they make a temporal journey as well as a physical one. As Marlow tells his listeners, "Going up
that river was like travelling back to the earliest beginnings of the world,
when vegetation rioted on the earth and the big trees were kings"
(p. 48). The incomprehensibility of the landscape and the people inhab-
iting it is caused because to travel to Africa is to travel to prehistoric
times.

We were wanderers on a prehistoric earth, on an earth that wore
the aspect of an unknown planet. We could have fancied ourselves
the first of men taking possession of an accursed inheritance, to be

subdued at the cost of profound anguish and of excessive toil. But suddenly, as we struggled round a bend, there would be a glimpse of rush walls, of peaked grass-roofs, a burst of yells, a whirl of black limbs, a mass of hands clapping, of feet stamping, of bodies swaying, of eyes rolling, under the droop of heavy and motionless foliage. The steamer toiled along slowly on the edge of a black and incomprehensible frenzy. The prehistoric man was cursing us, praying to us, welcoming us — who could tell? We were cut off from the comprehension of our surroundings; we glided past like phantoms, wondering and secretly appalled, as sane men would be before an enthusiastic outbreak in a madhouse. We could not understand because we were too far and could not remember, because we were travelling in the night of first ages, of those ages that are gone, leaving hardly a sign — and no memories. (pp. 50–51)

But Marlow eventually does comprehend these people. He can because, as different as they seem from civilized human beings, they constitute the prehistory of the West. If the veneer of civilization has made Westerners forget the truth of their prehistory, the function of Conrad's art is to make them remember what they have forgotten. As he writes in the preface to *The Nigger of the "Narcissus,"* his task is, "by the power of the written word," to present "that glimpse of truth for which you have forgotten to ask." The way he stimulates his readers' memories, however, is at odds with the way nineteenth-century historians tried to do so. As we saw, for the historians time constituted reality. The truth of an event had to do with the time in which it took place. To discover a truth we had forgotten was to reconstruct it historically. But Conrad has a different notion of temporality. For him truth has to be discovered by stripping it of "its cloak of time." The passage of history does not lead to continually new truths. Instead, it places a barrier between us and the memory of our prehistory. Truth is not to be found by remembering history but by forgetting it.

The belief that truth is located in a realm of a prehistory that is still present but disguised by modern life is typical of modernist writers. T. S. Eliot, for instance, praised the work of Wyndham Lewis for "sinking to the most primitive and forgotten, returning to the origin and bringing something back, seeking the beginning and the end" (Matthiessen 466). Whereas for nineteenth-century historians the past and present existed on different temporal planes, for many modernists past and present occupied the same plane. Flattening history in *The Waste Land*, Eliot continually juxtaposes past and present, just as in *Heart of Darkness* Marlow links the past of England with the present of Africa by comparing the Thames to the Congo: "And this also . . . has been one of the dark places of the earth" (p. 19).

Europeans like Conrad, then, possessed not only a progressive, Eurocentric vision of world history but also the temporal sense of the synchronicity of the nonsynchronic. It seemed to them, in other words, that by studying other, primitive-seeming cultures existing simultaneously (or synchronically) with their own, they could study something chronologically disparate, namely, their own deep, prehistoric past. Each culture, it seemed, had its own temporal logic. Whereas the West followed a fairly steady line of progress (despite a backward slide in the "Dark Ages"), other cultures plotted different curves. Thus, at any moment, the world's cultures were at different stages of development. To employ a widely used metaphor, some countries were developed, others underdeveloped. Since the standard of development remained European, cultures different from Europe were, almost by definition, underdeveloped, and the most underdeveloped land of all was Africa, which still existed in a prehistoric state. Drawing on this notion of the synchronicity of the nonsynchronic, Conrad is able to turn a story about a present journey to Africa into a journey to Europe's past, as well as one into each human being's primitive psyche.

Conrad's reliance on the temporal notion that allowed the West to absorb non-Western cultures into its view of history indicates how complicated his portrayal of Western imperialism is. One effect of his inversion of the West's narrative about "the Other" is to undercut its self-righteous superiority. Africa does not embody a lesser truth because it exists in an earlier stage of history. Instead, it embodies a more profound, if unspeakable, truth because it has not traveled as far from its prehistoric origins. Thus, like Freud and Nietzsche, Conrad subverts prevailing European values, offering a "counter-memory" to the belief in rationality and progress.

He also challenges accounts that have abandoned a belief in progress while holding onto a belief in European superiority. *Heart of Darkness* is in part a response to conditions that produced Charles Pearson's *National Life and Character* (1893). Just as Marlow notes that at the time of his journey Africa "was not a blank space anymore" (p. 22), so Pearson proclaims that at the end of the century there are no new lands for Europeans to explore and conquer. The result, this proud Englishman predicts, will be the inevitable and gradual decline of influence by Europeans and especially Anglo-Saxons, whose exemplary individualistic character is compatible with life in the temperate zones but not in the tropics, where future economic growth will occur. By having the heart of Africa conquer its would-be European conquerors, Conrad in part confirms Pearson's view. But Conrad offers a different reason for the European defeat. If Pearson argues that Europeans are constitutionally unfit for tropical climates, Conrad suggests that the European character that Pearson values is nothing more than the cloak of civilization. It is in Africa that Marlow discovers his "remote kinship" (p. 51) with "savages" that other Europeans dismiss as inhuman. Pearson stresses people's differences; Conrad stresses their commonality.

Nonetheless, Conrad's stress on commonality risks making Africans of interest to him only for what they reveal about Europeans. Conrad may challenge prevailing European narratives about "the Other," but by simply inverting them he remains within a Eurocentric logic. Indeed, Conrad's subversion of prevailing values yields a conservative, not a radical, social vision.

The political message of Conrad's encounter with the non-European may well be anti-imperialistic, but not because Conrad espouses liberation of the people he associates with a dark truth about human nature. Instead, for Conrad, European control of non-European cultures is a symptom of its inability to control "the Other" within itself. Conrad's political theory, like that of Hobbes, remains one of control and restraint. There is, it seems, a counter-memory to this narrative that reveals the counter-memory of Western notions of progress, enlightenment, and even decline. We can try to evoke it by examining Conrad's fictional forms.

4

For Conrad narrative has a function similar to that of history. Inevitably taking place within time, narrative, like history, disguises a truth that he feels exists prior to time. Just as the nature of European humanity is to be discovered in an encounter with Africans who exist in a state prior to history, so the meaning of Conrad's tale seems to exist in a realm prior to narrative time. Nonetheless, just as we have to travel through history to encounter our prehistory, so we have to travel through narrative to encounter a meaning that lies deeper than the tale's narrative surface.

To recognize the impossibility of bringing an atemporal truth into narrative representation is to start to understand the importance of one of the most noticeable formal characteristics of Conrad's narrative: its breaks and gaps. Disrupting the narrative flow, they suggest something that resists narrativization; that is, the glimpse of the truth we have forgotten to ask. For instance, the first interruption of Marlow's story occurs when Marlow cries out about his inability adequately to represent Kurtz in words.

> He was just a word for me. I did not see the man in the name any more than you do. Do you see him? Do you see the story? Do you see anything? It seems to me I am trying to tell you a dream — making a vain attempt, because no relation of a dream can convey the dream-sensation, that commingling of absurdity, surprise, and bewilderment in a tremor of struggling revolt, that notion of being captured by the incredible which is the very essence of dreams. . . . (p. 42)

Marlow's outcry is an obvious reminder to the reader of Conrad's own task as a novelist, for he must make his audience see not only Kurtz but also Marlow. And Conrad's task is even more difficult than Marlow's. Marlow's listeners have access to the voice of someone who has seen Kurtz. Conrad's audience confronts nothing but silent, black words on a white page. But Marlow's outcry does more than comment on the difficulty of representation in words.

To remain within narrative is to remain within the realm of consciousness that veils truth. By interrupting the flow of Marlow's narrative Conrad establishes contact with his readers, momentarily freeing them from the shackles of a linear narrative and throwing them back on their own imaginations. In their imaginations, which contain "all the past as well as the future," not in conscious attention to the story's surface, readers will be able to evoke the memory of their prehistory necessary to comprehend the story's meaning. It was, for instance, in a dreamlike state that Marlow was able to remember his kinship with prehistoric humanity. "There were moments when one's past came back to one, as it will sometimes when you have not a moment to spare to yourself; but it came in the shape of an unrestful and noisy dream, remembered with wonder amongst the overwhelming realities of this strange world of plants, and water, and silence" (p. 49). To relate a dream is to distort the dream-sensation. In *Heart of Darkness* Conrad's disruption of narrative forms works to recreate a dream-sensation in the reader.

But it is not quite so simple. If words seem to block us from a deeper truth accessible only through the imagination, it is words that provoke the imagination. It is, for instance, the mention of Kurtz's name that provokes Marlow's outcry over his inability to use words to make us see Kurtz. Since the very narrative that must be disrupted in order for us to have a glimpse of a forgotten truth is our only means to approach that truth, the gaps in Marlow's narrative can be said to serve a different function from the one we have examined. If, on the one hand, they suggest a truth that resists narrativization, on the other, they reveal Marlow's reluctance to continue his narrative journey toward the glimpse of truth he experienced at the heart of darkness. For Marlow to mention Kurtz is to recall all that Kurtz came to embody for him. Not yet capable of facing that horror, Marlow interrupts the story that inevitably leads to Kurtz. The very breaks and gaps that seem to be the only way to suggest the truth also indicate an avoidance of it.

If these two functions seem at odds, they ultimately converge, because for Conrad "the horror" is associated with the inability fully to represent the truth and what that inability implies about the human condition. So long as truth cannot fully be represented, lies become part of the truth of the world. Indeed, immediately preceding the first interruption of the story Marlow announces his hatred of lies. This hatred does not, however, stem from Marlow's love of truth over false-hood, for what he hates about lies is that they remind him of the inevitable truth of mortality. "There is a taint of death, a flavour of mortality in lies — which is exactly what I hate and detest in the world — what I want to forget" (p. 42). Marlow wants to forget the truth of human finitude that lies remind him of: the truth of our existence in a fallen state in which we cannot have full access to truth, a state making lies inevitable. The lie Marlow tells Kurtz's Intended at the end of the story signals Marlow's ability to overcome his hatred of lies and his accep-tance of a world of finitude. At odds with the Enlightenment's faith in humankind's ability through time to liberate itself by expanding its sphere of influence in the world in order to gain a fuller access to truth, Marlow's vision has affinities with a medieval view that a fallen human-kind will never have full knowledge of God's truth. For Conrad, as for many contemporary theorists, humanity's finitude is intricately related to humanity's existence within language. Language, our only access to truth, by its very nature offers only a trace of what it seeks to represent. To be within language is to be in a perpetual state of lost presence.

Politically for Conrad this necessitates the acceptance of a world in which lies and repression are inevitable, a political vision that is intri-cately linked to the seemingly contradictory functions of a narrative that, on the one hand, helps reveal the horror at the heart of darkness and, on the other, serves to cover it up and hold it at bay. Humanity, or the male part of it at least, must confront the horror Kurtz had the courage to face. Survival of the species, however, demands that unlike

Kurtz it must not succumb to it, but instead, like Marlow, learn to cover it up. The work of civilization is a lie, but since the alternative is so terrifying it must go on.

In a world in which all other values seem to be relativized, restraint, therefore, becomes an important value for Conrad. In *Heart of Darkness* restraint is by no means the sole property of Westerners. For Marlow the Africans who accompany him on the journey up the river display more restraint than any European when they resist "the devilry of lingering starvation" (p. 57) by not killing and eating the whites. Marlow, however, cannot explain this restraint, which he finds a mystery greater than the inexplicable sounds of savagery emanating from the primeval forest. He cannot explain it, because for Marlow restraint is associated with work, the work of civilization that separates the West from the savage forest. How much Marlow values work is made clear in another break in his narrative.

Interrupted by a skeptical grunt from one of his listeners, Marlow responds.

> You wonder I didn't go ashore for a howl and a dance? Well, no — I didn't. Fine sentiments, you say? Fine sentiments be hanged! I had no time. I had to mess about with white-lead and strips of woollen blanket helping to put bandages on those leaky steam-pipes — I tell you. I had to watch the steering, and circumvent those snags, and get the tin-pot along by hook or by crook. There was surface-truth enough in these things to save a wiser man. (pp. 51–52)

The necessity to work, just to keep the ship moving, not some idealistic values, keeps Marlow from participating in "unspeakable rites" (p. 65). And, as the reference to "surface-truth" reminds us, Conrad self-consciously compares Marlow's journey up the river to the act of narrating that journey. As a comment directly before another break in Marlow's tale makes even clearer, Conrad's narrative also offers a surface truth that hides a profounder truth. "When you have to attend to things of that sort, to the mere incidents of the surface, the reality — the reality, I tell you — fades. The inner truth is hidden — luckily, luckily" (p. 49).

Within the logic set up by the implied analogy between Marlow's journey and his narrative, the leaky steam-pipes that threaten to sink the ship invite comparison with the gaps and breaks in Marlow's narrative. Just as covering the holes in the steam-pipes allows the ship to continue its journey on the surface of the river, so filling the gaps in

Marlow's narrative allows the surface narrative to continue, thus protecting us from the groundless horror they suggest. Told by an agent at the station about "the necessity for every man to get on," Marlow responds, "Did I see it? I saw it. What more did I want? What I really wanted was rivets, by Heaven! Rivets. To get on with the work — to stop the hole. Rivets I wanted" (p. 43). But rivets, although in abundance at a station closer to shore, are not available. Thus, Marlow, like Conrad, must improvise techniques that will allow him to stop the holes so dangerously exposed and difficult to repair in this outpost of progress.

5

In the final two paragraphs of his preface to *The Nigger of the "Narcissus,"* Conrad explicitly compares his work as an artist to the work of civilization by referring to "the workman of art." But there is an important difference. Workers' hands are kept so busy that they never take a moment to glimpse "the truth." Thus, the hand of a writer must produce a work that arrests,

> for the space of a breath, the hands busy about the work of the earth, and compel men entranced by the sight of distant goals to glance for a moment at the surrounding vision of form and colour, of sunshine and shadows; to make them pause for a look, for a sigh, for a smile — such is the aim, difficult and evanescent, and reserved only for a very few to achieve. But sometimes, by the deserving and the fortunate, even that task is accomplished. And when it is accomplished — behold! — all the truth of life is there: a moment of vision, a sigh, a smile — and the return to an eternal rest.

What interests me most about this passage is the effect that the work of art has, according to Conrad, on the workers of the earth. The initial image is one of labor — hands busy at toil. The final image is one of tranquility — an eternal rest. That final image is clearly an image of death, but, as J. Hillis Miller points out, it also suggests a return "to the forgetful sleep of everyday life" (*Poets* 39). The implication is, therefore, that after people have had a glimpse of the truth of life provided by the workman of art their lives of everyday labor can be considered ones of rest. Arrested for the space of a breath, the hands busy about the work of the earth are set in motion again, returning to the world of time that, because it protects them from the truth at the heart of darkness, is actually one of repose. Serving to protect humanity from the horror it discovers when truth is stripped from the cloak of time, work not only takes place within history but also produces history. It is work, then, that constructs the lie of civilization that hides humanity, necessarily, from the prehistoric truth about itself.

But what if Conrad's location of truth in an atemporal realm is itself a lie? What if the horror of human existence is not to be found in a realm of savagery that we discover by escaping history, but instead lies within history itself — not a Eurocentric construction of a universal History, but one that refuses to indulge in Conrad's mystification that turns Africa into the mere site of Europe's prehistory? If this is the case, work might serve a very different function from the one Conrad attributes to it.

Just as the narrative Conrad uses to hold the horror at bay produces gaps and breaks that bring us face to face with it, so the very work that is supposed to cover up the horror might also produce it. Rather than protecting humanity from an unnameable horror, work might be part of the unnamed horror of Conrad's story. Whereas Conrad sees work providing Europeans with the restraint and discipline necessary to control the horror of "the Other" within themselves, European history records the horror of the enforced labor of others — European and non-European — to maintain structures of domination. Work does indeed restrain. Perhaps, however, the reason why people with hands busy about the work of the earth are restrained from seeing a glimpse of the truth is not because they repress an unconscious world of the imagination that contains an ahistorical truth about the reality of forms, but because they are given no time to become conscious of the history of how the time of their lives has been wasted. Or to put this another way, the unconsciousness of narratives about the unconscious might turn out to be the history of human labor.

As we have seen, Conrad's tale easily lends itself to psychoanalytical and poststructuralist analyses at the same time that it helps us place in a historical context both psychoanalysis's narrative about the journey to the unconscious and poststructuralism's narrative about the decentering of the West's logocentrism. Conrad's representation of work indicates the need to introduce another form of narrative explanation in our attempt to analyze *Heart of Darkness*: Karl Marx's insistence that historians tell the history of work. Whereas the affinities of Conrad's narrative with Freudian and Nietzschean narratives help explain how it serves as a counter-memory to prevailing Eurocentric narratives, its differences from the Marxist narrative help expose the counter-memory of such counter-narratives. To say this is not to argue that the Marxist narrative is the master narrative that explains all others. But so long as there are those who offer narratives of human history that neglect the role human labor has played in shaping history — or even more, who, like Conrad, offer a narrative in which human labor hides us from the "truth" of human experience — so long as such narratives influence our sense of history, Marx's narrative will serve as a reminder of acts of repression.

Like Conrad, Marx constructs a narrative in which human beings quite literally make history through their labor. But, unlike Conrad, Marx would consider any escape from that history to be an escape from the truth of human experience. People are prone to escape from the truth *within* human history because it is not a pleasant one. Human beings might make history, but they do not, Marx reminds us, make it under conditions of their own choosing. Humanity's lack of control over the conditions under which it labors makes history, as it is for Joyce's Stephen Dedalus, a nightmare from which we are trying to awake. The role the historian plays in helping us awaken from the nightmare of history is quite different for Conrad and Marx. In expounding human experience Conrad's novelist as historian becomes its "preserver" and "keeper." He does so by revealing a prehistorical, unchanging truth about humanity. In expounding human experience, Marx's philosopher as historian tries to help change it. He does so by providing explanations of the historical forces that keep humanity from laboring under conditions of its own choosing with the hope that consciousness of those conditions can help liberate humanity from them. Any new historical criticism worthy of its name will share in this goal of using historical analysis as a way to help those in the present work toward the construction of a new future, a future in which work is not only used as a means to control "the Other" within, but also directed toward liberating ourselves to help improve the lives of others truly different from us. In terms of Conrad's *Heart of Darkness* this means recognizing that, whereas Conrad's attempt to separate truth and history serves the important function of demystifying nineteenth-century notions of progress and European superiority, it generates a mystification of its own by absorbing the encounter with "the Other" into a narrative about European identity. Precisely because Conrad's narrative tells us more about Europe than the Africa it supposedly represents, it compels us, not to strip truth from the cloak of time, but to imagine a radically different form of temporal narrative that allows "the Other" to be represented.

WORKS CITED

Bann, Stephen. *The Clothing of Clio*. Cambridge: Cambridge UP, 1984.

Guerard, Albert J. *Conrad the Novelist*. Cambridge: Harvard UP, 1958. New York: Atheneum, 1967.

Iggers, George G. *The German Conception of History*. Middletown: Wesleyan UP, 1968.

Kosellek, Reinhart. *Futures Past*. Trans. Keith Tribe. Cambridge: MIT P, 1985.

Matthiessen, F. O. *American Renaissance*. New York: Oxford UP, 1941.

Miller, J. Hillis. *The Disappearance of God*. Cambridge: Harvard UP, 1963.

———. *Poets of Reality*. Cambridge: Harvard UP, 1965.

Pearson, Charles H. *National Life and Character: A Forecast*. London: Macmillan, 1893.

Postcolonial Criticism
and
Heart of Darkness

WHAT IS POSTCOLONIAL CRITICISM?

Postcolonial criticism typically involves the analysis of works by authors from regions of the globe subject to European colonization. Postcolonial criticism might just as easily have been referred to as "post-imperialist criticism," since the term *imperialism* refers to the extension of rulership or authority (almost always unsought and unwanted) by a politically and economically powerful empire or nation and its culture over a weaker, less "developed" foreign country or region and its culture, thereafter referred to as a "colony" or "dependency" of the imperialist[ic], colonizing ruler nation.

Usually, the prefix *post* in *postcolonial* signifies the period following the end of colonization and the achievement of national independence by a former colony, but sometimes it is used to refer to any point following the establishment of colonial rule. Thus, Chinua Achebe's *Things Fall Apart* (1959), a novel that implicitly opposes the ongoing colonial oppression of the Nigerian people, is often referred to as a postcolonial work. Although in such instances the prefix *post* seems to have secondary connotations of *anti*, its meaning is usually more strictly chronological. For one thing, postcolonial criticism sometimes engages texts produced by authors hailing from the colonizing culture. (Joseph Conrad's *Heart of Darkness*, written by an author Achebe has called a "bloody racist," is a case in point.) The intent of this type of post-colonial criticism is to expose colonialist attitudes held by the author and/or literary characters and to demonstrate the role such biases play in the representation of subjugated persons and cultures.

Emerging from an extraordinary variety of critical and theoretical discourses prevalent during the last half of the twentieth century, post-colonial criticism entered the twenty-first century as the predominant form of literary study. Because it may best be thought of as a convergence of discourses, postcolonial criticism may be best understood in relation to some of its antecedents.

One of these involved the study of so-called Commonwealth literature; that is, literature produced in and about areas colonized by the British Empire that at one point become part of the Commonwealth of Nations (to which, for instance, Canada still belongs). Another focused on what used to be called Third World Literature, a wider field of study since it included non-English cultures and texts (e.g., francophone studies of cultures once colonized by France). Important intellectuals associated with the development of postcolonial criticism include Achebe, mentioned earlier; Edward Kamau Brathwaite, a Caribbean writer from Barbados whose work will be described later; Aimé Césaire, and Frantz Fanon. Césaire, a francophone postcolonial intellectual best known for his book *Discours sur le colonialisme* (*Discourse on Colonialism*; 1950), experienced the brutality of French imperialism firsthand. He established the "Negritude" movement, the purpose of which was to increase political awareness and unite the pan-national interests among black victims of European colonization. Fanon, a French-educated black African psychiatrist who immigrated to Algeria, wrote a series of essays on the needs of colonized peoples, with particular emphasis on political independence from the imperialist, colonizing country.

When painting the background of contemporary postcolonial criticism with the very broadest brush strokes, it is impossible not to mention cultural criticism, or cultural studies. Indeed, in the most general sense, postcolonial criticism may be seen as a form of cultural criticism, an approach to literature and its manifold social and economic relationships that emerged in England in the 1950s and 1960s. Cultural critics notably opposed the general tendency to hear "culture" and think "high culture" — evenings at the symphony, gallery openings, *belles lettres*. They strived to make the term refer at least equally to popular, folk, even "street" culture. Raymond Williams, an early British cultural critic, famously suggested in his book *The Long Revolution* (1961) that "art and culture are ordinary"; he did so not to "pull art down" but rather to point out that there is "creativity in all our living. . . . We create our human world as we have thought of art as being created" (37). The idea that culture, including literature, is produced not only by the dominant or "official" culture but also by ordinary folk enabled and encouraged an interest in authors speaking from the vantage point — and often in the native language of — a colonized people.

Early cultural critics such as Williams followed the practices of Marxist criticism in viewing culture in relation to ideologies, which Williams defined as the "residual," "dominant," or "emerging" ways of viewing the world held in common by asocial groups or by individuals holding power. Williams's view that even repressive ideologies can evolve was linked to his belief in the resilience of subjugated individuals, in their ability to experience the conditions in which they find themselves and creatively respond to those conditions. These relatively hopeful views paralleled those of Michel Foucault, a mid-twentieth-century French theorist who greatly influenced the new historicism (see "What Is the New Historicism?," pp. 245–57), cultural criticism, and, ultimately, postcolonial criticism.

Like Williams, Foucault had been influenced enough by Marxist thought to study cultures in terms of power relationships. But Foucault refused to see power as something exercised by a dominant class or group over a subservient one. Instead, he viewed it as a whole web or complex of forces involving everything from "discourses" — accepted ways of thinking, writing, and speaking — and social practices. According to Foucault, not even tyrannical aristocrats wield power, for they are themselves formed by a network of discourses and practices that constitute power. Viewed by Foucault, power is that which produces what happens. It is positive and productive, not repressive and prohibitive. Furthermore no historical event, according to Foucault, has a single cause; rather, it is intricately connected with a vast web of economic, social, and political factors. Like Williams's view that culture is not, by definition, centered in "high" culture and reflective of dominant ideologies, Foucault's radically decentered view of both power relations and history — the history that power relations engender and are engendered by — reinforced the work of early postcolonial critics and enabled the development of postcolonial criticism by later practitioners.

For instance, Brathwaite, generally viewed as one of the first postcolonial critics, adopted a fluid and dynamic view of the power relations that develop between imperialistic nations and colonized cultures. In *The Development of Creole Society in Jamaica 1770–1820* (1971), he used the term *creolization* to describe what he viewed as a "two-way process," "a way of seeing the society, not in terms of white and black, master and slave, in separate nuclear units, but as contributory parts of a whole. . . . Here in Jamaica, fixed within the dehumanizing institution of slavery, were two cultures of people, having to adapt themselves to a new environment and to each other. The fiction created by this confrontation was cruel, but it was also creative" (153). Homi Bhabha, a leading contemporary cultural critic, focuses on the creative aspect of the colonial confrontation, making a Foucauldian argument that marginalized people subject to repressive power in fact wield positive and productive power of their own. In an essay entitled "Of Mimicry and Man: The Ambivalence of Colonial Discourse" (1987), he uses the term *hybridity* to refer to the process whereby subjugated people, having at first assimilated aspects of oppressor culture, eventually manage to metamorphose those elements, making them their own through a process of transformation. Bhabha, it should be noted, also adopts a decentered view of history made possible by Foucault, arguing that modern Western culture is best understood from the perspective of the postcolonial world, rather than *vice versa*, as Westerners (stereo)typically assume.

The overlap between postcolonial criticism and the cultural criticism from which it emerges is perhaps most evident in the work of Bhabha, who in his groundbreaking work *The Location of Culture* speaks cryptically of "culture's archaic undecidability" in arguing that "there can be no ethically or epistemologically commensurate subject of culture" (135). Since culture is thought to distinguish humanity from the rest of nature, to define the subject of culture generally one would have to begin with an impossibility, namely, a definition of humanity that is not derived from any particular culture's sense of values. Thus, just as there is no one set of practices that can be said definitively to constitute "culture" (as opposed to "pop culture" or "high culture"), so any larger definition of human culture is a dangerous undertaking doomed by a relativism that is inevitably myopic and potentially murderous, as when the values and practices operative within one social group (e.g., the native Africans represented in Conrad's *Heart of Darkness*) are viewed and represented by members of another group (e.g., Mr. Kurtz, the European manager of "the Company's" Inner Station) as sub- or even nonhuman. ("Exterminate all the brutes!" Kurtz writes in his postscript to a report written for the International Society for the Suppression of Savage Customs [p. 66].)

*   *   *

In theory, postcolonial criticism could analyze works about or arising from any colonized culture and could be written in the language of the imperialistic colonizers or in the colonized language. In fact, however, most postcolonial criticism is written in English and tends to concern itself with the following geographic areas: Africa and the Caribbean, as have been mentioned, but also the "East" (i.e., the Middle East and Asia) and the Indian subcontinent — areas in which, during the past century, liberation movements arose that ultimately led to national independence. To be sure, some attention has been paid to Australia, Canada, and New Zealand — often referred to as English "settler colonies" — and sometimes even the thirteen "settler" colonies that became the United States are viewed from the postcolonial perspective. (However, in this instance, the focus is far more likely to be on African American works and works by nonblack authors about African slaves brought to America and/or their free descendants than on, say, Thomas Jefferson as leader of a postcolonial rebellion!) Additionally, an occasional postcolonial reading of Irish literature has taken into account Ireland's status as a colony in all but name — but one that, unlike other colonies, was near the center of the empire with respect to matters such as location, race, and (for the most part) language.

With regard to the Middle East and Asia, the most powerful practitioner of postcolonial criticism is, indeed, one of its acknowledged founders: Edward Said. Said, like his cultural-critical precursor Williams, understood implicitly the role played by ideology in blinding the colonizer to the realities and conditions of the colonized. More specifically influenced by Foucault, Said laid the foundations of postcolonial criticism in *Orientalism* (1978), a book in which he analyzed European discourses concerning the exotic, arguing that stereotypes systematically projected on peoples of the East contributed to the establishment of European domination and exploitation of Eastern (Asian) and Middle Eastern cultures through colonization. Although *Orientalism* focuses on colonialist discourses, both Said and those scholars influenced by him have used its insights to interpret the aftermath of colonialism.

Gayatri Spivak, an Indian scholar, has examined the ways in which issues of class and, especially, gender pertain to the postcolonial situation, relationships that develop within it, and representations of it. In her groundbreaking essay "Can the Subaltern Speak?" (1988), Spivak uses "subalterns" — a British term used to refer to the lowest-ranking officers in the military — to refer to the colonized and, more specifically, to the most vulnerable of the groups comprising that population (e.g., women, racial minorities, immigrants, and underclass persons dominated by relatively powerful groups *within* the colonized culture). With regard to the position of women, subaltern scholars have pointed out their double oppression, both by traditional patriarchal attitudes and practices within their own culture and, beyond that, by attitudes and practices inherent in colonizing cultures that were in many cases more masculinist, sexist. Indeed, Michael Payne has said that subaltern critics in India, Ngugi wa Thiong'o of Kenya, and Rey Chow of China "have read imperialism as not only actively suppressing the more feminist and egalitarian of indigenous institutions and cultural practices, but also as driving the indigenous patriarchy to increasingly reactionary excesses against women and subalterns in an effort to maintain its strength *vis-à-vis* the colonizers" (425).

Issues Spivak raises concerning whether and how agency — the ability of postcolonial, subaltern subjects to choose and to speak independently — can survive the impact of long-term hierarchal situations are central to the understanding of individuals and groups in postcolonial contexts. But they also highlight the difficulties faced by postcolonial scholars whose goal is to give the voiceless a voice. Some of these scholars have resorted to such things as court testimony and prison memoirs, while others have studied popular cultural forms (e.g., oral literature and street theater) through which those who have been silenced may still be heard to speak. The Subaltern Studies Group has been particularly successful at producing revisionary historical accounts of life as experienced by once-silent or silenced colonial subjects. Ranajit Guha's "The Prose of Counter-Insurgency" (1983), for example, provides a critical alternative to accepted historical narratives by contrasting official documents with personal ones, contemporary accounts with retrospective ones, and European views with indigenous perspectives.

Feminist postcolonial critics have understandably focused on recovering the cultures of postcolonial women. In doing so, they have questioned whether the universal category "woman" constructed by certain French and American predecessors is appropriate to postcolonial women or the diverse groups of women comprising that general category. They have stressed that, while all women are female, they are something else as well (such as African, Muslim Pakistani, lesbian, working class, and so forth). This "something else" is precisely what makes them — including their problems and goals — different from other women. Some feminist postcolonial critics have focused on a particularly unique female postcolonial experience, namely, that of women marginalized not in their own colonized culture but, rather, in the imperialistic, colonizing culture to which they have immigrated or been forcibly taken. The so-called classics of white European novels may even tell, indirectly, of the experiences of these women. In "Three Women's Texts and a Critique of Imperialism" (1985), Spivak mines Charlotte Brontë's novel *Jane Eyre* for its numerous references to the West Indies, the slave trade, and Bertha Mason (often referred to as "the madwoman in the attic"), the insane Jamaican wife of the novel's hero, Mr. Rochester. Elsie Michie subsequently focused not on images of the colonized in *Jane Eyre* but, rather, on "the way the colonizers are represented in Brontë's novel because, as Edward Said and subsequent postcolonial critics have noted, images of the colonized are inextricably bound up with and determined by the attitudes of the colonizers" (584).

For the most part, however, the postcolonial women discussed by feminist postcolonial critics are not characters in novels written by white women. Amrit Wilson has written about the challenges faced by post-colonial Asian women living in London, pointing out, for instance, that they tend to be expected by their families and communities to preserve Asian cultural traditions; thus, the expression of personal identity through clothing involves a much more serious infraction of cultural rules than it does for Western women. Gloria Anzaldúa spoke person-ally and eloquently about the experience of women on the margins of Eurocentric North American culture. "I am a border woman," she wrote in *Borderlands: La Frontera = The New Mestiza* (1987). "I grew up between two cultures, the Mexican (with a heavy Indian influence) and the Anglo. . . . Living on the borders and in margins, keeping intact one's shifting and multiple identity and integrity is like trying to swim in a new element, an 'alien' element" (i).

Powerful though it is as a force in contemporary literary studies, postcolonial criticism has its critics. Even the name *postcolonial* has been deemed imprecise, due to the various, inconsistent ways in which the prefix *post* is used and the way *postcolonial* may be used to refer to politi-cal situations, writers writing from or about those contexts, and schol-ars and critics writing about those writers. Others find *postcolonial* mis-leading if not useless as an umbrella term because, in fact, the attitudes and practices of some colonizing countries differed so utterly from those of nations with dissimilar political values and economic purposes. Still others take the opposite view, arguing that postcolonial critics over-stress differences and undervalue attempts (for instance by the Negri-tude movement) to forge a shared collective (in this case African) his-tory of repression and revolt.

The use of *postcolonial* as an adjective to describe any and all so-called diaspora studies has been questioned — whether these studies concern slaves living in the American South, thriving but insular "black" communities in London, or Chinese American families like the one depicted in Amy Tan's novel *The Joy Luck Club* (1989). Critics have also objected to use of the term with reference to settler colonies in which the majority of the population came quickly to consist of colonists and use of the term in connection with minority groups living within a colonizing culture (e.g., the Irish) whose race and language they share.

Some critics of the postcolonial approach have argued that the focus on relations between imperialists and those they have colonized leaves entirely too much out of the picture, whether the picture in question is of postcolonial society or some literary representation or a postcolonial situation. Within this group are those who would prefer to see race, class, or gender difference privileged over the opposition *colonizer/ colonized*. Then there are various groups of detractors who find a misleadingly bright thread in various aspects of what has been called postcolonial studies. Some of these believe that, in so often telling the story of oppressed peoples who eventually gained independence from subjugating empires, postcolonial criticism misleadingly implies that oppression ends when political independence is gained.

In reality, however, most of the above-mentioned critics of postcolonial criticism are, in fact, in almost everyone else's view, postcolonial critics themselves, a fact that demonstrates the dynamic liveliness of the approach, the way in which, although we have the general rubric *postcolonial criticism*, it can mean as many different things (for the time being) as the prefix *post*.

In the example of postcolonial criticism that follows, Patrick Brantlinger begins by alluding to the now-famous claim — made in 1975 by African novelist Chinua Achebe — that Conrad was a racist and that *Heart of Darkness* is a racist work. He then summarizes the diametrically opposed view of Cedric Watts, one of the many critics who have rejected Achebe's assertion. Implicitly asking how the same text could strike different readers so differently, Brantlinger comes up with a compelling answer: "*Heart of Darkness* . . . offers a powerful critique of at least certain manifestations of imperialism and racism, at the same time that it presents that critique in ways that can only be characterized as both imperialist and racist" (p. 305).

Brantlinger draws a parallel between the mixed signals given out by *Heart of Darkness* and its author's lukewarm opposition to colonial oppression in real life. Conrad was sympathetic with the goals of the Congo Reform Association, founded by his friend Roger Casement (see pp. 113–16 in this volume), but generally "backed away from involvement," contributing less to the association's work than did writers such as Mark Twain and Sir Arthur Conan Doyle (pp. 112, 114). Furthermore, Brantlinger points out, "the worst feature of imperialism for Conrad may not have been its violence toward the 'miserable' and 'helpless,' but the lying propaganda used to cover its bloody tracks" (p. 307). What bothered Conrad more than the thought of starving, Congolese chain gangs was the realization that their exploitation was being characterized in Europe as a noble act of philanthropy.

One of the most interesting aspects of Brantlinger's essay is his claim that in writing *Heart of Darkness* Conrad drew as much on books and newspaper articles written after his return to Europe as upon his own experiences in the Congo in 1890. While in Africa, for instance, Conrad "probably saw little or no evidence of cannibalism, despite the stress upon it in his story" (p. 307); he would have learned about the savage practices of cutting off heads or limbs (see "Mutilated Africans," pp. 116–18) from "exposé literature" chronicling the horrors of the 1891 war between Arab slave traders and King Léopold's forces, both of which employed Congolese slave-soldiers. What doesn't come through, either in the accounts Conrad read or the novella he subsequently wrote, is that many of the atrocities described were not so much the traditional practices of the Congolese natives as they were the exploitative, intimidating tactics of their Belgian and Arab oppressors.

That "Conrad portrays the moral bankruptcy" of colonizing ventures by "showing European motives and actions to be no better than African fetishism and savagery" is a telling indication of the novel's at once anti-imperialist and racist tone, according to Brantlinger. He writes that Conrad "paints Kurtz and Africa with the same tarbrush. His version of evil — the form taken by Kurtz's Satanic behavior — is 'going native.' In short, evil *is* African in Conrad's story; if it is also European, that's because some number of white men in the heart of darkness behave like Africans" (p. 311)

Another important aspect of Brantlinger's postcolonial approach is a usage of Marxist thought regarding the relationship between repressive ideologies and oppressed cultures that recalls the work of Williams and Foucault. Brantlinger draws on Fredric Jameson's Marxist argument that another famous novel by Conrad, *Lord Jim*, is characterized by a split between a hollow, modernist "will to style" (which according to Jameson is the source of Conrad's "impressionism") and "the mass

culture tendencies of romance conventions" (p. 313). Brantlinger deconstructs Jameson's opposition, arguing that "on some level, the 'impressionism' of Conrad's novels and their romance features are identical"
(p. 314). Certainly, "romance conventions" and "heroic adventure
themes" do as much to advance colonialist propaganda as the modernist (and/or impressionist) will to style does to blur the depiction —
thereby obscuring the reader's awareness — of atrocities.

Brantlinger shows his debt to earlier practitioners of cultural criticism by using Marxist thought while *fusing* it with the thinking of non-
Marxist postcolonial critics such as Said. Tacitly agreeing with Williams
that "culture is ordinary," Brantlinger insists on seeing a Great Work
of Art like *Heart of Darkness* not only in terms of literary modernism
but also as a work informed by newspapers, exposé literature, and mass
culture romances. Finally, though, Brantlinger's essay exemplifies that
contemporary strain of cultural criticism best described as postcolonial
criticism insofar as it places the text in the context of postcolonial politics, seeing it not only in terms of the political reality it supposedly
represents but also in terms of the politically motivated *representations*
of that political reality.

POSTCOLONIAL CRITICISM:
A SELECTED BIBLIOGRAPHY

Postcolonial Criticism and Theory: General Texts

Ashcroft, Bill, Gareth Griffiths, and Helen Tiffin, eds. *The Empire
    Writes Back: Theory and Practice in Postcolonial Literatures.* New
    York: Routledge, 1989. Print.

Ashcroft, Bill, Gareth Griffiths, and Helen Tiffin, eds. *The Post-
    Colonial Studies Reader.* 2d ed. London: Routledge, 2006. Print.

Ashcroft, Bill, Gareth Griffiths, and Helen Tiffin. *Post-Colonial
    Studies: The Key Concepts.* London: Routledge, 2000. Print.

Barker, Francis, Peter Hulme, and Margaret Iversen, eds. *Colonial
    Discourse/Postcolonial Theory.* Manchester: Manchester UP, 1994.
    Print.

Boehmer, Elleke. *Colonial and Postcolonial Literature.* Oxford:
    Oxford UP, 1995. Print.

Castle, Gregory, ed. *Postcolonial Discourses: An Anthology.* Oxford:
    Blackwell, 2001. Print.

Chambers, Iain, and Lidia Curti, eds. *The Post-Colonial Question: Common Skies, Divided Horizons.* London: Routledge, 1996. Print.

Chrisman, Laura. *Postcolonial Contraventions: Cultural Readings of Race, Imperialism, and Transnationalism.* Manchester: Manchester UP, 2003. Print.

Desai, Gaurav, and Supriya Nair, eds. *Postcolonialisms: An Anthology of Cultural Theory and Criticism.* Piscataway: Rutgers UP, 2005. Print.

Featherstone, Simon. *Postcolonial Cultures.* Edinburgh: Edinburgh UP, 2005. Print.

Gandhi, Leela. *Postcolonial Theory: A Critical Introduction.* New York: Columbia UP, 1998. Print.

Gilbert, Helen, and Joanne Tompkins. *Post-Colonial Drama: Theory, Practice, Politics.* London: Routledge, 1996. Print.

Goldberg, David Theo, and Ato Quayson, eds. *Relocating Postcolonialism.* Oxford: Blackwell, 2002. Print.

Harrison, Nicholas. *Postcolonial Criticism: History, Theory, and the Work of Fiction.* Cambridge: Polity, 2003. Print.

King, C. Richard, ed. *Postcolonial America.* Urbana: U of Illinois P, 2000. Print.

Loomba, Ania. *Colonialism/Postcolonialism.* 2d ed. London: Routledge, 2005. Print.

López, Alfred J. *Posts and Pasts: A Theory of Postcolonialism.* Albany: State U of New York P, 2001. Print.

McLeod, John. *Beginning Postcolonialism.* Manchester: Manchester UP, 2000. Print.

Mongia, Padmini, ed. *Contemporary Postcolonial Theory: A Reader.* London: Arnold, 1996. Print.

Moore-Gilbert, Bart. *Postcolonial Theory: Contexts, Practices, Politics.* London: Verso, 1997. Print.

Moore-Gilbert, Bart, Gareth Stanton, and Willy Maley, eds. *Postcolonial Criticism.* London: Longman, 1997. Print.

Punter, David. *Postcolonial Imaginings: Fictions of a New World Order.* Edinburgh: Edinburgh UP, 2000. Print.

Quayson, Ato. *Postcolonialism: Theory, Practice or Process?* Malden: Blackwell, 2000. Print.

Rajan, Gita, and Radhika Mohanram, eds. *Postcolonial Discourse and Changing Cultural Contexts: Theory and Criticism.* Westport: Greenwood, 1995. Print.

Schwarz, Henry, and Sangeeta Ray, eds. *A Companion to Postcolonial Studies*. Malden: Blackwell, 2000. Print.

Sharp, Joanne. *Geographies of Postcolonialism*. London: Sage, 2008. Print.

Smith, Rowland. *Postcolonizing the Commonwealth: Studies in Literature and Culture*. Waterloo: Wilfrid Laurier UP, 2000. Print.

Sugirtharajah, R. S. *Postcolonial Criticism and Biblical Interpretation*. Oxford: Oxford UP, 2002. Print.

Syrotinski, Michael. *Deconstruction and the Postcolonial: At the Limits of Theory*. Liverpool: Liverpool UP, 2007. Print.

Williams, Patrick, and Laura Chrisman, eds. *Colonial Discourse and Post-Colonial Theory: A Reader*. Hemel Hempstead: Harvester Wheatsheaf, 1993. Print.

Young, Robert. *Postcolonialism: An Historical Introduction*. Oxford: Blackwell, 2001. Print. See especially Part V, "Formations of Postcolonial Theory."

Works by or about Homi K. Bhabha, Edward Said, and Gayatri Chakravorty Spivak

Ansell-Pearson, Keith, Benita Parry, and Judith Squires, eds. *Cultural Readings of Imperialism: Edward Said and the Gravity of History*. London: Lawrence & Wishart, 1997. Print.

Bhabha, Homi K. "Framing Fanon" (foreward). *The Wretched of the Earth*. Trans. Richard Philcox. New York: Grove, 2004. Print.

———. *The Location of Culture*. New York: Routledge, 1994. Print. See especially "Of Mimicry and Man: The Ambivalence of Colonial Discourse." 85–92.

———. *Nation and Narration*. New York: Routledge, 1990. Print. See especially "DissemiNation: Time, Narrative, and the Margins of the Modern Nation." 291–322.

———. "Of Mimicry and Man: The Ambivalence of Colonial Discourse." In *The Location of Culture*.

———. "Postcolonial Criticism." *Redrawing the Boundaries: The Transformation of English and American Literary Studies*. Eds. Stephen Greenblatt and Giles Gunn. New York: MLA, 1992. 437–65. Print.

Bhabha, Homi, and W. J. T. Mitchell, eds. *Edward Said: Continuing the Conversation*. Chicago: U of Chicago P, 2005. Originally published as a special issue, *Critical Inquiry* 31 (2005). Print.

Bové, Paul A., ed. *Edward Said and the Work of the Critic: Speaking Truth to Power*. Durham: Duke UP, 2000. Print.

Morton, Stephen. *Gayatri Chakravorty Spivak*. London: Routledge, 2003. Print.

Said, Edward. *After the Last Sky: Palestinian Lives*. New York: Pantheon, 1986. Print.

———. *Culture and Imperialism*. New York: Knopf, 1993. Print.

———. *The Edward Said Reader*. Eds. Moustafa Bayoumi and Andrew Rubin. New York: Vintage, 2000. Print.

———. *Joseph Conrad and the Fiction of Autobiography*. Cambridge: Harvard UP, 1966. Print.

———. *Orientalism*. New York: Pantheon, 1978. Print.

———. *The World, the Text, and the Critic*. Cambridge: Harvard UP, 1983. Print.

Spivak, Gayatri Chakravorty. "Can the Subaltern Speak?" *Marxism and the Interpretation of Culture*. Eds. Cary Nelson and Larry Grossberg. Urbana: U of Illinois P, 1988. 271–313. Print.

———. *A Critique of Postcolonial Reason: Toward a History of the Vanishing Present*. Cambridge; Harvard UP, 1999. Print.

———. *Death of a Discipline*. New York: Columbia UP, 2003. Print. Includes interpretation of *Heart of Darkness*.

———. *In Other Worlds: Essays in Cultural Politics*. New York: Methuen, 1987. Print.

———. *Other Asias*. Malden: Blackwell, 2007. Print.

———. *Outside in the Teaching Machine*. New York: Routledge, 1993. Print.

———. *The Post-Colonial Critic: Interviews, Strategies, Dialogues*. Ed. Sarah Harasym. New York: Routledge, 1990. Print.

———. *The Spivak Reader: Selected Works of Gayatri Chakravorty Spivak*. Eds. Donna Landry and Gerald MacLean. New York: Routledge, 1996. Print.

———. "Three Women's Texts and a Critique of Imperialism." *Critical Inquiry* 12.1 (1985): 243–61. Print.

Influential Texts in the Development of Postcolonial Criticism and Theory

Brathwaite, Edward Kamau. *The Development of Creole Society in Jamaica, 1770–1820*. Oxford: Clarendon, 1971. Print.

Césaire, Aimé. *Discours sur le colonialisme* (*Discourse on Colonialism*). Paris: Réclame, 1950. Print.

Derrida, Jacques. *La Dissémination* (*Dissemination*). Paris: Éditions du Seuil, 1972. Print.

Fanon, Frantz. *Les damnés de la terre* (*The Wretched of the Earth*). Paris: Maspero, 1961. Print. With a preface by Jean-Paul Sartre.

———. *Peau noire, masques blancs* (*Black Skin/White Masks*). Paris: Éditions du Seuil, 1972. Print.

Foucault, Michel. *Surveiller et punir: Naissance de la prison* (*Discipline and Punish: The Birth of the Prison*). Paris: Gallimard, 1975. Print.

Williams, Raymond. *Culture and Society, 1780–1950*. London: Chatto & Windus, 1958. Print.

———. *The Long Revolution*. New York: Columbia UP, 1961. Print.

Postcolonial Criticism and Theory with a Feminist or Gender Emphasis

Anzaldúa, Gloria. *Borderlands = La Frontera: The New Mestiza*. San Francisco: Spinsters/Aunt Lute, 1987. Print.

Jayawardena, Kumari. *Feminism and Nationalism in the Third World*. New Delhi: Kali for Women, 1986. Print.

Kwok, Pui-lan. *Postcolonial Imagination and Feminist Theology*. Louisville: Westminster John Knox P, 2005. Print.

Lewis, Reina, and Sara Mills, eds. *Feminist Postcolonial Theory: A Reader*. Edinburgh: Edinburgh UP, 2003. Print.

McClintock, Anne, Aamir Mufti, and Ella Shohat, eds. *Dangerous Liaisons: Gender, Nation, and Postcolonial Perspectives*. Minneapolis: U of Minnesota P, 1997. Print.

Mills, Sara. *Gender and Colonial Space*. Manchester and New York: Manchester UP, 2005. Print.

Mohanty, Chandra Talpade, et al., eds. *Third World Women and the Politics of Feminism*. Bloomington: Indiana UP, 1991. Print.

Sharpe, Jenny. *Allegories of Empire: The Figure of the Woman in the Colonial Text*. Minneapolis: U of Minnesota P, 1993. Print.

Wilson, Amrit. *Finding a Voice: Asian Women in Britain*. London: Virago, 1978. Print.

Subalternity, Subaltern Studies

Beverley, John. *Subalternity and Representation: Arguments in Cultural Theory*. Durham: Duke UP, 1999. Print.

Chaturvedi, Vinayak, ed. *Mapping Subaltern Studies and the Postcolonial*. London: Verso, 2000. Print.

Guha, Ranajit. "The Prose of Counter-Insurgency." *Subaltern Studies No. 2: Writings on South Asian History and Society.* Delhi: Oxford UP, 1983. 1–42. Print.

hooks, bell. "Marginality as a Site of Resistance." Eds. Russell Ferguson et al. *Out There: Marginalization and Contemporary Cultures.* Cambridge: MIT P, 1990. 341–43. Print.

Ludden, David, ed. *Reading Subaltern Studies: Critical History, Contested Meaning and the Globalization of South India.* Delhi: Permanent Black, 2001. Print.

Payne, Michael. *A Dictionary of Cultural and Critical Theory.* Oxford: Blackwell, 1996. Print. See entries on postcolonial studies, subaltern studies.

Subaltern Studies: Writings on South Asian History and Society. Delhi: Oxford UP, 1982–2005. Print. Series edited by Ranajit Guha et al., comprised of 12 numbered volumes, *Selected Subaltern Studies* (1988), and *A Subaltern Studies Reader: 1986–95* (1997). See especially Ranajit Guha's essays "On Some Aspects of the Historiography of Colonial India," vol. 1, 1–8, and "The Prose of Counter-Insurgency," vol. 2, 1–40.

Further Reading on Postcolonial Criticism and Theory

Bartolovich, Crystal, and Neil Lazarus, eds. *Marxism, Modernity, and Postcolonial Studies.* Cambridge: Cambridge UP, 2002. Print.

Bohata, Kirsti. *Postcolonialism Revisited: Welsh Writing in English.* Cardiff: U of Wales P, 2004. Print.

Centre for Contemporary Cultural Studies. *The Empire Strikes Back: Race and Racism in 70s Britain.* London: Hutchinson, 1982. Print.

Chakrabarty, Dipesh. *Provincializing Europe: Postcolonial Thought and Historical Difference.* Princeton: Princeton UP, 2000. Print.

Chow, Rey. *Writing Diaspora: Tactics of Intervention in Contemporary Cultural Studies.* Bloomington: Indiana UP, 1993. Print.

Dirlik, Arif. *Third World Criticism in the Age of Global Capitalism.* Boulder: Westview P, 1997. Print.

Gilroy, Paul. *The Black Atlantic: Modernity and Double Consciousness.* London: Verso, 1993. Print.

Hawley, John C., ed. *Postcolonial, Queer: Theoretical Intersections.* Albany: State U of New York P, 2001. Print.

Huggan, Graham. *The Postcolonial Exotic: Marketing the Margins.* London: Routledge, 2001. Print.

JanMohamed, Abdul, and David Lloyd, eds. *The Nature and Context of Minority Discourse*. New York: Oxford UP, 1991. Print.

Kaplan, Amy, and Donald Pease, eds. *Cultures of United States Imperialism*. Durham: Duke UP, 1983. Print.

Kelertas, Violeta. *Baltic Postcolonialism*. Amsterdam: Editions Rodopi B. V., 2006. Print.

Mbembé, Achille. *On the Postcolony*. Trans. A. M. Berrett et al. Berkeley: U of California P, 2001. Print.

McCallum, Pamela, and Wendy Faith. *Linked Histories: Postcolonial Studies in a Globalized World*. Calgary: U of Calgary P, 2005. Print.

Ngũgĩ wa Thiong'o. *Decolonising the Mind: The Politics of Language in African Literature*. London: J. Currey; Portsmouth: Heinemann, 1986. Print.

Parry, Benita. *Postcolonial Studies: A Materialist Critique*. London: Routledge, 2004. Print. Chapter 9, "Narrating Imperialism: Beyond Conrad's Dystopias," includes a section on *Heart of Darkness*. 132–39.

Pines, Jim, and Paul Willeman, eds. *Questions of Third Cinema*. London: BFI, 1989. Print.

Rajan, Gita, and Radhika Mohanram, eds. *English Postcoloniality: Literatures from Around the World*. Westport: Greenwood, 1996. Print.

Rooney, Caroline. *Decolonising Gender: Literature and a Poetics of the Real*. London: Routledge, 2007.

San Juan, E. (Epifanio), Jr. *Beyond Postcolonial Theory*. New York: St. Martin's, 1998. Print.

Singh, Amritjit, and Peter Schmidt, eds. *Postcolonial Theory and the United States: Race, Ethnicity, and Literature*. Jackson: UP of Mississippi, 2000. Print.

Talib, Ismail S. *The Language of Postcolonial Literatures: An Introduction*. London: Routledge, 2002. Print.

Young, Robert, ed. "Neocolonialism." *Oxford Literary Review* 13 (1991) (special issue). Print.

———. *White Mythologies: Writing, History, and the West*. 1st ed. and 2d ed. London: Routledge, 1990, 2004.

Postcolonial Readings

Arata, Stephen D. "The Occidental Tourist: Stoker and Reverse Colonialism." *Fictions of Loss in the Victorian Fin de Siècle*. Cambridge: Cambridge UP, 1996. 107–32. Print.

Bongie, Chris. *Islands and Exiles: The Creole Identities of Post/Colonial Literature.* Stanford: Stanford UP, 1998. Print.

Gorra, Michael Edward. *After Empire: Scott, Naipaul, Rushdie.* Chicago: U of Chicago P, 1997. Print.

Hogan, Patrick Colm. *Colonialism and Cultural Identity: Crises of Tradition in the Anglophone Literatures of India, Africa, and the Caribbean.* Albany: State U of New York P, 2000. Print.

Keown, Michelle. *Postcolonial Pacific Writing: Representations of the Body.* London: Routledge, 2005. Print.

Meyer, Susan. *Imperialism at Home: Race and Victorian Women's Writing.* Ithaca: Cornell UP, 1996. Print.

Michie, Elsie. "White Chimpanzees and Oriental Despots: Racial Stereotyping and Edward Rochester." In *"Jane Eyre": A Case Study in Contemporary Criticism.* Ed. Beth Newman. Boston: Bedford Books, 1996. Print.

Narain, Denise deCaires. *Contemporary Caribbean Women's Poetry: Making Style.* London: Routledge, 2002. Print.

Ní Loingsigh, Aedín. *Postcolonial Eyes: Intercontinental Travel in Francophone African Literature.* Liverpool: Liverpool UP, 2009. Print.

Park, You-me, and Rajeswari Sunder Rajan, eds. *The Postcolonial Jane Austen.* London: Routledge, 2000. Print.

Plasa, Carl. "Reading 'The Geography of Hunger' in Tsitsi Dangarembga's *Nervous Conditions*: From Frantz Fanon to Charlotte Brontë." *The Journal of Commonwealth Literature* 33 (1998): 33–45.

———. *Textual Politics from Slavery to Postcolonialism: Race and Identification.* New York: St. Martin's, 2000. Print.

Sabin, Margery. *Dissenters and Mavericks: Writings about India in English, 1765–2000.* Oxford: Oxford UP, 2002. Print.

Sharrad, Paul. *Postcolonial Literary History and Indian English Fiction.* Amherst: Cambria P, 2008. Print.

Thieme, John. *Postcolonial Con-texts: Writing Back to the Canon.* London: Continuum, 2001. Print.

Postcolonial Readings of Conrad and *Heart of Darkness*

Achebe, Chinua. "An Image of Africa." *Massachusetts Review* 18 (1977): 782–94. Print.

Bongie, Chris. "Exotic Nostalgia: Conrad and the New Imperialism." *Macropolitics of Nineteenth-Century Literature: Nationalism,*

Exoticism, Imperialism. Eds. Jonathan Arac and Harriet Ritvo. Philadelphia: U of Pennsylvania P, 1991. 268–85. Print.

Brantlinger, Patrick. "Epilogue: Kurtz's 'Darkness' and Conrad's *Heart of Darkness.*" *Rule of Darkness: British Literature and Imperialism, 1830–1914.* Ithaca: Cornell UP, 1988. 255–74. Print.

Caminero-Santangelo, Byron. *African Fiction and Joseph Conrad: Reading Postcolonial Intertextuality.* Albany: State U of New York P, 2005. Print. See especially chapter 4, "Subjects in History: Disruptions of the Colonial in *Heart of Darkness* and *July's People.*"

Collits, Terry. *Postcolonial Conrad: Paradoxes of Empire.* London: Routledge, 2005. Print. See especially chapter 5, "Conrad in the Postcolonial World," on the reception of Conrad's work in the field of postcolonial studies, and chapter 6, "*Heart of Darkness:* History, Politics, Myth, and Tragedy," the author's own reading of the novella.

Greiff, Louis K. "Soldier, Sailor, Surfer, Chef: Conrad's Ethics and the Margins of *Apocalypse Now.*" *Literature/Film Quarterly* 20 (1992): 188–98. Print.

Hamner, Robert D., ed. *Joseph Conrad: Third World Perspectives.* Washington, D.C.: Three Continents, 1990. Print.

Harrison, Nicholas. *Postcolonial Criticism: History, Theory, and the Work of Fiction.* Cambridge: Polity, 2003. Print. See especially chapters 1–2 for historical context and a close reading of *Heart of Darkness.*

López, Alfred J. "The Other! The Other!": Conrad, Wilson Harris, and the Postcolonial "Threshold of Capacity." *Posts and Pasts: A Theory of Postcolonialism.* Albany: State U of New York P, 2001. 43–64. Print.

McClure, John A. "A Late Imperial Romance." *Raritan* 10 (1991): 111–30. Print.

Parry, Benita. *Conrad and Imperialism: Ideological Boundaries and Visionary Frontiers.* London: Macmillan, 1983. Print. See especially chapter 2, which addresses *Heart of Darkness.*

Shetty, Sandya. "*Heart of Darkness:* Out of Africa Some New Thing Never Comes." *Journal of Modern Literature* 15 (1989): 461–74. Print.

Thieme, John. "Conrad's 'Hopeless' Binaries: *Heart of Darkness* and Postcolonial Interior Journeys." *Postcolonial Con-texts: Writing Back to the Canon.* London: Continuum, 2001. 15–52. Print. Considers a range of postcolonial responses to the novella.

Watts, Cedric. "'A Bloody Racist': About Achebe's View of Conrad."
    Yearbook of English Studies 13 (1983): 196–209. Print.

White, Andrea. *Joseph Conrad and the Adventure Tradition: Con-
    structing and Deconstructing the Imperial Subject.* Cambridge:
    Cambridge UP, 1993. Print. See especially chapter 9, "The
    African Fictions (II): 'Heart of Darkness.'" 167–92.

A POSTCOLONIAL CRITICAL PERSPECTIVE

PATRICK BRANTLINGER

Heart of Darkness: Anti-Imperialism, Racism, or Impressionism?

In a 1975 lecture at the University of Massachusetts, Nigerian novelist Chinua Achebe attacked *Heart of Darkness* as "racist." Conrad
"projects the image of Africa as 'the other world,' the antithesis of
Europe and therefore of civilization, a place where man's vaunted intelligence and refinement are finally mocked by triumphant bestiality"
(Achebe 783). Supposedly the great demystifier, Conrad is instead a
"purveyor of comforting myths" (Achebe 784) and even "a bloody
racist" (788). Achebe adds: "That this simple truth is glossed over in
criticisms of his work is due to the fact that white racism against Africa
is such a normal way of thinking that its manifestations go completely
undetected" (788). Achebe would therefore like to strike Conrad's
novella from the curriculum, where it has been one of the most frequently taught works of modern fiction in English classes from Chicago
to Bombay to Johannesburg.

Achebe's diatribe has provoked a number of vigorous defenses of
Heart of Darkness, which predictably stress Conrad's critical stance
toward imperialism and also the wide acceptance of racist language and
categories in the late Victorian period. Cedric Watts, for example,
argues that "really Conrad and Achebe are on the same side" (204).
Achebe simply gets carried away by his understandable aversion to racial
stereotyping. "Far from being a 'purveyor of comforting myths,'"
Watts declares, "Conrad most deliberately and incisively debunks such
myths" (197). Acknowledging that Conrad employed the stereotypic
language common in his day, Watts contends that he nevertheless rose
above racism:

Achebe notes with indignation that Conrad (in the "Author's Note" to *Victory*) speaks of an encounter with a "buck nigger" in Haiti which gave him an impression of mindless violence. Achebe might as well have noted the reference in *The Nigger of the "Narcissus"* . . . to a "tormented and flattened face — a face pathetic and brutal: the tragic, the mysterious, the repulsive mask of a nigger's soul." He might have noted, also, that Conrad's letters are sprinkled with casual anti-Semitic references. It is the same in the letters of his friend [R. B. Cunninghame] Graham. Both Conrad and Graham were influenced by the climate of prejudice of their times. . . . What is interesting is that the best work of both men seems to transcend such prejudice. (208)

Their work "transcends prejudice," Watts believes, partly because they both attack imperialism. Watts is one of the many critics who interpret *Heart of Darkness* as an exposé of imperialist rapacity and violence. Kurtz's career in deviltry obviously undermines imperialist ideology, and the greed of the "faithless pilgrims" — the white subKurtzes, so to speak — is perhaps worse. "The conquest of the earth," Marlow declares, "which mostly means the taking it away from those who have a different complexion or slightly flatter noses than ourselves, is not a pretty thing when you look into it too much" (p. 21). There is nothing equivocal about that remark; Conrad entertained no illusions about imperialist violence. But Marlow distinguishes between British imperialism and that of the other European powers: the red parts of the map are good to see, he says, "because one knows that some real work is done in there" (p. 24). *Heart of Darkness* is specifically about what Conrad saw in King Léopold's African empire in 1890; the extent to which his critique can be generalized to imperialism beyond the Congo is unclear.

The politics of Conrad's story are complicated by its ambiguous style. I will use "impressionism" as a highly inadequate term to refer to its language and narrative structure, in part because Fredric Jameson uses it in his diagnosis of the "schizophrenic" nature of *Lord Jim* (219). Conrad's "impressionism" is for some critics his most praiseworthy quality, while for others it appears instead to be a means of obfuscation, allowing him to mask his "nihilism," or to maintain contradictory values, or both. Interpretations of *Heart of Darkness* that read it as only racist (and therefore imperialist), or conversely as only anti-imperialist (and therefore antiracist), inevitably founder on its "impressionism." To point only to the most obvious difficulty, the narrative frame filters everything that is said not just through Marlow, but also through the anonymous primary narrator. At what point is it safe to assume that Conrad/Marlow express a single point of view? And even supposing that Marlow speaks directly for Conrad, does Conrad/Marlow agree with the values expressed by the primary narrator? Whatever the answers, *Heart of Darkness*, I believe, offers a powerful critique of at least certain manifestations of imperialism and racism, at the same time that it presents that critique in ways that can only be characterized as both imperialist and racist. "Impressionism" is the fragile skein of discourse that expresses — or disguises — this "schizophrenic" contradiction as an apparently harmonious whole.

I

In *Conrad and Imperialism* (1983), Benita Parry argues that "by revealing the disjunctions between high-sounding rhetoric and sordid ambitions and indicating the purposes and goals of a civilisation dedicated to global . . . hegemony, Conrad's writings [are] more destructive of imperialism's ideological premises than [are] the polemics of his contemporary opponents of empire" (10). Perhaps. It is at least certain that Conrad was appalled by the "high-sounding rhetoric" that had been used to mask the "sordid ambitions" of King Léopold II of Belgium, Conrad's ultimate employer during his six months in the Congo in 1890. *Heart of Darkness* expresses not only what Conrad saw and partially recorded in his "Congo Diary," but also the revelations of atrocities that began appearing in the British press as early as 1888 and that reached a climax twenty years later, when in 1908 the mounting scandal forced the Belgian government to take control of Léopold's private domain. During that period the population of the Congo was reduced by perhaps one half; as many as 6,000,000 persons may have been uprooted, tortured, and murdered through the forced labor system used to extract ivory and what reformers called "red rubber."[1] Conrad was sympathetic to the Congo Reform Association, established in 1903 partly by his friend Roger Casement whom he had met in Africa, and Casement got him to write a propaganda letter in which Conrad says: "It is an extraordinary thing that the conscience of Europe which seventy years ago . . . put down the slave trade on humanitarian grounds tolerates the Congo state today" (Morel, *Rule* 351–52). There

---

[1]For a history of British humanitarian protest against Léopold's policies, see S. J. Cookey, *Britain and the Congo Question, 1885–1913* (London: Longman, 1968).

follows some patronizing language contrasting the brutalities visited upon the Congolese with the legal protections given to horses in Europe, but Conrad's intention is clear enough.

There is little to add to Hunt Hawkins's account of Conrad's relations with the Congo Reform Association. Its leader, Edmund Morel, who quoted Conrad's letter to Casement in *King Leopold's Rule in Africa* (1904), called *Heart of Darkness* the "most powerful thing ever written on the subject" (Hawkins 293). But as Hawkins notes, apart from writing the letter to Casement, Conrad backed away from involvement with the Association. Other prominent novelists who'd never been to the Congo contributed as much or more to its work. Mark Twain volunteered "King Léopold's Soliloquy," and Sir Arthur Conan Doyle wrote a book for the Association called *The Crime of the Congo*. Hawkins notes that Conrad "had little faith in agitation for political reform because words were meaningless, human nature unimprovable, and the universe dying" — hardly views that would encourage engagement in a cause like that of the Association (292–93).

All the same, in at least one other work of fiction Conrad registered his abhorrence of King Léopold's rape of the Congo. This is the minor but highly revealing fantasy that Conrad coauthored with Ford Madox Hueffer, *The Inheritors: An Extravagant Story* (1901). Conrad's role in its writing may have been slight, but was still substantial enough to make plain that he shared the views expressed in it. Briefly, the protagonist meets a beautiful young woman who claims to come from the "fourth dimension" and to be one of those who "shall inherit the earth."

> The Dimensionists were to come in swarms, to materialise, to devour like locusts. . . . They were to come like snow in the night: in the morning one would look out and find the world white. . . . As to methods, we should be treated as we ourselves treat the inferior races. (Conrad and Hueffer 16)

Far from being meek, the "inheritors" are obviously modern-day imperialists, satirically depicted as invaders from a "spiritualist" alternative world. But apart from the young woman and one other character, the invasion does not occur during the course of the novel, although the satire upon imperialism is maintained through the portrayal of the Duc de Mersch and his "System for the Regeneration of the Arctic Regions" (46). Like King Léopold, "the foreign financier — they called him the Duc de Mersch — was by way of being a philanthropist on megalomaniac lines." He proves ultimately to be no philanthropist at all, but just the sort of "gigantic and atrocious fraud" that Conrad believed Léopold to be. All one needs to do to read *The Inheritors* as an attack on Léopold's African regime is to substitute "Congo" for "Greenland." The hero, journalist Arthur Granger, helps to expose "the real horrors of the système Groënlandais — flogged, butchered, miserable natives, the famines, the vices, diseases, and the crimes" (280). The authors are not even particular about the color of the Eskimo victims: one character says that the Duc "has the blacks murdered" (246–74).

Hueffer and Conrad write some scorching things in *The Inheritors* about "cruelty to the miserable, helpless, and defenceless" (282). But the facts of exploitation in the Congo are perhaps less distressing to them than the lying idealism which disguises it:

> More revolting to see without a mask was that falsehood which had been hiding under the words which for ages had spurred men to noble deeds, to self-sacrifice, to heroism. What was appalling was . . . that all the traditional ideals of honour, glory, conscience, had been committed to the upholding of a gigantic and atrocious fraud. The falsehood had spread stealthily, had eaten into the very heart of creeds and convictions that we learn upon our passage between the past and the future. The old order of things had to live or perish with a lie. (282)

I will come back to the possibility that the worst feature of imperialism for Conrad may not have been its violence toward the "miserable" and "helpless," but the lying propaganda used to cover its bloody tracks.

As Hawkins and others have pointed out, Conrad did not base his critique of imperialist exploitation in *Heart of Darkness* solely on what he had seen in the Congo. What he witnessed was miserable enough, and he was also made personally miserable and resentful by disease and the conviction that his Belgian employers were exploiting him. But, as he assured Casement, while in the Congo he had not even heard of "the alleged custom of cutting off hands among the natives" (Morel, *Rule* 117). The conclusion that Casement drew from this and other evidence was that most of the cruelties practiced in the Congo were not traditional, but were the recent effects of exploitation. The cutting off of hands was a punishment for noncooperation in Léopold's forced labor system, and probably became frequent only after 1890. And just as Conrad had seen little or no evidence of torture, so, Molly Mahood conjectures, he probably saw little or no evidence of cannibalism, despite the stress upon it in his story (Mahood 12).

It thus seems likely that much of the "horror" either depicted or suggested in *Heart of Darkness* does not represent what Conrad saw, but rather his reading of the literature that exposed Léopold's bloody system between the time of his return to England and the composition of the novella in 1898–99. While Conrad's "Congo Diary" and every facet of his journey to Stanley Falls and back has been scrutinized by Norman Sherry and others, much less attention has been paid to what Conrad learned about the Congo after his sojourn there. The exposé literature undoubtedly confirmed suspicions which Conrad formed in 1890; the bloodiest period in the history of Léopold's regime began about a year later. According to Edmund Morel: "From 1890 onwards the records of the Congo State have been literally blood-soaked. Even at that early date, the real complexion of Congo State philanthropy was beginning to appear, but public opinion in Europe was then in its hood-winked stage" (*Rule* 103).

The two events that did most to bring Léopold's Congo under public scrutiny after Conrad's time there were the 1891–94 war between Léopold's forces and the Arab slave-traders and the murder of Charles Stokes, English citizen and renegade missionary, by Belgian officials in 1895. The conflict with the Arabs — a "war of extermination," according to Morel — was incredibly cruel and bloody. "The first serious collision with the Arabs occurred in October 27, 1891; the second on May 6, 1892. Battle then succeeded battle; Nyangwe, the Arab stronghold, was captured in January, 1893, and with the surrender of Rumaliza in January, 1894, the campaign came to an end" (*Rule* 23). Conrad undoubtedly read about these events in the press and perhaps also in later accounts, notably Captain Sidney Hinde's *The Fall of the Congo Arabs* (1897). Arthur Hodister, whom Sherry claims as the original of Kurtz, was an early victim of the fighting, having led an expedition to Katanga that was crushed by the Arabs. According to Ian Watt, "*The Times* reported of Hodister and his comrades that 'their heads were stuck on poles and their bodies eaten'" (23). This and many similar episodes during the war are probable sources of Conrad's emphasis upon cannibalism in *Heart of Darkness*.

Cannibalism was practiced by both sides in the war, not just by the Arabs and their Congolese soldiers. According to Hinde, who must also be counted among the possible models for Kurtz, "The fact that both sides were cannibals, or rather that both sides had cannibals in their train, proved a great element in our success" (124–25). Muslims, Hinde points out, believe that they will go to heaven only if their bodies are intact, as opposed to mutilated, chopped up, eaten. So cannibalism was in part a weapon of fear and reprisal on both sides, and in part also a traditional accompaniment of war among some Congolese societies. Hinde speaks of combatants on both sides as "human wolves" and describes numerous "disgusting banquets" (69). A typical passage in his account reads: "What struck me most in these expeditions was the number of partially cut-up bodies I found in every direction for miles around. Some were minus the hands and feet, and some with steaks cut from the thighs or elsewhere; others had the entrails or the head removed, according to the taste of the individual savage . . ." (131). Hinde's descriptions of such atrocities seem to be those of an impartial, external observer, but in fact he was one of six white officers in charge of some four hundred "regulars" and "about 25,000" "cannibal" troops. His expressions of horror seem only what are expected of an Englishman, but they are also those of a participant and contradict more honest expressions of sadistic fascination with every bloodthirsty detail.

While it seems likely that Conrad read Hinde's lurid account, he must have known about the war from earlier accounts such as those in *The Times*. To cite one other example, in a series of journal extracts published in *The Century Magazine* in 1896–97, E. J. Glave documented "cruelty in the Congo Free State." According to Glave, "The state has not suppressed slavery, but established a monopoly by driving out the Arab and Wangwana competitors." Instead of a noble war to end the slave trade, which is how Léopold and his agents justified their actions against the Arabs, a new system of slavery was installed in place of the old. Glave continues: "sometimes the natives are so persecuted that they [take revenge] by killing and eating their tormentors. Recently the state post on the Lomami lost two men killed and eaten by the natives. Arabs were sent to punish the natives; many women and children were taken, and twenty-one heads were brought to [Stanley Falls], and have been used by Captain Rom as a decoration round a flower-bed in front of his house" (706). Captain Rom, no doubt, must also be counted among the possible models for Kurtz. In any event, the practice of seizing Congolese for laborers and chopping off the hands and heads of resisters continued and probably increased after the defeat of the Arabs, as numerous eyewitnesses testify in the grisly quotations that form the bulk of Edmund Morel's exposés. According to a quite typical account by a Swiss observer: "If the chief does not bring the stipulated number of baskets [of raw rubber], soldiers are sent out, and the people are killed without mercy. As proof, parts of the body are brought to the factory. How often have I watched heads and hands being carried into the factory" (Morel, *Rubber* 77).

II

When Marlow declares that "the conquest of the earth . . . is not a pretty thing," he goes on to suggest that imperialism may be "redeemed" by the "idea" that lies behind it. But in the real world idealism is fragile, and in *Heart of Darkness*, except for the illusions maintained by a few womenfolk back in Brussels, it has almost died out. In "going native," Kurtz betrays the "civilizing" ideals with which he supposedly set out from Europe. Among the "faithless pilgrims," there are only false ideals and the false religion of self-seeking. "To tear treasure out of the bowels of the land was their desire," says Marlow, "with no more moral purpose at the back of it than there is in burglars breaking into a safe" (p. 45). The true nature of European philanthropy in the Congo is revealed to Marlow by the chain gang and the "black shadows of disease and starvation," left to die in the "greenish gloom," whom he sees at the Outer Station (p. 31). These miserable "phantoms" are probably accurate depictions of what Conrad saw in 1890; they may also be taken to represent what he later learned about Léopold's forced labor system. In any case, from the moment he sets foot in the Congo, Marlow is clear about the meaning of "the merry dance of death and trade" (p. 29). It thus makes perfect sense to interpret *Heart of Darkness* as an attack on imperialism, at least as it was operative in the Congo.

But in the course of this attack, *all* "ideals" threaten to turn into "idols" — "something," in Marlow's words, that "you can set up, and bow down before, and offer a sacrifice to" (p. 21). Conrad universalizes "darkness" partly by universalizing fetishism. Lenin, Rosa Luxemburg, and other Marxist critics of empire described the era of "the scramble for Africa" — roughly 1880 to 1914 — as one when the "commodity fetishism" of "late capitalism" was most intense, a notion that Edward Said touches upon in analyzing *The Nigger of the "Narcissus"* (142–43). If the "natives" in their darkness set Kurtz up as an idol, the Europeans worship ivory, money, power, reputation. Kurtz joins the "natives" in their "unspeakable rites," worshipping his own unrestrained power and lust. Marlow himself assumes the pose of an idol, sitting on shipdeck with folded legs and outward palms like a Buddha. And Kurtz's Intended is perhaps the greatest fetishist of all, idolizing her image of her fiancé. Marlow's lie leaves Kurtz's Intended shrouded in the protective darkness of her illusions, her idol-worship.

But the difficulty with this ingenious inversion, through which "ideals" become "idols," is that Conrad portrays the moral bankruptcy of imperialism by showing European motives and actions to be no better than African fetishism and savagery. He paints Kurtz and Africa with the same tarbrush. His version of evil — the form taken by Kurtz's Satanic behavior — is "going native." In short, evil *is* African in Conrad's story; if it is also European, that's because some number of white men in the heart of darkness behave like Africans. Conrad's stress on cannibalism, his identification of African customs with violence, lust, and madness, his metaphors of bestiality, death, and darkness, his suggestion that traveling in Africa is like traveling backward in time to primeval, infantile, but also hellish stages of existence — these features of the story are drawn from the repertoire of Victorian imperialism and racism that painted an entire continent dark.

Achebe is therefore right to call Conrad's portrayal of Africa and Africans "racist." It is possible to argue, as does Parry, that Conrad works with the white-and-black, light-and-darkness dichotomies of racist fantasy in order to subvert them, but she acknowledges that the subversion is incomplete: "Although the resonances of white are rendered discordant . . . black and dark do serve in the text as equivalences for the savage and unredeemed, the corrupt and degraded . . . the cruel and atrocious. Imperialism itself is perceived as the dark within Europe. . . . Yet despite . . . momentous departures from traditional European usage . . . the fiction gravitates back to established practice, registering the view of two incompatible orders within a manichean universe" (23). The "imperialist imagination" itself, Parry suggests, works with the "manichean," irreconcilable polarities common to all racist ideology. Achebe states the issue more succinctly: "Conrad had a problem with niggers. . . . Sometimes, his fixation on blackness is . . . overwhelming" (789).

Identifying specific sources for Conrad's later knowledge of the horrors of Léopold's regime is less important than recognizing that there were numerous sources, swelling in number through the 1890s. Conrad reshaped his firsthand experience of the Congo in the light of these sources in several ways. As I have already suggested, the emphasis on cannibalism in *Heart of Darkness* probably derives in part from Conrad's reading about the war between Léopold's agents and the Arabs. At the same time, the war is not mentioned in the novella — indeed, the Arab rivals of the Belgians for control of the Congo are conspicuous only by their absence. The omission has the important effect of sharpening the light-and-dark dichotomies, the staple of European racism; "evil" and "darkness" are parceled out between only two antithetical sides, European and African, "white" and "black." But while Conrad/ Marlow treats the attribution of "evil" to the European invaders as a paradox, its attribution to Africans he treats as a given. Further, the omission of the Arabs means that Conrad does not treat cannibalism as a result of war, but as an everyday custom of the Congolese, even though he probably saw no evidence of it when he was there. Exaggerating the extent and nature of cannibalism is also standard in racist accounts of Africa.

In simplifying his memories and sources, Conrad arrived at the dichotomous or "manichean" pattern of the imperialist adventure romance, a pattern radically at odds with any realist, exposé intention. Perhaps *Heart of Darkness* expresses two irreconcilable intentions. As Parry says, "to proffer an interpretation of *Heart of Darkness* as a militant denunciation and a reluctant affirmation of imperialist civilisation, as a fiction that [both] exposes and colludes in imperialism's mystifications, is to recognise its immanent contradictions" (39). Moreover, the argument that Conrad was consciously anti-imperialist, but that he unconsciously or carelessly employed the racist terminology current in his day will not stand up, because he was acutely aware of what he was doing. Every white-black and light-dark contrast in the story, whether it corroborates racist assumptions or subverts them, is precisely calculated for its effects both as a unit in a scheme of imagery and as a focal point in a complex web of contradictory political and moral values.

Conrad knew that his story was ambiguous: he stresses that ambiguity at every opportunity, so that labeling it "anti-imperialist" is as unsatisfactory as condemning it for being "racist." The fault-line for all of the contradictions and ambiguities in the text lies between Marlow and Kurtz. Of course it also lies between Conrad and both of his ambivalent characters, not to mention the anonymous primary narrator. Is Marlow Kurtz's antagonist, critic, and potential redeemer? Or is he Kurtz's pale shadow and admirer, his double, and finally one more idolator in a story full of examples of fetishism and devil worship? Conrad poses these questions with great care, but he just as carefully refuses to answer them.

III

In the world of *Heart of Darkness*, there are no clear answers. Ambiguity, perhaps the main form of "darkness" in the story, prevails. Conrad overlays the political and moral content of his novella with symbolic and mythic patterns that divert attention from Kurtz and the Congo to "misty halos" and "moonshine." The anonymous narrator uses these metaphors to describe the difference between Marlow's stories and those of ordinary sailors:

> The yarns of seamen have a direct simplicity, the whole meaning of which lies within the shell of a cracked nut. But Marlow was not typical . . . and to him the meaning of an episode was not inside like a kernel but outside, enveloping the tale which brought it out only as a glow brings out a haze, in the likeness of one of these misty halos that sometimes are made visible by the spectral illumination of moonshine. (pp. 19–20)

The passage announces that locating the "meaning" of the story won't be easy, and in fact may be impossible. It seems almost to be a confession of defeat, or at least of contradiction. Conrad here establishes as one of his themes the problem of rendering any judgment whatsoever — moral, political, metaphysical — about Marlow's narrative. It is precisely this complexity — a theme that might be labeled the dislocation of meaning or the disorientation of values in the story — that many critics have treated as its finest feature.

In *The Political Unconscious*, Fredric Jameson argues that Conrad's stories — *Lord Jim* is his main example — betray a symptomatic split between a modernist "will to style," leading to an elaborate but essentially hollow "impressionism," and the reified, mass culture tendencies of romance conventions. In a fairly obvious way, *Heart of Darkness* betrays the same split, moving in one direction toward the "misty halos" and "moonshine" of a style that seeks to be its own meaning, apart from any "kernel" or center or embarrassingly clear content, but also grounding itself in another direction in the conventions of Gothic romance with their devalued mass culture status — conventions that were readily adapted to the heroic adventure themes of imperialist propaganda. This split almost corresponds to the contradiction of an anti-imperialist novel which is also racist. In the direction of high style, the story acquires several serious purposes, apparently including its critique of empire. In the direction of reified mass culture, it falls into the stereotypic patterns of race-thinking common to the entire tradition of the imperialist adventure story or quest romance. This double, contradictory purpose, characteristic perhaps of all of Conrad's fiction, Jameson calls "schizophrenic" (219).

By "the manichaeanism of the imperialist imagination," Parry means dividing the world between "warring moral forces" — good versus evil, civilization versus savagery, West versus East, light versus darkness, white versus black. Such polarizations are the common property

of the racism and authoritarianism that constitute imperialist political
theory and also of the Gothic romance conventions that were appropri-
ated by numerous writers of imperialist adventure tales — G. A. Henty,
Rider Haggard, Robert Louis Stevenson, Conan Doyle, John Buchan,
Rudyard Kipling, and Conrad among them. As Martin Green points
out, "Conrad of course offers us an ironic view of that genre. But he
affirms its value" (219). Conrad is simultaneously a critic of the imperialist adventure and its romantic fictions, and one of the greatest writers
of such fictions, his greatness deriving partly from his critical irony and
partly from the complexity of his style — his "impressionism." But the
chief difficulty with Jameson's argument, I think, is that the "will to
style" in Conrad's text is also a will to appropriate and remake Gothic
romance conventions into high art. On some level, the "impressionism" of Conrad's novels and their romance features are identical —
Conrad constructs a sophisticated version of the imperialist romance —
and in any case both threaten to submerge or "derealize" the critique
of empire within their own more strictly esthetic project. As part of that
project, providing much of the substance of "impressionism," the
romance conventions that Conrad reshapes carry with them the polarizations of racist thought.

   In analyzing Conrad's "schizophrenic writing," Jameson notes the
proliferation of often contradictory critical opinions that mark the
history of his reception: "The discontinuities objectively present in
Conrad's narratives have, as with few other modern writers, projected
a bewildering variety of competing and incommensurable interpretive
options. . . ." Jameson proceeds to list nine different critical approaches,
from "the 'romance' or mass-cultural reading of Conrad as a writer
of adventure tales [and] the stylistic analysis of Conrad as a practitioner of . . . [an] 'impressionistic' will to style," to the "myth-critical,"
the Freudian, the ethical, the "ego-psychological," the existential, the
Nietzschean, and the structuralist readings. Jameson leaves off of the
list his own Marxist-political reading; what he wishes to suggest is how
often criticism ignores or downplays the contradictory politics of Conrad's fiction (208–09). Raymond Williams voices a similar complaint:

> It is . . . astonishing that a whole school of criticism has succeeded
> in emptying *Heart of Darkness* of its social and historical con-
> tent. . . . The Congo of Léopold follows the sea that Dombey and
> Son traded across, follows it into an endless substitution in which
> no object is itself, no social experience direct, but everything is
> translated into what can be called a metaphysical language — the
> river is Evil; the sea is Love or Death. Yet only called metaphysical,

because there is not even that much guts in it. No profound and ordinary belief, only a perpetual and sophisticated evasion. . . . (145)

There are wonderfully elaborate readings of Marlow's journey as a descent into hell, playing upon Conrad's frequent allusions to Homer, Virgil, Dante, Milton, Goethe, and devil worship. And there are just as many elaborate readings of the story as an "inward voyage" of "self-discovery," in which its geopolitical language is treated as symbolizing psychological states and parts of the mind. Conrad, Albert Guerard reminds us, was Freud's contemporary, and in *Heart of Darkness* he produced the quintessential "night journey into the unconscious" (39). Guerard adds that "it little matters what, in terms of psychological symbolism, we . . . say [Kurtz] represents: whether the Freudian id or the Jungian shadow or more vaguely the outlaw" (39). Perhaps it matters just as little whether we say the story takes place in Léopold's Congo or in some purely imaginary landscape.

The point, however, is not to take issue with Guerard and other critics who concentrate on the "impressionism" of Conrad's story, but rather to restore what their readings neglect. In a great deal of contemporary criticism, words themselves have ceased to have external referents. Williams does not take Jameson's line in accusing Conrad's "will to style" of emptying *Heart of Darkness* of its "social and historical content"; instead, he accuses criticism of so emptying it. The "will to style" — or rather the will to a rarefied critical intelligence — devours us, too, leaving structuralists and deconstructionists, Althusserians and Foucauldians, and so forth. And yet Conrad has anticipated his critics by constructing a story in which the "meaning" does not lie at the center, not even at "the heart of darkness," but elsewhere, in "misty halos" and "moonshine" — forever beyond some vertiginous horizon which recedes as the would-be critic-adventurer sails toward it.

IV

The crowds [in one village] were fired into promiscuously, and fifteen were killed, including four women and a babe on its mother's breast. The heads were cut off and brought to the officer in charge, who then sent men to cut off the hands also, and these were pierced, strung, and dried over the camp fire. The heads, with many others, I saw myself. The town, prosperous once, was burnt, and what they could not carry off was destroyed. Crowds of people were caught, mostly . . . women, and three fresh rope

gangs were added. These poor 'prisoner' gangs were mere skele-
tons of skin and bone. . . . Chiyombo's very large town was next
attacked. A lot of people were killed, and heads and hands cut off
and taken back to the officers. . . . Shortly after the State caravans,
with flags flying and bugles blowing, entered the mission station
at Luanza . . . and I shall not soon forget the sickening sight of
deep baskets of human heads. (Morel, *Rubber* 49)

While the primary narrator and many critics seem to believe that the
meaning of *Heart of Darkness* lies in "the spectral illumination of moonshine," Marlow knows better. "Illumination" proves as false as most
white men — as false as white "civilization"; the "truth," or at least the
meaning of Conrad's story, lies in "darkness." That is why, once Marlow learns about the shadowy Kurtz, he is so impatient to get to the
Central Station. And yet Kurtz seems inadequate as a central character
or the goal of Marlow's quest — vacuous, a mere "shade," a "hollow
man." That, however, may be part of Conrad's point. Ian Watt has
identified at least nine possible models for Kurtz, including Henry
Morton Stanley, Arthur Hodister, and Charles Stokes, who left the
Church Missionary Society for an African wife and life as a gun-runner
and slave-trader (Watt 141–45). In 1895 Stokes was executed in the
Congo for selling guns to the Arabs, an event which, close on the heels
of the war, provided a focus for British public indignation. To Watt's
list of models for Kurtz I have already added Captain Hinde, author of
The Fall of the Congo Arabs, and Captain Rom, who decorated the bor-
ders of his flower garden with skulls. The Belgian officer responsible for
Stokes's illegal execution, Captain Lothaire, must also be counted.

But just as Conrad probably drew upon many sources in depicting
the horrors of the Congo, so he probably had many models for Kurtz
in mind. *All* of the white officers in charge of Léopold's empire were in
essence Kurtzes, as the eyewitness testimony published by the Congo
Reform Association demonstrates. And what about the eyewitnesses?
Were they always so objective or so morally appalled as they claimed to
be? What about Conrad himself? Although his role in the building of
Léopold's "Congo Free State" was minor and also prior to the worst
horrors, Conrad must have recognized his own complicity and seen
himself as at least potentially a Kurtz-like figure. In the novella, the
African wilderness serves as a mirror, in whose "darkness" Conrad/
Marlow sees a death-pale self-image.

The massive evidence of wholesale torture and slaughter under the
direction of Léopold's white agents suggests not only that there were
numerous Kurtzes in the "heart of darkness," but also that, as Hannah

Arendt contends in *The Origins of Totalitarianism*, nineteenth-century imperialism prepared the ground in which fascism and Nazism took root after World War I. Arendt has Kurtz and other Conrad characters in mind when she describes the appeal of "the phantom world of colonial adventure" to certain types of Europeans:

> Outside all social restraint and hypocrisy, against the backdrop of native life, the gentleman and the criminal felt not only the closeness of men who share the same color of skin, but the impact of a world of infinite possibilities for crimes committed in the spirit of play, for the combination of horror and laughter, that is for the full realization of their own phantom-like existence. Native life lent these ghostlike events a seeming guarantee against all consequences because anyhow it looked to these men like a "mere play of shadows. A play of shadows, the dominant race could walk through unaffected and disregarded in the pursuit of its incomprehensible aims and needs." The world of native savages was a perfect setting for men who had escaped the reality of civilization. (70)

A great many Kurtz-like Europeans "went native" in Africa, often to the extent of practicing genocide as a hobby; some were even rumored to practice cannibalism. According to Sir Harry H. Johnston, first governor of British Central Africa, "I have been increasingly struck with the rapidity with which such members of the white race as are not of the best class, can throw over the restraints of civilization and develop into savages of unbridled lust and abominable cruelty" (68). Kurtz is not a member of the *worst* "class" of the white race, however; Conrad is talking about a quite common pattern of behavior.

One of the most remarkable perversions of the criticism of *Heart of Darkness* has been to see Kurtz not as an abomination — a "hollow man" with a lust for blood and domination — but as a "hero of the spirit." That phrase is Lionel Trilling's. In his well-known essay describing the establishment of the first course in modern literature at Columbia University, Trilling explains why he put Conrad's novella on the reading list:

> Whether or not . . . Conrad read either Blake or Nietzsche I do not know, but his *Heart of Darkness* follows in their line. This very great work has never lacked for the admiration it deserves, and it has been given a . . . canonical place in the legend of modern literature by Eliot's having it so clearly in mind when he wrote *The Waste Land* and his having taken from it the epigraph to "The Hollow Men." ("Modern" 17–18)

Despite the "hollow man" association between Eliot's poem and Conrad's novella, Trilling claims that "no one, to my knowledge, has ever confronted in an explicit way [the latter's] strange and terrible message of ambivalence toward the life of civilization" (17). In *Sincerity and Authenticity* (1981), Trilling adds that Conrad's story is "the paradigmatic literary expression of the modern concern with authenticity," and continues: "This troubling work has no manifest polemical content but it contains in sum the whole of the radical critique of European civilization that has been made by [modern] literature" (106).

Although Trilling mentions the Congolese background of the story, it is less important to him than the larger question of the nature of "European civilization." Marlow's quest for Kurtz becomes a quest for the truth about that civilization. Trilling arrives at his view of Kurtz partly the way Marlow does, because Kurtz at the end of his satanic career seems to confront "the horror, the horror." "For Marlow," says Trilling, "Kurtz is a hero of the spirit whom he cherishes as Theseus at Colonus cherished Oedipus: he sinned for all mankind. By his regression to savagery Kurtz had reached as far down beneath the constructs of civilization as it was possible to do, to the irreducible truth of man, the innermost core of his nature, his heart of darkness. From that Stygian authenticity comes illumination . . ." (108).

Marlow does paradoxically come to admire Kurtz because he has "summed up" or "judged" in his final moments: "He was a remarkable man" (p. 86). Marlow's admiration for Kurtz, however, carries a terrific burden of irony that Trilling seems not to recognize. Kurtz has not merely lost faith in civilization and therefore experimented with "Stygian authenticity" — he is also a murderer, perhaps even a cannibal. He has allowed his idolators to make human sacrifices in his honor and, like Captain Rom, has decorated his corner of hell with the skulls of his victims. I suspect that Trilling arrives at his own evaluation of Kurtz as a "hero of the spirit" in part because he himself does not find "the horror" all that horrible, even though the deaths of 6,000,000 Congolese is a high price to pay for the "illumination" of "Stygian authenticity." But Trilling's interpretation of Kurtz's dying words — "the horror, the horror" — does not take account of what transpired in Léopold's Congo. "For me it is still ambiguous whether Kurtz's famous deathbed cry refers to the approach of death or to his experience of savage life" (Trilling, "Modern" 18).

According to Trilling's view, either Kurtz thinks death "the horror," or Kurtz thinks African "savagery" "the horror." There is another possibility, of course, which is that Kurtz's dying words are an outcry against himself — against his betrayal of civilization and his Intended, against the smash-up of his early hopes, and also against his bloody domination of the people he has been lording it over. No one would ever mistake Conrad's other traitors to civilization as "heroes of the spirit." I am thinking, for example, of Willems who goes wrong and then "goes native" in *An Outcast of the Islands*, or of the ironically sympathetic murderer Leggatt in "The Secret Sharer." Even Lord Jim is no "hero of the spirit," but a moral cripple who manages to regain a semblance of self-respect only after fleeing to Patusan. But how was it possible for Trilling to look past Kurtz's criminal record and identify "the horror" either with the fear of death or with African "savagery"? Achebe gives part of the answer: "white racism against Africa is such a normal way of thinking that its manifestations go completely undetected" — so normal that acts that are condemned as the vilest of crimes when committed in the supposedly civilized West can be linked to a "heroism of the spirit" and to "Stygian authenticity" when committed in Africa against Africans.

But the other part of the answer, it seems to me, is that Trilling is right. Conrad himself identifies with and ironically admires Kurtz. He, too, sees him as a "hero of the spirit," although "the spirit" for Conrad is perhaps not what Trilling thinks it is. For Conrad, Kurtz's heroism consists in staring into an abyss of nihilism so total that the issues of imperialism and racism pale into insignificance. It hardly matters if the abyss is of Kurtz's making. No more than Trilling or perhaps most Western critics, I think, did Conrad concern himself deeply about "unspeakable rites" and skulls on posts. These appear in Marlow's account like so many melodrama props — the evidence of Kurtz's decline and fall, yes — but it is still Kurtz who has center stage, with whom Marlow speaks, who is the goal and farthest point of the journey. Kurtz's black victims and idolators skulking in the bushes are also so many melodrama props.

Kurtz is not only the hero of the melodrama, he is an artist, a "universal genius," and a quite powerful, eloquent "voice" as well. As Achebe points out, the African characters are, in contrast, rendered almost without intelligible language. The headman of Marlow's cannibal crew gets in a few phrases of Pidgin-minstrelese, something about eating some fellow Africans. These are the black Kurtz worshippers, shrieking and groaning incoherently in the foggy shrubbery along the river. Kurtz's "superb and savage" mistress, though described in glowing detail, is given no voice, but in spite of this I like to imagine that she, at least, entertained no illusions about Kurtz or about imperialism, unlike the prim, palefaced knitters of black wool back in Brussels. "It's queer how out of touch with truth women are" (p. 27) says Marlow, but of course he means *white* women. Kurtz's black mistress knows all; it's just unfortunate that Marlow did not ask her for an interview.

The voices that come from the "heart of darkness" are almost exclusively white and male. As a nearly disembodied, pure "voice" emanating from the very center of the story, Kurtz is a figure for the novelist, as is his double Marlow. True, the "voice" that speaks out of the "heart of darkness" is a hollow one, the voice of the abyss; but Marlow still talks of Kurtz's "unextinguishable gift of noble and lofty expression." The "voice" of Kurtz has "electrified large meetings," and through it Kurtz "could get himself to believe anything — anything" (p. 88). Is Conrad questioning or mocking his own "voice," his own talent for fiction-making, for lying? Is he aware that the "will to style," his own tendency to "impressionism," points toward the production of novels that are hollow at the core — that can justify any injustice — that contain, perhaps, only an abyss, a Kurtz, "the horror, the horror"? Yes, I think so. It is just this hollow "voice," so devious and egotistical, so capable of self-deception and lying propaganda, that speaks from the center of "the heart of darkness" to "sum up" and to "judge."

Besides a painter, musician, orator, and "universal genius," Kurtz is also, like Conrad, a writer. What he writes can be seen as an analogue for the story and also its dead center, the kernel of meaning or non-meaning within its cracked shell. True, Kurtz has not written much, only seventeen pages, but "it was a beautiful piece of writing." This is his pamphlet for the "International Society for the Suppression of Savage Customs," which Marlow describes as "eloquent, vibrating with eloquence, but too high-strung, I think":

> The opening paragraph . . . in the light of later information, strikes me now as ominous. He began with the argument that we whites, from the point of development we had arrived at, "must necessarily appear to them [savages] in the nature of supernatural beings — we approach them with the might as of a deity," and so on, and so on. "By the simple exercise of our will we can exert a power for good practically unbounded," etc., etc. From that point he soared and took me with him. The peroration was magnificent, though difficult to remember, you know. It gave me the notion of an exotic Immensity ruled by an august Benevolence. It made me tingle with enthusiasm. This was the unbounded power of eloquence. [And here I will add, "This was the unbounded will

to style."] . . . There were no practical hints to interrupt the magic current of phrases, unless a kind of note at the foot of the last page, scrawled evidently much later, in an unsteady hand, may be regarded as the exposition of a method. It was very simple, and at the end of that moving appeal to every altruistic sentiment it blazed at you, luminous and terrifying, like a flash of lightning in a serene sky: "Exterminate all the brutes!" (pp. 65–66)

Viewed one way, Conrad's anti-imperialist story condemns the murderous racism of Kurtz's imperative. Viewed another way, Conrad's racist story voices that very imperative, and Conrad knows it. At the hollow center of *Heart of Darkness*, far from the "misty halos" and "moonshine" where the meaning supposedly resides, Conrad inscribes a text that, like the novel itself, cancels out its own best intentions.

But now Kurtz's dying words can be seen as something more than an outcry of guilt, and certainly more than a mere expression of the fear of death or of loathing for African "savagery." They can be seen as referring to the sort of lying idealism that can rationalize any behavior, to a complete separation between words and meaning, theory and practice — perhaps to the "impressionistic" deviousness of art and language themselves. On this metaphysical level, I think, Conrad ceases to worry about the atrocities committed in the Congo and identifies with Kurtz as a fellow-artist, a "hero of the spirit" of that nihilism that Conrad himself found so attractive.

On several occasions, Conrad compared the artist with the empire builder in a way that obviously runs counter to his critique of imperialism in *Heart of Darkness*. In *A Personal Record*, Conrad writes of "that interior world where [the novelist's] thought and . . . emotions go seeking for . . . imagined adventures," and where "there are no policemen, no law, no pressure of circumstance or dread opinion to keep him within bounds." And in the first manuscript of "The Rescuer," which as John McClure points out contains "by far" Conrad's "most sympathetic" treatment of imperialism, empire-builders are among "those unknown guides of civilization, who on the advancing edge of progress are administrators, warriors, creators. . . . They are like great artists a mystery to the masses, appreciated only by the uninfluential few" (McClure 89–90). Kurtz is empire-builder, artist, universal genius, and voice crying from the wilderness all in one. But he has lost the faith — vision or illusion — that can alone sustain an empire and produce great art. Nihilism is no basis upon which to found or administer a colony, and it is also no basis on which to write a novel, and again Conrad knows it. In suggesting his affinity to Kurtz, he suggests the moral bankruptcy of his own literary project. But once there were empire-builders and great artists who kept the faith. Conrad frequently expresses his admiration for the great explorers and adventurers, from Sir Walter Raleigh and Sir Francis Drake through James Brooke, the white rajah of Sarawak, and David Livingstone, the greatest of the many great explorers of the "Dark Continent."

Conrad's critique of empire is never strictly anti-imperialist. Instead, in terms that can be construed as conservative rather than nihilistic, he mourns the loss of the truth faith in modern times, the closing down of frontiers, the narrowing of the possibilities for adventure, the commercialization of the world and of art, the death of chivalry and honor. Here the meaning of his emphasis on the lying propaganda of modern imperialism becomes evident. What was once a true, grand, noble, albeit violent enterprise is now "a gigantic and atrocious fraud" — except maybe, Marlow thinks, in the red parts of the map, where "some real work is done." Staring into the abyss of his life, or at least of Kurtz's life, Conrad sees in his disillusionment, his nihilism, the type of the whole — the path of disintegration that is modern history. It is not just Africa or even just Kurtz who possesses a "heart of darkness"; Conrad's story bears that title as well.

But I am not going to end by announcing in "a tone of scathing contempt" the death of Conrad's story as a classic, like the insolent manager's boy announcing: "Mistah Kurtz — he dead." I agree with Trilling that "authenticity," truth-telling, so far from being a negligible literary effect, is the essence of great literature. The fact that there are almost no other works of British fiction written before World War I that are critical of imperialism, and hundreds of imperialist ones that are racist through and through, is a measure of Conrad's achievement. I do not believe, moreover, that the real strength of *Heart of Darkness* lies in what it says about atrocities in King Léopold's Congo, though its documentary impulse is an important counter to its "will to style." As social criticism, its anti-imperialist message is undercut both by its racism and by its impressionism. But I know few novels that so insistently invoke an idealism that they don't seem to contain, and in which the modernist "will to style" is subjected to such powerful self-scrutiny — in which it is suggested that the "voice" at the heart of the novel, the voice of literature, the voice of civilization itself may in its purest, freest form yield only "the horror, the horror."

WORKS CITED

Achebe, Chinua. "An Image of Africa." *Massachusetts Review* 18 (1977): 782–94.

Arendt, Hannah. *Imperialism*. New York: Harcourt, 1968.

Conrad, Joseph. *A Personal Record*. New York: Doubleday, 1924.

Conrad, Joseph, and Ford Madox Hueffer. *The Inheritors: An Extravagant Story*. New York: McClure, 1901.

Cookey, S. J. *Britain and the Congo Question: 1885–1913*. London: Longman, 1968.

Glave, E. J. "Cruelty in the Congo Free State." *Century Magazine* 54 (1897): 706.

Green, Martin. *Dreams of Adventure, Deeds of Empire*. New York: Basic, 1979.

Guerard, Albert J. *Conrad the Novelist*. Cambridge: Harvard UP, 1958. New York: Atheneum, 1967.

Hawkins, Hunt. "Conrad's Critique of Imperialism in *Heart of Darkness*." *PMLA* 94 (1979): 286–99.

Hinde, Captain Sidney L. *The Fall of the Congo Arabs*. London: Methuen, 1897.

Jameson, Fredric. *The Political Unconscious: Narrative as a Socially Symbolic Act*. Ithaca: Cornell UP, 1981.

Johnston, Sir Harry H. *British Central Africa*. London: Methuen, 1897.

Mahood, M. M. *The Colonial Encounter: A Reading of Six Novels*. London: Rex Collings, 1977.

McClure, John A. *Kipling and Conrad: The Colonial Fiction*. Cambridge: Harvard UP, 1981.

Morel, E. D. *King Leopold's Rule in Africa*. Westport: Negro Universities P, 1970.

———. *Red Rubber: The Story of the Rubber Slave Trade on the Congo*. London: Unwin, 1906.

Parry, Benita. *Conrad and Imperialism*. London: Macmillan, 1983.

Said, Edward W. *Joseph Conrad and the Fiction of Autobiography*. Cambridge: Harvard UP, 1966.

Sherry, Norman. *Conrad's Western World*. Cambridge: Cambridge UP, 1971.

Trilling, Lionel. "On the Modern Element in Literature." *Beyond Culture: Essays on Literature and Learning*. New York: Harcourt, 1965.

———. *Sincerity and Authenticity*. Cambridge: Harvard UP, 1981.

Watt, Ian. *Conrad in the Nineteenth Century.* Berkeley: U of California P, 1979.

Watts, Cedric. "'A Bloody Racist': About Achebe's View of Conrad." *Yearbook of English Studies* 13 (1983): 196–209.

Williams, Raymond. *The English Novel from Dickens to Lawrence.* New York: Oxford UP, 1970.

Combining Postcolonial, Feminist, and Gender Criticism with Queer Theory

Although you have been introduced to feminist and gender criticism as well as the postcolonial approach earlier, you have not been introduced to queer theory. Because the essay by Gabrielle McIntire that follows eventually takes a "queered" turn after combining the postcolonial approach, feminist and gender criticism (plus the postmodernist concept of the *differend*, which McIntire herself thoroughly explains), a brief introduction to queer theory commences the following lead-in to "The Women Do Not Travel: Gender, Difference, and Incommensurability in Conrad's *Heart of Darkness*."

WHAT IS QUEER THEORY?

Generally speaking, queer theory begins by assuming that homosexuality and heterosexuality are not mutually exclusive binary oppositions — fixed and exclusive modalities of personal identity — but, rather, points along a continuum of possible sexual practices. Most queer theorists would agree with feminist gender critics that gender differences by and large are not innate but, rather, constructed, which is to say that they are the result of long-standing assumptions about what constitutes feminine versus masculine behavior. But they take the constructionist viewpoint a step farther, arguing that the opposition homosexual/

heterosexual is also an either/or social construct that codifies and thereby misrepresents a range of behaviors and practices.

Rather than being a term used prejudicially, *queer* is used by queer theorists to refer to critical and philosophical positions taken outside the circle of conventional assumptions about sexuality and gender. As a result, some queer theorists are interested in the way in which prevailing discourses regarding sex, gender, and sexuality lump individuals and individual practices not only into boxes marked male/female, masculine/feminine, and straight/queer (heterosexual/homosexual) but also divvy the "queer" world up into boxes marked bisexual, transvestite, transgendered, sadomasochist, and so forth.

The philosophical roots of queer theory are deeply grounded in Michel Foucault's *Histoire de la sexualité* (*The History of Sexuality* [1976]), which maintained that the whole concept of homosexuality as the abnormal opposite of heterosexuality was an artifact of nineteenth-century Western thought. Those roots also may be found in philosopher Judith Butler's *Gender Trouble: Feminism and the Subversion of Identity* (1990) and Eve Kosofsky Sedgwick's landmark books *Between Men: English Literature and Male Homosocial Desire* (1985) and *Epistemology of the Closet* (1990), both of which paved the way to understanding how queer theory can undergird a critical approach to literary works. *Between Men* is particularly relevant to McIntire's reading of *Heart of Darkness*, insofar as it utilizes the terms of feminist and gender criticism to analyze relationships between men that involve levels of male bonding that, though not necessarily or even usually sexual per se, utterly leave women out.

Any definition of queer theory will inevitably elicit reasonable objections from various subsets of queer theorists. For instance, some might want to carve out exceptions, arguing that African American lesbian authors have more in common with other African American women authors than, say, with black male homosexual writers. And, certainly, there are queer theorists who write not from the constructionist but, rather, from an essentialist perspective, arguing that homosexual persons are naturally different from birth much in the way that there are essentialist feminists who insist that women and men are not just anatomically different but *essentially* different in a number of ways (e.g., the way in which they write).

In the opening pages of the essay excerpted below, Gabriella McIntire examines the representations of women found in *Heart of Darkness*, finding them to be "always positioned . . . in either the [African] colony *or* the [European] metropole," always "*here* or *there,*" "decidedly static and unable to wander between cultural, ideological, and national boundaries" (p. 332). Thus "placed, . . . Conrad's women" — from Marlow's aunt in her parlor serving tea to the gorgeous African woman looking "like the wilderness itself" — "reinforce a sense of extreme separation between the colony and the metropole, and as such they are crucial for guarding and preserving difference between Africa and Europe" (p. 332).

But because they are all women (in a world of traveling white men), they also underscore gender difference in *Heart of Darkness,* a topic previously addressed by Johanna M. Smith, whose 1989 essay "Too Beautiful Altogether" (pp. 189–204) represents feminist and gender criticism in this volume, and Bette London, whose essay (published the same year) "Reading Race and Gender in Conrad's Dark Continent" blends the feminist/gender approach with that of postcolonial criticism. Developing the ideas of Smith and London while extending her argument regarding the gap between Europe and Africa, McIntire writes: "While Conrad's text explicitly marks out incommensurable differences between Europe and Africa and between Europeans and those he calls 'savages,'" these are, in turn, "sustained and enforced by the incommensurabilities in knowing and speaking that he establishes along gender lines" (p. 335). For the "male protagonists possess both empirical and abstract knowledge of the colonial enterprise in *both* Africa and Europe" (p. 335); thus, when Marlow judges his aunt's enthusiasm for the European civilizing project to be evidence that she is "out of touch with truth," he criticizes her not for exhibiting European moral blindness but, rather, "he reads her indoctrination as a specifically feminine ignorance" (p. 336). Later, in "one of the few places in the text where Marlow interrupts his narrative with an aside to his [male] auditors," he "pushes this exclusion [of the feminine from knowledge] further to insist, with an intratextual echo of his own words, that women should be 'out of' his whole story."

> "I laid the ghost of his gifts at last with a lie," he began suddenly. "Girl! What? Did I mention a girl? Oh, she is out of it — completely. They — the women I mean — are out of it — should be out of it." (p. 337)

McIntire finds in the above-quoted passage what postmodernist theorist Jean François Lyotard refers to as a *differend,* which refers on one hand to "an unstable state and instant of language wherein something which must be able to be put into phrases cannot yet be" and, on the other, that which would be "put into phrases" — that is, "rhetorical or speech genre" (McIntire's phrase) which cannot be "translate[ed]" by those wielding the predominant discourse. In the first sense of *differend*, Marlow's language is unstable because he is trying to "put" the feminine "into phrases"; he "typically," as McIntire points out, "stutters and falters in his narration most explicitly at the moments when he is unable to make women part of his story" (p. 338). In the second sense of Lyotard's term, what women would "put into phrases" in speaking to power is also present as a trace in the passage — that is, as silence. Turning to Smith's account of the way in which the women in *Heart of Darkness* are either silenced by the patriarchal discourses from which they are excluded or reduced to parroting them weakly, McIntire then returns to Lyotard's *The Differend*, which argues that discursive interactions between two parties from heterogenous "phrase regimens" end with one party "reduced to silence." McIntire continues: "The voices Lyotard writes of are as unintelligible to the more powerful discourses that frame and contain them . . . as the women in *Heart of Darkness* are to Marlow's narration" (p. 339).

"Without framing his argument in feminist, queer, or racial terms," McIntire subsequently argues, "Lyotard goes very far in describing how institutional and societal modes disallow certain forms of speech or genres of expression by not making space for the possibility of their idiom" (p. 339). Before ever invoking *The Differend*, Mcintire framed her argument in linked, feminist and racial terms. "[N]either women nor Africans (regardless of gender)," she had earlier remarked, "are capable of navigating between types of knowledge, any more than they are capable of leaving the territory that defines them" (p. 336). Having introduced Lyotard's concept of the *differend*, she powerfully reframes her argument in homosocial, homoerotic, "queer" terms.

She does so most pointedly in her consideration of the story's ending, which "highlight[s]" Marlow's "desire for non-contact between his epistemological framework" and "women's in general." When Marlow visits Kurtz's Intended, he "return[s] things" (a portrait and her letters) but "cannot meet her with language." Instead of engaging the young woman in conversation, he "mimics her phrasing."

> In answer to her statement, "You knew him well," he echoes her in profoundly homoerotic language: "I knew him as well as it is possible for one man to know another." His echolalia effectively parodies her desire for knowledge about nothing less than *knowledge* itself by claiming a supreme (and possibly sexual) form of knowledge for himself. (p. 341)

As "their exchange continues," as Marlow "struggl[es] to piece words together in the hesitating language of discomfort, claiming 'He was a remarkable man [. . .] it was impossible not to . . . ,' the Intended interposes 'Love him'" (p. 342). In Lyotard's phrase, this is an attempt to "put into phrases" her love for the same man, to — in McIntire's words — "meet Marlow on his own discursive level by literally completing his sentence, . . . by echoing his language of love and desire." But this is "precisely the sort of thing Marlow does not want to hear from a woman; it is far too near to the 'truth' about his attraction to Kurtz. Marlow experiences this interpolation as a terrifying shutting down of his voice, feeling that she was 'silencing me into an appalled dumbness'" (p. 342).

Marlow soon recovers his voice. When the Intended subsequently asks him to "repeat" Kurtz's last words, to in effect share in Kurtz's and Marlow's language, he — in McIntire's words — "reinforces their difference by refusing to meet her in the same discursive territory of 'truth.'" Rather than tell her that Kurtz died muttering "The horror! The horror!" in what Marlow has called a "supreme moment of complete knowledge" that "had the appalling face of a glimpsed truth," he instead tells her that Kurtz died speaking her name. "As such," McIntire concludes, "Marlow ends his story on a differend by directing her away from knowledge to leave her believing in a false romantic vision of Kurtz's final words" (pp. 342–43).

WORKS CITED

Butler, Judith. *Gender Trouble: Feminism and the Subversion of Identity.* New York: Routledge, 1990. Print. For a new introduction by the author, see the 1999 edition.

Foucault, Michel. *The History of Sexuality.* Vol. 1. Trans. Robert Hurley. New York: Pantheon, 1978. Print.

London, Bette. "Reading Race and Gender in Conrad's Dark Continent." *Criticism* 31 (1989): 235–52. Print.

Lyotard, Jean François. *The Differend.* Trans. Georges Van Den Abbeele. Minneapolis: U of Minnesota P, 1988. Print.

Sedgwick, Eve Kosofsky. *Between Men: English Literature and Male Homosocial Desire.* New York: Columbia UP, 1988. Print.

———. *Epistemology of the Closet.* Berkeley: U of California P, 1991. Print.

Smith, Johanna M. "'Too Beautiful Altogether': Patriarchal Ideology in *Heart of Darkness.*" 189–204, this edition. Print.

GABRIELLE McINTIRE

The Women Do Not Travel:
Gender, Difference, and Incommensurability
in Conrad's *Heart of Darkness*

It is a story of the Congo. There is no love interest in it and no woman — only incidentally.
                                        –JOSEPH CONRAD, "To T. Fisher Unwin."

Despite Joseph Conrad's anxious confession to his publisher T. Fisher Unwin in 1896 that there would be "no love interest . . . and no woman" in *Heart of Darkness*, or at least "only incidentally," the novella he produced two-and-a-half years later is radically preoccupied with women and the ways they influence his "story of the Congo" (199). Yet Conrad allows women scarcely any narratological or thematic attention in *Heart of Darkness*; instead, women appear to function primarily as ancillary details to Marlow's narration about Kurtz and his adventure to the "heart" of Africa. However, despite women's near invisibility — a half-presence that echoes the text's preoccupation with shadows and darknesses[1] — they are an always-palpable presence in the background of the text. They tropologically illuminate the relationships of difference and distance that Conrad establishes between Europe and the Congo, and they figurally represent the incommensurability between different ideologies and different genres of speaking and knowing that are so central to the text's status as a framed oral narration.

The women in *Heart of Darkness* have, in fact, suffered from a double invisibility. First, Conrad invites his readers to participate in Marlow's insistence that the women are "out of it" (p. 63) by figuring women as palimpsestic, ghost-like, half-presences. At the same time, the women of the text have remained nearly invisible because so few critics have chosen to examine their roles. Once we begin looking (and we do have to look to find them), no less than eight women are present in *Heart of Darkness*: the Belgian aunt who secures Marlow a job when

---

[1]Since its initial publication and early reviews, critics have found *Heart of Darkness* excessively atmospheric, as well as structurally and adjectivally difficult, shadowy, and undecidable. Ross Murfin offers an excellent overview of some of these early- and mid-century critiques, pointing out that in 1903 John Masefield thought it consisted of "too much cobweb" (p. 139); in 1936 E. M. Forster considered it "a little *too* fuzzy" (p. 139); and in his highly influential work, *The Great Tradition* (1963), F. R. Leavis concurred with Forster, also stressing its "overwhelming sinister and fantastic 'atmosphere'" (Leavis, 173).

his prospects for work in Europe are exhausted; the two women sitting on "straw-bottomed chairs, knitting black wool" who appear to Marlow in the Company offices as guardians of "the door of Darkness" (pp. 24–25); the "wife of the high dignitary" to whom Marlow's aunt recommends him for employment in Africa (p. 26); the African laundress for the Company's chief accountant, who keeps him looking like a "vision" or a "miracle" (p. 32); the "wild and gorgeous apparition of a woman" (p. 76) at the Inner Station who "rushed out to the very brink of the stream" (p. 83) as Marlow leaves with Kurtz on board his steamer;[2] Kurtz's mother, who dies shortly after Marlow returns to Belgium (p. 87); and finally, Kurtz's Intended, the woman he might have married, whom he "intended" to be his final interpreter, and the woman to whom Marlow lies at the very end of the text.[3]

What is going on with these women? Perhaps most clearly, Conrad associates women with the cultures and geographies they inhabit as though by contiguous extension. The principal women of the text are always positioned in transitional spaces in either the colony or the

[2]Even though it has become something of a critical convention to call this woman "Kurtz's African mistress," she is never explicitly named or designated as such. Heteronormative biases have led critics to assume a sexual relation, but there is no substantial evidence in the text to indicate the precise nature of her relationship with Kurtz. Instead of characterizing her as his "mistress," then, I will simply refer to her as the woman at the Inner Station, or the African woman.

[3]Beginning with the opening words of the text — "The *Nellie*, a cruising yawl, swung to her anchor without a flutter of the sails, and was at rest" (p. 17) — every vessel that carries Marlow from one land to another is also gendered as feminine. While Conrad's use of feminine names for ships is of course quite conventional for the period, it nevertheless underscores the fact that he leaves every *woman* of his text unnamed. In pointing this out, we might note, though, that *Heart of Darkness* also participates in a more general absence of naming: other than Marlow and Kurtz, characters are known by *function* rather than by proper name. This tendency extends equally across boundaries of race and place. Marlow's audience for his tale consists of the "Director of Companies," the "Lawyer," the "Accountant," and the unnamed frame-narrator; while in Africa he speaks of figures like the "Manager," the "chief accountant," and the "helmsman." Even so, Conrad articulates gender differences through his unnaming since the men tend to be referred to by title or function, while the women are usually referred to by function *in terms of their relation to men*: Marlow's "aunt," Kurtz's "Intended," Kurtz's "mother," the "laundress" for the chief accountant. Furthermore, geographic place names are rarely specified either: neither the Belgian city nor the Belgian Congo is named; instead we hear only of "a city that always makes me think of a whited sepulchre" (p. 24), and, just once, of "Africa" (p. 22). The Congo itself is never named; when Marlow describes his childhood fascination with its representation on the map, he recalls only that it looked like "an immense snake, uncoiled" (p. 22). When he arrives in Africa after his ocean voyage, he simply remarks that he finally "saw the mouth of the big river" (p. 29). Conrad was well aware of this absence of naming place, at any rate, and in the same letter quoted above to T. Fisher Unwin, he notes that in his manuscript, "The exact locality is not mentioned" (qtd. in Kimbrough, 199).

metropole, while they are decidedly static and unable to wander between cultural, ideological, and national boundaries, as do Marlow and Kurtz. In terms of Marlow's understanding of his voyage, the women are neither *here* nor *there*; or rather, they are only ever *here* or *there*, since they are powerless to transgress the limit that such a boundary implies. Mostly the women are sedentary, stationary, and confined to their own territories, metonymically embodying the separate cultural, racial, and geographic identities at play in the novel. The aunt sits in her upper-middle-class domestic parlor in Belgium as she sends Marlow off to his adventure in Africa; the two knitting women sit in the outer room of the Company offices and glance at the men en route to the Congo; and, at the end of the text, Kurtz's Intended receives Marlow in a "lofty drawing-room" (p. 90) where they both "sat down" for their mournful exchange (p. 91). Even the movement Conrad grants to the African woman at the Inner Station only further emphasizes her essential immobility: she struts along the river bank as she wails at Kurtz's departure, but she, too, is confined to her own territory.

Placed as they are, Conrad's women reinforce a sense of extreme separation between the colony and the metropole, and as such they are crucial for guarding and preserving difference between Africa and Europe. Marlow's aunt embodies *whiteness* as well as the racist politics of the European colonizing mission, while she also represents the ignorance of the sedentary white Belgian masses who do not and cannot participate in Marlow's knowledge of the "dark" continent. Marlow's aunt is evidently very comfortable, ensconced in privilege, and capable of serious influence with people such as "the wife of the high dignitary" of King Léopold's Belgian Congo. Before he leaves for Africa, Marlow finds her "triumphant" as she praises his work for the Company, and they drink tea during "a long quiet chat by the fireside" (p. 26). Marlow, however, only mocks her flattery, considering her as a carrier for the ethics of the colonizing mission. In one of the many moments in the text when Conrad reveals his famous attention to the power of the written word, Marlow declares that his aunt has been sufficiently influenced by the "rot let loose in print and talk just about that time" to gain the sort of limited, ideologically saturated and very public knowledge of colonialism the Company wishes the general populace to possess (p. 27).[4] Suggesting both familial rootedness and European

---

[4]Conrad gives an exquisite disquisition on the relation of language to art in his "Preface to *The Nigger of the 'Narcissus.'*" Here he argues against the eroding power that "careless usage" can exert upon language, insisting that "it is only through complete,

cultural supremacy, the aunt upholds the "decency," order, calm, and "triumph" of the metropole without moving beyond the domestic space of her own parlor.[5]

Despite differences of race and place, yet with striking similarities in terms of her rootedness, the African woman at the Inner Station — the "wild and gorgeous apparition of a woman" who mirrors the "sorrowful land" (p. 76) — emblematizes and helps to inscribe the racist distinctions the text has already established between the colonial vision of native "savages" awaiting exploitation and the civilizing mission of the colonists, the white "emissar[ies] of light" (p. 27). Marlow describes her in terms of her physical beauty, her warrior-like posture and clothing, and her indecipherable language. Distinct from the ugliness of the white women who knit in the Company's offices — the "slim one" with a "dress as plain as an umbrella cover" (p. 24) and the "old one" with "a wart on one cheek" (p. 25) — the black native woman is granted a sexual and valuable body: she is "gorgeous," and laden with costly ornaments that "jingle and flash" as she moves in her slow procession. But while her beauty and confidence distinguish her, she too is restricted to her own territory, and Marlow describes her with a simile that links her to the land she represents, as though by contiguous extension:

> in the hush that had fallen suddenly upon the whole sorrowful land, the immense wilderness, the colossal body of the fecund and mysterious life seemed to look at her, pensive, as though it had been looking at the image of its own tenebrous and passionate soul.
>   She came abreast of the steamer, stood still, and faced us. Her long shadow fell to the water's edge. Her face had a tragic and fierce aspect of wild sorrow and dumb pain mingled with the fear of some struggling, half-shaped resolve. She stood looking at us without a stir and like the wilderness itself, with an air of brooding over an inscrutable purpose. (pp. 76–77)

---

unswerving devotion to the perfect blending of form and substance; it is only through an unremitting, never-discouraged care for the shape and ring of sentences that an approach can be made to plasticity, to color, and that the light of magic suggestiveness may be brought to play for an evanescent instant over the commonplace surface of words: of the old, old words, worn thin, defaced by ages of careless usage" (xlix).

[5] Ian Watt reads Marlow's misogyny as specifically directed to "women of the well-to-do and leisured class to whom his aunt and the Intended, and presumably the women-folk of his audience, belong." Treating Conrad's text in the context of Victorian ideology, Watt argues that "Marlow's perspective, in fact, assumes the Victorian relegation of leisure-class women to a pedestal of philanthropic idealism high above the economic and sexual facts of life" (*"Heart of Darkness" and Nineteenth-Century Thought* 114).

In more than one sense her valuable body "mirrors" the body of Africa and its "dark" wilderness that the colonists are plundering as they scramble for their hoards of ivory, since Marlow anthropomorphizes the wilderness at the expense of the woman by figuring her as co-extensive with place: both she and the land convey "sorrow," while the land itself "seemed to look at her" as though it were looking at itself. Conrad seems to bestow as much agency on the land as he does on the woman. Nevertheless, the African woman is given an important signi-fying power since as she struts along the river bank, holding "her head high" (p. 76), she represents the absolute distance and incommensura-bility between Marlow's colonial river steamer and her people's land, which she guards even as she later gives a fervent and sorrowful "send off" to Kurtz. Marlow tells his auditors that when she concluded her exchange of glances, "[s]he turned away slowly, walked on following the bank and passed into the bushes to the left. Once only her eyes gleamed back at us in the dusk of the thickets before she disappeared" (p. 77). Marlow's orientalizing terms here invoke visions of a valuable and hunted animal retreating back to its camouflaged zone of protec-tion: she disappears into the thickets to resume her spatial identification with the "dark" territory. That is, just as Marlow earlier feminizes the wilderness that surrounds the isolated colonial stations along the Congo by describing them as "clinging to the skirts of the unknown" (p. 50), the African woman here "passe[s]" back into the feminized indecipher-ability of the unknown which defines her.[6]

In contrast, at no point in the text are the colonists themselves iden-tified with the land of the Belgian Congo. Instead, the Congo always remains a discrete territory, epistemologically distanced from the pos-sibility of European identification. In this sense Conrad critiques the colonial project by suggesting that colonists are always interlopers on the space of others. Frantz Fanon would propose many years later that "[f]or a colonized people the most essential value, because the most concrete, is first and foremost the land: the land which will bring them bread and, above all, dignity" (44). Conrad perverts this relation be-tween the land and its people by problematically implying a fantasy of extension between race, gender, and territory to propose, in effect, that race and gender *are* the motherland. However, neither women nor

---

[6]Conrad invokes the valences of racial passing through his choice of words, which therefore ask us to consider for whom or for what he implies the African woman might have been "passing." Does having an autonomous and authoritative presence as a woman in this text necessarily entail a form of passing? When the African woman "passed" back into the wilderness, is Conrad suggesting that she "passes" back to her "real" identity?

natives ever control the land, nor does it grant them "dignity." Instead, the inscrutability of Africa's wilderness becomes another metaphor that repeatedly reinforces both the literal silence of its inhabitants and their imagined ignorance.

In an excellent article that does consider a range of female figures in *Heart of Darkness*, Bette London suggests that in Conrad's text we need to "consider gender and race as interlocking systems whose mutually authorizing relationships support the dominant cultural perspective" (235). The dominant cultural perspective is, of course, colonial imperialism, and Conrad uses race and gender together to enforce the distinct alterities between Belgium and the Congo and colonizer and colonized that a model of colonial subjugation demands for its successful operation. In similar terms, Jeremy Hawthorn proposes that "in *Heart of Darkness* issues of gender are inextricably intertwined with matters of race and culture" (183).

Even so, by placing women in these fixed yet liminal territories, Conrad goes further than merely accentuating the disparities and distances between Africa and Europe; he also emphasizes important incommensurabilities between different modes of knowing, speaking, and experiencing. That is, while Conrad's text explicitly marks out radical incompatibilities between Europe and Africa and between Europeans and those he calls "savages," these geographic, racial, and cultural differences are sustained and enforced by the incommensurabilities in knowing and speaking that he establishes along gender lines.

Part of what is at stake in Marlow's narration and his brief but recurring attention to women is a need to distinguish two entirely different communities of people predicated on modes of knowledge and experience. The male protagonists possess both empirical and abstract conceptual knowledge of the colonial enterprise in *both* Africa and Europe — while the five major women of the text (Marlow's aunt, Kurtz's Intended, the African woman, and the two knitting women in the Company offices) apparently possess only conceptual knowledge of *either* Africa *or* Europe. Because of his aunt's acceptance of the public ideologies in support of colonialism, Marlow claims that women in general are

> out of touch with truth. . . . They live in a world of their own and there had never been anything like it and never can be. It is too beautiful altogether, and if they were to set it up it would go to pieces before the first sunset. Some confounded fact we men have been living contentedly with ever since the day of creation, would start up and knock the whole thing over. (p. 27)

Instead of reading his aunt's complicity with the Company project as metonymically representative of the ethics of the colonizing mission — which he does elsewhere — he reads her indoctrination as a specifically feminine ignorance. This "world" of women that Marlow imagines is distinguished by its non-relation to "truth" and its excessive concern with aesthetics over practicality. In contrast, the "men" Marlow refers to as "we" (effectively interpellating both his audience on the *Nellie* and Conrad's early male readers) possess a sufficiently accurate version of the "facts" about the daily business of colonization to make theirs a world that does not "fall apart" — to use both Yeats's and Achebe's important phrase — at least not until well into the unimaginable twentieth century.[7] The functional world that men have constructed abides by a utilitarian and empirically tested logic simply because it pursues its ends effectively. It recognizes such details as the "fact" that the Company is "run for profit" (p. 27). The world Marlow imagines for women, however, is distinct from that of the men who actually go to the "heart" of the "dark" continent to set up their version of a "world" insofar as it is fixed, static, and domestic: neither the women's world nor the women themselves can migrate to different territories or do more than manage the incommensurable differences of colonial order that Marlow and Kurtz confront as they travel. That is, neither women nor Africans (regardless of gender) are capable of navigating between types of knowledge any more than they are capable of leaving the territory that defines them.

In a text that is on a very fundamental level about language and its limits, narrativization and narratability, and speech and speakability, some of the terms Jean-François Lyotard sets up in *The Differend: Phrases in Dispute* might help us diagnose how Conrad's constructions of gender, genres of knowledge, and modes of speech mutually reinforce the distance and incommensurability between the male and female "worlds" of *Heart of Darkness*. Lyotard suggests that a differend marks the failure or impossibility of translating one rhetorical or speech genre into another. He writes: "The differend is the unstable state and instant of language wherein something which must be able to be put into

---

[7]Edward Said is generally critical of the "politics and aesthetics" of *Heart of Darkness*, which "are, so to speak, imperialist" (24); yet he proposes that "[s]ince Conrad *dates* imperialism, shows its contingency, records its illusions and tremendous violence and waste (as in *Nostromo*), he permits his later readers to imagine something other than an Africa carved up into dozens of European colonies, even if, for his own part, he had little notion of what that Africa might be" (26).

phrases cannot yet be. This state includes silence, which is a negative phrase, but it also calls upon phrases which are in principle possible" (13). I want to propose that the incommensurability between Marlow and the women of his narration reveals a differend that in turn elucidates the broader incompatibilities between modes of knowing and speaking in the text. As I will show, the women participate in and inhabit a different discursive genre from men since they are most often silent, uncomprehending, and indecipherable. Lyotard further proposes — in terms that echo Conrad's articulation of the different "worlds" and "universes" of the sexes — that a differend describes "[i]ncommensurability, in the sense of the heterogeneity of phrase regimens and of the impossibility of subjecting them to a single law. . . . For each of these regimens, there corresponds a mode of presenting a universe, and one mode is not translatable into another" (128). In *Heart of Darkness*, Marlow's narrative mode of speech presents and reveals a "universe" in which women are untranslatable and quite literally unable to be told. Marlow is only capable of reading them as metaphorical and meets a limit precisely because he cannot translate them to the real.[8]

Later in the novella — after Marlow has claimed that his aunt and women in general are "out of touch with truth" (p. 27) — he pushes this exclusion further to insist, with an intratextual echo of his own words, that women should be "out of" his whole story. In the middle of his description about his steamer's dangerous approach to the Inner Station he happens to mention "the girl," but then catches himself:

> "I laid the ghost of his gifts at last with a lie," he began suddenly.
> "Girl! What? Did I mention a girl? Oh, she is out of it — completely.
> They — the women I mean — are out if it — should be out of it.
> We must help them to stay in that beautiful world of their own
> lest ours gets worse. Oh, she had to be out of it. You should have
> heard the disinterred body of Mr. Kurtz saying 'My Intended.'
> You would have perceived directly then how completely she was
> out of it." (pp. 63–64)

---

[8]In "Lying as Dying in *Heart of Darkness*," Garrett Stewart takes this point even further to argue that "both" women of the text (in this case the Intended and Kurtz's "mistress") "copresent in the narrator's mind's eye, are emanations of Marlow as well as of Kurtz" (328), and he proposes that the Intended's "black-draped mourning is Kurtz's darkness visible" (331). It would be going too far to pursue this line of thought further and propose that the women are never more than Marlow's symbolic projections, but Stewart is right to point out the consistent manner in which women function as a kind of tabula rasa on which Marlow's preoccupations are staged. As we will see, the women also take on qualities from the settings that surround them.

Quite strikingly, his insistent repetition in this passage that women are "out of it" marks one of the few places in the text where Marlow interrupts his narrative with an aside to his auditors. Indeed, he stutters and falters in his narration most explicitly at the moments when he is unable to make women a part of his story. Here he "suddenly" stops the articulate flow of his yarn to revise his own terms and preoccupations by asserting that women are not simply of a different world, but ought to be "out of" the story "completely." His tangent is so filled with hesitations and dramatic caesuras that his very language betrays how unsettling women are to Marlow's order of things: as figures that cannot quite make their way into narration, or even into language, they resemble Lyotard's differend because they present a problem — not simply of translation, but of an epistemological incommensurability with Marlow's genre of telling and knowing.

His repeated insistence that women are "out of it" ought to alert us to the fact that they might be more important to his story than he allows. Marlow's repetitive insistence on women being "out of it" actually seems to betray his own anxiety regarding women as guardians of difference and players in his own destiny, since they are, in fact, overly imbricated in his story. He confesses this predicament to his fellow sailors with embarrassment: "would you believe it? — I tried the women. I, Charlie Marlow, set the women to work — to get a job. Heavens!" (p. 23). Here he must not only repeat the personal pronoun, "I," but he feels compelled to name himself to the others in order to stress his own astonishment, to perform his alienation from ostensibly unusual behavior. Without his aunt's intervention, Marlow would never have gained his appointment to the river steamer in Africa in the first place; his aunt is, quite significantly, partly responsible for originating his story.

Not only are women "out of touch with truth," but Conrad also constructs the women of his story in terms of a different discursive genre from the men in *Heart of Darkness*. In contradistinction to Kurtz's "folds of a gorgeous eloquence" (p. 89), and Marlow's exquisite narration to his fellow sailors that takes places with scarcely a pause, the women's narration and their very narratability are severely restricted. Not a single woman has a name, women scarcely speak, and when they do speak they are misunderstood, deliberately misled, or represented as profoundly lacking a comprehensive understanding of the events in which they participate. The only women of the text who are granted a decipherable language are Marlow's aunt and Kurtz's Intended, and they are the only two with whom Marlow converses. Johanna M. Smith argues that Marlow chooses not to "silence" the Intended and the aunt simply because he needs them for his speech. "By mocking the lack of worldly experience which their words convey, he can recuperate that experience as a manly encounter with truth. By having them feebly echo the case Kurtz has made for imperialism, he can reverse the powerlessness evinced in his response to Kurtz's eloquence" (p. 196 in this volume). In contrast, the African woman is powerfully granted *sound* — a point I will return to later — though for Marlow the sound of her wailing is closer to the "howl" of the "bush" (pp. 60–61) that eerily takes his crew by surprise than it is to language.

In *The Differend* one of Lyotard's principal concerns is to explore how parties within discursive encounters involving heterogeneous "phrase regimens" are divested of the possibility of communicating, and are therefore "reduced to silence" (10). While he is interested especially in the philosophy of language and its discursive systems, he also includes a deeply ethical and political dimension to the differend, claiming, "What is at stake in a literature, in a philosophy, in a politics perhaps, is to bear witness to differends by finding idioms for them. In the differend, something 'asks" to be put into phrases, and suffers from the wrong of not being able to be put into phrases right away" (13). Without framing his argument in feminist, queer, or racial terms, Lyotard goes very far in describing how institutional and societal modes disallow certain forms of speech or genres of expression by not making space for the possibility of their idiom. That is, a differend occurs not simply when voices are not heard, but because those voices *cannot* be heard. The voices Lyotard writes of are as unintelligible to the more powerful discourses that frame and contain them (whether these are legal discourses, or whether they involve an exchange in which one of the parties — sometimes *a priori* — is refused the chance for self-articulation) as the women in *Heart of Darkness* are to Marlow's narration.[9]

For the majority of the text we do not and cannot know why women partake so completely of a different epistemological framework than the men, and it seems that Marlow is quite happy to allow this difference (which generates a differend) to remain unchallenged. He has virtually no desire to explore the incommensurabilities between their systems of

---

[9]In her recent study, *Conrad and Women*, Susan Jones points to a fascinating letter George Gissing wrote to Joseph Conrad in 1903 in which Gissing claims there is a pressure of speech behind the actual silence of Conrad's women: "Wonderful, I say, your mute or all but mute women. How, in Satan's name, do you make their souls speak through their silence?" (qtd. in Jones, 21). His point is idealistic and misogynistic at the same time, though he does touch upon some of the *work* these silent, or nearly silent, women do in Conrad's text.

knowledge and his own, establishing himself instead as an "Enlightened" reader, as Bette London points out, and "the voice of cultural
authority" (241). That is, he is capable of distinguishing between
epistemes while confidently remaining within his own. While his aunt is
making him "quite uncomfortable" with her naïve praise of the Company's project, for example, lauding their efforts to "wean those ignorant millions from their horrid ways," Marlow ventures a "hint that the
Company was run for profit" (p. 27). He stops short of a full explanation of his views, which he narrates to his male auditors, and he only
weakly expresses his discomfort through the always-ambiguous gesture
of a hint. Marlow thus not only allows his aunt to misread his own
ambivalence about the Company's capitalist ventures, but he seems to
wish this misreading upon her. He considers her, as with the Intended
at the end, incapable of any kind of complex logic or factual understanding. . . .

   At the very end of the text, Marlow's wish to retain a fundamental
disjunction between his epistemological framework and women's in
general is highlighted when he chooses to lie to Kurtz's Intended. Marlow's desire to visit her has been piqued by Kurtz's "small sketch in
oils" of the Intended — "a woman draped and blindfolded carrying a
lighted torch" (p. 40) — that Marlow first sees at the Central Station
before he meets Kurtz. The portrait of a deliberately blinded woman
who nevertheless functions as a carrier of light draws together Marlow's
general characterization of women as blinded, ignorant, and yet oddly
capable of illuminating the way into darkness, offering a parallel with
his aunt's procurement of his position and with the ways the women
of the story illuminate the epistemological structures and concerns of
Heart of Darkness.[10] Always one step away from truth and knowledge,
women can reflect their reasonable light, but not know where they
walk. Importantly, the painting also operates as a symbolic point of
currency for Marlow since together with Kurtz's letters, the blinded
figure of liberty provides a connecting bridge between Marlow and the
Intended, and gives him a reason for visiting her. Marlow chooses to

---

[10]Earlier in the story, when Marlow is first describing the trip toward the Inner Station on the river steamer, he associates himself with someone who is "blindfolded."
Defending his navigational skills he claims he "didn't do badly either since I managed not
to sink that steamboat on my first trip. It's a wonder to me yet. Imagine a blindfolded
man set to drive a van over a bad road. I sweated and shivered over that business considerably" (p. 49). When he later invokes the image of the "blindfolded" woman he again
offers the possibility to his readers that he and the women of his story are more intertwined — even metaphorically — than he would like to admit.

visit her on the pretence of returning what is rightfully hers — to "give her back her portrait and those letters myself" — while he simultaneously admits that his move is made equally out of "[c]uriosity," and a desire "to surrender personally all that remained of [Kurtz} with me," including "his memory" (p. 89).

When Marlow does visit the Intended, he is capable only of returning the portrait and her letters, not of giving her Kurtz's final words; he can return things, but he cannot meet her with language. Their dialogue takes place in a chiaroscuric setting of half-lights and shadows, and as elsewhere in the novella Marlow describes the Intended in terms that suggest she is co-extensive with her physical environment. The room they sit in has a "tall marble fireplace [that] had a cold and monumental whiteness. A grand piano stood massively in a corner with dark gleams on the flat surfaces like a sombre and polished sarcophagus" (p. 90), and the room grows increasingly "dark" as their conversation about Africa and Kurtz progresses. The Intended herself is still in mourning and dressed "all in black," yet she is also aligned with whiteness; she possesses a "pale head," "fair hair," a "pale visage," and she "seemed surrounded by an ashy halo" (p. 90).[11]

The Intended is predictably eager to hear all that Marlow has to tell about Kurtz's last days. But even though Marlow has already pronounced that "as it turned out [he] was to have the care of [Kurtz's] memory" (p. 66), he is unwilling to share either memory or truth with this woman. If Marlow is to insist on meeting Kurtz's Intended only in the language of lies, it appears he must foreclose communication altogether. Rather than giving the Intended the dignity of a conversation, he mimics her phrasing in a bizarrely sadistic wrestling match that belittles her hopes to learn about her once future husband.[12] In answer to her statement, "You knew him well," he echoes her in profoundly homoerotic language, "I knew him as well as it is possible for one man to know another" (p. 91). His echolalia effectively parodies her desire for knowledge about nothing less than *knowledge* itself by claiming a supreme (and possibly sexual) form of knowledge for himself. He has already conveyed a stuttering erotic homage to Kurtz that insists upon their eternal "intimacy," claiming that in his first words to Kurtz Marlow

---

[11]See Natalie Melas's "Brides of Opportunity: Figurations of Women and Colonial Territory in *Lord Jim*" for a brilliant discussion of the ways in which Conrad's Manicheistic dualisms echo structures of colonialism.

[12]Henry Staten reads this encounter as a sado-masochistic power conflict between Marlow and the Intended where Marlow possesses a "desire to inflict mourning on a woman and then to drink of her grief" (163).

said the "right thing," just at the "very moment when the foundations of our intimacy were being laid — to endure — to endure — even to the end — even beyond" (p. 81).

As their exchange continues he finds her responses deeply troubling and finally bars communication with her altogether, recognizing in the "appealing fixity of her gaze" (p. 91) the same language of "glances" he so detests in other women. As Marlow is struggling to piece words together in the hesitating language of discomfort, claiming Kurtz "was a remarkable man. . . . It was impossible not to —" the Intended interposes "Love him." This statement works simultaneously as a command, as an assertion of her own love for Kurtz, and as an attempt to meet Marlow on his own discursive level by literally completing his sentence to join his genre of praise. By echoing him in the language of love and desire, however, the Intended pushes his remembrance of Kurtz to its passionate and epistemological limits: her conclusion is precisely the sort of thing Marlow does not want to hear from a woman; it is far too near to the "truth" about his attachment to Kurtz. Marlow experiences this interpolation as a terrifying shutting down of his voice, feeling that she was "silencing me into an appalled dumbness" (p. 91). This is, of course, a distinctly feminine position in *Heart of Darkness*, and, along with the sudden revelation of her uncanny *knowledge*, produces a discomfort from which Marlow is unable to recover.

After a few more moments of an awkward, hesitating dialogue in which Marlow expresses a palpable jealousy about the Intended's devotion to Kurtz and her assurance of their mutual love, Marlow tells her that he was with Kurtz "[t]o the very end. . . . I heard his very last words," but then he suddenly "stopped in fright." The Intended, of course, asks him, with childlike repetitiveness, "Repeat them. . . . I want — I want — something — something — to — to live with" (p. 93). Again she is asking to participate in his language, to know the words he carries as memory. Marlow, however, is incapable of speaking. Rather than tell her the truth of Kurtz's astonishing last words, and thus uphold his promise to Kurtz to communicate his story to her on a decipherable level, Marlow reinforces their difference by refusing to meet her in the same discursive territory of "truth." Instead of telling the Intended that Kurtz died muttering "The horror! The horror!" — a statement that Marlow interprets as a "supreme moment of complete knowledge" (p. 85) that "had the appalling face of a glimpsed truth" (p. 86) — he tells her that Kurtz died muttering her (unspecified) name. As such, Marlow ends his story on a differend by directing her away from knowledge to leave her believing in a false romantic vision of

Kurtz's final words. Instead of allowing for the positivity of difference and otherness, Marlow refuses to risk the sort of incommensurability that might flourish if he tried to convey "the horror" to the Intended. Clearly he believes it would be impossible for her to understand his community of errantry and experience, and he chooses to close off an anticipated differend rather than to allow its free play: in effect, he will guard the difference between male and female forms of knowledge as vigilantly as the two knitting women guard "the door of Darkness."

His lie also binds him irrevocably and phantasmatically to Kurtz since it makes him the sole inheritor of Kurtz's story. By choosing to lie to the Intended, Marlow meddles with authorship and authority (he is a storyteller, after all) to impose his own revisions on Kurtz's final statement, thereby effectively authoring Kurtz's story himself. His lie uncannily marks the moment at which he is closest to Kurtz, yet simultaneously this refusal to honor Kurtz's contract for truth instantly dispels their community and their "Being in common." His lie to the Intended — which Marlow has already prematurely confessed to his auditors midway through his narration when it slips from his lips as a kind of premature ejaculation of the intention of the whole story — consequently marks the moment when Marlow has least control over language, narration, or his search for "the truth of things."

To mark the closure of his story, then, Marlow refuses the possibility of relation by purposefully remaining fixed in a differend as a means of resisting the frightful contact of knowledge between different modes of thought. In his mind we can hear him insisting that women do not travel, and they "live in a world of their own." His refusal to relate to the Intended is tantamount to claiming a continually shifting epistemological status that no one but himself can discern. By lying to her, and in the split moment that informs his decision to do so, he apparently finds her name (and perhaps the name of "women") translatable and *commensurable* with what otherwise seems to be the incommensurability of "the horror." Within his own mind he might even believe that he is telling her a kind of truth, leaving her ignorant of the "facts" of what really happened, but affirming to himself the affinity between women and "The horror!"

WORKS CITED

Achebe, Chinua. "An Image of Africa." *The Massachusetts Review* 18 (1977): 782–94.
Conrad, Joseph. *Heart of Darkness*. This edition.

————. "Geography and Some Explorers." 1926. Kimbrough 143.

————. "To T. Fisher Unwin." July 1896. Kimbrough 199.

————. "Preface to *The Nigger of the 'Narcissus.'*" *The Nigger of the "Narcissus."* By Joseph Conrad. Ed. Cedric Watts. London: Penguin, 1988.

Fanon, Frantz. *The Wretched of the Earth.* 1961. Trans. Constance Farrington. New York: Grove, 1963.

Forster, E. M. Rev. of *Heart of Darkness,* by Joseph Conrad. 1936. Murfin 139.

Hawthorn, Jeremy. *Joseph Conrad: Narrative Technique and Ideological Commitment.* London: Arnold, 1990.

Jones, Susan. *Conrad and Women.* Oxford: Clarendon P, 1999.

Kimbrough, Robert, ed. *Heart of Darkness.* By Joseph Conrad. New York: Norton, 1988.

Leavis, F. R. *The Great Tradition.* New York: New York UP, 1963.

London, Bette. "Reading Race and Gender in Conrad's Dark Continent." *Criticism* 31 (1989): 235–52.

Lyotard, Jean-François. *The Differend.* Trans. Georges Van Den Abbeele. Minneapolis: U of Minnesota P, 1988.

Masefield, John. Rev. of *Heart of Darkness,* by Joseph Conrad. 1903. Murfin 139.

Melas, Natalie. "Brides of Opportunity: Figurations of Women and Colonial Territory in *Lord Jim.*" *Qui Parle* 3 (1989): 54–75.

Murfin, Ross C, ed. Heart of Darkness: *A Case Study in Contemporary Criticism.* 3rd ed. New York: St. Martin's, 2011.

Said, Edward. *Culture and Imperialism.* New York: Vintage, 1993.

Smith, Johanna M. "'Too Beautiful Altogether': Patriarchal Ideology in *Heart of Darkness.* Heart of Darkness: *A Case Study in Contemporary Criticism.* Ed. Ross C Murfin. New York: Bedford, 2011. 189–204.

Staten, Henry. "Inflicting/Mourning: *Heart of Darkness.*" *Eros in Mourning: Homer to Lacan.* Baltimore: Johns Hopkins UP, 1995.

Stewart, Garrett. "Lying as Dying in *Heart of Darkness.*" *PMLA* 95 (1980): 319–31.

Watt, Ian. *Conrad in the Nineteenth Century.* Berkeley: U of California P, 1979.

————. "*Heart of Darkness* and Nineteenth-Century Thought." *Partisan Review* 45 (1978): 108–19.

Combining the New Historicism and Postcolonial Criticism with Psychoanalytic Criticism

Although you have been introduced to postcolonial criticism as well as the new historicism earlier, you have not been introduced to psychoanalytic criticism. Because the essay that follows mixes the postcolonial and a new historicist approach with psychoanalytic criticism, a brief explanation to psychoanalytic criticism has been incorporated into this introduction of Tony C. Brown's "Cultural Psychosis on the Frontier: The Work of the Darkness in Joseph Conrad's *Heart of Darkness.*"

WHAT IS PSYCHOANALYTIC CRITICISM?

Most psychoanalytic criticism is grounded in the theories of Sigmund Freud (1856–1939), who posited the importance of the unconscious. Freud called the predominantly unconscious, irrational, instinctual self the *id*, using the term *ego* to refer to the rational self, or "I," and *superego* to reference those aspects of the psyche that derive from external influences — parents, schools, churches or synagogues or mosques, and so forth.

The conscious mind, according to Freud, acts as a censor, driving underground, as it were, unconscious or conscious thoughts or instincts that it deems unacceptable. Repressed (and therefore psychologically significant) thoughts or desires often emerge in dreams, a subject Freud took up in *The Interpretation of Dreams* (1900). But they also can be in language (for instance, through so-called Freudian slips), in creative activity (art, including literature), or, of course, in neurotic behavior. One of the unconscious wishes we have all suppressed, according to Freud, is the childhood wish to displace the parent of our own sex and take his or her place in the affections of the parent of the opposite sex. (These wishes Freud referred to as "oedipal," naming a psychological complex after the Greek tragic hero Oedipus, who unwittingly killed his father and married his mother.) But Freud identified other fixations (oral and anal), compulsions (the compulsion to repeat traumatic events), and instincts (the death instinct) as well.

Psychoanalytic critics writing before 1950 tended to psychoanalyze individual authors; poems and novels were read as fantasies that allowed authors to indulge repressed wishes, to protect themselves from deep-seated anxieties, or both. Then the focus shifted to the psychology of readers and their individual responses to texts. Still later, literary critics employing the psychoanalytic approach used not only Freud's ideas but also those advanced in the seminars and writings of Jacques Lacan, who discussed "the gaze" — the human tendency to want to see and be seen — and who developed Freud's concept of the "mirror stage" in human development, a pre-oedipal stage during which the child comes to recognize him or herself in the mirror as a separate entity and therefore develops the concept of the Other, which eventually includes even the mother.

Additionally, Lacan theorized that there are three "orders" of "subjectivity" pertaining to the ways in which the individual self, or psyche, takes in and/or colors its world: the Imaginary Order, the Symbolic Order, and the Real. Although Lacan's conceptions of the Imaginary and the Symbolic probably differ from what you may imagine them to be, based on common understandings of the meanings of those terms, his conception of the Real is not only most unusual but also most relevant to Brown's essay. Specifically, Lacan's Real is the intractable and substantial world of traumatic knowledge that resists and exceeds interpretation. The Real cannot be imagined, symbolized, or known directly. It constantly eludes our efforts to name it (death, gravity, sexual difference, and the physical effects of trauma are examples). The Real is fundamentally "Other," the mark of the cut, or divide, within conscious and unconscious life and is signaled in language by gaps, slips, speechlessness, and the sense of the uncanny.

Other major theorists who have influenced psychoanalytic criticism include Carl Jung, who studied broad-based archetypes as they express themselves in individual human lives and mythological and literary representations, and D. W. Winnicott, whose ideas have more recently led psychoanalytic critics to view reader and text not in "either/or" terms but, rather, in terms of a "dyadic" relationship, not unlike the mother/child relationship they have posited in place of Freud's destructively powerful oedipal bond.

Tony C. Brown begins the essay that follows by citing the work of two postcolonial cultural critics: Homi K. Bhabha, who has noted with irony "the long shadow" that Conrad's *Heart of Darkness* casts over postcolonial studies, and Edward Said, who wrote of the "ambivalent status" of colonialism in the text, which at once offers a subversive, critical perspective on colonial discourse and serves as a central example *of* that discourse. (Brown points out that even the view of *Heart of Darkness* as a subversive critique of colonialism involves a "repetition" of Western, anti-African prejudice, since in order for Marlow, on his return home, to realize and reveal "the darkness at home in the very heart of Europe" he "must still uphold, as it were, the first term" — i.e., the view of Africa as the "primal seat of darkness.")

Brown's own perspective, as becomes apparent as his argument unfolds, is not entirely or even primarily that of postcolonial criticism; it also offers a distinctly psychoanalytic perspective. His focus is on "the peculiar conceptualization of the darkness in Conrad's writings," the "way the darkness works," and "what . . . is produced through the work it does." Brown views the darkness — which he several times calls "the cause of the horror" — as a "cultural psychosis" and, more specifically, as a "frontier phenomenon," that is, a culturally generalized psychotic phenomenon which Marlow comes to recognize in far-flung colonial places but also "at home in Europe."

In order to understand "the operation of darkness" as a culturally generalized psychosis, Brown adopts an historical perspective as he reviews accounts of atrocities being carried out in the Congo that were "appearing in an ever increasing quantity" in the European press toward the end of the nineteenth century. An "image of the Congo as an abject zone of horrors," Brown writes, "became embedded in the European social imagination," serving as "a kind of shorthand for a frontier-zone of brutality and terror" (p. 354). But the "cause of the horror" had, in Brown's words, "an ambivalent status," for "it was not the case that reports of atrocities in the Congo Free State shocked their European audiences simply because they reported hideous events; rather, what was so abhorrent about these events was that they occurred as *part of* what was supposed to be the actions of a civilizing mission" (p. 354; this is where Brown's historicist account becomes new historicist). The "dominant role played by colonial forces in the production of the horror of the Congo," he goes on to say, "disturbed a commonplace conception of the colonial zone as itself inherently barbaric" (p. 354).

In order to understand "the operation of darkness" on Conrad specifically, Brown points out that his editor, Edward Garnett, suggested that the author's own, actual "Congo experiences were the turning-point of his mental life," bringing about his "transformation from a sailor to a writer. . . . The sinister voice of the Congo with its murmuring undertone of human fatuity, baseness and greed," Garnett wrote, "had swept away the generous illusions of his youth, and left him gazing into the heart of an immense darkness" (pp. 357–58). Conrad admitted as much in his essay "Geography and Some Explorers," in which he said that his trip to the Congo brought about an abrupt "end to the idealized realities of a boy's daydreams!" (25).

"What Garnett and Conrad both articulate," Brown goes on to state, "is the collapse of Conrad's experiential organization," in other words of "fantasies" that had heretofore "structured Conrad's reality." More specifically, this "traumatic event" occurs due to what the psychoanalytic theorist Jacques Lacan called *"the encounter with the real"* (p. 359), a term he uses to refer not to reality as we ordinarily think of it but, rather, to that which cannot be known directly, imagined, symbolized, or interpreted (such as death, gravity, the physicality of objects). Relating James Clifford's claim that *Heart of Darkness* bears witness to a subjectivity grounded in cultural codes and conventions, particularly language, Brown asserts that "an irruption [i.e., an incursion, invasion, or breaking in] which forces an emptying out of culture's conventions would also force an emptying out of the fashioned self" (p. 360). He proceeds by arguing that Conrad's and Marlow's — and especially Kurtz's — Congo experience involved just such an irruption. "In Kurtz's case death was the result of the experience. By contrast, the experiences of Conrad and Marlow, though involving a confrontation with the threat of dissolution, were not as extreme as Kurtz's, and they both survive to tell their tales — though undergoing . . . a significant transformation of self" (p. 360).

In discussing their traumas and recoveries, Brown recounts "a famous dream" recorded by psychoanalytic theorist Sigmund Freud, a dream in which Freud "peer[ed] down the throat" of a female party guest to see "the flesh one never sees, the foundation of things, the other side of the head, of the face, of the secretory glands, . . . the flesh from which everything exudes" (p. 361). The subsequent, literally nightmarish anxiety — *"You are this, which is so far from you, this which is the ultimate formlessness"* — Brown likens to the Congo trauma that left Conrad "gazing into the heart of an immense darkness." Brown subsequently likens the conclusion of Freud's dream — in which he finds himself among friends who are fellow doctors — to the scene that initiates Conrad's plot and ends Marlow's story: "In the place of Freud's fellow doctors, . . . Conrad had his readers and Marlow [had] his four ship-deck listeners (the Lawyer, the Accountant, the Director of Companies, and the anonymous framing narrator)" to "giving . . . signification" (p. 362) to what has been said, to "attempt . . . some kind of management and control of the trauma" (p. 362) that has been experienced in the Congo.

But such attempts are not always successful, as Brown points out; in fact, within Marlow's narrative — and at "a heightened, climactic point" in Conrad's novel — "there is revealed the absolute and terrifying failure of signification and its attendant authority in the midst of the dark wilderness" (p. 362). While recounting his nighttime search of the jungle for Kurtz, who has escaped the steamer and returned to the wilderness, Marlow appeals to his listeners by saying "don't you see, the terror of the position was not in being knocked on the head — though I had a very lively sense of that danger, too — but in this, that I had to deal with a being to whom I could not appeal in the name of anything high or low" (p. 82).

From the perspective of cultural as well as psychoanalytic criticism, the phrase "in the name of" is doubly significant. First, it acknowledges that "it was precisely because the authority of civilized codes lay elsewhere that Kurtz, in his isolation, was 'found out' by the wilderness." Second, " 'in the name of' calls forth a recognition of the arbitrary aspect of language." Throughout his narrative, Marlow has seen "the expressly arbitrary naming of natives as 'enemies,' 'criminals,' and 'rebels' " — and how these names are used by the culture of colonialism to "legitimate" everything from forced work to executions. But when Marlow confronts Kurtz in the jungle and finds himself unable to "appeal in the name of anything," even this lowest-level form of signification proves impossible; as Brown puts it, "the relational and qualitative terms of sense-making — high and low — have become indistinguishable, without anchorage in any stable system of language: words . . . have lost the power to point beyond themselves" (p. 364). Calling this "the space of civilization's dissolution or foreclosure," Brown writes: "Marlow encounters Kurtz in a space beyond signification and is left without recourse to the distinguishing codes of civilization, with their controlling influence and authority. The reality structured through these codes has slipped, fallen away to reveal, in Lacanian terms, the monstrous grimace of the real" (p. 365).

WORKS CITED

Conrad, Joseph. "Geography and Some Explorers." In *Last Essays.* Ed. Richard Curle. London: Dent, 1926. Print.

Freud, Sigmund. *The Interpretation of Dreams.* Trans. A. A. Brill. New York: Macmillan, 1913. Print.

Lacan, Jacques. *Écrits: A Selection.* Trans. Bruce Fink. New York: W. W. Norton, 2002. Print.

———. "The Eye and the Gaze." In *Fundamental Concepts of Psychoanalysis.* Trans. Alan Sheridan. New York: Norton, 1978. Print.

TONY C. BROWN

Cultural Psychosis on the Frontier: The Work of the Darkness in Joseph Conrad's *Heart of Darkness*

> Therein consists the most elementary formal definition of psychosis: the massive presence of some real that fills out and blocks the perspective openness which is constitutive of "reality."
>
> –SLAVOJ ŽIŽEK, "Grimaces of the Real"[1]

Heart of Darkness has perversely proved a central document in postcolonial discourse. As Homi K. Bhabha puts it, "the long shadow of Conrad's *Heart of Darkness* falls on so many texts of the postcolonial pedagogy."[2] Notably, Bhabha cites Edward W. Said's *Culture and Imperialism* as an exemplary example of such a text:

---

[1] Slavoj Žižek, "Grimaces of the Real, or When the Phallus Appears," *October* 58 (Fall 1991): 52.

[2] Homi K. Bhabha, "How Newness Enters the World: Postmodern Space, Postcolonial Times and the Trials of Cultural Translation," in *The Location of Culture* (London: Routledge, 1994), 212.

Heart of Darkness is the novel that invites the most comment and interpretation. It serves as a resource for many of the central arguments in the book. In Said's early discussions of the complex address and consolidation of the imperial idea as ideology, *Heart of Darkness* features prominently. In the later, postcolonial perspectives that deal with resistance and opposition, Said demonstrates the "anxiety of influence" generated by the novel on the anti-colonialist fictions of Ngugi wa Thiongo, *The River Between*, and Tayeb Salih, *Season of Migration to the North.*[3]

When we turn to Said's book, Bhabha's comments are clearly borne out as Conrad's novel takes on a privileged and at times pervasive role. Importantly, however, there is a particular tension running throughout Said's discussion and use of *Heart of Darkness* to which Bhabha does not immediately direct our attention. This tension emerges from Said's recognition of an ambivalent status afforded colonialism in Conrad's novel, as it at once offers critics a perspective from which can be gained critical leverage on the discourse of colonialism and yet is itself one of the most concentrated and influential documents of modern colonial discourse."[4] In terms of the former, *Heart of Darkness* has commonly been seen to present a subversive perspective through Marlow's perversion of the West's image of itself as the place of light and civilization. After his up-river journey into the heart of darkness, the Western metropolis is revealed to Marlow cloaked in the folds of darkness he encountered at the ends of the earth: the white woman, the Intended, resembles Kurtz's African woman; the tall houses lining the city streets appear in the profile of the posts with human heads on them outside Kurtz's Inner Station; and the pounding of his heart echoes the beat of primitive drums heard in the depths of the jungle. As Bhabha himself observes, in Marlow's revelation of the darkness at home in the very heart of Europe through such a "discourse of daemonic doubling," he "beholds the everyday reality of the Western metropolis through the veil of the colonial fantasm."[5] In doing so Marlow performs a perversion of the West's ideal-image of itself as the true seat of civilization and light — a perversion which offers a certain critical leverage for interrupting the perpetuation of this self-image.

---

[3] *Ibid.*, 272, n. 1.
[4] See Edward W. Said, *Culture and Imperialism* (London: Chatto and Windus, 1993), esp. 20–35.
[5] Bhabha, "How Newness Enters the World," 213.

In line with the latter pole of the ambivalent status of colonialism recognized by Said, the "long shadow" of Conrad's novel has also been seen in far less positive terms. Most famously, Chinua Achebe has argued *Heart of Darkness* constitutes a document of high European racism to be rejected and purged of all cultural currency. In these terms the "long shadow" of its influence is felt more as a dark mantle to be cast off than a critically enlightening experience. For Achebe, Africa functions in the novel as a "foil" for Europe, constituting a negative, blank space onto which is projected all that Europe does not want to see in itself, everything that is abhorrent and abject.[6] The difference between this position and the former, which locates a subversive potential in the text, has largely to do with the respective degree of attention paid to the place of Africa in *Heart of Darkness*. It is with the place of Africa Achebe is notably most concerned, focusing on the way this place is marked by racial abjection. But in the invocation of a subversive potential in the novel's "discourse of daemonic doubling," the place of Africa is largely ignored — a situation resulting from a failure to adequately take into account the continued repetition of Africa as a zone of abhorrence and abjection. What occurs in Marlow's viewing of the Western metropolis through "the veil of the colonial fantasm" is what might be called a "metonymy of the veil," as one fantasy (Western metropolis as civilized place of light) is displaced by another (Western metropolis as horrific place of darkness). While this might correctly recognize the perversion of the West's ideal self-image, it ignores what must remain the constant repetition of Africa as the primal seat of darkness: in Marlow's perverse or ironic presentation of Europe *qua* the darkness, he must still uphold, as it were, the first term (i.e., Africa as darkness). So while Marlow effectively questions the West's self-image, he maintains, at every point, the West's image of Africa as a negative space of darkness.

A consequence of ignoring the repetition of Africa as primal darkness is a failure in critical terms to ascertain what kind of place "the darkness" actually occupies. Much, of course, has been said of the horror of the darkness in Conrad's novel; little, however, has been done to trace its precise conceptualization. Critics (postcolonial or not) have by and large simply seen the darkness as horrible, stopping short of asking how it operates to generate "the horror" in the conceptual organization

[6]Chinua Achebe, "An Image of Africa: Racism in Conrad's *Heart of* Darkness," in *Hopes and Impediments: Selected Essays, 1965–1987* (Oxford: Heinemann, 1988), 1–13.

of *Heart of Darkness*. J. Hillis Miller's work on Conrad might be cited as an exception, as Miller, more than anyone else, has sought to trace the peculiar conceptualization of the darkness in Conrad's writings.[7] However, what largely remains missing from Miller's account of the darkness is a specific consideration of how the darkness works to *produce* the horror in *Heart of Darkness*. I want to ask in what way does the darkness thus work, and what is it that is produced through the work it does. An examination of the darkness not simply as horrible but as the horror's *cause* will, I suggest, show how it works to effect for Conrad what can be called "cultural psychosis." I will specifically examine this psychosis as a frontier phenomenon in *Heart of Darkness* — a phenomenon which is later recognized by Marlow at home in Europe as a latent threat of a larger cultural psychosis. As we shall see, through the interruption of Europe's civil codes on the frontier the darkness — to bend Slavoj Žižek's words to my purposes — "fills out and blocks the perspective" of civilization and its constitutive codes.

In order to approach the operation of the darkness, it is worthwhile, first of all, to take into account the historical situation which gave rise to the text of *Heart of Darkness* and Marlow's journey up-river presented in it — a journey which has been readily recognized as set in the Congo Free State since the novel's first publication.[8] In *fin de siècle*

---

[7]Between his earlier phenomenological reading of Conrad's darkness and later deconstructive approach, Miller presents a sustained engagement with the role darkness plays for Conrad. What I have referred to as Miller's earlier reading of Conrad's darkness can be found in *Poets of Reality: Six Twentieth-Century Writers* (Cambridge, MA: Harvard Univ. Press, 1965), 13–39. Here Miller argues that Conrad's darkness is not only "the origin from which things come, and the end toward which they go. It is a metaphysical entity": "The darkness is present at every moment and in every thing and person, underlying them as their secret substance" (28). In his later reading, J. Hillis Miller, "*Heart of Darkness* Revisited," in *Tropes, Parables, Performatives: Essays on Twentieth-Century Literature* (London: Harvester Wheatsheaf, 1990), 181–94, Miller shifts attention from the content of the darkness to its textual inscription, examining the figuration of darkness in the text. According to this reading the "darkness" is that which can ever be revealed in itself, only referred to indirectly — that is, the darkness is strictly unpresentable literally or figuratively (see 186).

[8]Though as Christopher L. Miller has observed, the Congo Free State or even Africa is nowhere mentioned in Conrad's novel as the location of Marlow's up-river journey: "The referent of *Heart of Darkness* is so commonly understood to be Africa, and specifically the Congo Free State at the time of King Léopold II's reign of terror and profit at the end of the nineteenth century, that it may come as a surprise to learn that 'Africa' is never specifically named as its referent." But as he goes on to point out, Africa returns in the phrase "heart of darkness": "in a text where every detail points to Africa, 'Africa' alone is missing, encoded in a new phrase, 'heart of darkness.'" Christopher L. Miller, *Blank Darkness: Africanist Discourse in French* (Chicago: Univ. of Chicago Press, 1985), 170.

Europe, accounts of grotesque atrocities occurring in Léopold II's Congo Free State were appearing in an ever increasing quantity. A notable effect of this was the recurrence of an image of the Congo as an abject zone of horrors. The degree to which this image became embedded in the European social imagination is indicated by a headline from a 1909 edition of the London-based magazine *Truth.* "The Devil's Paradise: A British owned Congo" introduced a series of articles detailing the brutality of representatives of the Arana Brothers' Anglo-Peruvian rubber company in their treatment of the native populations of the Putumayo area in south-western Colombia.[9] The "Congo" of this headline is specifically Léopold's Congo Free State, and it functions as a kind of shorthand for a frontier-zone of brutality and terror — a condition, it should be realized, that is perceived to have been brought about by the abhorrent actions in the area of European colonialists. The use of the name "Congo" in this way clearly suggests that by 1909 the Congo Free State had come to be a readily recognizable and repeatable signifier of an horrific and corrupt colonial violence: the Congo Free State always returned, so to speak, to the same place in the topography of the European social imagination, constantly occupying that special place so often marked in European conceptions of overseas colonial domains: Hell on earth.

There is, however, in the context of the late-nineteenth- and early-twentieth-century discourses of colonialism, a distinctive feature of the Congo Free State's recurring image that must be observed. In the production of the Congo Free State's image as a Hell on earth, it is noticeable that the cause of the horror has an ambivalent status. It was not the case that reports of atrocities in the Congo Free State shocked their European audiences simply because they reported hideous events; rather, what was so abhorrent about these events was that they occurred as *part of* what was supposed to be the actions of a civilizing mission. The explicit and quite dominant role played by colonial forces in the production of the horror of the Congo disturbed a commonplace conception of the colonial zone as itself inherently barbaric. In the discourse of colonialism — particularly in a late-nineteenth-century context where the noble savage had all but disappeared[10] — when it was a space of terror being spoken of, it was so typically the "daemonic" environments of the far-off colonies which were perceived as the terror's

---

[9]Michael Taussig, *Shamanism, Colonialism, and the Wild Man: A Study in Terror and Healing* (Chicago: Univ. of Chicago Press, 1987), 21.
[10]See George Stocking, *Victorian Anthropology* (New York: The Free Press, 1987).

source. It was, of course, such an abhorrent condition which the civilizing force of European colonization was supposed to set right. In the
case of Léopold's Congo Free State, though, *la mission civilisatrice*
appeared to perform the hideous barbarism it was supposed to eradi-
cate, effecting a degree of confusion as to the cause of those horrors
reported as occurring in the colony.

It is this historical context that *Heart of Darkness* both emerges
from and extends. Indeed, the ambivalent status of what I have called
the horror's "cause" in the Congo is perhaps nowhere more famously
brought out than in *Heart of Darkness*. In Marlow's account of his
journey up-river there can be observed an obscure vacillation between
the horror as an effect of colonial intervention and the location of the
horror's cause as the environment itself. It could be argued there is a
sense in which these two dimensions of the horror's cause double what
has already been seen as the simultaneous perversion and repetition of
the novel. Firstly, to show the horror of the situation as generated by
European intervention suggests the colonial mission is not so much a
project of bringing light to benighted savages as it is itself a process of
darkening, thus perverting the West's image of itself as bearer of light
and civilization. Then, secondly, locating the cause of the horror in the
African wilderness would appear a fairly clear repetition of Africa as *the*
hideous primal darkness. The first notably offers evidence for the presence of a critical view of colonialism in Conrad's novel, and is at first
sight a more obvious source of "critical leverage" on the discourse of
colonialism than the perversion of the West's self-image I began by
discussing. However, in the oscillation between the cause *qua* colonial
intervention and the arguably more dominant cause *qua* wilderness,
the former loses its possible critical edge by remaining an account
merely of atrocious things happening in the colonies. This contrasts to
the perversion of the West's self-image which intimates the irruption of
the darkness *at home in Europe*, representing not so much a perversion,
as a repetition of the image of the colonial frontier as a place of barbarity — a barbarity, in fact, marked most notably in the distorted bodies
of African men.

The cause *qua* colonial intervention is most clearly presented when
Marlow first arrives in the colonial zone and surveys the desolation of
the Company Station. The hideous panorama confronting Marlow as
he makes his way unguided through the Company Station appears the
direct result of the colonialists' actions in the area. What Marlow calls
"the grove of death," for instance, is a product of "The work!" as he sar-
donically puts it, directly recalling the grandiose rhetoric of the civilizing

mission used earlier in the novel by his aunt.[11] The natives he finds in the grove had been "helpers" in the building of a railroad, that great self-monument of nineteenth-century imperial expansion. But they were made to work under such poor conditions they inevitably got fatally sick, and were left to crawl away and wait for death in various poses of geometric distortion, embodying for Marlow the barbarity of the colonial forces:

> Black shapes crouched, lay, sat between the trees, leaning against the trunks, clinging to the earth, half coming out, half effaced within the dim light, in all the attitudes of pain, abandonment, and despair. . . . These moribund shapes were free as air — and nearly as thin. I began to distinguish the gleam of the eyes under the trees. Then, glancing down, I saw a face near my hand. The black bones reclined at full length with one shoulder against the tree, and slowly the eyelids rose and the sunken eyes looked up at me, enormous and vacant, a kind of blind, white flicker in the depths of the orbs, which died out slowly. . . . Near the same tree two more bundles of acute angles sat with their legs drawn up. One, with his chin propped on his knees, stared at nothing, in an intolerable and appalling manner: his brother phantom rested its forehead, as if overcome with a great weariness; and all about others were scattered in every pose of contorted collapse, as in some picture of a massacre or a pestilence. (pp. 31–32)

The further up-river Marlow goes, though, the more the cause of the hideous situation resides in the dark wilderness, which becomes *the* heart of darkness itself. If the darkness overtakes the colonialist, as in the privileged case of Kurtz, it is as a quality otherwise latent, lodged deep within him, but which irrupts *due to* intimate contact with the lawless wilderness. When the "civilized" person resides in Europe, where Conrad believes behavior is effectively structured and censored by the policing mechanisms of civilization, the subterranean darkness is held at bay (and it should be recalled at this point that the great perversion of *Heart of Darkness* is, of course, the revelation that the darkness *does* exist in Europe, albeit in a restrained form). This condition is, for Conrad, a positive restraining or foreclosure of something truly abhorrent. But he also believes that once the civilized soul is displaced onto the colonial frontier of the Congo, these structuring and screening

---

[11] See Joseph Conrad, *"Heart of Darkness" and Other Tales*, ed. Cedric Watts (Oxford: Oxford Univ. Press, 1990), 160, 156, and 149. All further references are cited parenthetically in the text.

mechanisms too are displaced and ultimately distorted into mere shadows of their original form as the policing practices and institutions necessary to uphold them are markedly absent. The wilderness becomes then, in opposition to the state of instituted civilization in Europe, a lawless, thoroughly uncivilized place: it manifests as an unrestrained savagery which by its very nature threatens as a massive presence that will "block" the imposition of civilized order. Indeed, *Heart of Darkness* can be seen to suggest that the wilderness will destroy those foolish enough to attempt such an imposition.

Of course, European civilization can stumble at home, so to speak. It certainly does not need to go beyond itself to the colonial frontier in the far-off places of the world (as one stands in Europe) to become displaced from itself through the loss of an ordering consistency. However, the perception of the frontier as a place where this readily happens persists as a common perception, and *Heart of Darkness* in particular stands out as one of the most influential representations of such a frontier. In other words, Conrad's novel presents a singularly sustained and influential account of what I have called "the loss of an ordering consistency" upon the displacement of the codes and conventions of civilization onto the colonial frontier. As will become clear, the colonial frontier manifests as a stumbling block for civilization in *Heart of Darkness* in the form of, or rather in the formless presence of, a void which forecloses upon European culture. And it is as such a formless presence that the darkness operates as the horror's cause in the novel. The terms with which to begin to think through this foreclosing of civilization come from the life of Conrad as it emerges in certain written sources.

One of the most significant accounts of the effect Conrad's Congo encounter had on him comes from his close friend and editor, Edward Garnett. Recalling conversations he had with Conrad, Garnett suggests "Conrad's Congo experiences were the turning-point of his mental life and . . . [their] effects on him determined his transformation from a sailor to a writer."[12] Conrad himself had said to Garnett that he thought his time in the Congo responsible for a personal transformation, though not from sailor to writer. Rather, Conrad believed he had undergone a metamorphosis from "a perfect animal" without "a thought in his head," to a thinking, reflecting being who could mobilize the mechanisms of a critical reason.[13] From such comments, Garnett received the

---

[12]Edward Garnett, "[Art drawn from memory]" [1928], in Robert Kimbrough, ed., *Heart of Darkness*, Norton Critical Edition, 3d ed. (New York: Norton, 1988), 195.
    [13]*Ibid.*

startling impression that in the Congo Conrad's youthful "illusions" had been "swept away," leaving him gazing into "the heart of an immense darkness": "The sinister voice of the Congo with its murmuring undertone of human fatuity, baseness and greed had swept away the generous illusions of his youth, and left him gazing into the heart of an immense darkness."[14]

Support for Garnett's observation can be found in Conrad's essay "Geography and Some Explorers," where he writes of his African-river journey in terms which suggest a similar collapsing of youthful illusions that leave him confronting a dark void. Writing late in life (this essay was one of Conrad's final pieces of writing), Conrad recalls how as a boy he had a passion for the modern, accurate maps of what he calls the "geography militant." To his youthful imagination these maps presented unmarked, unknown spaces, to which he dreamed of going as an explorer — explorers being, for the young Conrad, heroic men who he believed searched earnestly for the Truth. Conrad remembers one day pointing to a particularly inviting blank spot and saying he would "go there" (a gesture also performed by Marlow in *Heart of Darkness*).[15] About eighteen years after making this bold declaration, Conrad found himself on the deck of "a wretched little stern-wheel steamboat . . . moored to the bank of an African river."[16] This was the very place he

---

[14] *Ibid.*, 195–96. Notably, Garnett does not isolate the cause of Conrad's loss of "the generous illusions of his youth": the "sinister voice of the Congo" could refer to either the forces of colonial intervention or the wilderness, or indeed to both. On the impact of Conrad's "gazing into the heart of an immense darkness" on his view of colonialism, see Sooyoung Chon, "Writing as an Exodus from Two Empires," in *Under Postcolonial Eyes: Joseph Conrad After Empire*, ed. Gail Fincham and Myrtle Hooper (Cape Town: Univ. of Cape Town Press, 1996), 43; and Andrea White, "Conrad and Imperialism," in *The Cambridge Companion to Joseph Conrad*, ed. J. H. Stape (Cambridge: Cambridge Univ. Press, 1996), 181. Other relevant discussions of the traumatic impact of Conrad's Congo experience include: Zdzislaw Najder, "[Introduction to 'The Congo Diary' and the 'Upriver Book']," in *Heart of Darkness*, ed. Kimbrough, 155; Hunt Hawkins, "Conrad and Congolese Exploitation," *Conradiana* 13 (1981): 94–100; Albert J. Guerard, "[From life to art]," in *Heart of Darkness*, ed. Kimbrough, 192–93; and Taussig, *Shamanism, Colonialism, and the Wild Man*, 16–17.

[15] Joseph Conrad, "Geography and Some Explorers," in *Last Essays*, ed. Richard Curle (London: Dent, 1926), 24. This scene with the map was a deeply significant experience for Conrad and he returned to it several times in his writings. Most notably, Marlow recalls an identical episode in *Heart of Darkness*: "Now when I was a little chap I had a passion for maps and I would look for hours at South America, or Africa, or Australia, and lose myself in all the glories of exploration. At that time there were many blank spaces on the earth, and when I saw one that looked particularly inviting on a map (but they all looked like that) I would put my finger on it and say, When I grow up I will go there" (142). See also Joseph Conrad, "[When I grow up I shall go *there*]," in *Heart of Darkness*, ed. Kimbrough, 148.

[16] Conrad, "Geography and Some Explorers," 24.

had declared he would go those many years before: the center of the African continent, deep in the Congo Free State. Despite this achievement, however, Conrad did not feel satisfied or triumphant. Instead, he felt a great melancholy descend upon him, and was confronted with the brutal "end to the idealised realities of a boy's daydreams!"[17]

What Garnett and Conrad both articulate to greater or lesser degrees is the collapse of Conrad's experiential organization. They each speak of this collapse in terms of the destruction of certain fantasies — Garnett referring to Conrad's youthful "illusions," and Conrad to the "idealised realities" of his boyhood "daydreams." But importantly they recognize that these fantasies framed and therefore structured Conrad's reality: it was in terms of these fantasy-frames that Conrad experienced experience, so to speak; he had taken them with him to the Congo, expectantly, as frames organizing his perception. Traumatically for him, he was thrown awry when they proved inadequate. In other words, upon his encountering something which — in Žižek's phrase — "fills out and blocks the perspective . . . constitutive of 'reality,' " Conrad lost the fantasy-frames structuring his experience of and in the world. As we have seen, according to Garnett this traumatic event "left him gazing into the heart of an immense darkness" — that is, into a blank space beyond any possible imaginary identification.

The terms of Conrad's traumatic encounter point us in the direction of the Lacanian *tuché*, or *"the encounter with the real."*[18] Put most simply, to encounter the real is to reach a point at which "reality" — including its structuration in relation to the fantasy-frame — loses its consistency, collapsing and dissolving. Of course, for Lacan, the encounter with the real is always and necessarily missed in the case of the "normal" person, who most typically is lured towards the encounter with the real at that fleeting, transitory moment *in-between* dreaming and waking, but manages to awake and escape into "reality." In the everyday run of things, then, the real is passed-over.[19] The specific characteristic to be noted of Conrad's "encounter," however — and as we shall

---

[17] *Ibid.*, 25.

[18] See Jacques Lacan, *The Four Fundamental Concepts of Psycho-Analysis*, ed. Jacques-Alain Miller, trans. Alan Sheridan (London: Hogarth Press, 1977), 53–64.

[19] For a full treatment of this, see Slavoj Žižek, *Looking Awry: An Introduction to Jacques Lacan through Popular Culture* (Cambridge, MA: The MIT Press, 1991), 29–34; and Slavoj Žižek, *The Sublime Object of Ideology* (London: Verso, 1989), 43–49. Lacan discusses the subject who does not miss the encounter with the real, and who thus escapes from symbolization, in his "On a Question Preliminary to any Possible Treatment of Psychosis," in *Écrits: A Selection*, trans. Alan Sheridan (New York: Norton, 1977), 179–225.

see later, Marlow's too — is the failure to pass-over "the real": rather, it "fills out" the frame, foreclosing on the ideal order and orderings of civilization. Or, to put it another way, Conrad's "gazing into the heart of an immense darkness" upon losing the structuring "illusions" of "reality" corresponds to the sense of a *traumatic event* as an encounter with the real that is not missed but confronted in all its unbearable terror.

When we consider the enormously important role of language and other cultural structures of understanding in Conrad's conception of subjectivity, the traumatic significance of the event which effectively evacuates them becomes acutely apparent. With great insight James Clifford has suggested that Conrad presents with *Heart of Darkness* one of the first and one of the most powerful articulations of a subjectivity anchored in the constitutional codes of culture and language.[20] For Clifford, Conrad "built into his work a vision of the constructed nature of culture and language" and of the "arbitrariness of conventions," which included a belief in the individual as an entity that is fashioned by such conventions and constructions.[21] Accordingly, an irruption which forces an emptying out of culture's conventions and constructions would also force an emptying out of the fashioned self. The loss of language and its aligned structures of understanding is effectively, then, a loss of the self which has been fashioned in the co-ordinates of culture. In *Heart of Darkness* such an experience of dissolution is caught, in its most extreme form, in the horror of Kurtz's fall, and in Kurtz's case death was the result of this experience. By contrast, the experiences of Conrad and Marlow, though involving a confrontation with the threat of dissolution, were not as extreme as Kurtz's, and they both survive to tell their tales — though undergoing, as we have seen with Conrad, a significant transformation of self.

There is a notable paradox — or at least seeming paradox — in Conrad's and Marlow's repetition of the event through narration in that, to do so, they must call upon the conventions and constructions of a culture whose limits this event had painfully exposed to them. Indeed, the event in question threatened the very collapse of these cultural codes constituting both themselves as individuals and the reality in which they move. In *Lord Jim*, Marlow articulates an analogous situ-

---

[20]James Clifford, "On Ethnographic Self-Fashioning: Conrad and Malinowski," in *The Predicament of Culture: Twentieth-Century Ethnography, Literature, and Art* (Cambridge, MA: Harvard Univ. Press, 1988), 92–113.
[21]*Ibid.*, 95–96.

ation using the ship as metaphor for a properly ordered culture: "When your ship fails you, your whole world seems to fail you; the world that made you, restrained you, took care of you."[22] But in representing the event which threatened, so to speak, the destruction of the "ship" in *Heart of Darkness*, Conrad and Marlow are seeking to re-institute the authority of culture's codes, and thereby foreclose the threat of dissolution. There is a famous dream of Freud's which best enables us to think through this situation: the dream of Irma's injection. In the first part of the dream, Freud encounters, in Lacanian terms, "the real" — an encounter which disturbs, in this case, the specular dual-relationship held between Freud and Irma up until that point. The "encounter" occurs when a curious Freud, propelled by his desire, peers down the throat of his party guest Irma:

> There's a horrendous discovery here, that of the flesh one never sees, the foundation of things, the other side of the head, of the face, of the secretory glands *par excellence*, the flesh from which everything exudes, at the very heart of the mystery, the flesh in as much as it is suffering, is formless, in as much as its form in itself is something which provokes anxiety. Spectre of anxiety, identification of anxiety, the final revelation of *you are this — You are this, which is so far from you, this which is the ultimate formlessness.*[23]

The encounter with the real, it will be recalled, is an encounter which threatens an acute dissolution. In this case the cause of that threat appears as the night of the absolute origin, where no distinctions can be made and no conventions determine behavior. Supporting the use of Freud's dream in reading *Heart of Darkness*, it can be said that in Marlow's journey up-river in *Heart of Darkness* he traveled down an analogue of this throat, witnessing the very "foundation of things": "[g]oing up that river," he says at one point, "was like travelling back to the earliest beginnings of the world" (p. 48).

In the second part of Freud's dream there is an abrupt switch as he finds himself in a space populated by his doctor friends. As Joan Copjec notes, in the passage from the first to the second part of his dream

---

[22]Joseph Conrad, *Lord Jim*, ed. Cedric Watts and Robert Hampson (Harmondsworth: Penguin, 1986), 103.

[23]Jacques Lacan, *The Seminar of Jacques Lacan, Book II: The Ego in Freud's Theory and in the Technique of Psychoanalysis 1954–1955*, ed. Jacques-Alain Miller, trans. Sylvanna Tomaselli (Cambridge: Cambridge Univ. Press, 1988), 154–55. See also Slavoj Žižek, *Tarrying with the Negative: Kant, Hegel, and the Critique of Ideology* (Durham: Duke Univ. Press, 1993), 118.

Freud "*flees* from the real . . . into the symbolic community of his fellow doctors."[24] In doing so, he guards against the terrifying real by escaping to a determined place *from where he can discuss "the real" with other figures of qualified authority*. In short, Freud's dream suggests that by discussing the real, and giving it signification within an authoritative context, a defense against it can be erected.[25]

In the place of Freud's fellow doctors, it can be said that Conrad had his readers and Marlow his four ship-deck listeners (the Lawyer, the Accountant, the Director of Companies, and the anonymous framing narrator). And though Conrad once described the interior experience of the creative artist in precisely the same terms he used to describe the lawless solitude of the wilderness in *Heart of Darkness*,[26] it is, as he was aware, in the distinctly public and structured domain of civilized intercourse that the text's signification is given, and which I have in mind when I refer to the possibility of giving signification to the event of Conrad's experience. It is in the public domain that an "artistic product" such as *Heart of Darkness* circulates — and it is also in this domain, albeit a small and fictionalized one, that Marlow tells his story: in an "objective" relationship established as such by the presence of his listeners. In the exchange between Conrad and his readers, or between Marlow and his listeners, there occurs the "giving" of signification to the event as they each call upon the conventions and constructions of language and culture in an attempt to enable some kind of management and control of the trauma.

Sown into the conceptual economy of *Heart of Darkness*, however, there is a sharp problematization of the ability to successfully manage and control the "content" of a trauma through its signification — a problematization rendered in the pervading problematic of representation. At a heightened, climactic point in the novel there is revealed the absolute and terrifying failure of signification and its attendant authority in the midst of the dark wilderness; an examination of this heightened moment will make explicit what I earlier referred to as the foreclosure of European culture and reveal to us the operation of the darkness.

---

[24]Joan Copjec, "Vampires, Breast-Feeding, and Anxiety," *October* 58 (Fall 1991): 27.
[25]*Ibid.*, 28.
[26]In *A Personal Record* (1912), Conrad writes: "And least of all can you condemn an artist pursuing, however humbly and imperfectly, a creative aim. In that interior world where his thought and his emotions go seeking for the experience of imagined adventures, there are no policemen, no law, no pressure of circumstance or dread of opinion to keep him in bounds." Cited in Michiel Heyns, " 'Like People in a Book': Imaginative Appropriation in *Lord Jim*," in Fincham and Hooper, eds., *Under Postcolonial Eyes*, 78.

As Marlow tells the part of his story where he searched for Kurtz in the jungle at night after Kurtz had escaped from the steamer to return to the wilderness, moving "towards the gleam of fires, the throb of drums, the drone of weird incantations" (p. 82), he asks his listeners to see the terror of the situation not in the threat of being knocked on the head but in the confronting of a man to whom no appeal could be made through the received civil codes of Europe. In the immense solitude of the jungle, Kurtz's soul has lost contact with the governing order of civilization as it exists in Europe: "don't you see, the terror of the position was not in being knocked on the head — though I had a very lively sense of that danger, too — but in this, that I had to deal with a being to whom I could not appeal in the name of anything high or low."

The phrase "in the name of" is crucial here, and possesses a double significance. Firstly, Marlow's use of the phrase bears witness to the deferral necessary in asserting the authority of civilization's codes when displaced to the fundamentally different location beyond civilization's margins. Civilization does not move out to the frontier zone and repeat itself in its full presence, as if achieving the sublation of the other in the dialectical advance of the selfsame. "In the name of" reveals that the source of authority lies elsewhere, not present on the colonial frontier, but to be deferred to from this place of difference. It was precisely because the authority of civilized codes lay elsewhere that Kurtz, in his isolation, was "found out" by the wilderness; the hollow core left by the absence of civil law left him open to the wiles of the wilds.[27] Of course, the discursive repetition of the colonial sphere as different is a major strategy of colonial power: marked by the trace of its difference-as-inferiority in relation to Europe, the frontier zones need to be subject to the redeeming forces of colonialist imposition.[28] The philanthropic rhetoric of Léopold II, for instance, made sense in Europe not because the frontier zone of the Congo was the repeatable signifier of identity or superiority, but because it was constituted in colonial discourse as an abhorrent, inferior difference *to be* eliminated.

---

[27]Conrad makes this connection between hollowness and the absence of civil law clear in his only other work set in Africa, "An Outpost of Progress": "It was not the absolute and dumb solitude of the post that impressed them [the European agents Kayerts and Carlier] so much as an inarticulate feeling that something from within them was gone, something that worked for their safety, and had kept the wilderness from interfering with their hearts." Conrad, "An Outpost of Progress," in *"Heart of Darkness" and Other Tales*, 24.

[28]See Homi K. Bhabha, "Signs Taken for Wonders: Questions of Ambivalence and Authority under a Tree Outside Delhi, May 1817," in *The Location of Culture*, 111.

Secondly, "in the name of" calls forth a recognition of the arbitrary aspect of language so important to Conrad generally, but acutely revealed here in the peculiar displacement of European language away from Europe in the depths of the night-time jungle. Notably the act of naming itself appears throughout Marlow's narrative as the most obvious of language's arbitrary practices, as various nouns are used in a way that, Marlow implies, constitutes a series of mis-namings.[29] Furthermore, these mis-namings appear an imposition — an often brutal, physical imposition by imperial forces. Thus, what Marlow sees as the expressly arbitrary naming of natives as "enemies," "criminals," and "rebels" is shown to legitimate, and even incite, their murder or their enforcement into "chain gangs."[30] But in Marlow's night-time jungle confrontation with Kurtz, in not being able to "appeal in the name of anything high or low," the relational and qualitative terms of sense-making — high and low — have become indistinguishable, without anchorage in any stable system of language: words appear emptied of meaning, doomed only to float detached in the overwhelming confusion of the scene. In short, they have lost the power to point beyond themselves.

Leading up to his night-time encounter with Kurtz, Marlow's general sense of indistinguishability had become increasingly prominent the further up-river he traveled. Most explicitly it had been figured in spatial terms when the steamer was stranded mid-stream amidst a heavy fog. The disorientation of the fog contrasts though with the confusion in confronting Kurtz in the wilderness in an important respect. The former presents the disorientation of a blinding whiteness, while the latter is an encounter with an impenetrable darkness; the differing effects of these two states have to do primarily — though by no means exclusively — with epistemology and signification respectively. The indistinguishability of the fog is an expressly epistemological disorientation in the sense that due to its blinding aspect it cuts Marlow off from enlightenment. That is, it is the difficulty of *knowing* in the midst of the fog that is of concern for Marlow. In the tradition of metaphysics beginning with Aristotle and arguably running through Conrad at this point, the situation of blindness and deafness engendered by the fog is a

---

[29]Paul Armstrong, "*Heart of Darkness* and the Epistemology of Cultural Differences," in *Under Postcolonial Eyes*, ed. Fincham and Hooper, 25.

[30]See Anthony Fothergill's discussion of the "politics of linguistic representation" in *Heart of Darkness* in his essay "Cannibalising Traditions: Representation and Critique in *Heart of Darkness*," in *Under Postcolonial Eyes*, ed. Fincham and Hooper, 106.

situation rendering knowledge impossible.[31] Cut off visually and aurally from everything beyond the blurred edges of the steamer, the rest of the world "was nowhere," without "a whisper or a shadow":

> What we could see was just the steamer we were on, her outlines blurred as though she had been on the point of dissolving, and a misty strip of water, perhaps two feet broad, around her — and that was all. The rest of the world was nowhere, as far as our eyes and ears were concerned. Just nowhere. Gone, disappeared; swept off without leaving a whisper or a shadow behind. (p. 55)

In short, Marlow is faced here with an epistemological problem generated by the redundancy of the senses necessary for generating knowledge, and as a result "the world [is] nowhere."

In the case of Marlow's night-time confrontation with Kurtz, though, the failure to distinguish is more specifically a confusion produced by a failure of signification and its corresponding identifying practices. Marlow becomes acutely aware that the arbitrary identifying practices of civilization fall short at this point: they lack the authority and power to impose themselves in this frontier colonial situation. Kurtz, in the darkness, occupies the space of civilization's dissolution or foreclosure, being, in his "alignment" with the wilderness, out of joint with civilization. "I could not appeal in the name of anything high or low" (p. 82): Marlow encounters Kurtz in a space beyond signification and is left without recourse to the distinguishing codes of civilization, with their controlling influence and authority. The reality structured through these codes has slipped, fallen away to reveal, in Lacanian terms, the monstrous grimace of the real. In the confusion of the colonial situation's extremity, then, the authority of the "symbolic community" of civilization is rendered problematic through the inability of words to properly take hold, as it were, in the resistance of the situation to signification.

It has to be emphasized, though, that the scene of the night-time encounter is a climactic, heightened moment in the narrative. It depicts a privileged moment among a series of strange happenings — happenings

---

[31]As Jacques Derrida notes: "Starting with its first words, Metaphysics associates sight with knowledge." But as Derrida adds, sight is never enough for the metaphysician, who says: "We must also know how to hear, and to listen." Jacques Derrida, "The Principle of Reason: The University in the Eyes of Its Pupils," *Diacritics* 13 (3): 4 (1983). On the importance of sight in *Heart of Darkness*, see John W. Griffith, *Joseph Conrad and the Anthropological Dilemma: "Bewildered Traveller"* (Oxford: Clarendon Press, 1995), 36–37.

so strange, in fact, Marlow repeatedly doubts their occurrence. It is the heightened aspect of the scene that explains how Kurtz could manifest, at this point, the dissolution of civilization and its language, and yet have been virtually defined, the further up-river Marlow went, by his supremely seductive eloquence. Of all of Kurtz's "gifts," Marlow says, "the one that stood out preëminently, that carried with it a sense of real presence, was his ability to talk, his words" (p. 62). But in leaving the steamer to return to the jungle, Kurtz becomes "utterly lost" as the darkness of the wilderness overtakes him, sucking him into a void beyond recognition and beyond any code. This is the horror as foreclosure, the horror of a void resulting from the voiding of civilization; and this is Africa as the first term in Marlow's ironic "perversion": the primal site of the void.

Africa as this "first term" has to be repeated as such for the "metonymy of the veil" — that is, the displacement of Europe's ideal self-image as the place of pure light and civilization — to take place. Without the organizational and conceptual force of Africa as a nodal point, the perversion of Europe's ideal self-image makes no sense. Thus, importantly, it does not allow a reconsideration or reconfiguration of Europe's image of Africa as its primal other, but only the repetition and reinforcement of this image. In short, the perversion of *Heart of Darkness* is limited to the revelation that Europe already *contains* this "otherness" which it vigorously tries — through its philanthropic discourse, for example — to put beyond the frame of its own proper reality. We might say in conclusion, then, that Marlow's perversion is, perhaps as perversion always is, ambivalent: as much an undoing as a repetition.

Glossary of Critical
and Theoretical Terms

Most terms have been glossed parenthetically where they first appear in the text. Mainly, the glossary lists terms that are too complex to define in a phrase or a sentence or two. A few of the terms listed are discussed at greater length elsewhere (feminist criticism, for instance); these terms are defined succinctly and a page reference to the longer discussion is provided.

AFFECTIVE FALLACY First used by William K. Wimsatt and Monroe C. Beardsley to refer to what they regarded as the erroneous practice of interpreting texts according to the psychological responses of readers. "The Affective Fallacy," they wrote in a 1946 essay later republished in *The Verbal Icon* (1954), "is a confusion between the poem and its *results* (what it *is* and what it *does*). . . . It begins by trying to derive the standards of criticism from the psychological effects of a poem and ends in impressionism and relativism." The affective fallacy, like the intentional fallacy (confusing the meaning of a work with the author's expressly intended meaning), was one of the main tenets of the New Criticism, or formalism. The affective fallacy has been contested by reader-response critics, who have deliberately dedicated their efforts to describing the way individual readers and "interpretive communities" go about "making sense" of texts.

See also: Authorial Intention, Formalism, Reader-Response Criticism.

AUTHORIAL INTENTION Defined narrowly, an author's intention in writing a work, as expressed in letters, diaries, interviews, and conversations. Defined more broadly, "intentionality" involves unexpressed motivations, designs, and purposes, some of which may have remained unconscious.

The debate over whether critics should try to discern an author's intentions (conscious or otherwise) is an old one. William K. Wimsatt and Monroe C.

Beardsley, in an essay first published in the 1940s, coined the term "intentional fallacy" to refer to the practice of basing interpretations on the expressed or implied intentions of authors, a practice they judged to be erroneous. As proponents of the New Criticism, or formalism, they argued that a work of literature is an object in itself and should be studied as such. They believed that it is sometimes helpful to learn what an author intended, but the critic's real purpose is to show what is actually in the text, not what an author intended to put there.

See also: Affective Fallacy, Formalism.

BASE *See* Marxist Criticism.

BINARY OPPOSITIONS *See* Oppositions.

BLANKS *See* Gaps.

CANON Since the fourth century, used to refer to those books of the Bible that the Christian church accepts as being Holy Scripture. The term has come to be applied more generally to those literary works given special status, or "privileged," by a culture. Works we tend to think of as "classics" or the "Great Books" produced by Western culture — texts that are found in every anthology of American, British, and world literature — would be among those that constitute the canon.

Recently, Marxist, feminist, minority, and postcolonial critics have argued that, for political reasons, many excellent works never enter the canon. Canonized works, they claim, are those that reflect — and respect — the culture's dominant ideology and/or perform some socially acceptable or even necessary form of "cultural work." Attempts have been made to broaden or redefine the canon by discovering valuable texts, or versions of texts, that were repressed or ignored for political reasons. These have been published both in traditional and in nontraditional anthologies. The most outspoken critics of the canon, especially radical critics practicing cultural criticism, have called into question the whole concept of canon or "canonicity." Privileging no form of artistic expression that reflects and revises the culture, these critics treat cartoons, comics, and soap operas with the same cogency and respect they accord novels, poems, and plays.

See also: Cultural Criticism, Feminist Criticism, Ideology, Marxist Criticism.

CONFLICTS, CONTRADICTIONS *See* Gaps.

CULTURAL CRITICISM A critical approach that is sometimes referred to as "cultural studies" or "cultural critique." Practitioners of cultural criticism oppose "high" definitions of culture and take seriously popular cultural forms. Grounded in a variety of continental European influences, cultural criticism nonetheless gained institutional force in England, in 1964, with the founding of the Centre for Contemporary Cultural Studies at Birmingham University. Broadly interdisciplinary in its scope and approach, cultural criticism views the text as the locus and catalyst of a complex network of political and economic discourses. Cultural critics share with Marxist critics an interest in the ideological contexts of cultural forms.

DECONSTRUCTION A poststructuralist approach to literature that is strongly influenced by the writings of the French philosopher Jacques Derrida. Deconstruction, partly in response to structuralism and formalism, posits the undecidability of meaning for all texts. In fact, as the deconstructionist critic J. Hillis Miller points out, "deconstruction is not a dismantling of the structure of a text but a demonstration that it has already dismantled itself." *See* "What Is Deconstruction?" pp. 205–21.

DIALECTIC Originally developed by Greek philosophers, mainly Socrates and Plato, as a form and method of logical argumentation; the term later came to denote a philosophical notion of evolution. The German philosopher G. W. F. Hegel described dialectic as a process whereby a thesis, when countered by an antithesis, leads to the synthesis of a new idea. Karl Marx and Friedrich Engels, adapting Hegel's idealist theory, used the phrase "dialectical materialism" to discuss the way in which a revolutionary class war might lead to the synthesis of a new social economic order. The American Marxist critic Fredric Jameson has coined the phrase "dialectical criticism" to refer to a Marxist critical approach that synthesizes structuralist and poststructuralist methodologies.

See also: Marxist Criticism, Poststructuralism, Structuralism.

DIALOGIC *See* Discourse.

DISCOURSE Used specifically, can refer to (1) spoken or written discussion of a subject or area of knowledge; (2) the words in, or text of, a narrative as opposed to its story line; or (3) a "strand" within a given narrative that argues a certain point or defends a given value system.

More generally, "discourse" refers to the language in which a subject or area of knowledge is discussed or a certain kind of business is transacted. Human knowledge is collected and structured in discourses. Theology and medicine are defined by their discourses, as are politics, sexuality, and literary criticism.

A society is generally made up of a number of different discourses or "discourse communities," one or more of which may be dominant or serve the dominant ideology. Each discourse has its own vocabulary, concepts, and rules, knowledge of which constitutes power. The psychoanalyst and psychoanalytic critic Jacques Lacan has treated the unconscious as a form of discourse, the patterns of which are repeated in literature. Cultural critics, following Mikhail Bakhtin, use the word "dialogic" to discuss the dialogue *between* discourses that takes place within language or, more specifically, a literary text.

See also: Cultural Criticism, Ideology, Narrative, Psychoanalytic Criticism.

FEMINIST CRITICISM An aspect of the feminist movement whose primary goals include critiquing masculine-dominated language and literature by showing how they reflect a masculine ideology; writing the history of unknown or undervalued women writers, thereby earning them their rightful place in the literary canon; and helping create a climate in which women's creativity may be fully realized and appreciated. *See* "What Are Feminist and Gender Criticism?" pp. 163–76.

FIGURE *See* Metaphor, Metonymy, Symbol.

FORMALISM Often equated with the New Criticism, formalism reached its height during the 1940s and 1950s, but it is still practiced today. Formalists treat a work of literary art as if it were a self-contained, self-referential object. Rather than basing their interpretations of a text on the reader's response, the author's stated intentions, or parallels between the text and historical contexts (such as the author's life), formalists concentrate on the relationships *within* the text that give it its own distinctive character or form. Special attention is paid to repetition, particularly of images or symbols, but also of sound effects and rhythms in poetry.

Because of the importance placed on close analysis and the stress on the text as a carefully crafted, orderly object containing observable formal patterns, formalism has often been seen as an attack on Romanticism and impressionism, particularly impressionistic criticism. It has sometimes even been called an "objective" approach to literature. Formalists are more likely than certain other critics to believe and say that the meaning of a text can be known objectively. For instance, reader-response critics see meaning as a function either of each reader's experience or of the norms that govern a particular "interpretive community," and deconstructors argue that texts mean opposite things at the same time.

The New Criticism was originally based on essays written during the 1920s and 1930s by T. S. Eliot, I. A. Richards, and William Empson. It was significantly developed later by a group of American poets and critics, including R. P. Blackmur, Cleanth Brooks, John Crowe Ransom, Allen Tate, Robert Penn Warren, and William K. Wimsatt. Although we associate these critics with certain principles and terms (such as the "Affective Fallacy" and the "Intentional Fallacy" as defined by Wimsatt and Monroe C. Beardsley), formalists were trying to make a cultural statement rather than establish a critical dogma. Generally southern, religious, and culturally conservative, they advocated the inherent value of literary works (particularly of literary works regarded as beautiful art objects) because they were sick of the growing ugliness of modern life and contemporary events. Some recent theorists even suggest that the rising popularity of formalism after World War II was a feature of American isolationism, the formalist tendency to isolate literature from biography and history being a manifestation of the American fatigue with wider involvements.

See also: Affective Fallacy, Authorial Intention, Deconstruction, Reader-Response Criticism, Symbol.

GAPS When used by reader-response critics familiar with the theories of Wolfgang Iser, the term refers to "blanks" in texts that must be filled in by readers. A gap may be said to exist whenever and wherever a reader perceives something to be missing between words, sentences, paragraphs, stanzas, or chapters. Readers respond to gaps actively and creatively, explaining apparent inconsistencies in point of view, accounting for jumps in chronology, speculatively supplying information missing from plots, and resolving problems or issues left ambiguous or "indeterminate" in the text.

Reader-response critics sometimes speak as if a gap actually exists in a text; a gap is, of course, to some extent a product of readers' perceptions. Different readers may find gaps in different texts, and different gaps in the same text. Furthermore, they may fill these gaps in different ways, which is why, a reader-response critic might argue, works are interpreted in different ways.

Although the concept of the gap has been used mainly by reader-response critics, it has also been used by critics taking other theoretical approaches. Practitioners of deconstruction might use "gap" when speaking of the radical contradictoriness of a text. Marxists have used the term to speak of everything from the gap that opens up between economic base and cultural superstructure to the two kinds of conflicts or contradictions to be found in literary texts. The first of these, they would argue, results from the fact that texts reflect ideology, within which certain subjects cannot be covered, things cannot be said, contradictory views cannot be recognized as contradictory. The second kind of conflict, contradiction, or gap within a text results from the fact that works don't just reflect ideology: they are also fictions that, consciously or unconsciously, distance themselves from the same ideology.

See also: Deconstruction, Ideology, Marxist Criticism, Reader-Response Criticism.

GENDER CRITICISM Developing out of feminist criticism in the mid-1980s, this fluid and inclusive movement by its nature defies neat definition. Its practitioners include, but are not limited to, self-identified feminists, gay and lesbian critics, queer and performance theorists, and poststructuralists interested in deconstructing oppositions such as masculine/feminine, heterosexual/homosexual. This diverse group of critics shares an interest in interrogating categories of gender and sexuality and exploring the relationships between them, though it does not necessarily share any central assumptions about the nature of these categories. For example, some gender critics insist that all gender identities are cultural constructions, but others have maintained a belief in essential gender identity. Often gender critics are more interested in examining gender issues through a literary text than a literary text through gender issues. *See* "What Are Feminist and Gender Criticism?" pp. 163–76.

GENRE A French word referring to a kind or type of literature. Individual works within a genre may exhibit a distinctive form, be governed by certain conventions, and/or represent characteristic subjects. Tragedy, epic, and romance are all genres.

Perhaps inevitably, the term *genre* is used loosely. Lyric poetry is a genre, but so are characteristic *types* of the lyric, such as the sonnet, the ode, and the elegy. Fiction is a genre, as are detective fiction and science fiction. The list of genres grows constantly as critics establish new lines of connection between individual works and discern new categories of works with common characteristics. Moreover, some writers form hybrid genres by combining the characteristics of several in a single work.

Knowledge of genres helps critics to understand and explain what is conventional and unconventional, borrowed and original, in a work.

HEGEMONY Given intellectual currency by the Italian communist Antonio Gramsci, the word (a translation of *egemonia*) refers to the pervasive system of assumptions, meanings, and values — the web of ideologies, in other words — that shapes the way things look, what they mean, and therefore what reality *is* for the majority of people within a given culture.

See also: Ideology, Marxist Criticism.

IDEOLOGY A set of beliefs underlying the customs, habits, and/or practices common to a given social group. To members of that group, the beliefs seem obviously true, natural, and even universally applicable. They may seem just as obviously arbitrary, idiosyncratic, and even false to outsiders or members of another group who adhere to another ideology. Within a society, several ideologies may coexist, or one or more may be dominant.

Ideologies may be forcefully imposed or willingly subscribed to. Their component beliefs may be held consciously or unconsciously. In either case, they come to form what Johanna M. Smith has called "the unexamined ground of our experience." Ideology governs our perceptions, judgments, and prejudices — our sense of what is acceptable, normal, and deviant. Ideology may cause a revolution; it may also allow discrimination and even exploitation.

Ideologies are of special interest to sociologically oriented critics of literature because of the way in which authors reflect or resist prevailing views in their texts. Some Marxist critics have argued that literary texts reflect and reproduce the ideologies that produced them; most, however, have shown how ideologies are riven with contradictions that works of literature manage to expose and widen. Still other Marxists have focused on the way in which texts themselves are characterized by gaps, conflicts, and contradictions between their ideological and anti-ideological functions.

Feminist critics have addressed the question of ideology by seeking to expose (and thereby call into question) the patriarchal ideology mirrored or inscribed in works written by men — even men who have sought to counter sexism and break down sexual stereotypes. New historicists have been interested in demonstrating the ideological underpinnings not only of literary representations but also of our interpretations of them. Fredric Jameson, an American Marxist critic, argues that all thought is ideological, but that ideological thought that knows itself as such stands the chance of seeing through and transcending ideology.

See also: Cultural Criticism, Feminist Criticism, Marxist Criticism, New Historicism.

IMAGINARY ORDER One of the three essential orders of the psychoanalytic field (see Real and Symbolic Order), it is most closely associated with the senses (sight, sound, touch, taste, and smell). The infant, who by comparison to other animals is born premature and thus is wholly dependent on others for a prolonged period, enters the Imaginary Order when it begins to experience a unity of body parts and motor control that is empowering. This usually occurs between six and eighteen months, and is called by Lacan the "mirror stage" or "mirror phase," in which the child anticipates mastery of its body. It does so by identifying with the *image* of wholeness (that is, seeing its own image in the mirror, experiencing its mother as a whole body, and so forth). This sense of oneness, and also difference from others (especially the mother or primary caretaker), is established through an image or a vision of harmony that is both a mirroring and a "mirage of maturation" or false sense of individuality and independence. The Imaginary is a metaphor for unity, is related to the visual order, and is always part of human subjectivity. Because the subject is fundamentally separate from others and also internally divided (conscious/ unconscious), the apparent coherence of the Imaginary, its fullness and grandiosity, is always false, a *mis*recognition that the ego (or "me") tries to deny by imagining itself as coherent and empowered. The Imaginary operates in conjunction with the Real and Symbolic and is not a "stage" of development equivalent to Freud's "pre-oedipal stage," nor is it prelinguistic.

See also: Psychoanalytic Criticism, Real, Symbolic Order.

IMPLIED READER A phrase used by some reader-response critics in place of the phrase "the reader." Whereas "the reader" could refer to any idiosyncratic individual who happens to have read or to be reading the text, "the implied reader" is *the* reader intended, even created, by the text. Other reader-response critics seeking to describe this more generally conceived reader have spoken of the "informed reader" or the "narratee," who is "the necessary counterpart of a given narrator."

See Reader-Response Criticism.

INTENTIONAL FALLACY *See* Authorial Intention.

INTENTIONALITY *See* Authorial Intention.

INTERTEXTUALITY The condition of interconnectedness among texts. Every author has been influenced by others, and every work contains explicit and implicit references to other works. Writers may consciously or unconsciously echo a predecessor or precursor; they may also consciously or unconsciously disguise their indebtedness, making intertextual relationships difficult for the critic to trace.

Reacting against the formalist tendency to view each work as a freestanding object, some poststructuralist critics suggested that the meaning of a work emerges only intertextually, that is, within the context provided by other works. But there has been a reaction, too, against this type of intertextual criticism. Some new historicist critics suggest that literary history is itself too narrow a context and that works should be interpreted in light of a larger set of cultural contexts.

There is, however, a broader definition of intertextuality, one that refers to the relationship between works of literature and a wide range of narratives and discourses that we don't usually consider literary. Thus defined, intertextuality could be used by a new historicist to refer to the significant interconnectedness between a literary text and nonliterary discussions of or discourses about contemporary culture. Or it could be used by a poststructuralist to suggest that a work can only be recognized and read within a vast field of signs and tropes that is *like* a text and that makes any single text self-contradictory and "undecidable."

See also: Discourse, Formalism, Narrative, New Historicism, Poststructuralism, Trope.

MARXIST CRITICISM An approach that treats literary texts as material products, describing them in broadly historical terms. In Marxist criticism, the text is viewed in terms of its production and consumption, as a product *of* work that does identifiable cultural work of its own. Following Karl Marx, the founder of communism, Marxist critics have used the terms *base* to refer to economic reality and *superstructure* to refer to the corresponding or "homologous" infrastructure consisting of politics, law, philosophy, religion, and the arts. Also following Marx, they have used the word *ideology* to refer to that set of cultural beliefs that literary works at once reproduce, resist, and revise.

METAPHOR The representation of one thing by another related or similar thing. The image (or activity or concept) used to represent or "figure" something else is known as the "vehicle" of the metaphor; the thing represented is called the "tenor." In other words, the vehicle is what we substitute for the tenor. The relationship between vehicle and tenor can provide much additional meaning. Thus, instead of saying, "Last night I read a book," we might say, "Last night I plowed through a book." "Plowed through" (or the activity of plowing) is the vehicle of our metaphor; "read" (or the act of reading) is the tenor, the thing being figured. The increment in meaning through metaphor is fairly obvious. Our audience knows not only *that* we read but also *how* we read, because to read a book in the way that a plow rips through earth is surely to read in a relentless, unreflective way. Note that in the sentence above, a new metaphor — "rips through" — has been used to explain an old one. This serves (which is a metaphor) as an example of just how thick (another metaphor) language is with metaphors!

Metaphor is a kind of "trope" (literally, a "turning," that is, a figure of speech that alters or "turns" the meaning of a word or phrase). Other tropes include allegory, conceit, metonymy, personification, simile, symbol, and synecdoche. Traditionally, metaphor and symbol have been viewed as the principal tropes; minor tropes have been categorized as *types* of these two major ones. Similes, for instance, are usually defined as simple metaphors that usually employ "like" or "as" and state the tenor outright, as in "My love is like a red, red rose." Synecdoche involves a vehicle that is a *part* of the tenor, as in "I see a sail" meaning "I see a boat." Metonymy is viewed as a metaphor involving two terms commonly if arbitrarily associated with (but not fundamentally or intrinsically related to) each other. However, deconstructors such as Paul de Man and J. Hillis Miller have questioned the "privilege" granted to metaphor and the metaphor/metonymy distinction or "opposition." They have suggested that all metaphors are really metonyms and that all figuration is arbitrary.

See also: Deconstruction, Metonymy, Oppositions, Symbol.

METONYMY The representation of one thing by another that is commonly and often physically associated with it. To refer to a writer's handwriting as his or her "hand" is to use a metonymic "figure" or "trope." The image or thing used to represent something else is known as the "vehicle" of the metonym; the thing represented is called the "tenor."

Like other tropes (such as metaphor), metonymy involves the replacement of one word or phrase by another. Liquor may be referred to as "the bottle," a monarch as "the crown." Narrowly defined, the vehicle of a metonym is arbitrarily, not intrinsically, associated with the tenor. In other words, the bottle just happens to be what liquor is stored in and poured from in our culture. The hand may be involved in the production of handwriting, but so are the brain and the pen. There is no special, intrinsic likeness between a crown and a monarch; it's just that crowns traditionally sit on monarchs' heads and not on the heads of university professors. More broadly, "metonym" and "metonymy" have been used by recent critics to refer to a wide range of figures and tropes. Deconstructors have questioned the distinction between metaphor and metonymy.

See also: Deconstruction, Metaphor, Trope.

NARRATIVE A story or a telling of a story, or an account of a situation or of events. A novel and a biography of a novelist are both narratives, as are Freud's case histories.

Some critics use the word "narrative" even more generally; Brook Thomas, a new historicist, has critiqued "narratives of human history that neglect the role human labor has played."

NEW CRITICISM *See* Formalism.

NEW HISTORICISM First practiced and articulated in the late 1970s and early 1980s in the work of critics such as Stephen Greenblatt — who named this movement in contemporary critical theory — and Louis Montrose, its practitioners share certain convictions, primarily that literary critics need to develop a high degree of historical consciousness and that literature should not be viewed apart from other human creations, artistic or otherwise. They share a belief in referentiality — a belief that literature refers to and is referred to by things outside itself — that is fainter in the works of formalist, poststructuralist, and even reader-response critics. Discarding old distinctions between literature, history, and the social sciences, new historicists agree with Greenblatt that the "central concerns" of criticism "should prevent it from permanently sealing off one type of discourse from another, or decisively separating works of art from the minds and lives of their creators and their audiences."

See also: "What Is the New Historicism?" pp. 245–57; Authorial Intention, Deconstruction, Formalism, Ideology, Poststructuralism, Psychoanalytic Criticism.

OPPOSITIONS A concept highly relevant to linguistics, since linguists maintain that words (such as "black" and "death") have meaning not in themselves but in relation to other words ("white" and "life"). Jacques Derrida, a poststructuralist philosopher of language, has suggested that in the West we think in terms of these "binary oppositions" or dichotomies, which on examination turn out to be evaluative hierarchies. In other words, each opposition — beginning/end, presence/absence, or consciousness/unconsciousness — contains one term that our culture views as superior and one term that we view as negative or inferior.

Derrida has "deconstructed" a number of these binary oppositions, including two — speech/writing and signifier/signified — that he believes to be central to linguistics in particular and Western culture in general. He has concurrently critiqued the "law" of noncontradiction, which is fundamental to Western logic. He and other deconstructors have argued that a text can contain opposed strands of discourse and, therefore, mean opposite things: reason *and* passion, life *and* death, hope *and* despair, black *and* white. Traditionally, criticism has involved choosing between opposed or contradictory meanings and arguing that one is present in the text and the other absent.

French feminists have adopted the ideas of Derrida and other deconstructors, showing not only that we think in terms of such binary oppositions as male/female, reason/emotion, and active/passive, but that we also associate reason and activity with masculinity and emotion and passivity with femininity. Because of this, they have concluded that language is "phallocentric," or masculine-dominated.

See also: Deconstruction, Discourse, Feminist Criticism, Poststructuralism.

PHALLUS The symbolic value of the penis that organizes libidinal development and which Freud saw as a stage in the process of human subjectivity.

Lacan viewed the Phallus as the representative of a fraudulent power (male over female) whose "law" is a principle of psychic division (conscious/unconscious) and sexual difference (masculine/feminine). The Symbolic Order (*see* Symbolic Order) is ruled by the Phallus, which of itself has no inherent meaning *apart from* the power and meaning given to it by individual cultures and societies, and represented by the name of the father as lawgiver and namer.

POSTCOLONIAL CRITICISM An approach to literature that typically involves the analysis of works by authors from regions of the globe subject to European colonization. Usually, the prefix *post-* in *postcolonial* signifies the period following the end of colonization and the achievement of national independence by a former colony, but sometimes it is used to refer to any point following the establishment of colonial rule. Sometimes postcolonial criticism engages texts produced by authors hailing from the colonizing culture (e.g., Joseph Conrad). The intent of this type of postcolonial criticism is to expose colonialist attitudes held by the author and/or literary characters and to demonstrate the role such biases play in the representation of subjugated persons and cultures. Because postcolonial criticism arose from a convergence of approaches (the "Negritude" movement; early, Marxist-leaning cultural criticism; the writings of Michel Foucault; the study of so-called Commonwealth literature; feminist criticism and theory, and so forth), it may best be understood in relation to its antecedents. Among the best-known postcolonial critics and writers are Edward Said, Homi Bhabha, Gayatri Spivak, and Gloria Anzaldúa. *See* "What Is Postcolonial Criticism?" pp. 285–94.

POSTSTRUCTURALISM The general attempt to contest and subvert structuralism initiated by deconstructors and certain other critics associated with psychoanalytic, Marxist, and feminist theory. Structuralists, using linguistics as a model and employing semiotic (sign) theory, posit the possibility of knowing a text systematically and revealing the "grammar" behind its form and meaning. Poststructuralists argue against the possibility of such knowledge and description. They counter that texts can be shown to contradict not only structuralist accounts of them but also themselves. In making their adversarial claims, they rely on close readings of texts and on the work of theorists such as Jacques Derrida and Jacques Lacan.

Poststructuralists have suggested that structuralism rests on distinctions between "signifier" and "signified" (signs and the things they point toward), "self" and "language" (or "text"), texts and other texts, and text and world that are overly simplistic, if not patently inaccurate. Poststructuralists have shown how all signifieds are also signifiers, and they have treated texts as "intertexts." They have viewed the world as if it *were* a text (we desire a certain car because it *symbolizes* achievement) and the self as the subject, as well as the user, of language; for example, we may shape and speak through language, but it also shapes and speaks through us.

See also: Deconstruction, Feminist Criticism, Intertextuality, Psychoanalytic Criticism, Semiotics, Structuralism.

PSYCHOANALYTIC CRITICISM Grounded in the psychoanalytic theories of Sigmund Freud, it is one of the oldest critical methodologies still in use. Freud's view that works of literature, like dreams, express secret, unconscious desires led to criticism that interpreted literary works as manifestations of the authors' neuroses. More recently, psychoanalytic critics have come to see literary works as skillfully crafted artifacts that may appeal to *our* neuroses by tapping into our repressed wishes and fantasies. Other forms of psychological criticism that diverge from Freud, although they ultimately derive from his insights, include those based on the theories of Carl Jung and Jacques Lacan. *See* "What Is Psychoanalytic Criticism?" pp. 345–50.

READER-RESPONSE CRITICISM An approach to literature that, as its name implies, considers the way readers respond to texts, as they read. Stanley Fish describes the method by saying that it substitutes for one question, "What does this sentence mean?" a more operational question, "What does this sentence do?" Reader-response criticism shares with deconstruction a strong textual orientation and a reluctance to assign a single meaning to a work. Along with psychoanalytic criticism, it shares an interest in the dynamics of mental response to textual cues.

REAL One of the three orders of subjectivity (*see* Imaginary Order and Symbolic Order), the Real is the intractable and substantial world that resists and exceeds interpretation. The Real cannot be imagined, symbolized, or known directly. It constantly eludes our efforts to name it (death, gravity, the physicality of objects are examples of the Real), and thus challenges both the Imaginary and the Symbolic orders. The Real is fundamentally "Other," the mark of the divide between conscious and unconscious, and is signaled in language by gaps, slips, speechlessness, and the sense of the uncanny. The Real is not what we call "reality." It is the stumbling block of the Imaginary (which thinks it can "imagine" anything, including the Real) and of the Symbolic, which tries to bring the Real under its laws (the Real exposes the "phallacy" of the Law of the Phallus). The Real is frightening; we try to tame it with laws and language and call it "reality."

See also: Imaginary Order, Psychoanalytic Criticism, Symbolic Order.

SEMIOLOGY, SEMIOTIC *See* Semiotics.

SEMIOTICS The study of signs and sign systems and the way meaning is derived from them. Structuralist anthropologists, psychoanalysts, and literary critics developed semiotics during the decades following 1950, but much of the pioneering work had been done at the turn of the century by the founder of modern linguistics, Ferdinand de Saussure, and the American philosopher Charles Sanders Peirce.

Semiotics is based on several important distinctions, including the distinction between "signifier" and "signified" (the sign and what it points toward) and the distinction between "langue" and "parole." *Langue* (French for "tongue," as in "native tongue," meaning language) refers to the entire system within which individual utterances or usages of language have meaning; *parole* (French for "word") refers to the particular utterances or usages. A principal tenet of semiotics is that signs, like words, are not significant in themselves, but instead have meaning only in relation to other signs and the entire system of signs, or langue.

The affinity between semiotics and structuralist literary criticism derives from this emphasis placed on langue, or system. Structuralist critics, after all, were reacting against formalists and their procedure of focusing on individual words as if meanings didn't depend on anything external to the text.

Poststructuralists have used semiotics but questioned some of its underlying assumptions, including the opposition between signifier and signified. The feminist poststructuralist Julia Kristeva, for instance, has used the word "semiotic" to describe feminine language, a highly figurative, fluid form of discourse that she sets in opposition to rigid, symbolic masculine language.

See also: Deconstruction, Feminist Criticism, Formalism, Oppositions, Poststructuralism, Structuralism, Symbol.

SIMILE *See* Metaphor.

SOCIOHISTORICAL CRITICISM *See* New Historicism.

STRUCTURALISM A science of humankind whose proponents attempted to show that all elements of human culture, including literature, may be understood as parts of a system of signs. Structuralism, according to Robert Scholes, was a reaction to "'modernist' alienation and despair."

Using Ferdinand de Saussure's linguistic theory, European structuralists such as Roman Jakobson, Claude Lévi-Strauss, and Roland Barthes (before his shift toward poststructuralism) attempted to develop a "semiology" or "semiotics" (science of signs). Barthes, among others, sought to recover literature and even language from the isolation in which they had been studied and to show that the laws that govern them govern all signs, from road signs to articles of clothing.

Particularly useful to structuralists were two of Saussure's concepts: the idea of the "phoneme" in language and the idea that phonemes exist in two kinds of relationships: "synchronic" and "diachronic." A phoneme is the smallest consistently significant unit in language; thus, both "a" and "an" are phonemes, but "n" is not. A diachronic relationship is that which a phoneme has with those that have preceded it in time and those that will follow it. These "horizontal" relationships produce what we might call discourse or narrative and what Saussure called "parole." The synchronic relationship is the "vertical" one that a word has in a given instant with the entire system of language ("langue") in which it may generate meaning. "An" means what it means in English because those of us who speak the language are using it in the same way at a given time.

Following Saussure, Lévi-Strauss studied hundreds of myths, breaking them into their smallest meaningful units, which he called "mythemes." Removing each from its diachronic relations with other mythemes in a single myth (such as the myth of Oedipus and his mother), he vertically aligned those mythemes that he found to be homologous (structurally correspondent). He then studied the relationships within as well as between vertically aligned columns, in an attempt to understand scientifically, through ratios and proportions, those thoughts and processes that humankind has shared, both at one particular time and across time. One could say, then, that structuralists followed Saussure in preferring to think about the overriding langue or language of myth, in which each mytheme and mytheme-constituted myth fits meaningfully, rather than about isolated individual paroles or narratives. Structuralists followed Saussure's lead in believing what the poststructuralist Jacques Derrida later decided he could not subscribe to — that sign systems must be understood in terms of binary oppositions. In analyzing myths and texts to find basic structures, structuralists tended to find that opposite terms modulate until they are finally resolved or reconciled by some intermediary third term. Thus, a structuralist reading of Milton's *Paradise Lost* and *Paradise Regained* would show that the war between God and the bad angels becomes a rift between God and sinful, fallen man, the rift then being healed by the Son of God, the mediating third term.

See also: Deconstruction, Discourse, Narrative, Poststructuralism, Semiotics.

SUPERSTRUCTURE *See* Marxist Criticism.

SYMBOL A thing, image, or action that, although it is of interest in its own right, stands for or suggests something larger and more complex — often an idea or a range of interrelated ideas, attitudes, and practices.

Within a given culture, some things are understood to be symbols: the flag of the United States is an obvious example. More subtle cultural symbols might be the river as a symbol of time and the journey as a symbol of life and its manifold experiences.

Instead of appropriating symbols generally used and understood within their culture, writers often create symbols by setting up, in their works, a complex but identifiable web of associations. As a result, one object, image, or action suggests others and often, ultimately, a range of ideas.

A symbol may thus be defined as a metaphor in which the "vehicle," the thing, image, or action used to represent something else, represents many related things (or "tenors") or is broadly suggestive. The urn in Keats's "Ode on a Grecian Urn" suggests many interrelated concepts, including art, truth, beauty, and timelessness.

Symbols have been of particular interest to formalists, who study how meanings emerge from the complex, patterned relationships between images in a work, and psychoanalytic critics, who are interested in how individual authors and the larger culture both disguise and reveal unconscious fears and desires through symbols. Certain French feminists have also focused on the symbolic. They have suggested that, as wide-ranging as it seems, symbolic language is ultimately rigid and restrictive. They favor semiotic language and writing, which, they contend, is at once more rhythmic, unifying, and feminine.

See also: Feminist Criticism, Metaphor, Psychoanalytic Criticism, Trope.

SYMBOLIC ORDER One of the three orders of subjectivity (see Imaginary Order and Real), it is the realm of law, language, and society; it is the repository of generally held cultural beliefs. Its symbolic system is language, whose agent is the father or lawgiver, the one who has the power of naming. The human subject is commanded into this preestablished order by language (a process that begins long before a child can speak) and must submit to its orders of communication (grammar, syntax, and so forth). Entrance into the Symbolic Order determines subjectivity according to a primary law of referentiality that takes the male sign (phallus; *see* Phallus) as its ordering principle. Lacan states that both sexes submit to the Law of the Phallus (the law of order, language, and differentiation) but their individual relation to the law determines whether they see themselves as — and are seen by others to be — either "masculine" or "feminine." The Symbolic institutes repression (of the Imaginary), thus creating the unconscious, which itself is structured like the language of the symbolic. The unconscious, a timeless realm, cannot be known directly, but it can be understood by a kind of translation that takes place in language — psychoanalysis is the "talking cure." The Symbolic is not a "stage" of development (as is Freud's "oedipal stage") nor is it static throughout human life. We constantly negotiate its threshold (in sleep, in drunkenness) and can "fall out" of it altogether in psychosis.

See also: Imaginary Order, Psychoanalytic Criticism, Real.

SYNECDOCHE *See* Metaphor, Metonymy.

TENOR *See* Metaphor, Metonymy, Symbol.

TROPE A figure, as in "figure of speech." Literally a "turning," that is, a turning or twisting of a word or phrase to make it mean something else. Principal tropes include metaphor, metonymy, personification, simile, and synecdoche.

See also: Metaphor, Metonymy.

VEHICLE *See* Metaphor, Metonymy, Symbol.

About the Contributors

THE VOLUME EDITOR

Ross C Murfin, general editor of the *Case Studies in Contemporary Criticism* and volume editor of Joseph Conrad's *Heart of Darkness* and Nathaniel Hawthorne's *The Scarlet Letter* in the series, was provost and vice president for academic affairs from 1996 until 2005 at Southern Methodist University, where he is now professor of English. He has taught at the University of Miami, Yale University, and the University of Virginia, and has published scholarly studies of Joseph Conrad, Thomas Hardy, and D. H. Lawrence.

THE CRITICS

Patrick Brantlinger, James Rudy Professor Emeritus at Indiana University, edited *Victorian Studies* for a decade. Besides *Rule of Darkness: British Literature and Imperialism* (1988), his scholarly works include *Dark Vanishings: Discourse on the Extinction of Primitive Races* (2003) and *Victorian Literature and Postcolonial Studies* (2009).

Tony C. Brown is assistant professor of English at the University of Minnesota, Twin Cities, where he teaches courses in literary theory. He is the author of scholarly articles on topics as diverse as early eighteenth-century aesthetic theory, contemporary globalization, and

North American burial mounds. He is currently completing a book entitled *The Primitive, the Aesthetic, and the Savage: An Enlightenment Problematic.*

Gabrielle McIntire is associate professor in the Department of English at Queen's University, Canada. She is author of *Modernism, Memory, and Desire: T. S. Eliot and Virginia Woolf* (2008), and her articles and book reviews have appeared in journals such as *Modern Fiction Studies, Modernism/modernity, Narrative,* and *University of Toronto Quarterly.* She has also published poetry in journals and collections including *The Literary Review of Canada, The Cortland Review, Van Gogh's Ear,* and *Kingston Poets' Gallery.*

J. Hillis Miller is UCI Distinguished Research Professor of Comparative Literature and English, University of California, Irvine. He has published many books and articles on nineteenth- and twentieth-century literature and on literary theory. His latest books include *For Derrida* (2009) and *The Medium Is the Maker* (2009). He is writing two books on communities in literature. He is a fellow of the American Academy of Arts and Sciences and a member of the American Philosophical Society.

Johanna M. Smith is associate professor of English at the University of Texas–Arlington, where she teaches eighteenth- and nineteenth-century British literature and culture. She is coeditor of an anthology of eighteenth-century British women's life-writings and author of a book on Mary Shelley in Twayne's British Authors series, as well as numerous articles on writers from Aphra Behn to Eliza Cook. She is currently working on a study of women's interventions in British and Indian public spheres from 1762 to 1868.

Brook Thomas is a Chancellor's Professor of English at the University of California, Irvine. He has been awarded fellowships from the Alexander von Humboldt Stiftung, the Woodrow Wilson Center, the ACLS, and the NEH. Winner of a number of teaching awards, he has also published numerous articles and books, including *The New Historicism and Other Old-Fashioned Topics* (1991) and, most recently, *Civic Myths: A Law and Literature Approach to Citizenship* (2007).

Kayla Walker Edin is a Ph.D. candidate at Southern Methodist University, Dallas, Texas, where she studies nineteenth- and twentieth-century transatlantic literature, with a special interest in the way that gender shapes and informs space. A native Northwesterner, she earned her MA at Portland State University and has subsequently presented work on Conrad at national and international conferences.

(continued from p. iv)

"Heart of Darkness: Anti-Imperialism, Racism, or Impressionism?" by Patrick Brantlinger. Copyright © Patrick Brantlinger. Reprinted with permission of the author.

"Heart of Darkness Revisited" by J. Hillis Miller. Copyright © 1983 by J. Hillis Miller. Reprinted by permission of the author.

Excerpts from *Conrad: The Critical Heritage* by Norman Sherry. Copyright © 1973 Routledge, UK.

"Was Joseph Conrad Really a Racist?" by Caryl Phillips. Reprinted from *Philosophia* 10.1 (March 2007): 59–66. Copyright © 2007. Reprinted by permission of the author.